The Rise of the Global Imaginary

The Rise of the Global Imaginary

Political Ideologies from the
French Revolution to the
Global War on Terror

Manfred B. Steger

OXFORD
UNIVERSITY PRESS

OXFORD
UNIVERSITY PRESS

Great Clarendon Street, Oxford OX2 6DP
Oxford University Press is a department of the University of Oxford.
It furthers the University's objective of excellence in research, scholarship,
and education by publishing worldwide in
Oxford New York
Auckland Cape Town Dar es Salaam Hong Kong Karachi
Kuala Lumpur Madrid Melbourne Mexico City Nairobi
New Delhi Shanghai Taipei Toronto
With offices in
Argentina Austria Brazil Chile Czech Republic France Greece
Guatemala Hungary Italy Japan South Korea Poland Portugal
Singapore Switzerland Thailand Turkey Ukraine Vietnam

Oxford is a registered trade mark of Oxford University Press
in the UK and in certain other countries
Published in the United States
by Oxford University Press Inc., New York

ISBN 978-0-19-928694-2

Printed in the United Kingdom by
Lightning Source UK Ltd., Milton Keynes

To Perle, with love

Contents

Preface and Acknowledgments

Neoliberalism. Neoconservatism. Neofascism. Postmarxism. Postmodernism. Postcolonialism. ... The remarkable proliferation of conventional "isms" adorned with these two prefixes casts a shadow on the contemporary relevance of traditional political ideologies. As Eric Hobsbawm notes in his magisterial history of the twentieth century, when people face what nothing in their past has prepared them for, they grope for words to name the unknown, even if they can neither define nor understand it.[1] No longer confined to the ivory towers of academia, this gnawing sense of sailing into uncharted conceptual waters pervades today's public discourse. Add fears of transnational terrorism and global climate change and you get the existential insecurity that has gripped the world in the opening decade of the twenty-first century. And yet, some sanguine voices continue to hail our global age as humanity's best chance to realize the liberal ideals of peace, democracy, and free markets.[2] For these inveterate optimists, the New World Order that has emerged after the Cold War is still teeming with opportunity—despite the terrible setback of 9/11.

Is there, indeed, something genuinely "neo" about today's isms? Have we really moved "post" our familiar political ideologies and social imaginaries? These are the fundamental questions animating my exploration of an ideological landscape that stretches from the French Revolution to the Global War on Terror. Shuttling back and forth between text(s) and context(s), this book suggests that there is, in fact, something different about today's political belief systems: a new global imaginary is on the rise. It erupts with increasing frequency within and onto the familiar framework of the national, spewing its fiery lava across all geographical scales. Stoked, among other things, by technological change and scientific innovation, the global imaginary destabilizes the grand political ideologies codified by social elites during the national age. Thus, our changing ideational landscape is intimately related to the forces of "globalization," defined here as the expansion and intensification of social relations across world-time and world-space.

The rising global imaginary finds its political articulation in the ideological claims of contemporary social elites who reside in the privileged spaces of our global cities and also fuels the hopes, disappointments, and demands of migrants who traverse national boundaries in search of their piece of the global promise. Thus, the global is nobody's exclusive property. It inhabits class, race, and gender, but belongs to none of these. Nor can it be pinned down by carving up geographical space into watertight compartments that reflect outdated hierarchies of scale.[3] The multiple inscriptions and incomplete projections of the global on what has been historically constructed as the national have become most visible in the proliferation and reconfiguration of "community." For this reason, one of globalization's most profound dynamics has been the messy and incomplete superimposition of the global village on the conventional nation-state. At a bare minimum, we are witnessing the destabilization of taken-for-granted meanings and instantiations of the national.

Consider, for example, today's asymmetric wars pitting shifting alliances of nation-states and non-state actors against amorphous transnational terrorist networks that nonetheless operate in specific localities— usually in "world cities" like New York, London, Madrid, or Delhi. New global pandemics expose the limits of our national public health systems. Nationally framed environmental policies cannot respond adequately to accelerating global climate change. Conventional educational and immigration schemes based on national goals and priorities are incapable of preparing shifting populations for the pressing tasks of global citizenship. Large-scale sports events like the soccer World Cup, originally designed for competing national teams, no longer make sense in a global environment in which the best athletes play for city-based teams, thus pushing their fans' divided loyalties to the limit. And the list goes on.

It is, therefore, all the more surprising to find that our changing ideological landscape has not been adequately described or analyzed in pertinent literature. Well-intentioned attempts to "update" modern political belief systems by adorning them with prefixes resemble futile efforts to make sense of digital word processing by drawing on the mechanics of moveable print. In the past two decades, there have been only three comprehensive attempts to reassess political ideologies. Focusing on the crucial role of electronic mass communication, John B. Thompson's *Ideology and Modern Culture* sparkles with insights, but appeared a decade too early to assess the full impact of globalization. Michael Freeden's magisterial *Ideologies and Political Theory* constitutes the most exciting effort in recent times to outline a sophisticated new theory of ideology, but his analytic spotlight rests primarily on the grand ideologies of the national age. Finally, John Schwarzmantel's discerning *The Age of Ideology* makes a valiant attempt to link ideologies to the conditions of postmodernity and globality, but the author's conclusion—the ideologies of modernity must be "reinvented" to respond to our globalizing world—fails to recognize that these changes are already in full swing.[4] However, the failure to redraw our ideological maps appears most glaringly in leading academic textbooks where the grand ideologies of the national age—complemented by various neoisms—continue to be presented as the dominant political belief systems of our time.[5]

Offering a long-overdue reassessment of the ideological landscape in the global age, this book is based on two general premises. The first is rooted in the assumption that political ideas are not just pale reflections of economics or technology but powerful forces capable of affecting profound social change at the opportune moment. Nevertheless, we must not fall into the idealist trap of treating political ideas as metaphysical entities floating above material practices and social institutions. Neither idealist reductionism nor materialist determinism can capture the complexities of our globalizing world. The second premise is the imperative of reaching out to a broad readership. Hence, this book has been written for both academics with a scholarly interest in the subject matter and general readers keen to explore ideology's journey. My desire to engage both audiences led me to adopt a compressed narrative that unfolds not as a continuous track of historical detail but as a series of linked snapshots that illuminate the "big picture." Settling on such a method is a notoriously risky business, for it is vulnerable to charges of selectivity and simplification. If executed well, however, it allows the author to tell a complex story in accessible language that sacrifices neither analytical rigor nor explanatory power. Adding color, character, and movement to otherwise rather abstract political and philosophical interpretations, it stimulates the generalist without boring the specialist. The reader will be the ultimate judge as to the success of my efforts.

This book is the culmination of a decade of thinking and writing about the ideological dimensions of globalization. In the process, I have accumulated a heavy intellectual debt to colleagues, students, and friends around the world. Although I cannot list all of these individuals, let me at least acknowledge some of them: Mark Amen, Benjamin Barber, Clyde Barrow, Larry Besserman, Roland Bleiker, Steve Bronner, Franz Broswimmer, Zac Callen, Joe Camilleri, Terrell Carver, Lane Crothers, John Ehrenberg, Cynthia Enloe, Michael Freeden, Barry Gills, James Goodman, Mary Hawkesworth, Chris Hudson, Brien Hallett, Tim Luke, Mike Lutzeler, Brad Macdonald, Peter Manicas, Khalil Marrar, Larry and Elaine May, Eduardo Mendieta, Jim Mittelman, Jamal Nassar, Ken Panfilio, Carlos Parodi, Jan Nederveen Pieterse, Sherri Replogle-Stone, Ravi Roy, Saskia Sassen, Nisha Shah, Chenshan Tian, Amentahru Wahrab, and "Frank" Xinhua Zhang.

I received tremendous support from RMIT University, particularly from my colleagues at the Globalism Institute, the Global Cities Institute, and the Global Studies Discipline Group: Todd Bennett, Mike Berry, Tony Dalton, Elizabeth Grierson, Kim Humphery, Brian Morris, Martin Mulligan, Yaso Nadarajah, Tom Nairn, Heikki Patomäki, Peter Phipps, Joe Siracusa, Deb Verhoven, and Chris Ziguras. My heartfelt thanks go to Paul James, the Director of the Global Cities Institute. His friendship means a lot to me and his generosity never ceases to amaze me. There are only very few academics working in the fledgling field of global studies whose intellect equals the breadth and depth of Paul's.

I appreciate the opportunity to hone my arguments in many invited lectures and academic presentations around the world. I am especially grateful to my students and colleagues at RMIT University, the University of Hawai'i at Manoa, and Illinois State University—three fine institutions I have had the pleasure to be affiliated with during the last decade. RMIT's former Pro-Vice-Chancellor Alan Cumming and Bruce Wilson, Head of the School of Global Studies, Social Science and Planning, deserve special recognition for their unwavering support of my research. I am grateful to my friends and colleagues at the University of Hawai'i's Globalization Research Center. Codirectors Mike Douglass and Jim Spencer, as well as former Director Deane Neubauer, provided me with an ideal professional environment during protracted periods of research between 2004 and 2007. As an affiliate graduate faculty member of the Department of Political Science at the University of Hawai'i at Manoa, I have had the privilege and pleasure to interact regularly with friends and first-rate scholars such as Hokulani Aikau, Kathy Ferguson, Manfred Henningsen, Jon Goldberg-Hiller, Sankaran Krishna, Noenoe Silva, Nevi Soguk, and

Phyllis Turnbull. Mike Shapiro, a towering intellectual presence at the University of Hawai'i for many years, has been a wonderful friend and great source of inspiration.

Sue Bennet, my tireless Executive Assistant at RMIT, deserves much credit for her enthusiastic support, professional competence, and encouraging words. My thanks go to Dominic Byatt and his superb team at Oxford University Press, as well as to the three anonymous reviewers for their insightful comments and suggestions. Finally, and most importantly, I embrace Perle Besserman, my soul mate. Her love and willingness to provide me with valuable feedback on all aspects of my academic work have sustained my efforts during the long and difficult process of writing this book. This book is for you, Perle. Many people have contributed to improving the quality of this study; its remaining flaws are my own responsibility.

Introduction: Political Ideologies and Social Imaginaries

Ideologies may be power structures that manipulate human action, but they are also ideational systems that enable us to choose to become what we want to become.

Michael Freeden (1996)

The social imaginary is that common understanding which makes possible common practices, and a widely shared sense of legitimacy.

Charles Taylor (2007)

Both self-evidently global and denationalizing dynamics destabilize existing meanings and systems.

Saskia Sassen (2006)

I.1. Disparaging Ideology: From Napoleon Bonaparte to George W. Bush

Ideology is a loaded word with a checkered past. Most people today regard it as a form of dogmatic thinking or political manipulation. Virtually no one associates it with analytic clarity or scientific rigor. And yet, this is precisely how *idéologie* was envisioned by an imprisoned French aristocrat awaiting execution at the height of the Reign of Terror. Count Destutt de Tracy coined the term for his rationalist method of breaking complex systems of ideas into their basic components. Consciously directed against established religion and its transcendental claims to absolute Truth, the ultimate purpose of Tracy's new "science of ideas" went far beyond intellectual contemplation. The postulation of ideology's

1

scientific truths was to guide the practical improvement of the new French Republic that emerged from the convulsions of the Revolution. Brandished as the infallible instruction manual for political and social reform, *idéologie* was the rallying cry of Tracy's small circle of Enlightenment thinkers affiliated with the newly founded National Institute of Arts and Sciences in Paris. Young Napoleon Bonaparte, too, embraced ideology on his rise to power, but swiftly discarded its social prescriptions when members of the Institute dared to impede his political ambitions. To add insult to injury, he accused the Institute's absentminded *idéologues* of failing to grasp the imperatives of modern statecraft. The ensuing battle over the "real" meaning of ideology was decisively won by the wily Emperor, for it was his pejorative connotation that stuck in the public mind.

As the nineteenth century progressed, the term acquired additional derogatory punch in radical circles inspired by the revolutionary ideas of Karl Marx and Friedrich Engels. Their *German Ideology* defined it as a deliberate distortion of material reality that served the ruling classes as a convenient cloak for economic exploitation and political oppression. At the dawn of the twentieth century, ideology continued to be condemned as a tool of mass manipulation employed with equal skill by ruthless captains of industrial capitalism and radical left-wing revolutionaries. The crimes of these ideologues—a term now reserved for modern dictators and their unscrupulous propagandists—reached new heights in their genocidal regimes, ghastly concentration camps and sprawling gulags. As political philosopher Hannah Arendt put it in the early 1950s, "Not before Hitler and Stalin were the great political potentialities of ideologies discovered."[1] Attentive to the public's disaffection with these "ideological" excesses, shrewd postwar politicians quickly fell back on Bonaparte's successful strategy of presenting themselves as levelheaded solvers of concrete problems with nothing but contempt for anything that smacked even remotely of ideological thinking. And yet, their professed pragmatism was belied by an Iron Curtain that split the world along the seams of its two opposing isms.

Academics, too, found themselves deeply entangled in the sticky web of Cold War ideology. Soviet dialecticians invented new categories for the many degradations of "bourgeois ideology," while their Western counterparts contrasted the "highly emotive" content of (communist) ideology with the "value free" character of (liberal) social science. Claiming to analyze politics and society in a strictly objective manner, they disparaged ideology as the pernicious product of tyrannical minds obsessed with discovering "how populations and nations can be mobilized and manipulated all along the way that leads to political messianism and fanaticism."[2] Following Arendt's influential conflation of ideology with "totalitarianism," Western academics developed new typologies and classification systems designed to capture the essential features of "pathological" political belief systems. The least derogatory meaning bestowed upon ideology during these polarizing Cold War years was "party affiliation," used by public opinion researchers as a scientific measure for voters' electoral preferences. Reduced to this label, ideology managed to eke out a living in a small corner of the political science discipline.[3] At the same time, however, media-savvy campaign managers returned to the old stereotype by hurling ideology at their opponents' cheap political rhetoric, biased views, and self-interested spin.

With the sudden collapse of the Soviet Union and its Eastern European satellites precisely two centuries after the French Revolution, communism was pronounced dead and the Anglo-American variant of liberal democracy was elevated to the "final form of human government."[4] Triumphalist voices in the West celebrated the "end of ideology" as though competing political ideas had overnight turned into curious relics of the past. China's gradual shift to a party-directed capitalism and the rapid decline of Third-World Marxism only seemed to confirm the "passing of an illusion," as a nonchalant French commentator referred to the demise of communism.[5] It took the al-Qaeda attacks of September 11, 2001, to expose the naïveté of such premature hopes for a de-ideologized world. The familiar Cold War equation of ideology with the totalitarian schemes of depraved minds received a new lease on life in George W. Bush's characterization of jihadist terrorists as the "heirs of all murderous ideologies of the twentieth century."[6] Although the President's administration has come under severe criticism for its policies in Iraq, many people today support Bush's assertion that the Global War on Terror amounts to an "ideological war that is going to last for a while."[7]

I.2. Two Conceptions of Ideology

Moving beyond the invective, this book considers ideology as evolving and malleable political belief systems that emerged during the American and French Revolutions and competed with religious doctrines over what ideas and values should guide human communities. Although ideology offers a "secular" response to these fundamental questions, it also resembles religion in its attempts to link the various ethical, cultural, and political dimensions of society into a fairly comprehensive belief system. Imitating its rival's penchant for trading in truth and certainty, ideology also relies on narratives, metaphor, and myths that persuade, praise, condemn, cajole, convince, and separate the "good" from the "bad." Like religion, it thrives on human emotions, generating rage, fear, enthusiasm, love, sacrifice, altruism, mass murder, torture, and rape much in the same way as religious doctrines have run through the gamut of human virtues and vices.[8] Hence, it would be unfair to confine ideology to its harmful manifestations. What, for example, about its moral influence on human conduct or its crucial role of generating bonds of solidarity that result in enduring human communities? Its pejorative connotations notwithstanding, ideology deserves a more balanced hearing—one that acknowledges its integrative role of providing social stability as much as its propensity to contribute to fragmentation and alienation; its ability to supply standards of normative evaluation as much as its tendency to oversimplify social complexity; its role as guide and compass for political action as much as its potential to legitimize tyranny and terror in the name of noble ideals.

In this spirit, sociologist John Thompson usefully distinguishes between scholars employing critical or neutral conceptions of ideology.[9] The former approach ideology as systems of ideas that are necessarily misleading, illusory, or one-sided, whereas the latter refuse to do so. This book subscribes to a neutral conception, for it takes seriously the indispensable functions of political belief systems irrespective of their particular contents or political orientations. As Marxist philosopher Louis Althusser suggested some time ago, "Human societies secrete ideology as the very element and atmosphere indispensable to their historical respiration and life."[10] Still, to opt for "neutrality" does not necessarily imply withholding value judgments from what the analyst might consider harmful or beneficial commitments of various political ideologies. Under the guise of value-neutrality, declarations of "fact" can obscure or ignore normative aspects crucial for gaining an understanding of the phenomenon in question. A neutral approach to German Nazism, for example, might begin with an acknowledgment that this ideology operates on the same functional levels as, say, German liberalism, but it does not foreclose sustained ethical criticism of Hitler's genocidal vision. The same critical approach might be applied to classical British liberalism's tendency to neglect social welfare in the name of individual liberty. The same goes for French conservatism's defense of patriarchal hierarchies. Advancing such a neutral conception of ideology allows the student of ideology to use "the investigation of ideology as a critical tool for interpreting institutions, practices, and social thought-patterns all at once."[11]

Drawing on this critical spirit of conceptual neutrality, let us define ideology as comprehensive belief systems composed of patterned ideas and claims to truth. Codified by social elites, these beliefs are embraced by significant groups in society.[12] All political belief systems are historically contingent and, therefore, must be analyzed with reference to a particular context that connects their origins and developments to specific times and spaces. Linking belief and practice, ideologies encourage people to act while simultaneously constraining their actions. To this end, ideological codifiers construct claims that seek to "lock in" the meaning of their core concepts. Michael Freeden refers to this crucial process as "decontestation." Although successfully decontested ideas always require more explanation and justification, they are held as truth with such confidence that they no longer appear to be assumptions at all. Ultimately, major ideational claims give each ideology its unique fingerprint:

This configuration teases out specific conceptions of each of the concepts involved. Its precision of meaning, while never conclusive, is gained by the specific and constricted interaction among the concepts it employs. An ideology attempts to end the inevitable contention over concepts by *decontesting* them, by removing their meanings from contest. "This is what justice means," announces one ideology, and "that is what democracy entails." By trying to convince us that they are right and that they speak the truth, ideologies become devices for coping with the indeterminacy of meaning....That is their semantic role. [But] [i]deologies also need to decontest the concepts they use because they are instruments for fashioning collective decisions. That is their political role.[13]

Ideological "morphologies" can thus be pictured as decontested truth-claims that facilitate collective decision-making. Their interlinked semantic and political roles suggest that control over language translates directly into power, including the decision of "who gets what, when, and how."[14] As we shall see in the ensuing chapters, ideologies are not merely justifications of economic class interests, but fairly comprehensive programs designed to shape and direct human communities in specific ways.[15]

I.3. Ideology and the Social Imaginary

Chapter 1 opens with Destutt de Tracy's attempt to establish *idéologie* as the foundational discipline of all sciences. It traces the early career of the concept in postrevolutionary France and the unexpected reversal of its fortunes at the hands of Napoleon and Marx. Chapters 2 and 3 analyze the central truth-claims made by some prominent codifiers of the five grand ideologies—liberalism, conservatism, socialism, communism, and fascism/Nazism—by taking into consideration the crucial national context in which they grew to maturity.[16] Most importantly, this study links political ideologies to their overarching "social imaginary." Constituting the macromappings of social and political space through which we perceive, judge, and act in the world, this deep-seated mode of understanding provides the most general parameters within which people imagine their communal existence. Drawing on Benedict Anderson's account of the imagined community of the nation, Charles Taylor argues that the social imaginary is neither a theory nor an ideology, but an implicit "background" that makes possible communal practices and a widely shared sense of their legitimacy. It offers explanations of how "we"—the members of the community—fit together, how things go on between us, the expectations we have of each other, and the deeper normative notions and images that underlie those expectations. These background understandings are both normative and factual in the sense of providing us both with the standards of how things usually go on and how they ought to go on.[17] Much in the same vein, Pierre Bourdieu notes that the social imaginary sets the prereflexive framework for our daily routines and our commonsense social repertoires.[18]

Consider, for example, how the social imaginary provides the deep matrix for our meaningful participation in a public celebration of a national holiday. Here we find a smiling young woman waving a flag as the marching band passes by playing patriotic songs. There sits an old man on the side of the street, mouthing with gusto the words that go along with the tune. Around the corner we can observe throngs of patriotically dressed school children purchasing candy and soft drinks from a street vendor. Behind the long row of excited onlookers, we can make out two young men in uniform pointing proudly to the military planes roaring overhead. In the blink of an eye, language, symbols, space, and action flow into each other in ways that make immediate sense to all participants. The crowd does not seem to expend any conscious effort in navigating this familiar ocean of circulating symbols and their corresponding spatial orders as the social imaginary endows people's holiday celebrations with a background aura of normality.

Despite such apparent intangibility, however, social imaginaries are quite "real" in the sense of enabling common practices and deep-seated communal attachments. Though capable of facilitating collective fantasies and speculative reflections, they should not be dismissed as phantasms or mental fabrications.[19] Social imaginaries acquire additional solidity through the (re)construction of social space and the repetitive performance of certain communal qualities and characteristics. And yet, they are temporary constellations subject to change. At certain tipping points in history, such change can occur with lightning speed and tremendous ferocity.[20] This happened at the end of the eighteenth century when in intellectual circles, there arose in modernizing states on both sides of the Atlantic the conceptual template of the "nation." Its political message was as clear as it was audacious: henceforth, it would be "the people"—not kings, aristocrats, or clerical elites—that exercised legitimate authority in political affairs. Over time, the will of the people would replace monarchical forms of communal authority based on transcendental powers emanating from a divine realm beyond the nation. Thus, modern nationhood found its expression in the transformation of subjects into citizens who laid claim to equal membership in the nation and institutionalized their sovereignty in the modern nation-state. But who really counted as part of the people and what constituted the essence of the nation became the subject of fierce intellectual debates and political struggles. Seeking to remake the world according to the rising national imaginary, citizens exhibited a restlessness that became the hallmark of modernity. As William Connolly observes, "Modern agencies form and reform, produce and reproduce, incorporate and reincorporate, industrialize and reindustrialize. In modernity, modernization is always under way."[21]

Countless meanings and definitions of modernity have been put forward in the past two centuries. They extend far beyond familiar designations, referring to a historical era in the West characterized by its radical rupture with the past and its ensuing temporal reorientation toward notions of infinite progress, economic growth, and enduring material prosperity. As philosopher Jürgen Habermas reminds us, modernity is inextricably intertwined with an expanding "public sphere"—the incubator of modernity's tendency to "create its own normativity out of itself."[22] Various thinkers have elaborated on the main dynamics of modernity: the separation of state and civil society; conceptions of linear time; progressive secularization; individualism; intensifying geopolitical rivalries that facilitated the formation and multiplication of nation-states; new orders of rationality and their corresponding domains of knowledge; the uneven expansion of industrial capitalism; the rapid diffusion of discursive literacy; the slow trend toward democratization; and so on. The detailed genealogy of these features need not concern us here, although its involvement with the story of ideology will become apparent in later chapters. What we ought to consider straightaway, however, is the centrality of the national in the modern social imaginary.

I.4. Ideology and the National Imaginary

New treatments of nationality and nationalism appearing on the academic scene since the early 1980s have advanced convincing arguments in favor of a tight connection between the forces of modernity, the spread of industrial capitalism, and the elite-engineered construction of the "national community" as a cultural artifact. As Eric Hobsbawm notes, "The basic characteristic of the modern nation and everything associated with it is its modernity."[23] Even scholars like Anthony Smith, who reject the modernist view that nations were simply "invented" without the significant incorporation of premodern ethnic ties and histories, concede that nationalism represents "a modern movement and ideology, which emerged in the latter half of the eighteenth century in Western Europe and America...."[24] Smith's definition of nationalism as an "ideological movement for the attainment and maintenance of a nation" usefully highlights the idiosyncratic ways of processing and disseminating secular ideas that emerged in the nineteenth century as a distinctive feature of modernity. As Tom Nairn explains, "An ism ceased to denote just a system of general ideas (like Platonism or Thomism) and evolved into a proclaimed cause or movement—no longer a mere school but a party or societal trend."[25] In other words, ideas acquired alluring banner headlines and truth-claims that resonated with people's interests and aspirations and thus bound them to a specific political program. Having to choose sides in these proliferating battles of political ideas, like-minded individuals organized themselves into clubs, associations, movements, and political parties with the primary objective of enlisting more people to their preferred normative vision of the national.

There is, however, a serious downside to Smith's definition: it turns nationalism into an ideology of the same ilk as liberalism or conservatism. This begs the question of how nationalism can be both a distinct political ideology and a common source of inspiration for a variety of political belief systems. Sensing the overarching stature of the national, Benedict Anderson and other social thinkers with an anthropological bent have resisted the idea that nationalism should be seen as a distinct ideology. Instead, they refer to it as a "cultural artifact of a particular kind," that is, a relatively broad cultural system more closely related to "kinship" and "religion" than to "liberalism" or "conservatism."[26] For this reason, the national has often been described as an overarching *esprit general* capable of integrating different layers of the social into a cultural unity. Reaffirmed in a "daily plebiscite," it is said to underpin modern collective identities forged by common memories and common acts of forgetting.[27] In the same vein, sociologist Liah Greenfeld has likened the national to a powerful cultural system that produced the major structures of modernity, including the modern nation-state.[28] In spite of some remaining differences, most of these perspectives share the conviction that the national decisively colors the modern social imaginary.

Hence, we ought to treat the national not as a separate ideology but as the background to our communal existence that emerged in the Northern Hemisphere with the American and French Revolutions. Indeed, it gave the modern social imaginary its distinct flavor in the form of various factual and normative assumptions that political communities, in order to count as "legitimate," had to be nation-states.[29] Benedict Anderson, for example, speaks of "modern imaginings of the nation" as a limited and sovereign community of fundamentally equal members whose knowledge of each other is, in most cases, not direct, but mediated in linear time through the diffusion of discursive literacy and other factors.[30] The national imaginary, then, refers to the taken-for-granted understanding in which the nation—plus its affiliated or to-be-affiliated state—serves as the communal frame of the political.[31]

What, then, is the precise relationship between the national and ideology? Or, to reverse the question, what is the connection between political belief systems and the national imaginary? As I will seek to demonstrate in the first part of this book, the explicit grand ideologies gave political expression to the implicit national imaginary. To be sure, each ideology deployed and assembled its core concepts—liberty, progress, race, class, rationality, tradition, community, welfare, security, and so on—in specific and unique ways. But the elite codifiers of these ideational systems pursued their specific political goals under the background umbrella of the national imaginary. Liberalism, conservatism, socialism, communism, and Nazism/fascism were all "nationalist" in the sense of performing the same fundamental process of translating the overarching national imaginary into concrete political doctrines, agendas, and spatial arrangements. In so doing, ideologies normalized national territories; spoke in recognized national languages; appealed to national histories; told national legends and myths; or glorified a national "race." They articulated the national imaginary according to a great variety of criteria that were said to constitute the defining essence of the community.[32]

As we shall see shortly, the essentialism of race gained tremendous traction in the second half of the nineteenth century. Anthropologist Arjun Appadurai even goes so far as to argue that, "No modern nation, however benign its political system and however eloquent its public voices may be about the virtues of tolerance, multiculturalism, and inclusion, is free of the idea that its national sovereignty is built on some sort of ethnic genius."[33] But whatever ideologies purported the essence of the nation to be, they always developed their truth-claims by decontesting their core concepts within the national imaginary. Liberals, for example, spoke of "freedom" as applying to autonomous individuals belonging to the same national community, that is, the liberties of *French*, *Colombian*, or *Australian* citizens. The conservative fondness for "law and order" received its highest expression in the notion of *national* security. Tellingly, even the ostensibly internationalist creed of socialists and communists achieved its concrete political formulation only as *German* social democracy or Soviet *Russia's* "socialism in one country." For two centuries, the partisans of political ideologies clashed with each other over such important issues as participation, the extent of civil rights, the purposes and forms of government, the role of the state, the significance of race and ethnicity, and the scope of political obligations. Clinging to their different political visions, they hardly noticed their common embeddedness in the national imaginary.[34]

I.5. Ideology and the Global Imaginary

In the aftermath of World War II, new ideas, theories, and practices produced in the public consciousness a similar sense of rupture with the past that had occurred at the time of the French Revolution. Novel technologies facilitated the speed and intensity with which these ideas and practices infiltrated the national imaginary. Images, people, and materials circulated more freely across national boundaries. This new sense of "the global" that erupted within and onto the national began to undermine the normality and self-contained coziness of the modern nation-state—especially deeply engrained notions of community tied to a sovereign and clearly demarcated territory containing relatively homogenous populations.[35] Identities based on national membership became destabilized. During the early decades of the Cold War, the changing social imaginary led prominent thinkers in the First World to proclaim the "end of ideology." As evidence for their assertion, they pointed to the political–cultural consensus underpinning a common Western "community of values" and the socioeconomic welfare state compromise struck between liberalism and democratic socialism. Conversely, detractors of the end-of-ideology thesis seized upon the decolonization dynamics in the Third World as well as the rise of the countercultural "new social movements" in the 1960s and 1970s as evidence for their view that the familiar political belief systems were being complemented by "new ideologies" such as feminism, environmentalism, and postcolonialism.

I argue in Chapter 4 that the most fundamental novelty of these "new ideologies" lay in their sensitivity toward the rising global imaginary, regardless of whether they were formulated by the forces of the New Left or the cohorts of the New Right. Starting in the late 1970s, and especially after the 1991 disintegration of the Soviet Union, the ideas of the New Right gained the upper hand across the globe. By the mid-1990s, a growing chorus of global social elites was fastening onto the new buzzword "globalization" as the central metaphor for their political agenda—the creation of a single global free market and the spread of consumerist values around the world. Most importantly, they translated the rising social imaginary into largely economistic claims laced with references to the global: "global" trade and financial markets, "worldwide" flows of goods, services, and labor, "transnational" corporations, "offshore" financial centers, and so on.

But globalization was never merely a matter of increasing flows of capital and goods across national borders. Rather, it constitutes a multidimensional set of processes in which images, sound bites, metaphors, myths, symbols, and spatial arrangements of globality were just as important as economic and technological dynamics. The "objective" acceleration and multiplication of global material networks occurs hand in hand with the intensifying "subjective" recognition of a shrinking world. Such heightened awareness of the compression of time and space influences the direction and material instantiations of global flows. As sociologist Roland Robertson points out, the compression of the world into a single place increasingly makes the global the frame of reference for human thought and action.[36] Globalization involves both the macrostructures of community and the microstructures of personhood. It extends deep into the core of the self and its dispositions, facilitating the creation of new identities nurtured by the intensifying relations between the individual and the globe.[37]

Like the conceptual earthquake that shook Europe and the Americas more than 200 years ago, today's destabilization of the national affects the entire planet. The ideologies dominating the world today are no longer exclusively articulations of the national imaginary but reconfigured ideational systems that constitute potent translations of the dawning global imaginary. Although my account of this transformation emphasizes rupture, it would be foolish to deny obvious continuities. As Saskia Sassen notes, "the incipient process of denationalization and the ascendance of novel social formations depend in good part on capabilities shaped and developed in the national age."[38] Today's discursive preeminence of the "market," for example, harkens back to the heyday of liberalism in mid-Victorian England. And yet, this concept is no longer exclusively tied to the old paradigm of self-contained national economies but also refers to a model of global exchanges among national actors, subnational agencies, supranational bodies, networks of nongovernmental organizations, and transnational corporations. Our New World Order contains a multiplicity of orders networked together on multiple levels. Disaggregating nation-states struggle to come to grips with relational concepts of sovereignty while facing unprecedented challenges to their authority from both subnational and supranational collectivities.[39]

In Chapter 5, I contend that "market globalism" emerged in the 1990s as a comprehensive ideology extolling, among other things, the virtues of globally integrating markets. It discarded, absorbed, and rearranged large chunks of the grand ideologies while at the same time generating genuinely new ideas. The outcome was a hybridized political belief system capable of articulating the global imaginary in concrete political programs and agendas. But no single ideational system ever enjoys absolute dominance. Battered by persistent gales of political dissent, the small fissures and ever-present inconsistencies in political ideologies threaten to turn into major cracks and serious contradictions. As the Roaring Nineties drew to a close, market globalism found itself challenged on the political left by "justice globalism," an alternative translation of the rising global imaginary.

Although some political commentators have suggested that virulent forms of national populism embodied by the likes of Jean-Marie Le Pen and Jörg Haider constitute the most powerful right-wing challenge to market globalism, I argue in Chapter 6 that this designation belongs to "jihadist globalism." Far from being a regionally contained "last gasp" of a backward-looking, militant offshoot of political Islam, jihadism of the al-Qaeda variety represents a potent globalism of worldwide appeal. In response to the ascent of jihadist globalism epitomized by the terrorist attacks of 9/11, market globalism morphed into imperial globalism. This "hard-powering" of market globalism has been widely read as clear evidence for the staying power of the national, most clearly reflected in American Empire and its unilateral desire to remake the world in its own image. Analyzing a number of key texts produced by imperial globalists, I will attempt to show that American Empire is not at all incompatible with the rising global imaginary.

The book ends with a brief consideration of the current convergence of religion and ideology. Are we witnessing a reversal of the powerful secularization dynamic that served two centuries ago as the midwife of ideology? Is the rising global imaginary more hospitable to religious articulations than its predecessor? If so, then perhaps today's destabilization of the national also implies the unsettling of the ideological.

Attentive readers will notice that I refer to all three ideological translators of the global imaginary as "globalisms"—even though I previously argued against considering "nationalism" as a distinct ideology. Since the global possesses the same overarching stature as the national why should it be reduced to its concrete ideological articulations? The reason I use "globalism" on the level of ideology has to do with the difficulty of expressing the articulations of the global imaginary in familiar terms. For example, it was not until the 1820s that "liberal" was first used by aristocratic European elites as referring to the "ideology" adopted by Spanish *liberales* who opposed the restoration of autocratic monarchy under Ferdinand VII. Still, throughout the first half of the nineteenth century, the conventional meaning of "liberal" as a derivative of "liberality" (a synonym for the aristocratic virtues of generosity and open-mindedness) continued to circulate in the public discourse side by side with its new meaning.[40] Similarly, the old British party labels "Whigs" and "Tories" did not give way to their modern ideological significations of "Liberals" and "Conservatives" until the 1830s. In fact, "Tory" is still in use today. It is, therefore, my hope that "globalism," too, will eventually be known by different terms referring to the various ideological articulations of the global imaginary. In the meantime, however, I continue to rely on "market globalism," "justice globalism," and "jihadist globalism" much in the same way as one could refer to the grand ideologies as liberal nationalism, conservative nationalism, socialist nationalism, and so on.

Finally, before turning to the opening chapter, let me anticipate two objections raised at almost every public presentation of this book's main thesis. The first alleges that my narrative (re)produces modernist categories unsuitable for capturing the ideational dynamics of a globalizing world. Obviously, there is some truth to the charge that my efforts to analyze and describe the ideologies of the rising global imaginary rely on an established conceptual toolbox. To some degree, the modernist urge to force complex social phenomena into tight classification schemes and precise typologies dovetails with the nationalist impulse to draw rigid boundaries around collective identities and territories. But observers of transitional times necessarily retain a foothold in the old while struggling to find a toehold in the new. To that extent, then, my reliance on an established toolbox appears to be unavoidable. Nevertheless, I have made a conscious attempt to couch my understanding of the global in fluid metaphors of interdependence rather than fixed "zombie categories."[41]

The second objection involves a reading of my thesis as yet another variation on the familiar theme of the death of the nation-state.[42] That is not at all what I am arguing. In fact, to pronounce the national dead would be both inaccurate and premature, just as it would be myopic to deny the eruption of the global on all geographical scales. The best way of characterizing what I have in mind is to speak of a destabilization of the national that goes hand in hand with the spotty and uneven superimposition of the global. Ulf Hedetoft and Mette Hjort put it well in their discerning exploration of transnational identity:

"Globality"—for want of a better term—spells significant changes in the cultural landscapes of belonging, not because it supplants the nation-state ... but because it changes the contexts (politically, culturally, and geographically) for them, situates national identity and belonging differently, and superimposes itself on "nationality" as a novel frame of reference, values, and consciousness, primarily for the globalized elites, but increasingly for "ordinary citizens" as well.[43]

Potent as they are, the dynamics of denationalization at the heart of globalization neither propel the world to an inevitable endpoint nor have these forces dispensed entirely with the vast ideational and material arsenals of the nation-state. Today, the national and the global rub up against each other in myriad settings and on multiple levels. Putting the analytic spotlight on the changing ideological landscape not only yields a better understanding of the dominant political belief systems of our time but also helps us make sense of the profound and multidimensional dynamics that go by the name of globalization.

Part I

The National Imaginary

1

Ideology and Revolution: From Superscience to False Consciousness

Ideology is a system of truths closely tied together.

Antoine Louis Claude Destutt, Comte de Tracy (1798)

Yes, they are obsessed with meddling in my government, those windbags! My aversion for this race of *idéologues* amounts to disgust.

Napoleon Bonaparte (1802)

We start with real, active humans, and, on the basis of their real life-process, we demonstrate the development of ideological reflexes and echoes of this life-process. The phantoms inhabiting the human brain are necessary sublimations of empirically verifiable life-processes tied to material premises. Morality, religion, metaphysics, and the rest of ideology as well as their corresponding forms of consciousness thus no longer retain the appearance of independence.

Karl Marx and Friedrich Engels (1846)

1.1. Ideology and the French Revolution

The social and industrial revolutions that swept across Europe and the Americas between 1776 and 1848 served as midwives to the birth of a new social imaginary decisively colored by the national. The role played by the French Revolution in this process was even more crucial than what essentially amounted to a large-scale tax rebellion across the Atlantic. But this is not to downplay the significance of the American Revolution. French revolutionaries proudly invoked the example of the United States of America when linking their new language of patriotism and republicanism to the central notion of popular sovereignty. After all, the

American framers of the 1787 Constitution chose "We the People" as the opening words of their cherished document. Article III of the 1789 French Declaration of the Rights of Man and the Citizen expresses the same sentiments: "The nation is essentially the source of all sovereignty; nor can any individual, or any bond of men, be entitled to any authority which is not expressly derived from it."

Indeed, the modern concept of a nation based on popular sovereignty proved its powers of social mobilization and political legitimation for the first time in the great revolutions of the eighteenth century.[1] Within a few years, French revolutionary leaders would seize upon Jean-Jacques Rousseau's notion of a unifying "general will" to summon citizen-soldiers to a war for the defense and the glory of *la Grande Nation*. Pervaded by bloody images of battle and death, their ferocious war songs rang out in tandem with loving hymns to the motherland symbolized in the new Holy Trinity of Nation, Republic, and Revolution. Taking their cues from France, republican-minded elites across Europe seized upon the powerful template of nationhood to push for a fundamental political reorganization of their states.

For many generations preceding these cataclysmic events, powerful cultural systems had reproduced political and social hierarchies in the form of tribes, clanships, trading city-states, fiefdoms, dynastic empires, and absolutist monarchies. Although the administrative centralization of the state began well before the age of revolution, the authority of government was rooted in the person of the ruler. Likewise, the "nation" had been a part of the European experience since at least the sixteenth century. But its meaning was inextricably connected to monarchical rule. Henri IV of France and Elizabeth I of England, for example, served as the paradigmatic emblems of their respective nations.[2] Two centuries later, French revolutionaries would refer to the traditional aristocratic "society of orders" in pejorative fashion as *ancien régime*—an antiquated order based on the arbitrary powers of the king and his vassals and backed by a well-endowed Catholic clergy that monopolized religious worship and education.[3] Thus presided over by privileged elites, the old regimes of Europe were embedded in an ideational framework deeply colored by religious imaginings, which expressed themselves in potent symbols, metaphors, myths, narratives, rituals and festivals, as well as a sacred liturgy. As Pierre Manent observes, "In the beginning, Europe was dominated by the idea of Christian salvation."[4]

Politics and religion formed an inseparable but often tense whole, with the clergy invoking timeworn formulas of Divine Right to buttress fixed aristocratic hierarchies. Ultimate meaning was not to be found in this world but in the far distant regions of God's realm. The terrifying magnificence of this overarching transcendental order could only be hinted at in awe-inspiring arrangements of social space such as the magnificent cathedrals of Christendom that towered over the bowed heads of nameless worshipers. God served as the master concept that united the cognitive, aesthetic, and ethical dimensions of society into a totality, politically expressed in the singularity and indivisibility of monarchical rule.

The Revolution shook the old social imaginary to its foundations. Expanding the fledgling "secular" sphere of politics in the name of the people of the French nation, the revolutionaries searched for the best institutional expression of the will of the people. Already in its early phase—from the storming of the Bastille in July 1789 to the flight and capture of Louis XVI in June 1791—the Revolution had produced a National Assembly which voted overwhelmingly for such drastic measures as its seizure of sovereign power; the abolition of ancient feudal rights and privileges; the establishment of a Constitution that granted the king only limited veto powers on new laws; and, perhaps most tellingly, a radical reorganization of the Church calling for lay elections of priests and bishops and the nationalization of ecclesiastical boundaries. Having been assigned a meaningless honorific role befitting his status as a "foreigner," Pope Pius VI angrily denounced these developments, shivering at the thought of "constitutional priests" administering the Holy Sacraments to the faithful.

Little did the Pontiff know that much worse was to come in the next phase of the Revolution. Within three short years, the royal couple and thousands of aristocrats and commoners had lost their heads to the nationalist version of the feudal ax invented by the physician Joseph Guillotine. The proclamation of the Republic had been marked with the introduction of a secular calendar beginning with Year I of Liberty. Civil and foreign wars had devastated the country, devouring its economic and human resources. Terror had been officially adopted as the guiding policy of government. Virtually every Church in France had been closed down. Reminiscent of the Great Persecution unleashed by the Roman Emperor Diocletian at the outset of the fourth century, Maximilien Robespierre's Reign of Terror aimed at nothing less than the eradication of Christianity. And yet, the Jacobin Cult of the Supreme Being infused society with hymns, prayers, and festivals modeled on Christian liturgy. It substituted the Goddess of Reason for the Virgin Mary; the Temple of Reason for the Cathedral of Notre Dame; and Nature for Providence. The induction of revolutionary heroes like slain *sans-culottes* leader Jean-Paul Marat into the new pantheon of martyred patriots was eerily reminiscent of Catholic saint worship. The emergence of such practices during the Revolution should therefore serve as a cautious warning to scholars fond of drawing hard and fast boundaries between "secular ideologies" and "religious and magical beliefs."[5]

In 1795, at last, a new republican constitution placed France's executive powers into the hands of a politically moderate Directory. The Revolution was drifting into calmer waters, rekindling people's hopes of returning to some semblance of normalcy. And yet, the traditional social imaginary had been permanently destabilized as the certitudes of religion and the *ancien régime* went up in smoke. Reluctant to return to the past but unsure of the future, the new guardians of the Revolution struggled to convey a fresh sense of certainty in a language that left behind the excesses of the "French catastrophe," as Edmund Burke had sneeringly referred to the revolutionary events in a speech to the British Parliament. Obviously, the Enlightenment legacy loomed large, but Reason had been badly bruised by the murderous actions of the Jacobins. While "nation" and "the people" remained the buzzwords of the time, they were still in the public mind tied to the Reign of Terror. Slowly, the social elites on whose shoulders the postrevolutionary political and intellectual leadership had fallen stumbled into what looked like the most sensible ideational foundation for the new era: a pragmatic mixture of *la science* and *la patrie* anchored in the political values of a republican France.

A happy marriage of the rational with the national, however, required renewed efforts to stabilize the Revolution.[6] The new Constitution was a step in the right direction, but much work remained to be done. The most pressing task was the creation of pragmatic policies aimed at maximizing public utility. After all, public morale was still low. Inflation was running exorbitantly high. Food prices in the cities had gone through the roof. Selling confessions to the highest bidders, itinerant priests blamed the "godless Republic" for their misfortunes. Dangers to the centrist republican regime lurked everywhere. An uprising of disorganized *sans-culottes* in the spring of 1795 was rapidly followed by a botched royalist *coup d'état*. A few months later, Gracchus Babeuf and his radical followers launched their "communist" revolt. These unsuccessful attempts to unseat the government quickly convinced its five Executive Directors to articulate a moderate political vision that steered clear of a radical left ready to unleash a new wave of terror, while simultaneously suppressing a reactionary right eager to restore the Bourbon monarchy.

The influential distinction between the political left and right had originated in the French National Assembly in 1789 when its members had faced the vexing issue of the royal veto over legislation. At stake was, of course, the principle of popular sovereignty. The seating patterns in the chamber reflected the major political division between those representatives congregating on the right side who favored providing the king with an unrestricted veto and those on the left who categorically opposed it. Deputies supporting a conditional royal veto sat at the center of the chamber. These spatial arrangements solidified into French parliamentary assemblies permanently seated in tiered and semicircular formations, thus providing a template for parliamentary seating arrangements in several other countries, including the US Congress in Washington.[7]

Recognizing the crucial importance of courting "public opinion," the Directory unleashed a publicity campaign built around the claim that the fate of the country hung in the balance. The viability of the French nation, they argued, depended on clear and balanced ideas. After all, flawed concepts and faulty thinking had been responsible for the excesses of both royal despotism and Jacobin violence. Hence, social stability and public happiness demanded the firm rejection of religious metaphysics as well as half-baked radical notions. Seeking to enlist the brightest minds in the nation in this new quest for certitude, lawmakers passed a comprehensive public education law which established the National Institute of Sciences and Arts to replace the old royal Academies that had been abolished in the tumultuous summer of 1793. Divided into three disciplinary clusters or "classes" charged with "uniting all of human knowledge," the Institute's declared mission was to conduct scientific research, publish discoveries, correspond with other learned societies, and advise the Directory about "scientific and literary works of general utility and promoting the glory of the Republic."[8]

On April 4, 1796, France's political and intellectual elites gathered for the festive inauguration of the Institute. Pierre-Claude Daunou, a former prisoner of the Jacobins and now Head of the Institute, invoked the legacy of the French Enlightenment to promise the scientific advancement of "public happiness." The Institute's first task, he declared, was to develop a new system of public education dedicated to the growth of the human sciences within the political framework of the current French Republic.[9] Daunou's utilitarian sentiments resonated with the objectives of the Republic's Directors who held high expectations for the Institute's Second Class of Moral and Political Sciences. At stake was nothing less than the invention of a scientific project that would "purify national morals" and disclose "to the prudence of the legislators the future destiny of people in the tableau of their past virtues and even their past errors."[10]

Count Antoine Destutt de Tracy, an ambitious Research Associate of the Second Class' "Section on the Analysis of Sensations and Ideas," rose to the challenge. A vague notion of a new "science of ideas" had been simmering in Tracy's mind long before he introduced its basic principles in a series of papers read at the Institute between 1796 and 1798. Disparaging the old truth-claims of theology as "metaphysics," the Count equally rejected the fledgling discipline of "psychology" as a pseudoscience built around the unempirical concept of "soul." Instead, he proposed "ideology" as a genuinely scientific program capable of eliminating "faulty concepts" from society. The new project was to be built upon the method of scientific analysis pioneered by Antoine Lavosier who had founded the modern science of chemistry on the disaggregation of chemical composites into their constituent parts. Treating human thought the same way, Tracy hoped to discover the basic ideational elements by analyzing complex human concepts. If successful, ideologists would be in the position to provide the theoretical basis of the Directory's political agenda of building a cohesive Republican nation on empirically verifiable certainties strictly based on reason.

Initially, Tracy's program generated considerable enthusiasm among his academic peers. But his bold new vision ultimately foundered on the political ambitions of a dashing Corsican general determined to block the path of progressive political and social reform recommended by the Institute's "ideologues." Forced to endure the persistent humiliations of Napoleon Bonaparte's self-serving jabs at ideology, Tracy's death in 1836 spared him from witnessing the still greater impact of another negative stereotype leveled against his science by the founders of "scientific socialism," Karl Marx and Friedrich Engels.

1.2. Destutt de Tracy's Superscience of Ideas

Born into a noble French family in 1754, Antoine Destutt de Tracy joined the Royal Cavalry at the tender age of 16 and was promoted quickly through its commissioned ranks. He proved to be popular with his peers, mostly for the lavish parties he hosted on many occasions. Despite his obvious fondness for the pleasures of the body, however, the young Count was deeply committed to the cultivation of the mind. Shortly before entering the army, he had embarked on a pilgrimage to worship at the altar of Reason propagated by Voltaire, his philosophical hero. The aged *philosophe* received him warmly "with all the seductions of his grace and mind." The Count would later claim that his idol even touched his forehead—a gesture the impressionable youth interpreted as an auspicious act of philosophical benediction. Voltaire's influence would remain visible throughout Tracy's work, particularly in his later attacks on religious prejudice and his rejection of Leibnizian optimism and its central idea of Providence.[11]

Enthusiastically embracing the libertarian ideals of the American Revolution, the young officer thrived in the Enlightenment atmosphere he encountered at Strasbourg University. Engrossed in the works of Montesquieu, Diderot, Rousseau, and Helvétius, he later recalled, "My eyes were dazzled and my mind was astonished.... I felt myself swept along in a moral and intellectual movement as violent and as rapid as the physical movement of the earth."[12] When the first rumblings of the coming revolution rolled across the country in May 1788 in the form of stiff opposition against King Louis XVI's controversial suspension of the provincial *parlements*, Colonel Tracy refused to order his reluctant troops to move against the rebellious regional assemblies. He supported the convocation of the Estates General, and, after a series of meetings with leading moderate aristocrats, which included the American hero Marquise de Lafayette, delivered rousing speeches in favor of greater provincial participation in government. "True representatives of the nation," Tracy argued, had to be "legally and freely elected" within the emerging framework of three separate orders in the Estates General. Once again, the Count drew his inspiration from the American example embodied in Benjamin Franklin and Thomas Jefferson, whom he almost certainly met in Paris between 1776 and 1789. Three decades later, Jefferson would translate the final volume of Tracy's seminal *Elements of Ideology*, recommending it to American readers as a "production of the first order in the science of our thinking faculty, or of the understanding."[13]

In the meantime, the budding French politician spent most of his time drawing up *cahiers des doléances* demanding the freedom of the press and commerce, the establishment of public education, and a drastic reduction in government spending.[14] Promptly elected to the National Assembly, Tracy supported the abolition of all feudal privileges—including his own—and praised the Declaration of the Rights of Man and the Citizen as "the best ever made." At the same time, however, he managed to avoid heated debates in the Assembly, seeking to steer clear of factions and parties. Emphasizing in general terms the virtues of liberty and patriotism, he concerned himself mostly with administrative detail, while his cautious stance at the political Center was reflected in his membership in moderate constitutionalist clubs such as the Society of 1789.[15]

Two of Tracy's speeches survive in the form of printed political pamphlets. The first is an impassioned rebuttal of Edmund Burke's attack on the principles of the French Revolution, dismissing the English model of gradual parliamentarianism as an "incomplete process" unfit to serve as a role model for France. Blaming royal despotism for his nation's violent upheavals, the patriotic Count ends his polemic by sneering at unwanted "lessons from foreigners" with little direct knowledge of the "marvels of French citizenship."[16] The second pamphlet offers an eloquent defense of the political rights of free Blacks in the Caribbean island of Saint Dominique (Santo Domingo), then a French colony plagued by chronic social unrest and violence. In addition to relying on familiar notions of natural rights, Tracy also advanced the utilitarian argument that racial equality in Saint Dominique would increase the happiness of both the French people and the majority of the island's inhabitants.[17]

Following his brief parliamentary stint in the Assembly, Tracy reported for active duty as Brigadier General under Lafayette's command in the impending war against Austria. Incensed by the chaotic situation on the front that found many French soldiers without adequate food or equipment, the Count took unlimited leave of absence and returned to Paris in what must have appeared to many of his comrades as an act of treachery second only to desertion.[18] Taking immediate precautions against possible acts of political retribution, Tracy moved to the Parisian suburb of Auteuil where he passed his time reading and socializing with fellow intellectuals in the chic Enlightenment salon of Madame Helvétius. Sensing real danger to his life after the arrest of some salon members, the Count resorted to dramatic public displays of his republican patriotism by paying for the salary and equipment of army volunteers from Paris and returning his Royal Cross of Saint Louis to the local authorities. Ultimately, however, even his willingness to part with most of his liquid assets did not save him from arrest on charges of "*incivisme* and aristocracy." Continuing his unsuccessful attempts to prove his innocence from prison, Tracy penned a long memoir highlighting his loyalty to the nation and the Republic.[19]

Resorting to voracious bouts of reading to take his mind off his seemingly inevitable rendezvous with "Madame Guillotine," the despondent prisoner struck one day upon Etienne de Condillac's study, *Traité des Systèmes*. Offering a utilitarian defense of natural law doctrine, the Enlightenment *philosophe* urged his readers to abandon metaphysical speculation in favor of sound rational analysis and empirical observation. Tracy had long admired Condillac, but this time, the book's central message struck deeper than ever before. Walled up in his cell, no longer distracted by the social and political whirlwind raging beyond his prison walls, the Count experienced an epiphany in which it was suddenly revealed to him that all major intellectual advances in history had been the result of uncovering "in the facts those important and very general truths which have not yet been detected." Tracy further realized that all genuine scientific innovators possessed the rare gift of grasping these certainties and expressing them in the form of precisely ordered chains of ideas that corresponded to the factuality of the material world. Consequently, the accumulation of knowledge depended on the mind's ability to lay bare the "main truths which result from analysis of thought."[20]

Elated by this unexpected jolt of insight, the prisoner hastily scribbled down a "summary of truths" in the form of algebraic equations beginning with the deductive claim that "the faculty of thinking or perceiving = knowledge = truth." Adding to this formula " = virtue = happiness, sentiment of loving," he ended his deductive chain with " = liberty = equality = philanthropy."[21] The reliance on mathematics to elucidate social phenomena had been pioneered by the *philosophe* Jean de Condorcet whom Tracy had met at Madame Helvétius' salon. Though the Count's prison equations were based on the same core insight of John Locke's "sensationalist philosophy" that had inspired Condorcet and Condillac, his initial enthusiasm for their "social mathematics" would later be tempered, and eventually rejected as a peculiar form of reasoning that considered ideas only under the limited principles of quantity and numbers.

For the moment, however, the grandeur of Tracy's philosophical breakthrough only seemed to magnify the pointlessness of his impending death. On the very day he committed to his diary his summary of ideological truths—the fifth of Thermidor of the Year II (July 23, 1794)—forty-five of his fellow prisoners were carted off to the guillotine. With the Revolutionary Tribunal expected to pronounce unfavorably on his case within a week, Tracy was convinced that he would not live to see another autumn, his favorite season. Then, only four days later, fate unexpectedly intervened with the overthrow and execution of Robespierre. Released from prison, Tracy arrived in Auteuil in surprisingly good physical condition, except that his hair had turned stark white.[22]

Two years later, the politically rehabilitated Count accepted the call to join the new National Institute of Sciences and Arts. Eager to put some flesh on the conceptual skeleton of his prison vision, Tracy reaffirmed Locke's proposition that sensations are both the source and the origin of our ideas. Raising the fundamental epistemological question of what humans can truly know, he drew a sharp line of demarcation between "positive knowledge" and "metaphysical pretensions." Only those insights extracted from a rigorous analysis of mental operations, he insisted, should count as "positive science."[23] However, since Tracy held that all concepts were but transformed sensations, he assumed that ideas originated in the "factuality" of material reality. Acknowledging his intellectual debt to Francis Bacon's scientific paradigm, the Count emphasized that all positive knowledge was ultimately derived from empirical observation and experience: "[I]n this world, you never do anything but see facts and draw consequences from them, receive impressions and notice their circumstances; in a word, sensing and deducing (which is still a form of sensing). These are your only means of instruction, the only sources of truth you can ever acquire...."[24]

Uniting the externality of the empirical world with the internality of mental operations, Tracy suggested that the physical laws underlying the intricate combinations of physical entities were, in principle, not different from the forces governing the myriad constellations of ideas and sensations. But what, exactly, was the substance of these forces? Tracy argued boldly that "the whole science of logic" could be reduced to two "irrefutable facts," both of which resulted "manifestly from the scrupulous examination of our intellectual operations." A key to his philosophy, the following passage is worth citing in its entirety:

The first [fact] is, that our perceptions being every thing for us, we are perfectly, completely, and necessarily sure of all that we actually feel. The second [fact], which is but a consequence of that, is that none of our judgments, taken separately, can be erroneous, since, for the very reason that we see one idea in another, it must be actually there; but that their falsity, when it takes place, is purely relative to all anterior judgments, which we permit to subsist, and consists in this, that we believe the idea, in which we see a new element, to be the same we have always had under the same sign, while it is really different, since the new element we actually see there is incompatible with some of those which we have seen previously there. So that, to avoid contradiction, it would be necessary either to take away the former, or not admit the latter.[25]

Tracy's "first fact" clearly serves to throw out, once and for all, the old sources of certainty that had been blackened by the flames of the Revolution. Anchored in the Enlightenment tradition, his new certitude was the human ability to sense or perceive the "truth" of an objective natural world utterly devoid of God or divine Providence. Our "basic ideas"— preliminary sense data—were "true" insofar as they accurately reflected the factuality of our empirical environment. This reality could be perceived through its tangible "resistance" to the "movement" of our senses, like the sensations of solidity we feel when our fingers pass over a rock. Hence, Tracy suggested that Descartes' famous phrase "I think, therefore I am" ought to be amended to "I sense, therefore I exist."[26] This recognition of humans as primarily sensing beings inhabiting an empirical universe, the Count argued, would have saved the great French philosopher from his dualistic blunder of separating ideas from matter. But how did such serious mental "errors" arise even in the minds of geniuses like Descartes?

Tracy's response relates to the "second fact," namely our imperfect faculty of memory that goes hand in hand with the human propensity to create imprecise signs. While the sensations we receive from the external world are accurate and reliable, the mental operations involving the ordering of ideas corresponding to sensations may be faulty. The process of reasoning, Tracy suggested, involves the rapid succession of complex ideas that are connected to each other through constant acts of "judgment," that is, the ability of our mind to link related ideas in ordered conceptual chains. But this rapid mental matching of current ideas with older impressions yields "correct judgments" only if past impressions are recalled accurately, thus producing logical chains of concepts. However, as the memory of our sensations fades with the passage of time, it results inevitably in the construction of erroneous chains made up of unrelated ideas. To make matters worse, Tracy argued, all thought processes rely heavily on language, that is, systems of signs that attempt to fix ideas in memory. Given the multiplicity of associations related to each sign, we could never be sure if our understanding of a word or a sentence corresponded precisely to similar understandings held by other groups and individuals—even within our own cultural environment. Finally, the Count conceded that all languages evolved in haphazard fashion, causing additional misunderstandings and errors. Ideally, of course, correct chains of ideas would correspond exactly to logical sequences of speech just as precise language would be reflected in related clusters of ideas. In practice, however, our imperfect memory combines with our sloppy use of language to produce chains of ideas in which "truth" cohabited with incoherence and error.[27]

At this critical juncture in his theory of ideology, Tracy wrestled with what Michael Freeden calls the "indeterminacy of meaning," that is, the inevitable susceptibility of thought and language to a multiplicity of understandings and interpretations. There are two possible strategies to cope with this predicament. First, one might restrict interpretive possibilities to those few options that are deemed "correct" on account of some higher standard like "divine revelation," "reasoned deduction," "sound observation," or "scientific analysis." If such narrow attempts to "lock in" meanings became widely accepted in society, then those ideas would have been successfully "decontested," that is, successfully removed from further challenges. Such decontested ideas would count as "truth" not just in a semantic sense but also politically since they now constituted powerful instruments for fashioning collective decisions. Signaling finality and closure of discussion, they would form the backbone of a concrete political agenda.[28] These claims would combine into full-blown "ideologies" in the modern sense of the word, that is, into fairly coherent political belief systems accepted as truth by social groups.

A second way of dealing with conceptual indeterminacy might be to accept or even embrace the inevitable multiplicity of meanings, and, at best, strive for greater conceptual clarity without aiming for arbitrary closure. One of the politically salient outcomes of such an open-ended procedure would be the creation of more flexible ideologies based on the valorization of doubt—that is, the recognition and appreciation of the social benefits that often accrue from a good dose of constructive skepticism injected into all claims to truth. At the same time, however, we should note that destabilized societies like late eighteenth-century France were ill-equipped to cope with perpetual challenges to political authority that emerge from the cultivation of doubt. Hence, narrow ideologies defending single-minded truths might be more effective avenues toward stability and law and order.

In his less dogmatic moments, notably toward the end of his life, Tracy opted for the second, more flexible, strategy. In his early career, however, he embraced the first option, promising his audience to rectify and purify the French language by making its words correspond to their "true ideas." Bestowing on the moral and political sciences "as much certitude as the mathematical sciences," ideology would prove "by facts what Locke and Condillac have shown by reasoning, that morality and politics are capable of demonstration."[29] Since all sciences consisted of different combinations of ideas and concepts, Tracy argued that *idéologie* was "incontestably" the "first of all the sciences in the genealogical order," which made it *"la théorie des théories"*—an overarching "super-science." Serving as both a means and an end—a scientific method and a body of scientific truths—ideology was the medicine required to "cure the moral and political sciences from centuries of prejudice and error."[30]

Tracy's unshakable confidence in his science of ideas was matched only by his boundless contempt for religion and the clergy as rival disseminators of truth-claims. He was especially fond of the provocative thesis offered by his contemporary Charles Dupuis that all religions, including Christianity, represented irrational forms of zodiac worship. Even Jesus Christ, Tracy quipped, was "just one of a thousand versions of the sun god." Ideology, not religion, he thundered, ought to form the basis of ethics in society, for morality "is only an application of the science of the generation of our sentiments and of our ideas from which it derives."[31]

It was on this very question of religion that Tracy fought a high-profile intellectual battle with François de Chateaubriand, a staunch defender of Catholicism and future Foreign Minister of the restored Bourbon monarch, Louis XVIII. Engaged in a passionate mission to rehabilitate Christianity in France, Chateaubriand furiously attacked the "materialist" and "soulless" character of Tracy's ideology. Christianity, he argued in a surprisingly utilitarian spirit, was "true" because it promoted beauty, harmony, and moderation. In response, Tracy enlisted the Republican journal *Décade Philosophique* to promote his rationalist ideal of an empirical world objectively discernible by scientific analysis. But both thinkers were united in their attempts to find certitudes in a postrevolutionary world. For Chateaubriand, it was the splendor of an imagined past to be revived by the restoration of a constitutional Bourbon monarchy. Tracy, on the other hand, held fast to his secular vision of a progressive Republic guided by intellectual elites. As Joseph Byrnes notes, the quarrel between these two men defined the polarities of the ideational temperament that pervaded the early decades of the nineteenth century. Chateaubriand's "conservatism" was anchored in an unconditional nostalgia for a nation based on the unity of throne and altar, while Tracy's "liberalism" was steeped in the secular pursuit of the scientific ideal.[32]

Tracy's dogmatic attempts to discredit religion also reflect the tremendous pressure exerted by the regime on the Institute's researchers to produce alternative moral certainties. The Count believed that he had delivered what the Directors had wished for, namely irrefutable principles of reason formulated in the new language of science and nation. Hence, it is not surprising that his ideology initially caught on like wildfire among his colleagues. Two of the Institute's most influential sections were soon dominated by "ideologists."[33] Moreover, Tracy's attempt to narrow down ideas to their correct meaning implied that only experts properly trained in ideology were capable of separating truth from falsehood. As long as it remained within the walls of academia, the potential damage inflicted by this "ideological" version of Platonic elitism might have remained confined to relatively trivial matters. But the trouble with Tracy's vision was that he never meant for it to be confined to a mere exercise in philosophical abstraction. His correct analysis of ideas revealed that politics was neither a metaphysic of terror nor a classical art of prudent statecraft, but a positive science to be applied to the nation. Linking his science of ideas to a politics of secular republicanism and social reform, the Count praised ideology's ability to enhance the "knowledge of effects and their practical consequences." The foundation of education and morality, ideology, was, therefore, political in its efforts to provide firm standards for "regulating society."[34]

Inspired by Helvétius' dictum that the good is always what is useful to the nation, Tracy proceeded to elaborate on the applied dimensions of his science. With respect to education, he called for a new national system of secondary "central schools" in France based on a curriculum intended primarily for the offspring of the propertied classes. Each subject was to be taught according to the "true principles of ideology," which protected students from past moral and metaphysical errors. However, children of the "working class destined for laborious toil" required only terminal primary schooling. With regard to economics, ideological truth prescribed the radical liberalization of commerce and industry according to market principles as well as the application of scientific principles to the nation's productive processes. As for politics, the only correct form of government was a secular republic led by enlightened elites committed to safeguarding the rights and freedoms of individuals, but willing to resort to repressive measures to uphold law and order.

Translating the national imaginary into a concrete political program of action that would later become part of liberalism's agenda, Tracy's science was sweeping in its reach yet riddled with oversimplifications that left it prone to mockery. Similarly, his grandiose vision of intellectual elites providing political authorities with policy recommendations based on timeless certainties opened itself up to caricature and derision by political leaders who thought otherwise. The first and most famous of these detractors was the soon-to-be Emperor of the French whose articulation of the national imaginary became known as Bonapartism.

32

1.3. Bonaparte's Shadowy Metaphysics

In March 1796—only weeks before Destutt de Tracy presented his first programmatic paper on *idéologie* to his colleagues at the Institute—a 26-year-old Corsican artillery general was appointed commander of the French Army in Italy. The series of spectacular military victories over the combined Austrian and Sardinian forces that followed over the next eighteen months made Napoleon Bonaparte a respected leader with his troops and a popular hero back home in France. Owing his meteoric rise to a peculiar mix of audacity, charisma, opportunism, and sheer luck, the young officer had been affiliated with various republican political factions ranging from Jacobin radicals to moderate supporters of the Directory. When the royalists attempted their *coup d'état* in October 1795, Bonaparte revived his sagging military career by assisting republican efforts to crush the insurrection. During the four-year rule of the Directory, he carefully nurtured his new public image as a supporter of the regime while implementing his own ideas of how to administer the newly annexed territories of the Cisalpine Republic in Northern Italy.

Keenly aware of the political and intellectual influence wielded by the Institute, Napoleon sought to cultivate personal relations with "ideologists" like Pierre Daunou, and Emmanuel-Joseph Sieyès, the revolutionary champion of the Third Estate. A master of flattery, the general praised these savants as having "revealed so many secrets, destroyed so many prejudices. . . . We must love scholars and protect the sciences." Naturally, such generous tribute to the life of the mind coming from a popular military hero was music to the ears of the ideologists, who, in 1797, promptly rewarded him with an honorary membership in the Institute. His response testifies to the steadfastness of his political strategy: "The election by the distinguished men who compose the Institute honors me. I feel that long before I am their equal, I will be their pupil. . . . The true conquests, the only ones which cause no regret, are those made over ignorance."[35] Bonaparte's flattery made significant inroads with the intellectuals of the Institute, but, more importantly, he managed to get the Directory in his debt that same year by dispatching some of his troops to Paris and thwarting an attempted royalist *coup d'état* following on the heels of the government's brazen annulment of election results revealing unexpected gains for both monarchist and radical factions.

Having emerged as the dominant military custodian of the Republic, Napoleon proved his superb political instincts by resisting the temptation to seize power in this hour of crisis. Further polishing his image of military hero, he set off to Egypt at the head of the French Army of the Orient. While the stated goal of the expedition was to challenge the regional supremacy of the British and the Ottomans, Bonaparte invited dozens of distinguished scientists to join him in what he glorified as "France's civilizing mission", including the founding of a scientific institute in Cairo dedicated to the "study of the Orient". Suspicious of the General's ambitions, Tracy had rejected his offer to join the campaign as a Brigadier General. On returning to Paris in October 1799, Napoleon found in Director Sieyès a more willing partner for the creation of an "imposing alliance of philosophy and bayonets."[36] A month later, the duo overthrew the unpopular Directory. The chief collaborators of the "Eighteenth Brumaire" were hailed by nearly all Institute members, including Tracy, who expressed his hopes for a more effective rule of republican elites under the new leadership. Within a few weeks, however, Napoleon outmaneuvered his former ally by trimming down Sieyès' draft of a new Constitution, which had retained a weak version of representative assemblies and individual liberties. Bearing Bonaparte's fingerprints, the final draft was an authoritarian document that vested the supreme executive power in a First Consul not responsible to the Senate. Seeing the writing on the wall, Sieyès handed over this post to Napoleon in return for a luxurious estate near Versailles. At the same time, however, the parting politician managed to fill the still influential ranks of the Senate and the Tribunate with fellow ideologists like Destutt de Tracy, who was appointed Senator at a lucrative annual income of 25,000 francs.

Aware of the remaining political strength of committed republicans like Benjamin Constant, who courageously protested the demise of civil liberties in the Tribunate, Bonaparte sought to discredit his opponents by instigating a nasty smear campaign in the Parisian press. The Institute was attacked as a "College of Atheists" led by "windbags who have always fought the existing authority." Ideologists were portrayed as pie-in-the-sky *idéologues* responsible for the failings of the previous regime. Napoleon's henchmen in the press soon escalated their efforts by suggesting that the ideologues had betrayed "true science" for vicious sectarianism, secretly plotting with Jacobins to devise a new Reign of Terror.[37] At the same time, however, the First Consul shrewdly refrained from ordering openly repressive political measures against his opponents. Instead, he showered them with honors and gifts, thus buying their silence through the potent combination of public ridicule and money.

As Emmet Kennedy notes, Bonaparte correctly judged that public opinion was turning against the prospect of more political violence. People seemed to be ready to accept a new strongman as long as he was willing to pay lip service to the revolutionary rhetoric of patriotism and popular sovereignty. And, of course, Napoleon's spectacular military victories helped to sustain his political authoritarianism. Translating favorable popular sentiments into concrete political action, the First Consul restored religious holidays and practices, even allowing exiled refractory priests to return to France. He signed a Concordat with the Vatican that made state-controlled Catholicism once again the official religion of the nation. Finally, he moved to suppress sixty of the seventy-three journals published in Paris.[38] Despite these repressive measures, most ideologists remained stubbornly confident in the ultimate triumph of their vision. One of Tracy's young students captured the undiminished optimism of his teacher and his close friend and collaborator, Pierre-Georges Cabanis, during a brief visit to their homes in Auteuil: "These two friends seem to have only one opinion, they live only for their families and ideology, the progress of which interests them above all else. Ideology, they told me, would change the face of the earth, and that's exactly why those who wish the world to remain stupid (and with good cause) detest ideology and the idéologues."[39]

In January 1803, five months after a plebiscite had made Bonaparte Consul for Life, the dictator felt strong enough to deal the final deathblow to the institutional bastion of ideology. He simply abolished the Second Class of Moral and Political Science, thus utterly depoliticizing the Institute. Although Bonaparte encountered very little resistance to this drastic action, he continued his verbal attacks against ideology, even going so far as to warn the defeated Prussian regime not to tolerate the emergence of republican-minded ideologues in the German states:

They are dreamers and dangerous dreamers; they are all disguised materialists and not too disguised. Gentlemen, philosophers torment themselves to create systems; they will search in vain for a better one than Christianity, which in reconciling man with himself assures both public order and the peace of states. Your ideologues destroy all illusions, and the age of illusions is for individuals as for people the age of happiness.[40]

Now at the zenith of his power, the Emperor could openly launch his authoritarian translation of the rising national imaginary into a political program that eliminated the extremes of both the left and the right by placing itself above "faction." Bonapartism was built upon a flexible strategy of political repression and ideological reconciliation. It glorified the Emperor's strong leadership on behalf of the French nation that had sustained, for the time being, public order and security. Limiting political participation, Bonapartism remained firmly anchored in the new postrevolutionary certitudes of science and nation while utilizing state-controlled religion as an antidote to the secular forms of morality associated with republicanism. Still, it was under the Emperor of the French that the venerable Holy Roman Empire met its official demise. Two popes and the entire College of Cardinals were incarcerated, monasteries and convents were closed down by the thousands across Catholic Europe, and the Spanish Inquisition was forcibly abolished. Invoking the legacy of the Revolution by cultivating its rhetoric of popular sovereignty, Bonapartism masterfully utilized the highly manipulative device of the plebiscite.

Moreover, it relied on the centralized state as the principal vehicle for forging a French nation, striving to build a uniform culture upon the veneration of the army and its associated discourse of patriotic service and sacrifice. The Emperor oversaw the founding of a Legion of Honor based on individual merit; the creation of public institutions of secondary and higher education; the promulgation of a new Civil Code reconciling custom, written law, and revolutionary legislation; a more efficient system of tax collection devised by a modernized state bureaucracy; and a sprawling network of wealthy notables appointed to national and local offices. By appearing to reconcile disparate class interests, Bonapartism also held a strong appeal for the peasantry. Its ambiguous blend of Enlightenment rationalism, traditionalism, and militaristic authoritarianism therefore makes it difficult to place in the conventional left-right spectrum. For this reason, some French historians have put it "more in the cadre of enlightened absolutism than of modern, right-wing Caesarism."[41] On the other hand, Bonapartism's increasing rhetoric of dynasty and militarism—especially after the establishment of the Empire in 1804—attested to its strong affinities with the right.

Long before his regime's final demise in 1815, Napoleon had successfully recast ideology as a "shadowy metaphysic" associated with the misguided Republican political agenda of ideologues. Alexander Lemare, a defrocked priest and failed coconspirator in an unsuccessful *coup d'état*, was the first to challenge the Emperor's exclusive association of ideology with Enlightenment republicanism. Extending its meaning to other "ideational systems" like "royalism," Lemare referred in 1812 to ideology in the plural, thus pioneering a neutral conception of the term.[42] In the same year, Napoleon endeavored to turn ideology one last time into a convenient scapegoat for the failings of his imperial regime. Returning to a gloomy Paris from his disastrous Russian campaign, the Emperor watched with disgust as his disheveled troops were mobbed by anxious crowds bemoaning the loss of nearly half a million of their compatriots. Furious at such signs of "national weakness," the defeated leader disavowed any responsibility for the calamity, blaming instead the destructive influence of the ideologues. At a hastily convened meeting of the Council of State, the ill-tempered Emperor vented his frustration:

We must lay blame for the ills that our fair France has suffered on ideology, that shadowy metaphysics which subtly searches for first causes on which to base the legislation of peoples, rather than make use of the laws known to the human heart and of the lessons of history. These errors must inevitably and did in fact lead to the rule of bloodthirsty men.[43]

At the time of the Emperor's outburst, however, Tracy's scientific program of *idéologie* was already a spent intellectual force in France. Idealism and romanticism had eclipsed the Count's rationalist-materialist aspirations. For this reason, it seems rather ironic that two self-proclaimed historical materialists would add to Bonaparte's stereotype.

1.4. Marx and Engels' *Camera Obscura*

In the three decades that passed between Napoleon's final defeat at Waterloo in 1815 and the drafting of Karl Marx and Friedrich Engels' *The German Ideology* in 1846, Europe had become a very different place. The industrial revolution was spreading from Britain to the European mainland, creating national economies operating increasingly on capitalist principles. The rural masses streamed into sprawling urban centers that provided but substandard housing for a starving proletariat whose labor created immense wealth for the few. Spending most of their waking hours toiling in dreary factories under conditions dangerous to their health, these laborers not only produced a vast array of commodities destined for a rapidly expanding market but also built the canals, roads, railways, and ships that opened the door to the mass transportation of goods and people. Politically, Continental Europe had gone through a brief period of reaction that strengthened monarchical rule, albeit tempered by some token concessions to constitutionalism. A driving force behind the rise of industrial capitalism, the middle classes continued their inexorable social ascent, assembling embryonic political parties built on their core commitments to individualism, property, liberty, and national self-determination. Enriching the intellectual and aesthetic aspects of bourgeois society, philosophers like Georg W. F. Hegel, composers like Ludwig van Beethoven, and novelists like Alexandre Dumas poured their boundless energies into the creation of a romantic sensibility dominated by Ideas, Spirits, Feelings, and the Will.

Paralleling these dynamics, ideology's journey had been similarly eventful. Napoleon's derogatory usage of the term had spread as far as the United States. In 1816, former US President John Adams inquired sarcastically of Thomas Jefferson whether the term "ideology" would be a more fitting designation for a "science of lunacy" or a "theory of delirium." Fully aware of his correspondent's close ties to the French ideologists that had culminated in Jefferson's 1801 election to Destutt de Tracy's Section of the Institute, Adams used his sarcastic query to ridicule the abstract philosophical inclinations of his former political adversary.[44] Crossing into Prussia with the sweeping conquests of the French armies, ideology maintained its Napoleonic associations with "vacuous metaphysics" and "utopian republicanism." In the 1830s, it gained additional currency as a term of derision directed at politically progressive German idealists like the so-called Young Hegelians. These left-leaning republicans, atheists, and self-appointed philosophical heirs of Hegel had convinced themselves that the success of social and political reform in Germany rested solely on their ability to change people's consciousness.

In August 1844, the 26-year-old Rhineland journalist Karl Marx and the slightly younger Westphalian industrialist Friedrich Engels—both lapsed Young Hegelians—met in Paris for the second time to establish what they called facetiously a "company business" devoted to the promotion of revolutionary "communism." By that time, the pair was aware of the multiple usages of ideology as referring to (*a*) an illusory abstraction; (*b*) a political belief system supportive of French-derived republicanism; (*c*) coherent political belief systems supportive of specific political programs; or (*d*) a political program based on a radical Young Hegelian reading of their master's idealism. Marx and Engels also knew that John Stuart Mill had attacked the "ideology of Condillac and his school" as the "shallowest set of doctrines which perhaps were ever passed off upon a cultivated age as a complete psychological system." Thus, the British empiricist had added philosophical weight to the dominant judgment that Destutt de Tracy's science of ideas constituted "a set of verbal generalizations explaining nothing, distinguishing nothing, leading to nothing."[45] Indeed, shortly before his fateful meeting with Engels, Marx had digested Tracy's writings on political economy, which he later derided as "bourgeois idiocy in all its glory." A few years later, his sarcastic pen struck again, ridiculing the Count as a "fish-blooded bourgeois doctrinaire" for calling social inequalities generated by capitalism "unavoidable facts."[46]

Forged in the crucible of early nineteenth-century romanticism and industrialism, the Marx–Engels partnership reflected both the refreshing élan and harsh contradictions of its time. Born into respectable bourgeois families, both men came to reject their preordained careers—law or academia in Marx's case, industrial management or the military for Engels—for seemingly more adventurous lives as freewheeling radical journalists and philosophical gadflies. Ironically, their biting criticisms of bourgeois society were generously financed by liberal industrial capitalists from the Rhineland. In their late teens, Marx and Engels had exchanged their Young Hegelian creed for a qualified materialism and an openly hostile attitude toward religion and the authoritarian Prussian regime. Despite, and perhaps because of, the relative economic backwardness of their *Heimat*, both men romanticized Germany as the "home of true philosophy" destined to lead all nations in a "complete revolution." Clothing the political struggle for equality in romantic garments, they nonetheless approached the study of society in the detached spirit of scientific objectivism. Speaking several languages fluently, both men had found kindred spirits abroad—Marx in Paris, where he socialized with exiled German workers and French radicals, and Engels in England, where he had come in contact with utopian laborites and democratic Chartists. Finally, both were voracious readers who had recently turned to the discipline of political economy as the key to understanding the coming triumph of the industrial proletariat, the active agent of human emancipation.[47]

In the spring of 1845, the two young radicals reconnected in Brussels shortly after Marx had been expelled from France on suspicion of political subversion. They looked forward to continuing their fertile intellectual partnership, which had already resulted in the publication of their fiercely anti-Young Hegelian polemic *The Holy Family*. But Bruno Bauer, one of their primary philosophical targets, was quick to respond to their assault with a harangue of his own. Stung by this venomous retaliation, Marx and Engels vowed to deal a decisive blow to the distorted "ideological" perspective of the Young Hegelians. Abandoned in draft form in 1846, the various related manuscripts that came to be known as *The German Ideology* offered a comprehensive criticism of the "most recent German philosophy according to its representatives [Ludwig] Feuerbach, [Bruno] Bauer, and [Max] Stirner."[48] The manuscript fragments remained unpublished in their entirety until 1932, but their authors were at the time convinced that their efforts had achieved their objective of "self-clarification." Thus, as Marx put it humorously, they were more than happy to leave the manuscript "to the gnawing criticism of mice."[49] A watershed in the history of modern political thought, their treatise articulated for the first time the enduring features of Marxist ideology—ironically organized around their sustained criticism of "ideology."[50]

Feigning contrition, the authors open their book with an implicit admission that their previous work had sometimes suffered from their deplorable tendency to use abstract "philosophical phraseology." Eager to rectify their mistake, Marx and Engels sound eerily like Tracy in their promise to build their arguments on unshakable scientific foundations, namely "the actions and material conditions of real human beings." In their view, this "real premise" establishes the uniqueness of humans as a species in its capability of producing its means of subsistence in a conscious way. In the course of its historical development, humanity ascends to new levels of production determined by its productive forces, that is, its skill and the effectiveness of its tools. Refining their mode of production largely as a result of population growth and the increasing division of labor, human communities end up creating class-based social structures that correspond to various forms of property such as tribal ownership in prehistoric times, landed property under feudalism, and the private property arrangements of capitalism.[51]

Positing the primacy of socioeconomic relations and activities, Marx and Engels present ideas and mental representations not as independent forces shaping the world, as Hegel had suggested, but as secondary phenomena dependent on the "real" material basis of human existence. As they state famously,

Consciousness can never be anything but conscious existence and the existence of humans is their real life process. If in all ideology humans and their circumstances appear upside down as in a *camera obscura*, this phenomenon arises just as much from their historical life-process as the inversion of objects on the retina does from the physical life-process.[52]

Invented in the late seventeenth century, the *camera obscura* was a relatively simple box of lenses and mirrors that produced a realistic, but inverted image of objects put in front of it. According to Marx and Engels, ideology, too, produced an upside-down mirror picture of a world in which ideas and concepts appeared to possess an independent existence and a separate history. "In truth," they asserted, "they have no history and no development. Quite to the contrary, as humans develop their material productions and material relations, their changing material reality also

alters their thinking and the products of their thinking. It is not consciousness that determines life, but life that determines consciousness."[53]

Marx and Engels emphasize the separation of physical and intellectual
labor—a particular manifestation of the more general division of labor—
as the critical historical moment when ideology was born. This separation
enabled the rise of "professional ideologists" who engaged on a full-time
basis in abstract forms of mental activity like philosophy, religion, politics,
law, and art. Cut off from the "real life" of economic production, these
"ideologues" postulated erroneously the primacy of ideas and concepts
and proceeded to draw up grand histories of ideas. Their concealment
of the material basis of human existence occurs both unconsciously—
in the sense that their "real" motives remain unknown to them—and
consciously, in deliberate fashion. After all, ideologues benefited directly
from the division of physical and intellectual labor, hence it was in their
material interest to present the dominant ideas of their age in the form
of universal claims to truth. As Marx and Engels put it, "The ideas of the
ruling class are in every epoch also the ruling thoughts, that is, the class
constituting the ruling *material* power in society represents at the same
time the ruling *mental* power."[54]

Potent instruments in the hands of the ruling class, these ideological
constellations generate in the minds of the oppressed classes the illusion
that the interests of the rulers ultimately coincide with theirs. Both the
metaphysical truth-claims of religion that correspond to the feudal mode
of production and the universalistic language of human rights born in
the capitalist era impart on the oppressed classes a "false consciousness."
Coined by Engels a few years later, this phrase does not signify a "mental
error" in the cognitive sense, but the production of a distorted or inverted
image of reality. Distracted from the material basis of their existence,
working people internalize an ideational system that contributes to the
reproduction of their misery. Such "wrong thinking" could be cured
neither by the application of Tracy's scientific method of analyzing ideas
leading to the rectification of language, nor by the abstract somersaults of
the Young Hegelians aimed at changing people's consciousness without
changing the material world. The only remedy was an alteration of the
relations of production as a result of an organized political struggle led
by the working class. As Marx had proclaimed a few months earlier in his
famous *Theses on Feuerbach*, "Philosophers have only *interpreted* the world
in different ways; the point, however, is to *change* it."[55]

Thus, Marx and Engels arrive at the core of their theory, the "materialist
conception of history." Rejecting as "ideology" the primacy of ideas while

at the same time chastising conventional materialists for failing to explain how material circumstances determining ideas change in the first place, the authors identify as the central force in human history the changes in the mode of material production and exchange, ultimately resulting in class struggle and revolution. Underscoring the scientific character of historical materialism, their prediction of the coming socialist revolution rests on empirical observation of historical development—"real-life depictions" that can be demonstrated "in a purely empirical mode that avoids all dogmas and fantasies."[56] The cofounders of scientific socialism never considered their own theory to be ideological, although it clearly contains authoritative claims on behalf of the proletariat and its material interests. In their view, communism was not merely an ideal to which reality had to conform, but an actual movement bound to usher in a new period in human history characterized by the abolition of the division of labor and its affiliated oppressive class system. As philosopher Leszek Kolakowksi points out, "Communism does away with false consciousness, not by substituting a correct image of the world for an incorrect one, but by dispelling the illusion that thought is or can be anything other than the expression of a state of life."[57]

The authors of *The German Ideology* had a hard time distinguishing historical materialism from the traditional materialist position that consciousness merely constitutes a form of matter. At times, their hesitancy undermines the notion that ideas are mere epiphenomena to material motions. Indeed, by suggesting that ideas might sometimes interact with reality as distinct forces—especially through the sustained efforts of ideologists who disseminate ruling ideas—Marx and Engels imply that concepts can be influenced and amplified by other ideas and, therefore, that the material determination of ideas can be altered by other ideas.[58]

Naturally, this qualification opened the floodgates to a host of questions that would expose Marxism's Achilles heel. If ideas cannot be reduced to material conditions, don't they retain at least some measure of independence? If ideas can influence other ideas to *some* extent, how is it possible to predict the course of history without lapsing into idealist philosophy or a distinct history of ideas? Isn't it possible for scientific concepts—including the materialist conception of history—to be mediated, and, therefore, "tainted" by other, metaphysical ideas? If this is feasible, how can we distinguish science from metaphysics or ideology? It took Engels almost fifty years to acknowledge the existence of such "substantial holes" in the materialist conception of history as presented in *The German Ideology*. "We [Marx and Engels] have neglected the formal side in favor of the content: the mode in which mental representations arise."[59] But rather than offering a substantive clarification of the role of consciousness in relation to economic factors, Engels' brief remarks on the topic a few years before his death remained deeply ambiguous and open to a number of conflicting interpretations. As soon as he granted that the material basis of society could be impacted by relatively autonomous ideas, it is not difficult to see why it required only a small change in emphasis for his intellectual heir, Eduard Bernstein, to drive home his full-blown "revisionist" proposition: "[I]t is neither possible nor necessary to give socialism a purely materialist basis."[60]

Finally, there remains the matter of *The German Ideology*'s "Germanness." The original manuscript contains a crucial paragraph stating that "German idealism can not be differentiated or isolated from the ideology of other nations which also present the world as ruled by ideas."[61] Tellingly, however, the authors later decided to cross out this passage without offering an explanation. Biographers and historians of socialist thought have long advanced sharply conflicting opinions on how the national impacted the various dimensions of Marx and Engels' philosophy. Oscar Hammen, for example, argues that *The German Ideology* fiercely criticizes "German socialists" for their "ideological" tendencies, but he also notes that it nonetheless holds firm to the authors' previous conviction that Germany would play a far more important role in the coming communist revolution than was warranted by its actual economic development. In support of his position, Hammen points to Marx's tendency to invoke invidious national comparisons. He insisted, for example, that the 1844 revolt of German workers in Silesia displayed a more advanced "*theoretical* and *conscious* character" than had been evident in any workers' uprisings in France or England.[62]

Regardless of how one chooses to interpret Marx and Engels' attachments to their *Heimat*, it is hard to ignore that their treatise contains many significations of and references to the national. Despite its celebration of the coming abolition of classes and nations, *The German Ideology* took shape from within the bowels of the rising national imaginary. It comes, therefore, as no surprise that Marxist socialism would find its most powerful expression in German social democracy and similar political parties organized along national lines. Vehemently opposing liberal and conservative ideas, most European socialists would nonetheless greet the outbreak of the Great War in 1914 with the same enthusiasm as their ideological competitors.

2

The Grand Ideologies of the Nineteenth Century: British Liberalism, French Conservatism, and German Socialism

Where the sentiment of nationality exists in any force, there is a *prima facie* case for uniting all the members of the nationality under the same government, and a government to themselves apart.... [I]t is in a general necessary condition of free institutions that the boundaries of governments should coincide in the main with those of nationalities.

John Stuart Mill (1861)

The French monarchy, that is, the Royal House of France, indissolubly unites the nation. My fathers and yours have traversed the centuries, working together to develop our beautiful motherland. For fourteen hundred years, alone among all the peoples of Europe, the French have always been led by the princes of their nation and their blood. The history of my ancestors is the history of enduring French grandeur.

Comte de Chambord (1852)

The working class must constitute itself as an independent political party and inscribe on its banner as its principal slogan the universal, equal, and direct suffrage. The representation of the working class in the legislative bodies of Germany is the sole means of satisfying its legitimate interests politically. To reach this goal, the political program of the workers' party must be peaceful agitation by legal means.

Ferdinand Lassalle (1863)

2.1. Translating the National Imaginary

Deep-seated modes of understanding our communal existence are notoriously resistant to change. The rise of the national imaginary in the nineteenth century is thus a testimony to the strength of what Mill, following the discursive conventions of his time, called the "sentiment of nationality." Nevertheless, ideological typologies compiled by political philosophers often rest on the assumption that the national matrix from which they arose can be taken for granted.[1] Intellectual historians, on the other hand, have been more attentive to its generative power, insisting that ideologies such as classical liberalism should be examined against the background of their various national colors.[2] Unfortunately, however, such laudable attention to context tends to be purchased at the price of philosophical rigor. Our examination of ideological truth claims arising from within specific national contexts will seek to combine the virtues of both approaches. Most importantly, it inveighs against approaching grand ideologies as abstract ideational clusters, that is, apart from their concrete manifestations in nations. My choice of British liberalism, French conservatism, and German socialism is not meant to exclude equally pertinent ideational constellations existing elsewhere in Europe or the Americas. Belgian socialism or liberalism in the United States, for example, would be equally worthwhile objects of study.

Let us now return to ideology's journey, picking up the story with a brief comment on the relationship between ideology and religion. As we have seen in Chapter 1, the capacity of traditional religious narratives to respond effectively to the growing social problems diminished in the late eighteenth century. Ideologies represented new responses to this challenge. However, the new revolutionary truth of the nation continued to be celebrated in myths, metaphors, symbols, and festivals that corresponded closely with the Christian liturgical tradition. Resistance against religiously sanctioned forms of political absolutism stimulated the worship of the people in a new style George Mosse refers to as "secular religion."[3] Born as products of the eighteenth-century rebellion against religion, the framers of ideology struggled hard to escape the womb of Christian theology. The prototype of this secular rebellion was the liberalism of French revolutionaries who sought to break the stranglehold of the *ancien régime* by cutting its umbilical cord linking politics and religion. Revolutionary France quickly became a symbol for the modern liberal nation defined in political rather than religious terms as a sovereign body of citizens represented by an elected body guiding the affairs of a territorially based nation-state. In the eyes of its philosophical supporters, such as Immanuel Kant and Emmanuel-Joseph Sieyès, the revolutionary French nation would inspire the rest of Europe to throw off the shackles of despotism, while detractors like Edmund Burke and Joseph de Maistre saw it as the source of anarchy and irreligion. A few decades into the nineteenth century, these conflicting perspectives on the meaning of the revolutionary French nation exploded into the ideological antagonism between liberalism and conservatism.

For the remainder of the century, liberalism evolved in a decisively national-republican manner—a development rendered most visible in the countless adoptions of the French tricolor flag by social movements championing the cause of "national liberation." But the various liberal translations of the national imaginary thrived on brazen imitation just as much as on retreat to a haughty posture of defensive exceptionalism. Simón Bolívar, for example, an ardent admirer of British liberal institutions, dismissed Anglo-Saxon forms of liberalism as unsuitable for the newly emancipated nations of Latin America. Accusing the United States of "plaguing America with torments in the name of freedom," he advocated the adoption of a distinct Grand Colombian Constitution that reflected the cultural independence of South American nation-states.[4]

The tie binding ideology to nationality was emphasized as early as the 1790s when Edmund Burke and his fellow conservatives in Parliament warned against the influence of the three pernicious "French principles"—atheism, Jacobinism, and democracy—on their "nation great & happy." Over time, their critique opened up to the constructive task of assembling a counterimage of a more desirable "conservative nation" anchored in "British principles" of ancient freedom, constitutional monarchy, landed aristocracy, and resistance to social change. Contrasting English liberties with French license, such patriotic hyperbole struck a ready chord with British elites whose fears of revolution boosted the political fortunes of the Tory Party in the opening decades of the century. Thus, many political historians have located the origins of modern British conservatism in Burke's antirevolutionary vision of an "alliance of right-thinking men governing in the national interest."[5] However, fears of a French-style democratic revolution were not confined to the political right in Britain. Entertaining similar thoughts, many Whigs were happy to join the Conservatives' rhetorical bandwagon, thereby setting the stage for the strange ideological convergence of British political parties around a cautious agenda of "reformist gradualism." Naturally, political treatises penned across the Channel responded in kind to the anti-French construction of nineteenth-century British nationhood. Offering conflicting ideological appraisals of the "English model," French thinkers tended to disagree on its relevance for their nation.[6]

Thus, conservatism in its distinct national manifestations took shape in reaction to French-clad liberalism, in the process gaining confidence in itself as an ideological movement. Various brands of socialism, too, thrived on the fertile legacy of the Revolution, particularly on its democratic promise of extending the principles of *liberté, egalité*, and *fraternité* to all people, including the incipient working classes. But the revolutionary enthusiasm of bourgeois socialists like Karl Marx or Ferdinand Lassalle did not translate into their ideological support of liberalism. Deeply influenced by Hegel's critique of rights-based liberalism, both men attacked the irredeemable selfishness of civil society composed of alienated individuals and predicted that the bourgeois order would soon find itself at a historical dead end. By the end of the century, however, the pendulum would swing back as leading German social democrats imbibed enough neo-Kantian philosophy to consider socialism the "legitimate heir" of Enlightenment liberalism, fighting for social justice "in the name of the principles of the French Revolution, aiming to liberate the *citoyen* from his dependency on the Church, the repressive state, and the capitalist economy."[7]

Considerably contained by ideology, the spirit of Christianity still wielded some institutional and ideational clout throughout the nineteenth century, forcing the codifiers of the grand ideational systems to devise unique strategies for dealing with the "religious question." Rationalists at heart, most liberals were willing to tolerate expressions of faith as "opinions among other opinions"—as long as religious imperatives remained confined to the private sphere of individual conscience. Conservatives, on the other hand, celebrated Christian values as the normative bedrock of the nation. Yet, as reflected most clearly in German Chancellor Otto von Bismarck's unequivocal policy of state supremacy over the Church, which he escalated in the late 1870s into a determined *Kulturkampf* against Catholicism, conservatives kept a watchful eye on the political ambitions of the clergy—including those belonging to the established national churches. Some socialists who detected a social message in Christianity sought to incorporate it into their ideology while others hoped to abolish religion altogether by smashing its economic foundations. Many clerics also felt the mounting pressure to come to grips with ideology. However, their relationship with the modern nation remained uneasy, at any moment threatening to disintegrate into fierce political disputes that pitted liberals against conservatives over such contentious issues as the separation of church and state, public education, civil marriage, divorce, science, and race. It was not until the rise of

German Nazism and Russian communism that the national imaginary was articulated in totalitarian ideologies that brutally subordinated religion to a nation-state. But even then, these regimes frequently entertained pragmatic alliances with the Church.

At the dawn of the twentieth century, the nation (and its affiliated state) had established itself as the dominant framework of modern social life. The national began to pervade all dimensions of society—from economics to politics; from language to leisure; and from the sciences to the arts. Everyday concepts were inevitably qualified in national terms. People referred to German science, American technology, Argentinean beef, and French perfume. Even the rise of the novel as an art form was unthinkable without the national. As Nobel Prize winner Orhan Pamuk points out, "When the great novels of the nineteenth-century were being written, the art of the novel was in every sense a national art."[8] Despite sharpening disagreements over whether race, language, citizenship, territory, or history constituted the essence of the nation, the concept itself had become so obvious that it hardly required an explanation.[9] What did, however, require further elaboration was the course a nation should follow, that is, its plans, objectives, aspirations, purpose, destiny, and standing among other nations.

Thus, the major political debates in the second half of the nineteenth century revolved around issues emerging from this "national agenda." The first and most important of these questions revolved around the definition of the nation. Who belonged to the nation? Was it a community of free and equal citizens deliberating on their common welfare in a rational manner? Or an organic whole rooted in blood and soil that bound individuals to ancient and unique traditions? Other questions followed. Did everyone have the capacity to vote and participate in national politics? Which collectivities were entitled to form an independent nation? Were all nations entitled to a state? Did nations possess natural borders or was their territory to be determined artificially? How should the nation-state deal with internal dissent and external aggression? What were the limits of state power? Should a nation choose liberty and reform or order and public security to advance its cause? Did industry and commerce further or undermine the health of the nation? What was the proper relationship between the individual and the nation? What moral values and ethical norms should guide the nation? What was the best way of settling disputes among nations? Were nations obliged to lead "less civilized" collectivities toward nationhood?

Ultimately, it fell to ideologies to provide the concrete conceptual road maps necessary for navigating the difficult political and cultural terrain staked out by these questions. Turning now to the exploration of the three grand ideologies of the nineteenth century, we leave behind the negative stereotype whose origins and evolution constituted the subject of our previous discussion. Relying on a neutral conception of ideology, we will treat political belief systems as ubiquitous and necessary ideational structures that express the overarching national imaginary in compressed and explicit form as competing political doctrines. However, our search for ideological and historical meaning cannot commence without raising one final methodological question. Which textual sources should we consult? Political theorists tend to rely on canonical treatises authored by paradigmatic thinkers like Mill, Maistre, or Marx, while conceptual historians often turn to less philosophical writings found in newspapers, magazines, pamphlets, party programs, and political addresses. We will draw on both sources, with Part I leaning more heavily on canonical writings and Part II relying more on journalistic materials. Both sources, however, highlight the pivotal role of social elites as codifiers of ideational systems that mobilize large segments of the population behind a political vision.

2.2. British Liberalism

It is tempting to open the discussion of nineteenth-century British liberalism with a genealogical reflection on John Locke's classical treatises on limited government and religious toleration. After all, his writings are generally read as the standard vindication of the 1688 Glorious Revolution in England and its central principle of limited government. Moreover, his celebrated doctrines of natural rights and social contract incorporate the liberal core concepts of individualism and rationality in a seventeenth-century philosophical framework that conferred a distinct complexion on later Anglo-American traditions of liberalism.[10] On the other hand, however, there are also good reasons why our exploration of British liberalism should be limited to a passing nod to Locke's lasting influence on modern liberal conceptions.

The first reason derives from my central argument that modern ideologies engage in competing political translations of the overarching national imaginary. Since the national at the core of this imaginary did not cross a significant threshold until the late eighteenth century, we cannot properly speak of political ideologies—liberal or conservative—during Locke's lifetime. What might be conceded, however, is that Locke provided a "proto-liberal" elaboration of concepts that would later be welded into comprehensive political belief systems articulating conflicting visions for the national community. Second, as Michael Freeden points out, one cannot usefully refer to the emergence of ideologies prior to the development of mass means of dissemination and the political mobilization of large segments of the population. Since ideologies require reasonably wide audiences to function in the manner described in this book, they depend on a host of technological and social innovations that simply did not exist before the onset of the industrial revolution.[11] Third, social movements and political parties that consciously embraced liberalism did not arrive on the historical stage until the early decades of the nineteenth century. Thus, it makes sense to date the emergence of British liberalism not before the 1830s or thereabouts.

This final point requires further explanation, for it raises some crucial contextual matters without which any conceptual analysis of liberalism would remain hopelessly abstract. Some of the most celebrated liberal political achievements in nineteenth-century British history included the electoral reform laws of 1832, 1867, and 1884; the 1833 abolition of slavery in the British Empire; the repeal of the protectionist Corn Laws in 1846; the factory laws of 1842 and 1847; the Catholic and Jewish emancipation of 1829 and 1858; the 1867 British North America Act; the 1870 establishment of a national system of free elementary public education; the introduction of the secret ballot in 1872; the trade union laws of 1871 and 1875; and the Redistribution Act of 1885 establishing a uniform map of mostly single-member electoral constituencies. But these achievements would not have been possible without the exertion of strong reformist pressures. Perhaps the most significant reform agents turned out to be newly emerging social movements, which pioneered a distinctive way of pursuing politics on both local and national levels. Charles Tilly suggests that social movements engage in three core activities: mass campaigns of collective claims on target authorities; an array of claim-making performances including special-purpose associations, public meetings, media statements, and demonstrations; and public displays of their causes' worthiness, unity, numbers, and commitment.[12]

It is not difficult to see how the formulation of such claims for large numbers of people went hand in hand with the elite construction of a coherent political worldview explicable not merely as a philosophical system but also in simple terms that resonated with the interests and aspirations of these movement activists and sympathizers. Indeed, the formation of such ideological vehicles in the early part of the century made it easier for individuals to organize themselves into movements, like-minded social clubs, associations, and political parties with the primary objective of rallying more people behind their claims and thus increasing the pressure for the desired reconstruction of the nation. Nationwide campaigns for parliamentary reform arose in Britain from about 1812 in a political landscape characterized by a weakening monarchy and a rising Parliament dominated by the aristocracy and landed gentry. While conducting their political affairs in the name of the people, these elites controlled government through the restricted suffrage and "rotten borough" systems, which allowed them to name members of parliament without consultation.

Composed of the rising bourgeoisie as well as the incipient working classes, the new social movements demanded a broadened franchise, more equal representation of electors, removal of social disabilities from Catholics and Nonconformists, and the legal recognition of reformist "unions" like the Stockport Union for the Promotion of Human Happiness. The symbols and slogans employed by these movements reinforced the liberal themes of freedom and recognition. Many of these early activists joined protest marches wearing Liberty Caps—headgear with a long iconic history in England that originated in the Roman practice of publicly honoring emancipated slaves.[13] No doubt, these new ways of asserting popular sovereignty by making direct claims on the government from the streets contributed to the passage of the 1832 Reform Act. This momentous piece of legislation expanded the franchise to the middle classes on the basis of uniform and national property qualifications. Social movements also contributed to the transformation of the old Whigs and Tories into the modern Liberal and Conservative Parties. Ideological clubs and party committees sprang up for the purposes of raising election funds, providing strategic advice to candidates, circulating propaganda, and organizing public events. These innovations—together with the broadening of education, the falling price of newspapers, and the rapid rise of literacy—produced large national constituencies that were fought over by the major political parties. By mid-century, free-trade radical Richard Cobden observed that control over the nation's direction was quickly passing from the landed oligarchy into "the hands of the people themselves."[14]

But for most of the century, it was far from clear as to who really belonged to "the people," defined by Cobden as having a direct hand in the nation's political fate. Indeed, suffrage issues rapidly presented themselves as a key concern for British liberals. As a result, a "language of capacity" emerged as the common currency of liberal discussion.[15] The potential answer given to the question of political participation was of critical importance for the future ideological appeal of liberalism. After all, it pronounced a person or group "mature" enough to be included in political decision-making, and thus entrusted with the well-being of the nation. Indeed, the focus of the liberal debate was on "trust." Nineteenth-century British liberals like Whig Attorney General Sir James Scarlett asserted that suffrage was a "sacred trust" the government might confer on "a class to whom it might be safely given . . . for the common good." This interpretation distinguished liberals from conservatives who saw the vote as a kind of private property belonging to traditional elites as well as from democrats who claimed an all-encompassing "right to vote." Indeed, up until the passage of the 1832 Reform Act, liberal stalwarts like Lord Brougham had to work hard to assure skeptical peers that the middle classes were the "genuine repositories of sober, rational, intelligent, and honest English feeling."[16]

By mid-century, it was apparent that those "middle and industrious classes" had earned their government's trust, for they would not even dream of following the French revolutionary examples of 1789, 1830, and 1848. In fact, the bourgeoisie had begun to cut itself loose from radical working-class movements like the People's Charter whose members demanded, among other things, universal male suffrage and secret ballots in parliamentary elections. When some Chartists openly sympathized with the 1848 European revolutions by flying French tricolors at demonstrations calling for revolutionary change in Britain, middle-class liberals responded with strong patriotic appeals for law and order. Increasingly vilified and socially isolated, the Chartist movement faded from the political scene in a matter of years. Having demonstrated their distaste for revolutionary change, the British middle classes also shaped and sustained the powerful Victorian moral and economic discourse in praise of hard work, self-improvement, and character formation. It underpinned a variety of liberal political languages such as the economic libertarianism of Herbert Spencer and other Manchester School proponents, the moral-philosophical ideals of John Stuart Mill, and the ethical state interventionism of T. H. Green, L. T. Hobhouse, and other late-century New Liberals.

While the middle classes clearly represented British industrial and commercial interests, it would be too simplistic to accept narrow Marxist interpretations that reduced liberalism to a capitalist ideology of the bourgeoisie. To be sure, liberals were the drivers of the emergent capitalist system, but they were equally prone to engage in ethical critiques of its disruptive social and moral impact. By and large, they idealized their nation as a meritocratic society composed of self-reliant and industrious citizens committed to material progress and moral improvement. Hence, liberal ideology was shaped by ethical ideals at least as much as by economistic dogmas of free trade and laissez-faire. As Richard Bellamy points out, British liberalism may have been the ethos of the bourgeoisie, "but it cannot be regarded as a narrow economic doctrine."[17]

Our brief ideological analysis of John Stuart Mill's version of British liberalism will show that familiar socialist and conservative caricatures of liberal agents as narrowly self-interested proprietors hostile to communal obligations are just as exaggerated as liberal stereotypes of faceless socialist collectivism. My choice of Mill as the prime exponent of British liberalism reflects a nearly unanimous scholarly consensus on his unequalled status as liberalism's spokesperson in the middle decades of the nineteenth century.[18]

Michael Freeden identifies at the heart of Mill's liberal ideology seven core concepts—liberty, individualism, progress, rationality, the general interest, sociability, and limited and responsible power—as well as a range of adjacent and peripheral concepts that sustain and operationalize the core cluster. He then goes on to offer a close interpretation of Mill's decontestation efforts, that is, his attempts to attribute fixed meanings to these mutually defining concepts.[19] Rather than embarking on a similar full-blown morphological analysis, I will focus my interpretation on Mill's efforts to anchor his paramount conception of individual freedom in significations of the national. Indeed, his belief that liberty fosters the best aspects of both individuals and nations emerges as the central ideological claim of his liberal translation of the national imaginary. My interpretation of Mill as a thinker who consciously links "individuality of power and development" to a vigorous "principle of nationality" deviates sharply from influential readings of his liberalism as dominated by an "atomistic conception of individual liberty" based on utilitarian agents who deliberately break the solidarities of social ties in their unencumbered pursuit of personal happiness.[20]

The first sentence of Mill's seminal essay *On Liberty* (1859) decontests "civil," or "social, liberty" as "the nature and limits of power which can be legitimately exercised by society over the individual." But by the time the author concludes his opening paragraph, he has added the unquestioned claim that the "stage of progress into which the more civilized portions of the species have now entered...requires a different and more fundamental treatment [of liberty]."[21] In other words, while Mill portrays the struggle between "liberty" and "authority" as a general human phenomenon, he emphasizes that the many forms and meanings of freedom, power, and community always correspond to a particular historical context. But apart from admonishing his readers to pay attention to history, why does Mill privilege the current "stage of progress" to the extent that it requires "a different and more fundamental treatment" of liberty? He offers an answer a few pages later by pointing to the emergence of modern society based on popular sovereignty—the special moment in history when the "ruling power" was made to emanate from the periodical choice of the ruled. "What was now wanted," he continues, "was that the rulers should be identified with the people, that their interest and will should be the will of the nation." In other words, the power of the rulers became "but the nation's own power, concentrated and in a form convenient for exercise. This mode of thought, or rather perhaps of feeling, was common among the last generation of European liberalism...."[22]

Next, Mill addresses the possible dangers that might arise if this "will of the people" turns into a "tyranny of the majority." Borrowing this phrase from Alexis de Tocqueville's famous critique of American democracy, he does not merely apply it to openly oppressive measures taken by political authorities, but, more importantly, to subtle and, therefore, less detectable social pressures for conformity. Such "tyranny of the prevailing opinion and feeling" threatens to fetter what Mill considers the most precious gem in the crown of civilization: "individuality of power and development," for which liberty is but a "prerequisite."[23] Without genuine individuality, he asserts in rather utilitarian fashion, there can be no true happiness. Ending his long decontestation of liberty, Mill finally proposes his famous "very simple principle entitled to govern absolutely the dealings of society with the individual," namely, noninterference with individual choice and spontaneity except as "to prevent harm to others."[24] But once again, he immediately historicizes the absolute validity of this truth claim by noting that his principle "is meant to apply only to human beings in the maturity of their faculties." Such mature people must be "members of a civilized community"— the type of society found in those European nations based on popular sovereignty he alluded to earlier. He further elaborates on this crucial claim:

For the same reason we may leave out of consideration those backward states of society in which the race itself may be considered as in its nonage.... Despotism is a legitimate mode of government in dealing with barbarians, provided the end be their improvement and the means justified by actually effecting that end. Liberty, as a principle, has no application to any state of things anterior to the time when mankind have become capable of being improved by free and equal discussion.... [A] period long since reached in all nations with whom we need here to concern ourselves.[25]

Let us pause here for a moment and take stock of Mill's interconnected network of concepts and claims that has grown rather quickly into the ideational skeleton of British liberalism. First, he insists that the meaning of liberty—certainly the most important concept in the ideology bearing its name—must be contextualized. However, by asserting a progressive course of history that corresponds to the progressive nature of human beings, he assigns to the current era the most advanced degree of liberty. "Civil" liberty emerges in its full glory only in a society bearing the features of the modern "nation" based on popular sovereignty. The crucial social and political conditions that make liberty possible—"free and equal discussion" among rational individuals—are those prevailing in liberal European and American nation-states. And yet, Mill concedes that not all nations are equally "liberal," that is, they have not realized to the same degree the conditions in which liberty can thrive. For example, he alleges that Spain's "progress in intellect and society" has been "lagging behind." Germany's social progress, too, has been "slow." Italian society, in addition to "standing still" for a long time, has not shown itself to be as "practical as the English." Finally, Ireland's politicians and legislators have yet to recognize "the duty of civilizing her people" by learning "from the experience of nations how high a rank among civilizing agents belongs to the wide diffusion of property in land." Not surprisingly, Mill singles out England and France as the two nations that have lifted liberty to unprecedented heights. Both countries have evolved "nobly and brilliantly" as a result of the "internal and external elements of civilization" unfolding in a "parallel" and "harmonious" manner.[26]

Consequently, Mill's liberty manifests itself primarily in England and France as the relatively unimpeded cultivation of individuality conceived as the "formation of character." Drawing on Alexander von Humboldt's Enlightenment ideal of *Bildung*—one that he regards as insufficiently realized in the German states—Mill's liberal "character education" summons the powers of the will to raise the individual's dispositions from their "lower," animalistic instincts and passions to the "higher faculties" of mind reflected in the Victorian virtues of rationality, self-control, industry, frugality, integrity, and temperance. Correspondingly, he warns against confusing individuality with the alienated "individualism" of hedonistic pleasure-seekers. For Mill, individuality is inextricably linked to the nation—not only because the cultivation of character requires the liberties available only in the modern nation-state but also because the moral qualities of the nation reflect the character of the individuals comprising it. Since the ethical imperative for "sovereignty" applies equally to individuals and nations, Mill advocates a "strong and active principle of nationality" as the best guarantee for the cohesion and durability of liberal political societies.[27]

Samuel Smiles, perhaps the most successful popularizer of Victorian character-building discourse, concurs: "National progress is the sum of individual industry, energy and uprightness as national decay is of individual idleness, selfishness and vice."[28] Experienced as a "feeling of union and common interest" by mature people living "within the same natural and historical boundaries," the principle of nationality represents the very force of self-determination operating in "human beings in the maturity of their faculties." It is, therefore, a powerful historical manifestation of the indomitable human spirit thirsting for freedom. As Mill notes, "One hardly knows what any division of the human race should be free to do if not to determine with which of the collective bodies of human beings they choose to associate themselves."[29]

Richard Bellamy argues that this comprehensive Victorian discourse of character formation allowed British middle-class liberals to contrast their self-declared "national interests" with the "partisan interests" of the conservative landed gentry as well as the radical working class. To support his thesis, Bellamy quotes Mill's father James: "In this country at least, it is this [middle] class which gives the nation its character."[30] The son's wholehearted acceptance of the Victorian character discourse as applying equally to individuals and nations not on the basis of biology but civilizational achievement fueled his lifelong commitment to the creation of "national institutions of education and forms of polity, calculated to invigorate the individual character."[31] Once again, Mill operated on the unquestioned assumption that individuality could not do without the modern nation—in spite of the illiberal tendencies exhibited by an emerging mass society.

Mill's liberal articulation of the national imaginary thus supplied his middle-class audience with a concrete conceptual map necessary for navigating the difficult political terrain of the "national agenda." For example, his liberalism seems to meet the challenge of explaining the relationship between the individual and the nation as one based on free and equal discussion among educated citizens for the good of the whole. Likewise, to the crucial questions of political capacity and participation, British liberalism provides a rationalist response that nonetheless remains suspicious of "democracy" and the uneducated masses. Toward the end of his life, Mill warmed up to a more inclusive political system that nonetheless retained an elitist bias in favor of the educated and propertied classes. His ideological claims served British liberals well for a long time. Still, they contained serious limitations that contributed to their decline in the dawning era of mass politics.

Mill's elitism also reflects liberal attitudes toward "less civilized" peoples. While celebrating the universality of their political ideals, the British thinker nonetheless affirmed these very principles as particular historical achievements of the most progressive nations of the West.[32] In this context, Mill spoke of his nation's "duty" to educate "less fortunate" collectivities like India to full nationhood. His ideological claims in support of the Empire's civilizing mission of teaching "barbarians" the benefits of freedom and individuality reified a hierarchy of human experience built on limited assumptions about reason and historical progress. In the real world of colonial domination, these allegedly universalistic core concepts of British liberalism were brutally enforced. In due time, however, the logic of educating colonial subjects to nationhood would come back to haunt the colonizers when their subjects chose both violent and nonviolent strategies for their project of "national liberation," thus enforcing their right to take part in the national imaginary as equals alongside the European nations. We will consider these maneuvers in Chapter 4.

Toward the end of the nineteenth century, Mill's claim that the crucial principle of nationality underpinned the free association of individuals and their political institutions received further elaboration in the writings of New Liberals like T. H. Green and L. T. Hobhouse. Building on Mill's arguments, these British thinkers argued that since the national was constitutive of individual identity, it represented an indispensable feature of civilization worthy of respect and political support. While careful to avoid the extremes of collectivism or jingoism, New Liberals nonetheless put a strong emphasis on the concept of sociability expressed in the individual's embeddedness in the nation. Thus, they anticipated the arguments of late twentieth-century liberal political thinkers whose liberal nationalism emphasized the crucial role of national culture in the creation of individuality—and thus liberty.[33]

New Liberalism also provided powerful ideological arguments in favor of state intervention in order to remove social and economic obstacles to liberty and progress. Yet, its growing sympathy for communitarian values not only represented a potent response to the dire social consequences of capitalist development but also drew much strength from intensifying national liberation struggles in Ireland and elsewhere. Returning to the crucial question of the proper relationship between the individual and the nation, T. H. Green ultimately arrived at an ideological position closer to a collectivist model, which nonetheless retained the traditional liberal focus on individuality and self-improvement. Criticizing the extreme libertarian view that a nation was merely an aggregate of individuals, he objected in particular to its implication that individuals could be what they are independently of their existence in the nation. He felt that it was wrong to suppose that individuals could import their moral and intellectual qualities "ready-made into the national existence." Rather, the moral capacity of persons "is only actualized through the habits, institutions, and laws, in virtue of which the individuals form a nation." At the same time, however, Green claimed that it was equally true that "the life of the nation has no real existence except as the life of individuals composing the nation—a life determined by the intercourse with each other and deriving its peculiar features from the conditions of that intercourse."[34]

Writing on the eve of the Great War, L. T. Hobhouse further expanded on the crucial conception of the relationship between individual liberty and the principle of nationality. He opens his short 1912 essay in support of Irish independence with the observation that nineteenth-century national liberation movements in Greece, Italy, Hungary, and Poland provided a "powerful stimulus to British Liberalism." On the basis of this historical affinity, Hobhouse infers that "Nationalism, therefore, lay close to the heart of liberalism." Given that the "primary object of political Liberalism is to found Government on freedom," liberals should not close their eyes to the struggles of the Irish people, for they appear to possess the principle of nationality to a degree sufficient to make them eligible for independent nationhood. Again, the British thinker anchors his argument in history, which, in his view, provides the ultimate test of nationality. If a people shows itself capable of maintaining its demand for autonomy even through persistent adversity and coercion, then "liberty must make its account" with the "the proof that nationality is a vital principle, and a permanent force. . . ."[35] Hobhouse's early twentieth-century perspective on the escalating "Irish question" represents perhaps the most dramatic expression of British liberalism in decline, struggling to preserve the ideological core of John Stuart Mill's vision in an inhospitable environment increasingly dominated by both racialized perspectives on the nation and the economistic arguments of the left.

2.3. French Conservatism

In stark contrast to the relatively placid reformism that prevailed in Britain, the political development of the French nation in the nineteenth century proved to be much more stormy and unpredictable. After the collapse of Bonaparte's Empire in 1815, the country had to endure fifteen years of restored constitutional Bourbon rule until the 1830 revolution drove the autocratic Charles X into his permanent English exile. Eighteen years later, his successor, the "Citizen-King" Louis-Philippe, suffered the same fate when his Orleanist regime paid the ultimate price for its foolish decision to resist mounting pressures to expand the suffrage. Unlike Britain, however, France had to wait until mid-century to witness the emergence of cohesive social movements as a regular vehicle of popular politics. But even then, mass demonstrations and large-scale campaigns did not really become readily available ways of pressing ideological claims until the massive May Day mobilizations of the 1890s.[36]

Emerging from the upheavals of the 1848 Revolution, the Second Republic was dominated by rich landowners and social conservatives who had been elected to the Constituent Assembly by universal male suffrage. Worker-led insurrections against these social elites were brutally suppressed by the combined forces of the army and the National Guard at a cost of over 3,000 lives. Taking a lesson from his uncle's fondness for messy plebiscites, the newly elected President Louis Napoleon brought the sputtering republic to an ignoble end after only three years. Riding the mid-century economic boom generated by massive rail and road construction, he presided over the modernization of the country in authoritarian fashion as Emperor Napoleon III until his dynastic dreams were shattered by Prussian troops at Sedan. Attesting to the growing political power of the working classes, the radical Paris Commune flourished for a brief moment in the political vacuum generated by the collapse of the Empire only to be crushed by the remnants of the returning French army in the short 1871 Civil War that killed up to 25,000 Communards.

The ensuing Third Republic was widely seen as a mere prelude to yet another monarchy headed either by the Bourbon pretender, the Comte de Chambord, or by his Orleanist counterpart, the Comte de Paris. Instead, the political veteran Adolphe Thiers seized the reins of political leadership, downplaying his Orleanist past in exchange for the presidency. A sworn enemy of the Commune and social democracy, he reassured the skeptical royalists that the republic would be "conservative or it will not exist."[37] Although well-organized political parties of the British ilk failed to materialize in the early decades of the Third Republic, the political sympathies of most national deputies could easily be associated with the ideological claims and political programs of four major camps—the bourgeois factions of Opportunists and Radicals, the Royalists, and the Socialists. Riven by internal divisions and plagued by endemic corruption, the short-lived republican governments found themselves preyed upon by authoritarian Bonapartists like General Boulanger or by conservative "patriots" like Paul Dérouléde who skillfully exploited the widespread anti-Semitic sentiments generated in the traumatic Dreyfus Affair to attract support for his ultimately unsuccessful coup attempt of 1899. Perpetually tottering on the brink of extinction, the increasingly militaristic Third Republic nonetheless managed to confound its supporters and critics alike by refusing to die.

This remarkable political history underscores the strength of the political right in nineteenth-century France, punctured only on occasion by the divided forces of the liberal center and the democratic left. Still, some prominent historians have suggested that French conservatism amounts to little more than the reactionary doctrines of exiled aristocrats like Joseph de Maistre and Louis de Bonald. Lacking an intellectual core and abjuring all forms of political action, so this judgment goes, early French conservatism hardly deserves serious consideration as a comprehensive system of political thought.[38] This argument falls short in two important respects.

First, as theocratic as these early counterrevolutionary thinkers may have been, their ideas provided a solid ideological basis for conservative articulations of the national imaginary that pervaded French politics from the royalists of the 1820s to the right-wing radicals of the 1890s. In fact, the ideological claims of these Catholic "ultraroyalists" seeped into the public discourse on a regular basis as early as 1818 with the founding of influential weeklies like *Le Conservateur*, which admonished its readership to uphold the nation's "sacred principles" of "religion, the King, liberty, the Charter and respectable people."[39] Like their counterparts in Germany or Austria, ultraconservatives were profoundly influenced by Edmund Burke's *Reflections on the Revolution in France* (1790). But it would be a mistake to turn his distinct British perspective on monarchy, landed aristocracy, and established religion into a generic standard for all conservative ideology. French-Catholic and German-Protestant conservatives clearly shared some of Burke's ideological commitments, but they remained skeptical of some other claims, including his strong endorsement of capitalist economic development. Hence, Burke's political thought inspired Anglo-American conservative traditions to a far greater extent than the right in Continental Europe and Russia.[40] As our analysis of Maistre's ideological claims will show, their coherence and conceptual richness clearly inveighs against a dismissive reading of nineteenth-century French conservatism as the superficial ranting of an anachronistic reactionary.

Second, one must acknowledge the existence of multiple ideological currents in nineteenth-century French conservatism. For example, René Rémond's pioneering study of the French political right names Legitimism, Orleanism, and Bonapartism as its three constituent parts.[41] However, after General Boulanger's failed drive to power in the late 1880s, this tripartite division no longer captures the new social and political realities of the dawning era of mass politics. As Zeev Sternhell points out, these new conditions split French conservatism into two camps, one accepting the basic rules and principles of the established liberal order and the other rejecting liberal democracy along the lines of a new "radical conservatism" that found its political manifestation in the right-wing extremism of the *Action Française* and similar extremist groups in the 1890s. Indeed, Sternhell makes a convincing case for the influence of these radical-conservative fin-de-siècle French thinkers on the twentieth-century formulation of fascist ideologies in Italy and Germany.[42] For this reason, we will focus our analysis of this highly original strain in the French conservative tradition on its racist claims. It received its first systematic formulation in the mid-century writings of Arthur de Gobineau who linked the alleged decline of "Aryan" and "Indo-European" nations like his own to what he called the "calamity of blood-mixture." As we shall see, his claims were further radicalized and popularized in the anti-Semitic diatribes of late-century figures like Edouard Drumont and Maurice Barrès.

For most of the century, however, French conservative views tended to coalesce around their common aspiration to reconstruct the fallen nation of 1789 within the rising national imaginary. Arguing for the primacy of the organic whole over the individual, conservatives stressed the uniqueness of their nation rooted in the ancient past and its sacred traditions. France was assured continued greatness as long as the old ruling classes remained the guardians of its national spirit. Indeed, the royalist impulse at the heart of French conservatism even survived in the late-century radical conservatism of Charles Maurras. Almost by default, such traditionalist inclinations facilitated the formulation of ideological claims constructed around core concepts that stood in direct opposition to liberalism: anti-individualism, antirationalism, anticapitalism, Providence, social organicism, particularity, resistance to change, and inequality.[43] Joseph de Maistre, an attorney from the small principality of Savoy, was the first French thinker to solidify these ideas into a coherent conservative ideology.

Some commentators have seized upon Maistre's ferocious attack on the French Revolution and its Enlightenment ideals to portray him as a polemical thinker who "destroys better than he builds." Others have condemned his providential explanation of the revolution as both God's justified punishment of the nation for its sins and the mysterious divine tool for the resurrection of a more profound theocratic monarchy as proof for an impotent fatalism that pervades his reactionary vision.[44] But the fury and hyperbole unleashed in the pages of *Considerations on France* should not detract from its author's uncanny ability to give a distinctly conservative voice to the rising national imaginary. At the heart of this effort, one finds Maistre's central ideological claim, repeated in countless permutations: the "abstractions" and "generalities" pervading liberal conceptions of the nation must be replaced with the intuitions of a collective "national mind" cultivated by those unique prejudices and ancient traditions that alone give meaning to genuine French nationhood. Maistre typically constructs this claim by first exposing the alleged weaknesses of various liberal views. For example, he opens the second chapter of his best-selling *Considerations on France* (1796) with the Mill-like statement that "Every nation, like every individual, has received a mission that it must fulfill."[45] Still sounding very much like the Victorian liberal, he continues with the assertion that France's special mission corresponds to its unique character. Equally fond of such a character discourse, Mill had celebrated liberty—decontested as the rational cultivation of individuality—as the primary force shaping the character of both individuals and nations. Thus, for the British thinker, the essential quality of a nation was its promotion of individual freedom secured by a proper political constitution grounded in ethical universalism.

Maistre could not disagree more. In one of the more notorious passages of his book, he blasts the universalism underlying the liberal conception of human nature: "There is no such thing as *man* in the world. In my lifetime, I have seen Frenchmen, Italians, Russians, etc.; thanks to Montesquieu, I even know that *one can be Persian*. But as for *man*, I declare that I have never in my life met him; if he exists, he is unknown to me." Hence, any political contrivance anchored in the abstract notion "man" was bound to fail in practice, for it remained a "pure abstraction, an academic exercise made according to some hypothetical ideal, which should be addressed to *man* in his imaginary dwelling place."[46] Maistre singles out popular sovereignty, liberal constitutions, and representative government as examples of such abstract ideals that violate the concreteness of the divinely ordained order of things. Bearing the anemic fingerprints of its Enlightenment creators, he asserts, the liberal conception of the nation represents the prototype of an "imaginary dwelling place" cut off from the particularity of a country's mores, geographic location, political circumstances, and, above all, its religious traditions. Such abstract articulations of nationhood have led to the fateful separation of the "people" from their legitimate king. For Maistre, the "revolutionary heirs of Rousseau's philosophy" shrewdly invoked the "nation"—a "wonderfully convenient word"—to dupe the people into joining their "satanic revolt" against God and King.[47]

Claiming that "the French are made for monarchy," Maistre locates the special mission of his nation not in its provision of a rational-legal framework that encourages individual self-improvement, but in its providential status as the "most Christian" of all European countries. It is France's religious "spirit of proselytism"—manifested in her beautiful language and glorious history—that forms the abiding essence of its national character.[48] Thus, his ultraroyalist conservatism is rooted in a conformist conception of human sociability—the need for a secure collective existence not as atomistic individuals united by their rational consent to a social contract, but as obedient servants in God-given, organic hierarchies. Conversely, liberalism's emphasis on individual reason represents, "by its nature," the "mortal enemy of any association whatsoever because it gives birth only to divergent opinions."[49] Only the virtues of "submission and belief"—Maistre worships them as "infants of Heaven"— can set the nation on a secure and lasting foundation: "[I]f they unite, join their forces and together take possession of a nation, they exalt it, make it divine and increase its power a hundredfold. . . . " In short, the French thinker insists that nationhood cannot be constituted a priori in a rational manner. It is God who bestows on each nation its true Constitution, revealed in those unwritten laws and mores that frame a community's concrete "political way of life."[50]

It is tempting to read such theocratic pronouncements as "reactionary" in the sense of returning to a traditional social imaginary deeply colored by the sacred narratives of Catholicism. But Maistre knew perfectly well that the *ancien régime* was finished.[51] After 1789, the rule of hereditary kings could hardly be presented as a natural arrangement without justification. Any serious political effort to restore the monarchy had to be complemented by a modern ideology capable of countering liberal articulations of the national imaginary. Maistre in France and Burke in Britain provided the basic features of such a comprehensive ideational system. After all, winning the crucial battle of ideas against liberalism rested on a series of conservative ideological counter claims convincing enough to reassure old constituencies and attract new supporters. Fierce opponents of the Enlightenment, they were nonetheless prepared to fight rationalists on their own turf by relying on reason and empirical experience to prove the great truths revealed by their arguments. J. L. Talmon makes the same point: counterrevolutionary spokespersons found themselves challenged by the revolution to rationalize their attachments to traditional order, which precisely lacked Enlightenment notions of rationality at its source.[52]

Moreover, conservatives faced the challenge of providing their audiences with an alternative vision of how to cope with their changing world. If such a vision consisted of little more than a throwback to bygone days, it might elicit intense emotion for a brief period, but it would hardly be sustainable in the long run. In order to be successful, conservatism needed to correspond to the new imperatives and aspirations of the rising national imaginary. Maistre delivered, at least to some extent. For example, he asserted that Providence would return France to her "Christian magistracy over Europe" once the people had properly atoned for the sins committed during the revolution. This claim represented an effective rejoinder to liberalism's attempt to secularize the traditional idea of the nation's divine mission. In his later writings, Maistre even incorporated into his conservative ideology popular revolutionary imagery—an impressive testimony to the fact that conservatism could not help confronting liberalism with claims that necessarily circulated within the frame of reference of liberal-revolutionary thought. Maistre especially delved into the purifying effects of violence, the virtues of territorial expansion, and the glories of war. He praised "French patriots" for their willingness to sacrifice their lives for *la Grande Nation*—regardless of who happened to be at its helm. In his dark *Saint Petersburg Dialogues*, penned during his 1803–17 tenure as Sardinian ambassador to the Russian court, Maistre even goes so far as to celebrate war as the divine principle fueling the inevitable and ennobling struggle of nation against nation that "bathes them in blood."[53]

Ultraroyalist elites who returned triumphantly from exile in 1815 feasted on Maistre's ideas. The politically adroit Vicomte de Bonald, in particular, developed his brand of Catholic-inspired political conservatism by drawing extensively on the arguments assembled by the Savoy thinker. Bonald's original contribution came in the form of his sophisticated defense of organic agricultural communities against the combined atomizing social effects of industrialism, the centralized modern state, and the fledgling national market. In his view, the true value of a nation consists of its traditional means of existence and conservation—a claim he employed against Adam Smith's idea that the wealth of nations could be measured in terms of their material productivity.[54] Naturally, Bonald's paternalistic reflections on the dissolution of the elementary bonds of society brought on by industrialization not only resonated well with rural populations but also inspired the efforts of late-century conservatives to reach out to the urban proletariat. Likewise, the conservative distaste for commercial and industrial expansion constitutes the red thread running through the literary works of traditionalist writers such as Balzac and Flaubert, and culminates in Maurice Barrès' fin-de-siècle image of the uprooted, "deracinated" urbanite.

After the 1830 overthrow of the Bourbon monarchy, however, ultraroyalism lost its ideological dominance in the conservative camp, ceding ground to what José Merquior calls "conservative liberalism"—or "liberal conservatism"—propagated by thinkers like François Guizot and Charles de Rémusat who tried to steer a middle course between monarchical conservatism and liberal republicanism.[55] Staunchly opposed to the extension of the franchise beyond the upper bourgeoisie, these so-called "doctrinaires" dreamed of a new nation built on the foundation of "French character and national scrupulousness."[56] Put to the political test in the bourgeois monarchy of Louis-Philippe, this unstable ideological mixture expired at the Parisian street barricades of the 1848 Revolution. Indeed, French conservatism did not receive a significant infusion of new ideas until Arthur de Gobineau, a royalist with Bonapartist sympathies, embarked on his pioneering translation of the national imaginary in explicitly racial terms. His turn toward a singular national ethnos as the essence of the modern nation preceded the twentieth century's totalizing visions of ethnic purity and superior blood.

Published between 1853 and 1855, his four-volume tome, *Essay on the Inequality of Human Races*, contains claims that became the ideological foundation of the French Right in the 1890s.[57] The book fuses an ethnic history of France—as explained in the 1820s in the works of the Thierry brothers as ancient rivalries between Gauls, Romans, and Franks—with romantic speculations about "Aryan-Teutonic" language families and their corresponding "racial" groupings. Reducing all problems in human history to the "racial question," Gobineau turns race into the key variable for understanding such momentous events as the rise and fall of civilization, the outbreak of revolutions and wars, and, most importantly, the formation of nations.[58] In particular, he radicalizes the Swedish botanist Carl von Linné's subdivision of the human race into biologically distinct races based on different "colors," "temperament," and "intelligence" by arguing that humanity can "naturally" be divided into three unequal races. Possessing a largely instinctive "animal character" and "low intelligence," the "black" or "negroid" variety occupies the bottom of the Frenchman's racial hierarchy. Given to "apathy" and cultural "imitation," the "yellow race" inhabits the middle part. Predictably, the Aryan group of the "white races" occupies the biological pinnacle as a result of its "immense superiority" in all dimensions of human existence. Originally separated by geography, these three races gradually intermingled, in the process turning their present descendants into "racial mixtures." Only the "peasant stock" of a few nations in Northern Europe—mostly Germany, Scandinavia, France, and England—contains the "last remnants of the superior Aryan element," which allows them to delay, but not prevent, the inevitable cultural and political decline that follows from "the calamity blood mixture." Unsurprisingly, the French diplomat ends his deterministic discourse with the dire prediction that "complete degeneration" awaits humanity as its unalterable fate.[59]

Although the idea that "blood" carried sacred or magical properties making up the unalterable essences of an ethnic group goes back to the Middle Ages, it did not find its first legal formulation until the sixteenth century when a number of Church bodies and local governments in Spain issued "certificates of pure blood" for admission into many ecclesiastical institutions and state offices. These documents were based on the concept of *limpieza de sangre* (purity of blood), which held that to be truly Spanish one had to be of pure Christian blood. This exclusionary doctrine of blood purity was mainly directed against Jews and Jewish converts to Christianity, thus representing the stigmatization of an entire ethnic group on the basis of biological-spiritual deficiencies that allegedly could not be eradicated by conversion or assimilation.[60] But the modern concept of race used by Gobineau with reference to basic human types classified by physical characteristics like blood and skin color was not invented until the eighteenth century when naturalists like Linné and the Comte de Buffon and anthropologists like Johann Friedrich Blumenbach sought to establish scientific classifications of human types. In France, ethnological discourse in the early to mid-nineteenth century spread the belief that human beings were not of "one blood" but consisted of several species with greatly differing aptitudes and capacities that were indelibly inscribed in their respective biological constitutions.[61] Gobineau's arguments echoed this tradition, insisting that people belonged to unequal races whose biological essences were immune to assimilation.

George Fredrickson suggests that, paradoxical as it seems, even the egalitarian norms created by the French Revolution unwittingly furthered the development of modern racism. The nation, premised on equal rights for all citizens, permitted only special reasons for exclusion: "The one exclusionary principle that could be readily accepted by civic nationalists was biological unfitness for full citizenship."[62] The result was the strengthening of racism as a system of thought and political practice based on the belief that an ethnic group or historical collectivity can be dominated, excluded, or perhaps even eliminated on the basis of its hereditary and thus unalterable inferiority.[63] Indeed, Gobineau's arguments rest on his main ideological claim that race constitutes the "essential quality of a nation."[64] He conveys this immensely influential view in the following passage:

These racial elements impose their modes of existence on nations, circumscribing them within limits from which, like blind slaves, they do not wish to escape, although they would not even have the strength to do so. They dictate their laws, inspire their wishes, control their sympathies and stir up their hatreds and contempt. Always subject to ethnic influence, they create local triumphs by this immediate means; by the same means they implant the germ of national disasters.[65]

The potential appeal of such a monocausal explanation for conservatives becomes even more apparent in Gobineau's related claim that neither rational-legal contrivances like political constitutions or bills of rights nor forcible social change like revolutions or war are capable of altering the "true foundation" of nations. Only blood mixture could bring about lasting change—but always to the detriment of the superior white races. Thus, the radiant essence of the French nation lay in its remaining Aryan elements, to be found in their most concentrated form in ancient aristocratic families and old peasant stock. Consequently, it fell to them to safeguard their country through the protection of blood and soil.[66] Easing his readers into accepting as common sense his racist articulation of the national imaginary, Gobineau deploys throughout the *Essay* the terms "nation," "country," "state," "civilization," and "race" as interchangeable equivalents or related composites such as "Germanic race," "Aryan nations," or "French civilization." Imitated by countless popularizers of the Frenchman's ideas in the ensuing decades, this literary practice of equating race and nation greatly facilitated the normalization of ethnic stereotypes. Moreover, Gobineau's assertion that the historical study of particular nations must be based upon the more primary "ethnological" study of "successive racial intermixtures" serves to lend scientific legitimacy to his arguments. The fixation on race as the determining factor in the development of nations intensified after the publication of Charles Darwin's *Origin of Species* (1859) when biological concepts like "evolution" and "selection" exploded onto the political scene. By the end of the century, racial perspectives proliferated in the fledgling social sciences, particularly in disciplines such as "physical anthropology."[67] Indeed, as Niall Ferguson points out, pervasive scientific arguments in favor of maintaining "racial hygiene" led to a worldwide revulsion against "miscegenation" and any form of interracial social intercourse.[68]

Curiously enough, however, Gobineau's *Essay* was not particularly anti-Semitic. The idea of Jews as a separate race participating in the heinous conspiracy of the Freemasons, Illuminati, and atheist philosophers against the existing order did not appear in France in full force until the 1869 publication *Le Juif, le judaisme et la judaisation des peuples chrétiens*, authored by the conservative French aristocrat Gougenot des Mousseaux. Some fifty years later, his book was translated into German by the Nazi race theorist Alfred Rosenberg whose *The Myth of the Twentieth Century*, one of the founding books of Nazi ideology, is second only to Hitler's *My Struggle*.[69] However, Gobineau did strike up a friendship with Richard Wagner, whose Bayreuth circle provided a fertile ground for the expansion of the French diplomat's views. Indeed, Houston Stewart Chamberlain, Wagner's son-in-law, published in 1899 his tremendously influential book *The Foundations of the Nineteenth Century*, which portrayed history in terms of struggle for supremacy between the Germanic and Jewish "races." Fusing anti-Semitism with Social Darwinism and science, Chamberlain's polemic had a tremendous impact on the development of Nazi ideology.[70] Ludwig Schemann, another member of the virulently anti-Semitic Wagner circle in Bayreuth, translated Gobineau's treatise into German in 1898 after founding the Gobineau Society four years earlier, thus posthumously linking his name to its vulgar anti-Semitic program of Pan-Germanic expansionism. Indeed, the activities of Schemann's organization contributed greatly to popularizing Gobineau's term "Aryan" among German anti-Semites.[71]

In France, the 1890s marked the rise of a radical new conservatism stirred up by the Dreyfus Affair. Still reeling from its humiliating defeat by the Prussians at Sedan and rattled by a protracted economic crisis, France had found itself slowly descending into serious social unrest. This situation had been exacerbated by the increasing polarization of the political landscape into fiercely antagonistic political camps. As the alleged act of treason by the Jewish army Captain Alfred Dreyfus became increasingly implausible in light of new evidence pointing to a fraudulent conspiracy of anti-Semitic officers in the French military establishment, the right stubbornly clung to the case in an effort to revive its sagging political fortunes. A new generation of militant conservatives teamed up with right-wing Catholic clergy to defend the "honor of the armed forces and the nation." Their targets were left-liberal "intellectuals" like Emile Zola and Jean Jaurès who had publicly denounced the General Staff for intentionally perpetrating a false judgment against the innocent Dreyfus. The ensuing struggle for favorable public opinion raged for several years in high-circulation newspapers and magazines, attesting to the growing role of the mass media in the dissemination of ideology.[72]

The Affair served as the catalyst for the ongoing integration of old royalist sentiments yearning for the unity of throne and altar with nationalist appeals to the economically sinking lower middle class and the embittered proletariat. As we shall see in Chapter 3, this radical-conservative articulation of the national imaginary was one of the prototypes of "nationalism" based on ethnic essentialism and committed to the elimination of ethnic difference. It hinged on ideological claims that turned Jews like Dreyfus into convenient scapegoats for the alleged decline of the nation under the Third Republic. The growing anti-Semitic campaign of the anti-Dreyfusards provided the ideal meeting ground for Catholic and petty-bourgeois hostility to the liberal-republican conception of the nation— even though the Jewish community in France constituted less than a quarter of a percent of the total population. In keeping with the national mood, the 1898 elections returned more than a dozen of self-proclaimed "nationalist" deputies and many more mainstream conservatives who had made anti-Semitism the overriding campaign issue.[73] It appeared that the ideological battle over the soul of the nation was increasingly being won by those who claimed "France for the [ethnic] French."

For Edouard Drumont, the influential founder of the anti-Semitic paper *La Libre Parole* and author of the popular multivolume polemic *La France Juive*, this slogan referred solely to members of the Aryan race, which included "all nations of Europe, from which have sprung all the great civilizations." His long list of innate Aryan traits includes "enthusiasm, heroism, chivalry, disinterest, frankness, and trust to the point of naïveté," while members of the opposing "Semitic race" were characterized as "mercantile, covetous, scheming, subtle, and cunning." According to Drumont, Jews were obsessively scheming to "reduce the Aryan to a state of slavery." As a result of their opposing qualities, the two were doomed to clash. Drumont goes on to assert that this antagonism was quickly escalating into a momentous struggle over the "soul of the nation."[74] Predictably, he suggests that things were not going well for the French side. Jews were taking control of the nation by shrewdly exploiting "the abstract principles of 1789" that had led to their political emancipation. As the Dreyfus Affair showed, Jews had even infiltrated the army, the nation's last bastion of honor. Unfortunately, the French people—a "good-natured giant"—remained under the pernicious influence of abstract universalism preached by "scheming Semites" like the center-left republican leader Leon Gambetta. As a result, French Aryans had been unwilling to resort to the drastic measures taken by their determined ancestors, which included actually burning Jews, or, at the very least, closing their town gates to them and "covering them with scorn" and using "their name as the cruelest of insults." For Drumont, the shameful disintegration of the French spirit could only be reversed by the creation of a New France as the conscious embodiment of the "absolute negation of the Jewish character itself."[75]

The anti-Semitic journalist then delves into yet another long enumeration of alleged Jewish traits—a compilation of grotesque insults too vile to be reproduced here in more detail. However, he does show considerable skill in weaving together various racial and religious stereotypes designed to "prove once and for all" that Jews could never qualify for nationhood of any sort. Three ideological claims, in particular, stand out. First, Drumont declares that Jewish oppression and treachery are rooted in their racial elements as well as in their religion, which constitutes a "foreign element" in an Aryan-French nation anchored in Christianity. He presents the Jesuits—personified by their "pure Aryan" founder Ignatius of Loyola— as the "exact opposite of the Jews." This rather bizarre claim shows that

Drumont takes much care in connecting his racial claims to traditional Catholic ideas. Second, he activates the old myth of the "perpetually nomadic Jew" to argue that *patrie* remains a term devoid of meaning for the "inexorably universalistic Jew." Unlike a "genuine Frenchman," whose "feeling of the mother country is engraved in his heart," the Jew "can have no possible motive for being a patriot." After all, he concludes, "Patriotism cannot be improvised; it is in the blood and the bones." Finally, Drumont claims that Jews interfere with the "French way of life" by incessantly "preaching communism or socialism, and demanding that the wealth of old inhabitants be shared, while their coreligionists arrive barefoot, make their fortune, and do not show the least inclination of sharing anything."[76] These associations of Jews with both socialism and cosmopolitanism would become an ominous refrain in both the late German Empire and Hitler's Third Reich.

Maurice Barrès, a successful novelist and politician, represents another leading exponent of radical French conservatism. In addition to writing his immensely successful novel *Les Déracinés* ("The Uprooted"), he also served as an elected deputy who was the first to coin the term "national socialism" referring to the integration of the proletariat into the French nation. Sharing Gobineau's sense of national decline, he also adopts the gist of Drumont's anti-Semitism. Claiming that "Jews have no native land in the sense that we understand it," he admonishes the French people to acknowledge the "fact" that "the Jew is a creature apart." At the same time, however, Barrès is more reluctant than Drumont to frame his conservative articulation of the national imaginary exclusively in crude anti-Semitic terms. Combining his superior literary talent with his revulsion for the urban life, he pleads with his eclectic audience to remain rooted in those traditional values and images that seem to offer shelter from the harsh winds of rapid economic and cultural change.

Barrès defines the French nation as a political community rather than an exclusively ethnic group, although he retains a sense of ethnic superiority by speculating that the various "Anglo-Saxon and Teutonic groups" may be "progressively on the way of constituting themselves as a race."[77] At the same time, however, he regards France as ethnically far too mixed to claim nationhood *solely* on the basis of race. This means that the French people need more than race to find their sense of identity. What Barrès has in mind is what he calls a "particular point"—a "determinist perspective"—embedded in a "feeling of collectivity" rather than liberalism's rational-legal framework that unites sovereign individuals. Fiercely opposing individualism in all its forms, he even traces personal thoughts to a primeval substratum of common "physiological dispositions" forged over many generations. "Soil," a core concept in Barrès' emotionally charged organicism, is that which nourishes the body and soul of the living while at the same time providing the final resting place for the dead. Reflected in his lifelong fascination with graveyards and military cemeteries, the novelist's attachment to *la terre et les morts* emerges as the overriding sentiment powering his essentialist vision of the French nation: "The soil gives us the discipline we need: we are the extension in time of our dead. This is the concept of reality upon which to base our existence."[78]

At times, Barrès leaves behind the pessimism of his ideological predecessors, suggesting that the metaphysical abstractions of liberals and Dreyfusard intellectuals would lose their ability to distract people once they allowed themselves to tap into the nonrational wisdom of the soil. Theoretical truth would then turn into "French truth"; justice into "French justice"; and abstract reason into "French reason." By identifying their idea of the good solely with the well-being of the *patrie*, the French people would come to understand the profound truth expressed in Paul Déroulède's deterministic anti-Dreyfusard dictum: "It is highly improbable that Dreyfus is innocent, but it is absolutely certain that France herself is innocent."[79] However, Barrès' sense of the national in terms of primordial feelings anchored in the soil should not be confused with the patriotism of lofty idealists. A native of Alsace-Lorraine—French territory lost to Germany in 1870— Barrès understood perfectly that feelings of attachment could be implanted and cultivated over time by a variety of means. For example, the French patriotism of many Lorrainers was born of the pragmatic desire for lasting order and peace after centuries of territorial strife. In fact, principled loyalty to one's country rested on ephemeral ideals rather than deep-seated feelings and emotions. Thus, Barrès points to the enthusiasm generated by the spectacular military victories of Napoleon's troops as a major source of his intense identification with the French nation.[80]

With regard to ideology, the significance of late-century exponents of the French right like Drumont and Barrès lies in their ability to incorporate new alluring claims into the rather stagnant conservative translation of the national imaginary. Setting themselves clearly apart from their liberal nemesis and the rising socialists, radical-conservatives utilized the popular appeal of anti-Semitism amplified by the Dreyfus Affair for their conceptual reconfigurations of traditional conservative images and ideas. As they sought to give new meanings to the national in the dawning era of mass politics, conservatives like Barrès and Maurras welded together different strains of their ideology into a new synthesis that was at once traditionalist and radical. Thus, they managed to appropriate for their own ideological purposes the left's revolutionary language of popular sovereignty previously so abhorrent to ultraconservatives like Maistre or Bonald. What made the new conservatives both "populists" and "nationalists" (we shall elaborate on these concepts in the ensuing chapters) was their willingness to disregard the rights of minorities in the name of the people conceptualized primarily in terms of a national ethnos. Their populist appeal to the nation rather than to class enabled conservatives—particularly in France and Germany—to make successful forays into a proletariat that never gave up on the ideal of fatherland encompassing all classes. The growing susceptibility of industrial workers to what Barrès called "national socialism" exposed the Achilles heel of a European labor movement led by figures who professed their allegiance to the socialist vision of two infamous "internationalists": Karl Marx and Friedrich Engels.

2.4. German Socialism

England, France, and Belgium were the first European nations to produce an urban working class large enough to develop a distinct consciousness as a class-in-itself. Embryonic trade unions and workers' associations emerged in Britain in the early part of the century and achieved limited governmental recognition in 1825 with the repeal of the Combination Act. Similar labor organizations arose in France after the revolution of 1830. Their leaders drafted reform programs that drew on a variety of socialist ideas developed by social thinkers and activists like Robert Owen, Henri de Saint-Simon, Charles Fourier, Pierre-Joseph Proudhon, and Auguste Blanqui. Ranged from advocating a return to small-scale, agrarian communities to endorsing large-scale industrial producer cooperatives owned and managed by workers, their socialist schemes nonetheless shared an ethical commitment to end capitalist exploitation and fashion a more egalitarian society.

Both industrial development and the articulation of socialist ideology lagged far behind in the German Confederation, a loose conglomeration of more than thirty semifeudal sovereignties dominated by the dynastic regimes of Austria and Prussia. In sharp contrast to the politically unified *Staatsnation* (nation-state) prevailing in Western European countries, early nineteenth-century Germany was, at best, an amorphous *Kulturnation* (culture-nation), weakly united under the Holy Roman Empire and possessing a common stock of Germanic dialects. For a brief period under the Napoleonic occupation, however, large segments of the *Volk* transcended their traditional loyalties to particular states and warmed up to anti-French visions of nationhood articulated by public educators and self-proclaimed German patriots like Johann Gottlieb Fichte and Friedrich Ludwig Jahn. After having their political rule reconfirmed at the 1815 Vienna Congress, however, the old German aristocratic elites immediately proceeded to suppress liberal efforts to build a modern German nation. Intent on forestalling any political or territorial change in Central Europe, they understood clearly that popular sentiments of nationality could flourish only at the expense of aristocratic legitimacy.[81]

As the century wore on, however, mounting pressures to compete with British and Belgian industries added economic punch to the German bourgeoisie's drive for political unification. In 1834, the creation of a common national market with low tariffs was formalized in the Prussia-led *Zollverein*, which comprised nearly all the territories of northern Germany. Rapidly growing industries in the Rhine-Ruhr region, Saxony, and Silesia underscored the urgency of bourgeois demands for further political and economic liberalization. By the mid-1840s, liberal elites clamored once again openly for a unified, constitutional nation-state as the necessary framework for further progress in Germany. At the same time, however, industrial development served to highlight the plight of the working poor. Existing in the German lands for decades, the Fourth Estate was composed of journeymen and agricultural workers who had been emancipated from the chains of feudalism by the progressive reforms of the Napoleonic era. Unable to earn a decent living, these proletarians amounted to roughly 50 percent of the population.[82] Roaming the countryside in search of work, they became increasingly attracted to the fledgling industrial centers where factory labor promised at least regular meals and a roof over one's head. Increasingly worried by the ensuing proletarian concentration in urban areas, conservative and liberal elites alike began to contemplate possible "solutions" for this troubling "social question."

As we have seen in Chapter 1, radical democrats like Karl Marx were among the first radical bourgeois thinkers to recognize the growing political significance of the industrial proletariat. And he greeted it with enthusiasm rather than with the fear and consternation of his fellow *Bürger*. Often exiled in economically advanced countries, German radicals like

Marx found a far more receptive environment for their socialist ideas than in their homeland. Together with local radicals and itinerant German craftsmen working abroad, they founded small but energetic political associations such as the League of Communists or the League of the Just. Their programs called for the realization of social democracy through the violent overthrow of the existing political order. As if to confirm their political expectations, revolution promptly broke out in Europe in early 1848, only weeks after Marx and Engels published *The Communist Manifesto*. In German cities, journeyman and workers flocked to the street barricades, fighting the *ancien régime* shoulder to shoulder with radical liberals. Ultimately, the defeated aristocracy was forced to accept a Constituent National Assembly whose popularly elected representatives pondered constitutional reform and possible national unification.

During the following months, the debates in the Frankfurt Parliament dragged on without much progress. But workers throughout Germany used this short interval of political freedom to build organizations that went far beyond the strictly educational labor associations that had previously been encouraged by liberals as the most promising way to address the social question. In Berlin, for example, the printer Stephan Born managed to assemble national delegates from thirty-two workers' associations who voted for the creation of the General German Brotherhood of Workers (GGBW), the first national political workers' organization free of liberal influence. Ballooning quickly to over 200 local and regional associations, the GGBW even published its own newspaper, *Die Verbrüderung* ("The Fraternization"). While the high literacy rate among the GGBW members was an impressive testimony to educational progress in Germany, it also revealed a deep social gulf separating them from the growing *lumpenproletariat*, that is, the class of unskilled manual workers and day laborers.[83]

By and large, the publications of the GGBW spread ideological claims that decontested socialist core concepts such as class, work, equality, solidarity, welfare, and the democratic state in a manner that emphasized the capacity of the working class to act in unison as an autonomous political force in the soon-to-be unified nation: "The workers of Germany must strive to constitute a moral force in the state, to become a powerful body that weathers every storm.... Workers of Germany, we appeal to you once again: Be united, and you will be strong. Fear no obstacles; you will overcome them all, but only with the strength born of unity."[84]

But proletarian hopes for political participation evaporated in 1849 when the recuperating aristocracy, having managed to retain control over an army composed mostly of apolitical peasant recruits, felt secure enough to strike back. Exploiting the deepening divisions among liberal Frankfurt deputies over issues of Austrian or Prussian dominance over the new German nation, the old guard forcibly dissolved Parliament and reimposed its old hierarchical order. Likewise, the Prussian national assembly was replaced by a monarchical regime that granted a toothless "constitution" permitting legislative elections only in accordance with a restrictive class-based franchise that left the king in complete control of executive government.[85] In Austria, the Habsburgs did not even bother with sham constitutions as their troops restored the old unity of throne and altar under its Most Catholic Majesty, the 18-year-old Emperor Franz Josef and his ultraconservative advisor, Prince Felix Schwarzenberg.

In the short run, the political fallout of the failed 1848 Revolution proved to be disastrous for the fledgling German labor movement. With its associations dissolved, their leaders arrested or driven into exile, and their activities severely curtailed, the proletariat disappeared from the political stage for the next fifteen years. Only some of its educational leagues survived under the tutelage of well-meaning liberals like the philanthropist Hermann Schulze-Delitzsch who promoted workers' economic self-help organizations at the explicit exclusion of political agitation. Still, the aspiring bourgeoisie did not fare much better under the restored regime. Exposed in Frankfurt as an impotent debating club, liberals had failed to deliver on their promise of national unification, thus forfeiting any claims to political leadership. In addition, their defeat discredited their cherished ideals of constitutionalism and representative government. To make matters worse, broad sections of the bourgeoisie soon succumbed to political apathy and profitable accommodation with the regime, thus heightening a sense of abandonment and betrayal among the working classes. And yet, the revolution did succeed in one crucial respect by placing the cause of German national unity on the public agenda for good. The political advantages of unification even became apparent to ambitious young conservatives like Prince Otto von Bismarck whose strategy of "iron and blood" eventually forged a *kleindeutsches Reich* under Prussian hegemony.

In the early 1860s, however, unification was still a decade away. But the harsh years of the restoration were finally giving way to a New Era inaugurated by the cautious liberalizing efforts of the new Prussian King Wilhelm. In addition, the Italian struggle for national liberation rekindled hopes of unification among many liberals who recognized the importance of forming a common political alliance that could count on the loyal support of workers while steering clear of formal coalitions with the "dangerous classes." When three Saxon labor leaders applied for full membership in the newly founded liberal National Association (*Nationalverein*), they learned to their dismay that workers should content themselves with informal honorary membership. Such exclusionary practices sparked lively debates in working-class circles as whether to remain under the tutelage of the liberals or seek to reenter the political arena in separate workers' organizations. However, cutting the ties to the liberal camp constituted a risky strategy for the politically inexperienced proletariat. As the legendary socialist party leader August Bebel observed decades later:

The German workman of those days knew next to nothing of politics. During the years of reaction political activity was dead. There were a few workmen's clubs, but they did not meddle with politics. In some German states such clubs were prohibited, as they were supposed to propagate Socialism and Communism. As a matter of fact, these words meant nothing to us of the younger generation.[86]

The proletariat's desire for political guidance only gained in urgency when the American Civil War and the ensuing cotton blockade began to rattle the German textile industry. Determined to find effective political mentors in such a time of crisis, the three rejected labor leaders from Leipzig turned to the charismatic lawyer and self-appointed "champion of the workers," Ferdinand Lassalle. The son of a Jewish silk merchant from Breslau, Lassalle had been a revolutionary participant in the events of 1848 and an ensuing political prisoner who maintained regular contacts with Marx and other exiled social democrats. He had made headlines, as well as a small personal fortune, during the 1850s with his successful prosecution of the Countess Sophie von Hatzfeld's widely publicized divorce case. Highly ambitious and itching to leave his mark on history, the dashing democrat cultivated a public image as an uncompromising German patriot strongly supportive of national unification under Prussian leadership.

Having fallen under the spell of Hegel's dialectical philosophy as a young student in Breslau and Berlin, Lassalle responded to the fundamental question of what constituted the nation by arguing that the working classes represented its most vital component. Chosen by fate to serve as a "gigantic and powerful exemplar for the rest of Europe," the German proletariat was the latest manifestation of a "unique Germanic Folk Spirit," which attested to "the necessity and indestructibility of our national existence."[87] Thus, Lassalle had struck upon an ingenious solution to a crucial question arising in industrializing societies: was "class" or "nation" more deserving of people's solidarity? Fearful of the divisive and revolutionary potential of class discourse, both liberals and conservatives emphasized the national appeal of their respective ideologies. Marxist socialists, on the other hand, focused on class struggle at the expense of the national. However, as we shall see, their much-publicized commitment to internationalism rarely escaped the rarified realm of theory. In practice, of course, most German Marxists were firmly anchored in the national sphere. By lionizing the proletariat as "the rock upon which the church of the future will be built", Lassalle merged class and the national, thus foreshadowing a development that gave French conservatism new life in the 1890s and contributed to the rapid growth of fascist movements after the Great War.

Articulating the national imaginary in (working) class terms, Lassalle managed to alienate his liberal friends. Criticizing their timid parliamentary tactics during the 1862 Prussian constitutional conflict over the government's proposed military reforms, he escalated his antiliberal crusade in a series of public lectures that urged workers to liberate the nation by shaking off the arduous bourgeois yoke for good. When the Leipzig labor leaders asked him to present his "considered views on a suitable political strategy to be adopted by the German labor movement," the flamboyant agitator composed within a fortnight his legendary *Open Reply Letter* (1863), which implored the proletariat to establish its own national class-based political party at once. Two months after the publication of the pamphlet, Lassalle's enthusiastic followers elected him President of their newly founded General German Workers' Association (GGWA), an independent socialist organization destined to grow into the largest political party of the German Empire.

Lassalle prefaces his *Open Reply Letter* with his conviction that the bourgeoisie in all modern nations had lost both its capacity and its will for progressive political leadership. Fearing the democratic radicalism of the Fourth Estate more than the aristocratic whip, liberals were acting according to the motto, "Above all, no revolution from below; better despotism from above." While there still remained the possibility of a social struggle leading to German unification, such a national revolution had to be combined with a political revolution under the auspices of "a solid and class-conscious workers' party."[88] Eager to lead the proletariat toward this "ultimate goal", Lassalle expends much energy convincing his audience to discard the liberal injunction against their involvement in German politics. Emphasizing that the "fulfillment of the proletariat's legitimate interests can only be expected from its free political activities," he insists that any future political agitation carried out by the working class would require a careful strategy revolving around a "big idea." Accordingly, Lassalle proceeds to condense his "considered views" into his central ideological claim: political oppression and capitalist exploitation in Germany can only be ended through the proletariat's democratic seizure of state power by means of universal, equal, and direct suffrage. The rest of the pamphlet merely elaborates on this "single, all-important point."[89]

Lassalle draws on census data collected in 1851 by the Prussian Statistical Bureau to argue that nearly 90 percent of the German population earned incomes that put them squarely into the proletarian camp. Conveniently disregarding contrary evidence from the short-lived Second French Republic, he suggests that these numbers show that the introduction of general suffrage would necessarily lead to the capture of state power by the representatives of the working classes. Moreover, Lassalle relies on the Prussian statistics to emphasize the crucial importance of the state. As he puts it melodramatically, "The state belongs to you, gentlemen, the members of the needy classes, not to us, the members of the higher estates!"[90] Adopting Hegel's conception of the state as an ethical whole "indispensable for the free cultural development of the nation," he parts ways not only with the Marxist characterization of the state as an oppressive organ wielded by the enemies of the working class and destined to wither away with the proletarian establishment of a communist society but also with the liberal view of the state as a nightwatchman limited in its functions to the protection of citizens' life, liberty, and private property. In a celebrated speech to a gathering of Berlin workers later published as *The Workers' Program*, Lassalle links the state to the realization of proletarian solidarity in that it "unifies the individual with other individuals of his class, thus allowing us to reach a stage of education, power, and liberty that would remain unreachable by individual efforts alone."[91] Finding its highest expression as the political command post of the Fourth Estate, the state, in turn, has an obligation to help workers to establish producer cooperatives that would eventually replace the capitalist mode of production with a socialist system responsive to human needs rather than profits.

Lassalle's glorification of the nation-state, together with his intense dislike of the bourgeoisie, led him to pursue secret talks with Prussian Prime Minister Bismarck who had been seriously considering breaking the constitutional stalemate with the liberal Progressive Party by forging a short-term tactical alliance between conservatives and the working classes. However, Bismarck ended his negotiations with Lassalle as soon as he realized that his interlocutor's influence on the German proletariat was limited to scarcely a few thousand workers affiliated with the GGWA. As the Iron Chancellor confessed years later, "What could Lassalle have offered me? He had nothing behind him.... But he attracted me as an individual.... He was very ambitious and by no means a republican. He was very much a nationalist and monarchist. His ideal was the German Empire, and here was our point of contact."[92] Leaving aside the question of the accuracy of Bismarck's impressions, they nonetheless reveal some overlap between two competing ideological articulations of the same overarching national imaginary.

Lassalle's sudden death in 1864 in a silly duel over a torrid love affair with a young woman prevented him from witnessing the spectacular growth of the German labor movement—in spite of the Iron Chancellor's antisocialist legislation banning political workers' associations in Imperial Germany from 1878 to 1890. But Lassalle's political ideas continued to dominate the amalgamated Social Democratic Party of Germany (SPD), much to the chagrin of the exiled Marx in London, who subjected its inaugural 1875 Gotha Party Program to his biting criticism. Nevertheless, it took decades for Marx's brand of socialism to make inroads in German workers' circles under the sway of Lassalle. One reason for this delayed reception lies in the fact that the principal works of Marx and Engels— including *The Communist Manifesto* and *The Capital*—had been written abroad and were thus largely unknown to the German proletariat. Conversely, Lassalle, who referred to himself jokingly as "the last of the [1848] Mohicans," had elected to remain in Germany on pain of imprisonment, which allowed him to develop a stellar reputation and personal contacts with various local labor leaders. Second, in contrast to the popular pamphlets that drove home Lassalle's main ideas in accessible and passionate language, the writings of Marx and Engels struck the average worker as dry and abstruse. It was not until the 1880s that the aging Engels, assisted by his two intellectual heirs, Karl Kautsky and Eduard Bernstein, managed to produce a steady stream of Marxist essays suitable for wide circulation in the growing party press. These efforts were crowned in 1891 with the adoption of the SPD's Erfurt Program drafted by Kautsky and Bernstein. Anchoring social democracy in the compressed Marxism they had learned from Engels, his disciples highlighted the escalating class struggle between the bourgeoisie and the proletariat, the fatal economic contradictions leading to the collapse of capitalism, the coming workers' revolution, and the historical inevitability of socialism.

Third, and most significantly, unlike the uncompromising patriotic orientation of Lassalle's socialism, the Marxists never resolved the serious tension between their theoretical appeal to proletarian internationalism and their party's practical commitment to improving the conditions of the German working class. For example, in his popular commentary on the 1891 Erfurt Program, Kautsky prefaces a long section on the alleged "internationalism of social democracy" with the following remarkable concession:

The new socialism of Marx and Engels originated in Germany. Its two founders were Germans; its first pupils were Germans; and its first interpretative essays appeared in German. Although not the sole cause, these facts clearly show that it was Germany that provided the framework for the successful merger of the labor movement with socialism. It was in Germany that social democracy first took root, though it must be emphasized that Germany cannot be equated with the German Empire, but includes all territories inhabited by a majority of German-speaking workers.[93]

As we have seen in our previous discussion of *The German Ideology*, Kautsky's decontestation of socialist core concepts within a national framework was by no means unique among Marxist thinkers. While denying any "patriotic chauvinism" on his part, Engels nonetheless delighted in invidious comparisons that exalted the intellectual acumen of German workers—allegedly belonging to "the most theoretical nation in Europe"—while deriding the British labor movement as "slow" and "indifferent to theory." He characterized French and Belgian workers as "mischievous" and "confused," and stereotyped Spanish and Italian laborers as "imitative." Indeed, Engels' most successful publication, *Socialism: Utopian and Scientific* (1880), contains a passage that articulates the national in a language that clearly prefigures Kautsky's views: "[S]cientific socialism is indeed an essentially German product and could arise only in that nation whose classical philosophy had kept alive the tradition of conscious dialectics: Germany."[94]

Indeed, appeals to internationalist principles that went beyond mere window dressing could be a risky business for German labor leaders. Whenever they elevated solidarity with foreign workers over sentiments of loyalty to the fatherland in a time of crisis—as Marx, Bebel, and Liebknecht did in their notorious defense of the 1871 Paris Commune following the Franco-Prussian War—they alienated large segments of their core constituencies while at the same time providing useful ammunition to ideological competitors who delighted in portraying social democrats as "rootless fellows without a fatherland." Likewise, while international labor associations succeeded in organizing large meetings from time to time, they never lived up to their Marxist ideal of forging strong and lasting alliances among working people from all countries. Both the First International Working Men's Association (1864–76) and the Second International Working Men's Association (1889–1914) ultimately collapsed under the combined weight of chronic factionalism, petty personality contests, and recalcitrant national attachments.

During the lifespan of the Empire, German socialists were persecuted by both conservatives and liberals. These constant harassments forced workers into an isolated subculture whose organizations provided them with alternative activities in nearly all aspects of daily life outside the workplace. And yet, working people continued to feel themselves to be part of the nation, refusing to abandon their struggle for full recognition by a regime that had nothing but contempt for them. As we have seen, even convinced Marxist internationalists, realizing the depth of proletarian feelings for the *Heimat*, eventually heeded the political imperative by tailoring their ideological claims to the needs of the *German* proletariat. As the political situation in Europe deteriorated in the first decade of the twentieth century, the labor movement drew ever closer to a German Empire it had come to accept as the ground of its existence and the operational base it needed to preserve. August Bebel expressed these sentiments openly at the 1907 party conference:

If a time really comes when we have to defend the fatherland, then we shall do so because it is our fatherland; we shall defend it as the soil on which we live, as the country whose language we speak and whose customs we hold, and because we wish to make this fatherland of ours a land of such perfection and beauty as shall be unmatched in all the world.[95]

Bebel's death in 1913 spared him from witnessing how the outbreak of the Great War put socialist internationalism to the fatal test. Following their deceased party leader's intuition, the entire SPD leadership voted on August 4, 1914, in favor of the Imperial government's request for war credits. Socialists officially signaled their support of the German war effort, ostensibly directed at "destruction of Czarist despotism" and the "defense of freedom and our German culture." The SPD leadership went so far as to agree to uphold a general social truce—a *Burgfrieden*—thereby indicating its willingness to forgo its political opposition to its nonsocialist "class enemies" and its public criticism of the government for the duration of the war. International socialism had morphed back into a Lassallean national socialism. As Joshua Muravchik notes, "The single most fundamental idea of Marxism was that class is the most important political variable, yet the response to the war proved that nationality was a more powerful bond, and few socialists were able to resist its pull."[96] Historian Gary Steenson seconds this view: "The most obvious lesson of August 1914 was that German socialists were really Germans first and socialists second."[97] In short, the majority of workers were thinking in categories of national consciousness rather than class consciousness. However, if we understand the three grand ideologies to be articulations of the national imaginary, then Steenson's observation contains an even deeper insight: in order to be socialist (or conservative or liberal), one *had to be* German (or British or French) *first*. It was, therefore, precisely in Bebel's profound wish to "make the fatherland a land of perfection and beauty" that the grand ideologies of the nineteenth century found their common inspiration.

3

Twentieth-Century Totalitarianisms: Russian Communism and German Nazism

Complete equality of rights for all nations; the right of nations to self-determination; the unity of the workers of all nations—such is the national program that Marxism, the experience of the whole world, and the experience of Russia, teach the workers.

V. I. Lenin (1914)

What is meant by the *possibility* of the victory of socialism in one country? It means the possibility of solving the contradiction between the proletariat and the peasantry by means of the internal forces of our country, the possibility of the proletariat seizing power and using that power to build a complete socialist society in our country, with the sympathy and support of proletarians of other countries, but without the preliminary victory of the proletarian revolution in other countries.

J. V. Stalin (1926)

As National Socialists we see our program in our flag. In the *red* we see the social idea of the movement, in the *white* the nationalistic idea, and in the *swastika* the fight for the victory of the Aryan man and at the same time for the victory of the idea of creative work, which in itself always was and always will be anti-Semitic.

Adolf Hitler (1925)

3.1. The Decline of Grand Ideology and the Rise of Totalitarianism

In his history of the twentieth century as an "age of extremes," Eric Hobsbawm speculates that people born in the mid-nineteenth century who

84

survived into the gloomy interwar period were perhaps "most shocked by the collapse of the values and institutions of the liberal civilization whose progress their century had taken for granted, at any rate in 'advanced' or 'advancing' parts of the world." Listing some of those liberal values—distrust of absolute rule, commitment to constitutional government and rule of law, defense of civil liberties, and belief in progress and the power of rationality—the British historian goes on to present staggering evidence for the retreat of liberal political institutions, stating that between 1918 and 1939, legislative assemblies were dissolved or rendered ineffective in seventeen European nations.[1]

There are further reasons why older generations would have been puzzled by the decline of the liberal order. First, the advance of industry and technology in the second half of the nineteenth century resulted in efficient national economies that generated considerable wealth and prestige and fueled the frenzied expansion of European and American spheres of influence. Entering the public discourse in the 1890s as the fashionable buzzword "imperialism," these dynamics attested to the growing power of "developed" nations over the rest of the world. As historian Robert Young suggests, imperialism functioned through the exercise of political power from the colonial center "either through direct conquest or (latterly) through political and economic influence that effectively amounts to a similar form of domination: both involve the practice of power through facilitating institutions and ideologies."[2] The respective codifiers of the three grand ideologies were equally capable of rationalizing Western colonial domination of Africa and Asia under the auspices of an overarching civilizing mission discourse that presented these exploitative practices as benign attempts to uplift "savage," "barbaric," or "backward" peoples.[3] At the height of the colonial era in 1900, nearly 450 million people in Africa and Asia chafed under the colonial rule of European powers whose search for new markets and raw materials was inextricably linked to the enhancement of their national prestige. With the claim to racial superiority firmly built into the imperialist project, colonial subjects were taught to feel inherently inferior and to believe that their indigenous cultures were doomed to certain extinction. At the same time, the very process of European expansion also contributed to the outbreak of the Great War, which set into motion modern Third-World resistance movements against colonial rule and imperialist oppression.[4]

The second reason for the older generation's puzzlement at the sudden decline of liberalism was the gradual but steady extension of political participation to the previously excluded masses of workers, peasants, and women, a trend that seemed to support the liberal thesis of the inevitable advance of democracy. Third, the new constitutional nation-states arising from the smoldering remains of the collapsed Austro-Hungarian and Ottoman Empires seemed to vindicate US President Woodrow Wilson's boundless confidence in "making the world safe for democracy" through the benign powers of national self-determination. But Wilson's intentions only applied to Europe. At the 1919 Versailles Conference, for example, the pleas of Iranian delegates for independence were ignored by the British who made the ancient Persian lands their protectorate. And it was not until the appearance of the Bolshevik government in 1917 that those peoples struggling against colonialism and imperialism would find the support denied to them by any of the Great Powers, including the United States of America.[5] Yet, although the horrors of the Great War had done considerable damage to Enlightenment ideals, the victorious powers continued to express their optimism in the prospects for a peaceful League of Nations built on Western liberal principles.

Despite this deceptive facade of a rising democratic order, however, older people in Europe would have been prepared—at least to some extent—for the misfortunes that befell bourgeois society in the first half of the twentieth century. After all, the first symptoms of the malady had appeared as early as the 1870s and intensified in the ensuing decades. Economically, it began with the severe recession of 1873 that had ushered in a long period of social volatility: the long-term decline of world prices had hit agriculture especially hard; the productivity of industrial nations slowed down markedly; and international trade expanded only at a modest pace. Workers and farmers were thrown into turmoil and even petty artisans and small shopkeepers had begun to warm up to populist slogans directed against Big Capital. Ignoring these warning signs, however, the upper middle classes—the captains of the bourgeois order—showed little sympathy for the plight of the masses.

When the economic crisis finally subsided at the turn of the century, it left in its wake a series of lasting structural changes. Capital was more concentrated than ever before. The modern corporation was slowly coming into its own. Production had been rationalized to an unprecedented degree, and the reach of the state apparatus into the economy had been expanded. Today, it has become fashionable to refer to the *belle époque* preceding the Great War as an era of globalizing capital. Some commentators cite as evidence increasing economic integration and trade liberalization, the stabilizing reign of the gold standard, and the power of classical laissez-faire ideas. Others even go so far as to refer to the beautiful epoch as the "golden age of globalization" not unlike our own era.[6] But such a narrow conflation of globalization with economic dynamics fails to account for the vast political and cultural differences that separate the early twentieth century and our contemporary era. Still, even if we accepted the comparison in strictly economic terms, it would not hold. As Eric Hobsbawm has argued, the "global economy" before 1914 may have facilitated the worldwide movement of capital, goods, and labor, but there was no evidence for the emancipation of manufacturing and most agricultural products from the territory in which they were produced: "When people talked about Italian, British, or American industry, they meant not only industries owned by citizens of those countries, but also something that took place almost entirely in Italy, Britain, and America, and was then traded with other countries."[7]

Hence, in spite of flourishing world markets and the remarkable degree of economic openness that existed 100 years ago, the social imaginary in the industrialized world was painted in stark national colors. National economies—not global cities networks, transnational corporations, or global economic institutions—played the leading role. As economic competition between nations began to heat up, the ensuing political tensions fueled imperialist rivalries. Locked into permanent antagonisms, industrialized nations began to erect trade barriers to protect their national economies. In large part as a result of these restrictive measures, the United States and Germany managed to catch up with industrial powerhouse Britain. Argentina and Canada were closing in as well. Even traditional agricultural economies like Russia experienced the first birth pangs of the Industrial Revolution as steel production in the Romanov Empire multiplied by a factor of 6 in the waning years of the century.[8] No doubt, however, at the center of this explosive economic activity was the industrial development of the *nation*. It is, therefore, not surprising that the vast majority of early twentieth-century economists explained the macroeconomic dynamics of their time in terms of "national patterns of comparative advantage."[9]

Despite its growing strength in numbers, however, the industrial proletariat had made little headway. Even when the economy regained its health after 1896, workers in leading industrial nations like Britain and France were forced to put up with chronically falling wages. The plummeting purchasing power of the working class contrasted painfully with capitalism's overflowing cornucopia of mass-produced commodities. Abundantly displayed in expanding department stores, these enticing wares beckoned the proletariat's entry into the restricted sphere of bourgeois consumption. But in spite of the growing availability of credit, only very few workers were fortunate enough to join the ranks of the middle classes. Their real-life experiences remained profoundly at odds with the consumerist paradise conjured up by the fledgling mass advertisement sector. As their desire for material betterment remained largely unfulfilled, workers vented their frustrations against the "bourgeois class enemy" and the "capitalist system." Accusing Jews of conspiring against honest and hardworking people may have given some workers cathartic release, but such psychological self-indulgence came at the high cost of strengthening the vicious ethnic stereotypes then circulating in society. Keeping their distance from the despised proletariat, the lower middle classes, too, struggled to make ends meet. Blaming Jews and Big Business for their misfortunes, the petty bourgeoisie castigated liberal democracy and its squabbling parliamentarians. Even those lucky souls who obtained jobs as salaried employees or state bureaucrats never forgave the liberal establishment for its complicity in what they decried as the shameful decline of their civilization. Thus, despite their remaining differences, the proletariat and the lower middle classes found common ideological ground in the populist claim that the "little people" were being victimized by elites and outsiders too selfish and indifferent to bother with the real problems confronting their nation. Disillusioned with the status quo, charismatic demagogues appeared on the scene, prophesizing the coming of a new order built on both antiliberal and anti-Marxist principles.

Paradoxically, the political decline of the liberal order was helped along by the advance of democracy—a development most dramatically manifested in the gradual extension of the franchise to large segments of the working classes. Although full enfranchisement eluded most nations until after the Great War, the inclusion of the masses fundamentally altered the rules of the political game. The power of entrenched notables who acted as independent political entrepreneurs was slowly eclipsed by permanent mass party organizations, which selected suitable candidates. Emotional appeals to public opinion and racial prejudice made for juicy headlines in newspapers printed for mass consumption. Sensationalist political exposés trumped boring reports of politics-as-usual. Acerbic crowd pleasers spouting one-liners on the stump outshone polished orators trained to deliver witty speeches in the confines of parliament. Fear of exploding crime and economic crisis afflicting ordinary people overshadowed traditional middle-class concerns with status and character.

Slow to adapt to these new political conditions, old-style bourgeois politicians vowed never to give in to the vulgarity of the masses. But their elitism clashed with the outlook of a new generation determined to push the grand ideologies into a decidedly new direction. As we have seen, British New Liberals argued that the realization of individual liberty required comprehensive public welfare measures initiated and supervised by an interventionist state. Linking the traditional liberal ideal of the self-governing individual to the "self-governing state," they equated the advancement of liberty with a state-backed guarantee to offer all citizens steady employment at a living wage.[10] Exhausting themselves in interminable factional squabbles that pitted the younger generation against the laissez-faire traditionalists, liberal parties across Europe fell into disarray. Such was the fate of the British Liberal Party as it moved from its historic landslide election victory in 1906 to its virtual extinction thirty years later.[11] In the meantime, extremists at both ends of the political spectrum were remarkably successful in building mass parties that thrived on their relentless attacks on liberal democracy and Big Capital.

Intellectually, the crisis of the liberal order was exacerbated by the growing influence of thinkers who applied the biological categories of "evolution" and "race" to virtually all aspects of society. But hardly anyone objected to the proliferation of Social-Darwinist and racist terminology. In fact, intellectuals of all ideological stripes showed considerable fondness for metaphors of the "organic" that cast the nation as a holistic community existing prior to the individual. The crux of the debate was not about the suitability of biological terminology in politics, but the derivative question of whether Darwinian principles of evolution led to the cooperative development of human societies along rational lines or whether they fueled an instinctual struggle for survival by means of cutthroat competition and violence. The former position was dear to socialists and liberals, whereas conservatives and right-wing radicals vigorously defended the ideas of competition and struggle. There was, however, overwhelming agreement among all of these voices that collectivism was on the march in modern societies.

Evidence for the appeal of this new vitalism and irrationalism abounded in almost all academic disciplines and cultural circles. Philosophers like Henri Bergson and Friedrich Nietzsche and their numerous followers celebrated "élan" and "will" as promethean forces unencumbered by conventional morality that were capable of forging a new social ethos based on natural hierarchies not unlike those prevailing in the animal kingdom. Analysts of mass politics like social psychologist Gustave Le Bon postulated that modern crowds provided individuals with a convenient cover for reverting to their primordial selves, leaving them vulnerable to political manipulation by charismatic leaders. Le Bon suggested that political power in the new century would fall to the most skillful choreographers of crowds: "It is no longer in the council of princes but in the heart of the masses that the destiny of nations is being forged."[12] Revolutionary trade unionists like Georges Sorel welcomed the instinctive violence of crowds as a healthy antidote to the "poisonous stench of moral degeneration" emanating from the putrefied institutions of parliamentary democracy. Disputing the Marxist idea that material forces acted as the primary movers of history, Sorel instead postulated the political efficacy of "direct action" fueled by emotive "myths" impervious to rational refutation. Likewise, avant-garde artists like Filippo Marinetti looked forward to an illiberal future ushered in by aggressive nation-states reinvigorated by the dazzling beauty of war, speed, and technology.

The belief in the power of the irrational simmering just beneath the thin veneer of civilization received its most influential elaboration in Sigmund Freud's assertion that unconscious biological drives—primarily sex and violence—functioned as the twin-engines of human motivation. His thesis of the undisputed dominance of nature over the fragile social environment received further affirmation by "scientific eugenicists" like Sir Francis Galton and Karl Pearson. In 1905, the German doctor Alfred Plötz founded the Racial Hygiene Society to propagate his view that the protection of the superior Aryan race required draconian eugenic measures such as forced sterilization and infanticide in order to eliminate the "weak" and "worthless" from the *Volksgemeinschaft* (national community). Defining the nation-state in racial terms, General Friedrich von Bernhardi argued on the eve of the Great War that ruthless warfare between antagonistic races was a biological necessity designed by nature to prevent "inferior and decaying races" from "choking the growth of healthy budding elements."[13] Popularized in best-selling books like Ernst Häckel's *The Riddle of the World*, such *völkisch* renditions of hereditary determinism were passed on to a new generation of German anti-Semites eager to "weed out" the carriers of "Jewish blood."

Ideologically, the problems of the bourgeois order were reflected in the decline of the grand political belief systems and the concomitant meteoric rise of "nationalism." Entering the public discourse in France and Britain in the 1880s, this new term rapidly replaced the liberal phrase "principle of nationality." As we noted in the Introduction, however, nationalism does not constitute a separate political ideology. Rather, it refers to the fin-de-siècle radicalization of those milder translations of the national imaginary discussed in Chapter 2 as conservatism and socialism.[14] After the Great War, Italian fascism and German Nazism emerged as the most extreme articulations of the national. Whereas nineteenth-century ideologies were built around largely defensive and moderately pluralistic forms of patriotism, the new twentieth-century nationalisms were aggressive, xenophobic, antidemocratic, and racist.[15] As we have observed in the case of radical French conservatism, however, the last decade of the nineteenth century brought significant changes to the ideological landscape. As early as the 1870s, nationalist agitators had ignited the first large-scale campaigns of "ethnic cleansing" in the multiethnic Ottoman and Russian empires.[16]

Starting as ideological scavengers that often relied on a populist style of rhetoric, the new nationalisms fed on suitable concepts and claims torn from the flanks of conservatism and socialism. Their early dependence on their ideological hosts was dramatically demonstrated throughout the opening years of the twentieth century by the proliferation of hyphenated terms such as "national-socialist," "national-conservative," and, in the case of Germany, even "national-liberal." The power of these ideological hybrids lay in their ability to convert the grievances and prejudices of the masses into valuable political capital without having to invent an entirely new political language. Utilizing familiar metaphors of racial resentment and revenge, nationalists urged all "decent people of the fatherland" to join their political alliance of "Force and Blood against Gold."[17] The nationalist New Right in France, as we have seen, thrived on the glorification of blood, soil, war, manliness, and self-sacrifice. Semi-mythical martial figures like Nicolas Chauvin, the mutilated hero of the Franco-Prussian War, served as role models for boisterous "chauvinists" who brandished their national flag as the symbol of an imagined single ethnos at the core of French nationhood. Mixing flattery with pathos, the superpatriots bemoaned their respective nations' victimization at the hands of sinister forces both inside and outside of the borders. Inevitably, such harrowing populist tales of national downfall culminated in emotional pleas for the restoration of the national honor and the regeneration of the nation.

The growing mass appeal of nationalist extremism in the new century not only revealed the frailty of liberalism but exposed the vulnerability of conservatism and socialism as well. French national-socialists scored political points by accusing traditional conservatives of indulging in the decadent lifestyles of the bourgeoisie while hiding behind their hypocritical incantations of "Tradition, Property, Family, and Morality,"[18] while in Britain, old-style Tory conservatism limped along for years until it finally expired with the passage of the 1911 Parliamentary Act. With the stroke of a pen, the once powerful House of Lords found itself reduced to a politically impotent social club for nostalgic aristocrats and retiring bourgeois politicians with upper-class ambitions. A new generation of self-proclaimed pragmatic Conservatives grudgingly acknowledged the advance of democracy and resigned themselves to working with a broadened electoral base: "The Conservative Party hesitated to accept Democracy; but Democracy, having become established, has become the traditional form of government which Conservatives support."[19] But their reluctant embrace of the rules of mass democracy only added more fuel to the extremists' assertion that conservatives and liberals were, in fact, birds of a feather—a corrupt alliance of privilege committed to propping up a corroded system while ignoring the legitimate demands of ordinary people. While such charges acquired far more traction on the excitable continent than in imperturbable Britain, radicals everywhere delighted the masses by blasting the political status quo. In fact, their relentless attacks added much legitimacy to their claim that they alone constituted the sole alternative to the established order.

But why would socialism find itself in the same precarious situation as its ideological competitors? After all, social democratic organizations and the trade-union movement enjoyed solid growth rates in the years leading up to the Great War. Large working-class parties existed in virtually all industrial nations except the United States. In the 1912 German General Election, for instance, the SPD captured 35 percent of the vote, making it the largest political party in the Reichstag. Four years later, the Finnish Socialist Party surpassed this stunning achievement by garnering 47 percent of the national vote. And yet, with each electoral success, socialism moved closer to the liberal-conservative establishment. Built on a party platform that embraced the Marxist doctrine of revolutionary internationalism, the SPD subscribed nonetheless in practice to a parliamentarianism that operated largely within the confines of the nation-state.

As early as 1898, Eduard Bernstein had famously urged his comrades to reconcile Marxist theory with actually existing Party practice. Suggesting that capitalism was getting better at containing its structural weaknesses, he advocated an evolutionary road to socialism. Once and for all, the democratic ballot was to supersede insurrectionist tactics played out at the street barricades. Bernstein not only rejected the Marxist claim of the inevitable collapse of capitalist society but also cast doubt on the necessity of the proletarian revolution itself. Instead, he counseled his party to broaden its narrow class appeal to address the concerns of the growing middle strata as well. Once transformed into a genuine People's Party, the SPD would "raise the worker from the social position of a proletarian to that of a citizen, thus making citizenship universal." Turning against his late mentor Friedrich Engels, Bernstein attacked the notion that liberalism and socialism were diametrically opposed forces in modernity. Provocatively calling socialism "the legitimate heir of liberalism," he let it be known that he preferred the gradual extension of democracy and civil liberties over the nebulous "final goal" of his revolutionary comrades.[20]

Although Bernstein's revisionism was soundly rejected by the majority of delegates at two tumultuous party conferences in 1899 and 1903, the SPD continued to trot along its parliamentarian path. Sounding more reformist and patriotic by the day, German socialism was in danger of losing its ideological identity, just as British New Liberalism had gradually drifted into social democratic waters. Neither fully liberal nor socialist, the resulting ideological hodgepodge would ultimately take the world by storm as "social welfarism" built on the state-interventionist principles attributed to British economist John Maynard Keynes. In the meantime, however, reformist socialists like Bernstein unwittingly prepared the way. In 1899, the very year he published his revisionist *opus magnum*, Alexandre Millerand, a reliable Marxist stalwart of the French Independent Socialist Party, joined the cabinet of liberal Prime Minister Waldeck-Rousseau without bothering to obtain permission from his party. Accused of collaboration with the bourgeois class enemy, Millerand became the quintessential traitor in Marxist labor circles whereas their revisionist counterparts revered him as a beacon of social democratic moderation. Howling in triumph, antidemocratic extremists on both sides of the ideological spectrum seized upon the Millerand Affair as irrefutable evidence for the moral bankruptcy of socialism. Indeed, the remarkable spread of revisionist doctrines prompted disaffected militants like V. I. Lenin and Georges Sorel to embark on their own idiosyncratic interpretations of Marxist theory. Once the socialist genie had escaped its authoritative German bottle, radicals of all kinds, and of all nations, were free to lay claim to the revolutionary legacy of the nineteenth century. Thus, for a few short years before the Great War, there existed considerable ideological overlap between extremists on both the left and the right as both sides clung to the ideals of revolution, violence, youth, direct action, collectivism, militarism, dictatorship, hypermasculinity, and the creation of a New Man. Most significantly, radicals shared the conviction that the masses were incapable of shaking off the political reins of the bourgeoisie without the guidance of visionary leaders at the helm of the vanguard party.

The traumatic experience of the Great War only exacerbated the camp mentality separating antidemocratic revolutionaries intoxicated with the martial spirit of trench brotherhood from the dejected partisans of liberal democracy who vowed never to let peace slip away again. Each side found its ideological perspective confirmed by the ghastly conflagration of violence. For right-wing extremists, modern warfare bore out the falsehood of liberal values and the truth of the instinctive struggle for existence. For left-wing socialists, the trenches foreshadowed the collapse of capitalism and the coming of the workers' revolution. For the defenders of representative democracy, the war drove home the importance of rationality and the rule of law.

Much has been written about the horrors of the Great War—its industrialized and mechanized nature and its staggering human toll. But perhaps the war's most significant impact on our story of ideology was its totality, that is, the merciless involvement of the hearts and souls of entire national populations in the collective war effort. The ensuing militarization of public life went hand in hand with the further expansion of state power in the name of "national emergency." These developments left the representatives of the grand ideologies little choice but to enter into joint governments of "national unity"—a decision that later made it even easier for communists and fascists to paint their ideological competitors in identical polemical colors. Although the Great War was decidedly not the sole factor responsible for the birth of totalitarianism, it contributed greatly to the creation of a social environment that proved to be enormously susceptible to extremist translations of the national imaginary.[21] Indeed, when the Italian dictator Benito Mussolini coined the term "totalitarianism" in 1926, he intended it to serve as a positive signifier for the total subordination of the individual to the nation-state.[22] Yet, even at the height of its power in the 1930s, his fascist regime never exerted absolute control over Italy's population. Thus, we shall use the term "totalitarianism" to refer to the most extreme forms of twentieth-century dictatorship and their affiliated ideologies. Relying on the modern state apparatus to impose their political vision on society, totalitarians on the left and right attacked civil society and its sphere of free activity. Their preferred tactics were propaganda and terror.

Academic discussions about the nature and origin of totalitarianism peaked in the 1950s with the emergence of the Soviet Union as the world's second superpower. As we noted previously, during these early Cold War years, the use of the concept itself was often ideological—in Bonaparte's pejorative sense—since the label tended to be applied indiscriminately to all existing communist systems, regardless of their differing levels of political repression.[23] Little or no distinction was drawn, for example, between Castro's communism and Maoism—although the human rights violations in Cuba paled in comparison to the horrific crimes against humanity perpetrated in China. At the same time, however, the appalling right-wing military dictatorships in Chile or Argentina during the 1970s were merely classified as "authoritarian." Indeed, Jeane J. Kirkpatrick, the US ambassador to the UN in the 1980s, carefully distinguished between "authoritarian" governments such as Pinochet's Chile and "totalitarian" regimes like the Soviet Union, Cuba, and Hitler's Germany.[24] Nonetheless, the academic Cold War debate on totalitarianism generated lasting insights into the origins and development of modern despotism. Let us now turn to our analysis of the two most lethal ideological manifestations of twentieth-century totalitarianism: Russian communism under Lenin and Stalin and German Nazism.[25]

3.2. Russian Communism

Early twentieth-century Russia constituted a vast multiethnic empire inhabited by Great Russians who comprised nearly half of its population; non-Russian Slavs such as Ukrainians, Poles, and Byelorussians; and sizable non-Slav minorities including Georgians, Turkic peoples, Central Asians, Armenians, Finns, Baltic peoples, and Jews. Covering nearly one-sixth of the planet's land area and stretching across two continents, the Romanov Empire was the product of a continuous process of territorial expansion proceeding over four centuries at the average rate of 50 square miles a day.[26] Home to over 100 million people—of whom close to 80 percent were peasants—the Empire was administered as though it constituted a nationally homogenous unit by a vast state bureaucracy answerable only to hereditary nobles who made up less than 1 percent of the total population. The Tsar presided over both Church and State, imposing his will on his domains without being checked by representative assemblies or a proper cabinet government.[27] It was not until his regime found itself weakened by its military defeat in the 1904–5 Russo-Japanese War, and the ensuing wave of social protest, that Nicholas II reluctantly transferred some of his powers to a popularly elected Duma (National Parliament).

Soon thereafter, however, Russia's embryonic process of democratization came to a screeching halt when the Imperial government managed to assert its dominance over the Duma. The Tsar's restored powers would not be challenged again until 1917 when the liberal February Revolution put an end to the *ancien régime*.

With the arrival of industrialization in the late 1880s, Russia's economy had modernized rapidly, fueled by large construction projects like the Trans-Siberian railway. Gigantic industrial plants had sprung up in major urban centers, providing low-paying jobs for a proletariat numbering just over 3 million at the outbreak of the Great War. As might be expected, workers bore the brunt of the social evils associated with rapid industrialization. Abominable living and working conditions combined with political repression to make them extremely susceptible to Marxist doctrines, just as devastating famines, relentless taxation, and unheeded demands for land reform pushed the rural masses into the arms of the populist Social Revolutionaries. Tsarist ministers like Sergei Witte and Peter Stolypin attempted to coordinate agricultural and industrial policy across the Empire. In order to create a more homogenous cultural environment for these economic measures, they launched educational "Russification" programs. Applied to a multiethnic population sunk in mass illiteracy and plagued by endemic poverty, however, these policies did little to stoke the Great-Russian sentiments of poor peasants who, in many cases, thought of themselves as provincial natives rather than Russian nationals.[28] But the Tsarist authorities soon discovered that anti-Semitism was a much more effective tool for nation-building. As Walter Laqueur notes, the rapid emergence of nationalist-conservative parties and the appearance of militant nationalist organizations like the Black Hundred attest to the formation of a more homogenous national ethnos which expressed itself in radical opposition to Jews. Extremist agitators like Vladimir Purishkevich demonstrated the growing mass appeal of Great-Russian chauvinism by sparking horrific anti-Jewish pogroms that swept across the country in the first decade of the new century. The popularity of anti-Semitism was further boosted by countless smear pamphlets, like the *Protocols of the Learned Elders of Zion*, a vile forgery portraying Jews as members of an international conspiracy bent on the destruction of Christian civilization. First published in 1903, this influential tract was endorsed by Tsar Nicholas II and many high officials of the Orthodox Church. Their propagation of Great-Russian patriotism at the expense of Jews and other minorities served as one of the legitimizing props of the old order.[29]

Leading left-wing intellectuals like Georgii Plekhanov and Vladimir Ilyich Ulyanov ("Lenin") despised such contrivances of ethnic hatred. As committed Marxists, they condemned what they called "Great-Russian chauvinism" as a blunt ruling-class attempt to dull the political conscious-ness of the masses and thereby obfuscate common class interests among the international proletariat. Still, Lenin grasped from the beginning of his stellar political career the central importance of the national factor in contesting the legitimacy of Romanov rule. In his 1901 address to the Unity Conference of the Russian Social Democratic Labor Party (RSDLP), for example, he balanced his denunciation of the regime's nationalism with an unambiguous endorsement of the "principle of national self-determination."[30] Indeed, he even went so far as to affirm the right of each nationality in the Empire to secede and form its own sepa-rate nation-state. Thus, unlike Rosa Luxemburg and other Marxists who opposed the participation of socialists in any national project—even in the highly popular struggle for national liberation waged at the time in Polish Russia—Lenin never hesitated to utilize the nationalist aspirations of various ethnic groups for his own political purposes. In fact, he urged the RSDLP leadership to draft a national program outlining the party's revolutionary strategy in the multiethnic Empire.

Still, Lenin was prudent enough to allow for certain limitations in his theory of nationality. Most importantly, he inserted a clause stipulating that national self-determination could only be exercised by the van-guard party of the proletariat—the "highest expression of the will of the nation"—and not by the people as a whole. This reservation dovetailed with his emphasis on class unity in the form of a single national Marxist party operating in all parts of the Empire. But Lenin's obvious prefer-ence for political centralization clashed with his support of the national aspirations of various oppressed minorities. In 1913, the Bolshevik leader entrusted his loyal lieutenant Iosif Dzhugashvili ("Joseph Stalin") with the task of ironing out these wrinkles. Published under the title "Marxism and the National Question," Stalin's essay presented some new insights, but ultimately failed to solve the central problem of theoretical inconsistency. Some passages in the pamphlet reaffirmed in categorical terms the right of nations to self-determination, whereas others treated this principle as a mere tactical tool always to be subordinated to the shifting conditions encountered by the proletariat in its revolutionary struggle.[31] It was not until the Communist Party of the Soviet Union (CPSU) consolidated its hold on power in the early 1920s that these theoretical problems found their political solution in a blanket prohibition of secession. Lenin's explicit assurance that all nationalities retained a "right to a divorce" was turned into its exact opposite—the forcible subordination of national self-determination to the arbitrary dictates of the Kremlin. Enjoying autonomy on paper only, Russia's nationalities found themselves under the heel of a "democratic centralism" that eliminated any prospect of real federalism in the newly founded Union of Soviet Socialist Republics (USSR).

Lenin's brilliant translation of the national imaginary into an authoritative political ideology found its first systematic expression in his 1902 essay, *What Is to Be Done?* Although the author intended it as a comprehensive guide for the revolutionary activities of the RSDLP, his ambitions materialized only partially. At the 1903 Party Congress in Brussels, petty squabbles over membership regulations led to the formation of two competing factions which attracted roughly equal support from attending delegates. Lenin's Bolshevik ("Majority") group insisted on conferring membership only on those individuals who were willing to engage actively in the political struggle, whereas Yulii Martov's Menshevik ("Minority") faction favored less stringent rules. The ensuing de facto split of the RSDLP was finalized at the 1912 Bolshevik Conference in Prague. Five years later, Lenin's party formally adopted the designation "communist." Bolsheviks cultivated a public image as committed activists who closely followed their leader's interpretation of Marxist theory emphasizing the virtues of political activism linked to revolutionary change in *Russia*. Let us briefly consider three arguments in support of the thesis that the overarching national framework played a pivotal role in Lenin's formulation of Russian communism.

First, there is little doubt that the Bolshevik leader placed his doctrine wholeheartedly in the political tradition of Russian left-wing radicalism. He deliberately adopted the phrase "what is to be done?" from a rather mediocre work of fiction penned in 1862 by the radical Russian writer and educator Nikolai Chernyshevsky. This moralistic tale relates the imagined adventures of a small but heroic band of ascetic revolutionaries who fight Tsarist despotism in the name of the Russian people. Lenin's life-long fascination with the novel reflects his open admiration of radical Populist organizations like *Zemlia i Volia* ("Land and Freedom"), and, to a lesser degree, *Narodnaya Volya* ("People's Will")—a terrorist group responsible for the assassination of Tsar Alexander II in 1881.[32] Naturally, the Populists' belief in his country's special path to an idyllic peasant socialism based on an idealized model of the traditional Russian village commune clashed with the modernist vision of Lenin and Plekhanov, who put their revolutionary hopes in a proletarian socialism nurtured to maturity in Russia by the same capitalist forces that allegedly underpinned the formation of modern nation-states in Western Europe. In the decade-old intellectual battle between Russian "Westernizers" and "Slavophiles," Marxists like Lenin clearly sided with the former. And yet, they shared with Slavophile Populists like Chernyshevsky and anarchists like Mikhail Bakunin a strong attraction to the specifically *Russian* version of political insurrectionism which Robert Tucker refers to as "Russian Jacobinism." This doctrine stipulated that the revolutionary seizure of power from below should be followed immediately by the formation of a dictatorship of the revolutionary party prepared to use its political power to carry through from above a socialist transformation of Russian society.[33] Lenin repeatedly acknowledged the tremendous influence exerted by Russian Jacobins on his own intellectual development as well as that of his beloved brother Sasha, executed in 1887 for his membership in a clandestine terrorist organization accused of plotting to assassinate Tsar Alexander III.

Second, Lenin's writings contain occasional passages in support of national exceptionalism. To be fair, it must be said that, as a rule, the Bolshevik leader affirmed the internationalist character of revolutionary social democracy as a class-based movement firmly opposed to all manifestations of "chauvinistic and reactionary nationalism." And yet, like Engels, he was not above stoking his audience's sentiments of nationality with exceptionalist flattery at the opportune moment. At the end of 1914, for example, Lenin wrote a brief article, "On the National Pride of the Great Russians," which praises Russian revolutionaries for their love of country and their deep affection for the Russian language. More than a decade later, Stalin would use this essay to justify his efforts to build socialism in one country anchored in a single Great-Russian national ethnos. But already as early as 1902, Lenin had allowed himself to speak in glowing terms of a special "national task" awaiting the Russian working class:

History has now confronted us with an immediate task which is the *most revolutionary* of all the *immediate* tasks confronting the proletariat of any country. The fulfillment of this task, the destruction of the most powerful bulwark, not only of European, but (it may be said) of Asiatic reaction, would make the Russian proletariat the vanguard of the international revolutionary proletariat.[34]

Third, even a cursory perusal of Lenin's work reveals his consistent practice of carrying forward his major ideological claims in narratives of national development. The principal arguments of *What Is to Be Done?*

are linked to his idiosyncratic interpretation of Russian social democracy unfolding in successive historical stages that propel the nation toward socialism. Period One: the rise and consolidation of Marxist theory in Russia without the emergence of a corresponding working-class movement (1884–94). Period Two: the creation of a Russian socialist movement and its political party made possible by the upsurge of the masses (1894–98). Period Three: the ideological struggle between "opportunistic economists" and "revolutionary Marxists" (1898–1902). Enveloping Lenin's narrative, the ever-present national framework greatly enhances the appeal of his ideological claims. Indeed, we must remember that the ultimate purpose of his polemic was to sell his *Russian* audience on the idea that they could be delivered from political oppression and economic exploitation only by a disciplined vanguard of socialist revolutionaries who shouldered the dual task of overthrowing the Tsarist regime and smashing the party's "opportunistic rearguard." Thus, Lenin's reply to the question of what needed to be done to revolutionize the proletariat comes in the form of an imperative that makes sense only in the context of *Russian* history: "Put an End to the Third Period!"[35]

Let us now examine the central ideological claims that articulated the national imaginary in Marxist-Leninist terms. It should come as no surprise that *What Is to Be Done?* will serve as the central text of our analysis. After all, the Bolsheviks' rise to prominence in the Russian labor movement owes much to the extraordinary inspirational powers of this essay.[36] The literary virtues of the pamphlet lie chiefly in its ability to convey with exceptional brevity and clarity the author's vision of a new socialist Russia brought into being by a "committee of professional revolutionaries" sworn to strict secrecy. Lenin's rationale for writing this polemic stemmed from his desire to provide a systematic critique of the Russian version of Bernstein's revisionism espoused by Alexander Martynov and his group of exiled socialists in the pages of their influential journal, *Rabocheye Dyelo* ("The Workers' Cause"). Arguing that Russia's low level of industrial development left workers no choice but to abandon the idea of political revolution, these reformists subscribed—in Lenin's opinion—to an "Economism" that advocated workers' advancement in the form of a purely economic struggle for higher wages and better working conditions without challenging the existing political system. While Martynov and his comrades insisted that their trade-unionist views faithfully reflected the actual aspirations of the average Russian worker, the future leader of the Soviet Union accused him of turning the proletariat's apolitical cravings for immediate material improvement into admirable expressions of working-class "spontaneity." By slavishly bowing to the embryonic socialist consciousness of the toiling masses, Lenin thundered, Economists committed the unforgivable error of letting their opportunism drive socialist theory. Lacking theoretical sophistication, the *Rabocheye Dyelo* group reduced revolutionary socialism to the level of "trade unionism" in the name of "realism."[37]

The crux of the dispute can be found in clashing assessments of the relevance of *political theory* for the Russian labor movement. Repeatedly chastising Economists for belittling "the significance of theory," the Bolshevik leader plays up the role of the "conscious element" in guiding the proletariat to its ultimate victory: "For Russian Social-Democrats the importance of theory is enhanced...by the fact that our Party is only in the process of formation, its features are only just becoming defined, and it has as yet far from settled accounts with the other trends of revolutionary thought that threaten to divert the movement from the correct path."[38] Thus, Lenin relegates the fledgling RSDLP and its working-class constituency to but a preliminary stage of political development characterized by theoretical and political immaturity. Accordingly, he refers time and again to "the pressing needs of the working class for political knowledge and political training." Asserting that only Marxist theory contains "scientific knowledge"—and thereby implying that his own interpretation corresponds to the mature perspective of Marx and Engels—he raises the pivotal question that gives the pamphlet its title: " 'Everyone agrees' that it is necessary to develop the political consciousness of the working class. The question is *how* that is to be done and what is required to do it."[39]

One might reasonably expect that the author's answer would lay out in some detail the necessary steps in the process of maturation *within* the Russian proletariat to the point where workers could act as the conscious agents of their own emancipation. But Lenin has other ideas. In a short passage that deserves to be quoted in its entirety, he puts forward the central ideological claim of Russian communism:

We have said that *there could not have been* Social-Democratic consciousness among the workers. It would have to be brought to them from without. The history of all countries shows that the working class, exclusively by its own effort, is able to develop only trade-union consciousness, i.e., the conviction that it is necessary to combine in unions, fight the employers, and strive to compel the government to pass necessary labor legislation, etc. The theory of socialism, however, grew out of the philosophic, historical, and economic theories elaborated by the propertied classes, by intellectuals. By their social status, the founders of modern scientific socialism, Marx and Engels, themselves belonged to the bourgeois intelligentsia.

In the very same way, in Russia, the theoretical doctrine of Social-Democracy arose altogether independently of the spontaneous growth of the working-class movement; it arose as a natural and inevitable outcome of the development of thought among the revolutionary socialist intelligentsia.[40]

The historical significance of this paragraph can hardly be exaggerated. In the course of the twentieth century, the leaders of countless "communist" movements around the world would evoke the spirit of this passage— often in the name of national liberation—as the justification for the forcible introduction of a proper revolutionary consciousness by Marxist-Leninist intellectuals like themselves. Seeking to lend Marxist legitimacy to his assertion, Lenin takes refuge behind a similar view expressed by Karl Kautsky, at the time the dominant theorist of German social democracy. Much ink has been spilt in the ensuing dispute over whether Lenin's claim does in fact correspond to the views expressed by Marx and Engels, let alone Kautsky. It would go far beyond the purposes of this book to regurgitate the subtleties of this multifaceted debate that raged on for decades—let alone enter it. Today, most commentators agree that some aspects of Lenin's communism run counter to the standpoint of the German founders—such as his un-Marxist advocacy of an alliance between the revolutionary proletariat and the poor peasantry and his eagerness to affirm the socialist character of his seizure of power in October 1917 after declaring that the Russian revolution had passed through its bourgeois phase in a mere eight months.[41] Only a careful consideration of the different national and historical contexts that impacted the writings of Marx and Lenin might be able to shed light on the reasons for some of these staggering discrepancies. At the same time, however, it is also possible to identify some theoretical agreements. Most importantly for our purposes, the writings of the founders seem to corroborate, at least in part, Lenin's pivotal claim that workers needed to be imbued with a revolutionary socialist consciousness from without. For example, a crucial passage in *The Communist Manifesto* suggests that the proletariat required the assistance of "bourgeois thinkers who have worked out a theoretical understanding of the whole historical development [of capitalism]."[42]

While sharing some common ground on the issue of theoretical leadership, the respective views of these two seminal socialist figures nonetheless diverge dramatically when it comes to the subject of ideology. Their differences on this topic are of great significance, for one could argue that Lenin's rehabilitation of ideology represents one of the most fundamental features separating Russian communism from German socialism. As we have seen in Chapter 1, Marx and Engels conceived of ideology as an elite-engineered *camera obscura* that produced an inverted picture of the world in which ideas and concepts appear to possess an independent existence separate from the material-economic conditions that gave rise to them in the first place. Their binary model of an "ideological superstructure" resting on an "economic base" forms the centerpiece of their materialist conception of history. Ultimately, Marx and Engels saw "scientific social-ism" as the necessary means for dissolving workers' "false consciousness." This had to be done not by simply substituting a "correct" picture of reality for an "incorrect" one, but by eliminating, once and for all, the illusion that ideas can be anything other than the derivative products of more primary relations of production.

Lenin, on the other hand, worked out a theory of ideology that assigns socialist intellectuals the task of supplying the working class with correct images of the world. Retaining a Marxist-sounding rhetorical emphasis on the significance of a "materialist analysis of social life," he nonetheless ends up robbing economics of its primacy by highlighting the role of ideas in bringing about revolution. His fixation on "correct ideology" would later incur the charge that he had turned Marx's historical materi-alism into a political voluntarism incapable of conceiving of the historical inevitability of communism without the leadership of socialist ideologists. Whether one agrees with this objection or not, the fact remains that *What Is to Be Done?* accomplishes in less than three pages the remarkable feat of exorcising the pejorative Bonapartist–Marxist specter. Presenting correct socialist ideas as "profound scientific knowledge," Lenin resurrects Destutt de Tracy's old meaning of ideology as a system of truths closely tied together. However, for Lenin, this characterization holds true only for the "socialist" variant of ideology. The Bolshevik leader continued to use the term in its old derogatory meaning for its "bourgeois" manifestation—a false system of ideas that exerts its power over the proletariat because the ruling classes have superior means of dissemination at their disposal. Rejecting the possibility of a third ideology between socialism and bour-geois belief systems, Lenin puts revisionists on notice that their refusal to come around to his position places them squarely in the camp of the class enemy.[43]

Having rehabilitated the role of ideology in the proletariat's battle with capital, Lenin manages to transfer the primary locus of the class struggle from the economic arena to the ideational plane. This move forces him to devote a long section in *What Is to Be Done?* to the discussion of the pivotal role of "political educators" destined to "go among all classes of the population as theoreticians, as propagandists, as agitators, and as organizers." Thus, Lenin's rehabilitation of ideology also rids "propaganda" of its negative meaning—but only if the term is understood as the systematic dissemination of "brilliant and completed ideas" by committed communist writers and orators who have made "revolutionary activity their profession." Indeed, propaganda and ideology become indistinguishable terms—a development repeated twenty-three years later in Adolf Hitler's *My Struggle*. The objective of propaganda-ideology is to expose the entire nation to the truth of the doctrine—hence Lenin's notion that the party bears responsibility for developing all-Russia newspapers and educational pamphlets of nationwide circulation. However, given the obvious limits of the proletariat, agitators can treat workers only in one of two ways: either as empty vessels waiting to be filled with political knowledge or as patients to be cured of their virulent infection by bourgeois ideology. As Lenin explains, "Working-class consciousness cannot be genuine political consciousness unless the workers are trained . . . to respond from a Social-Democratic point of view and no other." In other words, the establishment of the communist political order depends on the correct theoretical education of the masses imparted to them by thousands of professional propagandists. These elites, in turn, have been instructed by "a dozen tried and talented leaders" who occupy the highest echelons of the party hierarchy by virtue of having learned even the most difficult lessons in Marxist revolutionary ideology provided by master-trainer Lenin himself.[44]

Despite Lenin's lifelong contempt for "intellectualism"—short for any rational argument that deviated from his ideas—it is not difficult to detect in his "socialist ideology" more than faint echoes of Plato's guardianship or Robespierre's virtuous rule by committee. The Bolshevik leader's equivalent is the "revolutionary-democratic dictatorship of the proletariat and the poor peasantry" exerted by the communist party. Accessing the highest forms of scientific knowledge, party leaders are the sole experts capable of developing the political consciousness of ignorant and misguided proletarians. The party's perpetual monopoly on wisdom means that its political directives always take precedent over the shortsighted spontaneity of the working class. Its ideological superiority makes the party more proletarian than the proletariat itself. Grasping the objective laws of social development, the party can never be wrong. It hardly takes a stretch of imagination to recognize in Lenin's socialist ideology the kernel of Soviet totalitarianism. The dictatorship of the proletariat—the unlimited dictatorship of a small, centralized party elite, and by the 1930s, that of a single man—constitutes the indispensable organ that coerces workers into the "freedom" that comes from recognizing their "objective class interests." The party also provides "reeducation" for revisionist dissenters, thus helping them to see the errors of their flawed ideology.

There can be no doubt that Lenin and the members of his innermost circle understood dictatorship to mean just that: "unlimited power based on force, not on law." From the very beginning of their political rule, they offered unapologetic rationales for the concentration of state power in the hands of party elites who secured the "achievements of the revolution" through the application of "the element of compulsion in all its forms, both the most gentle and the extremely severe."[45] Intimidation, imprisonment, and mass execution became perfectly legitimate means in the struggle against class enemies—scientifically categorized as "kulaks" (better-off peasants), "suspects," "counterrevolutionaries," "rebels," "bandits," "saboteurs," and "general undesirables." As Kolakowski points out, there is very little in the worst excesses of Stalin's Reign of Terror in the 1930s that cannot be justified on the basis of Leninist principles:

The essential difference between the "Lenin era" and the "Stalin era" is not that under Lenin there was freedom in the party and society and that under Stalin it was crushed, but that it was only in Stalin's day that the whole spiritual life of the peoples of the Soviet Union was submerged in a universal flood of mendacity. . . . The omnipotence of the Lie was not due to Stalin's wickedness, but was the only way of legitimizing a regime based on Leninist principles.[46]

The totalitarian structure of the Soviet Union grew out of Lenin's unshakable confidence in the historical correctness of his communist ideology and its flexible applicability to the shifting political conditions in postrevolutionary Russia. What made the Bolshevik regime so murderous was the iron determination of its leaders to put Lenin's ideological claims into practice. Within months of the October Revolution, a new state apparatus was erected around the great leader's views on the dictatorship of the proletariat. Designed to retain political power by all means necessary, the guardians of the Soviet state had to be tough and pitiless, openly committed to the systematic use of violence as the foundation of their power. The autocratic nature of Russian communism showed itself as early as January 1918 when Lenin ordered the forcible dissolution of the popularly elected Constituent Assembly in which his party held only one-quarter of the seats. The ensuing Civil War was not just the epic struggle of heroic Reds against vile Whites as portrayed in the Party press. Without glossing over the terrible atrocities committed by the counterrevolutionaries, it is important to acknowledge the ideological war waged by the Bolshevik minority against the majority who dared to entertain different political beliefs—even in the case of dissenting socialist views held by Mensheviks, Socialist Revolutionaries, or anarchists. During the bloody years of the Civil War, the government perfected its five principal methods of dealing with political dissent: reeducation, torture, imprisonment, deportation, or elimination. Resistance against the Bolshevik regime culminated in March 1921 in the uprising of thousands of soldiers and workers in the city of Kronstadt, but the regime managed to hang on to power. Its victory, however, came at the horrendous cost of descending into an abyss of violence that swallowed countless "enemies of the people."

In fact, one of the first decrees of the Soviet Council of People's Commissars—presided over by Comrade Lenin—had inaugurated the Cheka, the regime's secret police and forerunner of the OGPU, the NKVD, and the KGB. Ostensibly designated as the communist state's chief weapon to "combat counterrevolution, speculation, and sabotage," the new organization was headed by Felix Dzerzhinsky, an unscrupulous murderer to whom Lenin referred warmly as a "solid proletarian Jacobin." Having spent most of his life behind the bars of Tsarist prison cells where he gained first-hand experience of the brutal methods of the Okhrana (Tsarist secret police), Comrade Dzerzhinsky built his small contingent of cold-blooded killers into a powerful bureaucratic organization employing nearly 300,000 people in hundreds of local branches. Experts in what Lenin praised as the "systematic practice of organized terror," Cheka members executed, deported, and tortured tens of thousands of prisoners and hostages without trial and murdered hundreds of thousands of "rebellious" workers and peasants. During less than eight weeks in the autumn of 1918, they killed twice as many "undesirables" than the 6,321 political prisoners who perished at the hands of the Tsarist Okhrana between 1825 and 1917. When Nikolai Bukharin and other party leaders pleaded with their boss to curb the excessive bloodlust of Dzershinsky's executioners, Lenin defended them as the "iron fist of the dictatorship of the proletariat". Forbidding any further criticism of the organization and its homicidal methods, he reminded his comrades that "A good Communist is also a good Chekist."[47]

This episode by no means represents an isolated incident. Rather, it serves as a typical illustration of a common pattern of crime and repression that arose from the consistent application of Lenin's socialist ideology. And it was none other than Vladimir Ilyich Ulyanov himself who sat at the top of this pyramid of terror. It was he who ordered the execution and deportation of thousands of Cossacks of the Don and the Kuban region in 1919 and 1920. It was he who encouraged as early as 1918 the "use of the energy of mass terror" even against poor peasants whom he conveniently labeled kulaks for resisting forcible requisitions of food and livestock. It was he who signed off on the liquidation of thousands of political opponents including anticapitalist Socialist Revolutionaries and Mensheviks. It was he who cherished the newly invented concentration camp as the appropriate abode for such "doubtful elements" as "kulaks, priests, and White Guards." It was he who demanded in 1919 the "merciless squelching" of large-scale peasant uprisings in the regions of the mid-Volga and the Ukraine. It was he who characterized the Bolshevik-induced "Great Famine" of 1921–2 in mid-Russia that took the lives of 5 million people as a "mortal blow struck against our class enemies." And, finally, it was Lenin who reassured his comrades that the draconian Soviet penal code of 1922 reflected "a politically just principle that is the essence and motivation for terror. . . . The courts must not end the terror or suppress it in any way."[48]

In May 1922, the Party leader added to his repressive measures by rolling out his plans for the banishment and incarceration of suspicious intellectuals, teachers, and artists. This "definitive purge" was to proceed hand in hand with the establishment of a nationwide system of spies who were ordered to collect information on the activities of the "unreliable intelligentsia." As a result, countless individuals fell into various bureaucratic categories of suspicion that predisposed them to ill-treatment by the state. Setting the stage for Stalin's Great Terror in the 1930s, the ailing party leader ordered his Secretary-General to compile elaborate lists containing the names of the "worst enemies of Bolshevism." Once apprehended and interrogated, these persons were to be "rooted out without mercy." Thus, Lenin simply put into practice his closing appeal in *What Is to Be Done?*, which calls for the end of the old era and expresses confidence in the coming of a new period anchored in the truth-claims of socialist ideology. Once again, the national imaginary forms the overarching framework of Lenin's renewed appeal: "It is our duty to clean up Russia once and for all."[49]

To be sure, Stalin needed little persuasion to carry out his master's totalitarian designs. But first he had to prevail in the struggle for supreme leadership that heated up shortly after Lenin's death in January 1924. Expressing severe doubts in the abilities of all of his potential successors, the late leader's political testament was kept secret by the Party's inner circle. Although he had been chastised by his former boss as a "crude fellow" who had accumulated too much power and should be removed from the key post of Secretary-General of the CPSU, Stalin was hardly in the mood for tendering his resignation. Instead he chose to join the formidable Leningrad party boss Grigori Zinoviev and his Moscow counterpart Lev Kamenev in their efforts to dispose of the Red Army Chief and Civil War hero Leon Trotsky. Stalin's control of the vast party bureaucracy is often cited as the main reason for his ultimate political triumph. But there is more to his success, for he also outmaneuvered his rivals by means of ideology. Often ridiculed for his apparent lack of theoretical acumen, the former Orthodox seminarian managed to discredit Trotsky on the basis of his simple but brilliant interpretation of Lenin's internationalism as a mandate for the "building of socialism in one country." Although Stalin appropriated this phrase from Bukharin's defense of the New Economic Policies (NEP), which permitted the coexistence of public and private forms of ownership until 1929, the fact remains that it was the "crude fellow" who authored the three seminal essays that laid the ideological foundation of a dictatorship which would not come to an end until Stalin's death in 1953.[50]

How did the Secretary-General manage to sell the Party on "socialism in one country"? As we have seen, Lenin's internationalism was always tempered by his pragmatic sensitivity to relevant national dynamics. While espousing the grandiose thesis that his party acted as the vanguard of the international proletarian army by smashing world capitalism at its weakest link—in economically backward Russia—the Bolshevik leader envisioned the ensuing world revolution in rather pragmatic terms as a chain reaction of *national* revolutions unfolding at their own speed and according to particular *national* conditions. Before the Great War, Lenin had believed that his party would lead workers and poor peasants to the establishment of a liberal republic in a nation where the bourgeoisie was still too weak to accomplish this task on its own. After capturing political power in 1917, however, he had made the convenient suggestion that the revolution had passed through its bourgeois phase in a matter of mere months. Toward the end of the Civil War, Lenin had been widely interpreted as concurring with the dominant view in the party that a defense of its revolutionary achievements—especially the development of a socialist economy in Russia—depended on the spread of the revolution to other countries. After all, his reluctant acceptance of the NEP had been an embarrassing concession to acknowledging Russia's inability to reach the promised land of socialism without support from more advanced social democratic countries.

Determined to put the muscle of the Soviet state behind his hopes for world revolution, Lenin had encouraged the formation of the Communist International in 1920. A network of nationally organized communist parties tightly controlled by Moscow, the Comintern concentrated on supplying arms and expertise to professional revolutionaries throughout Europe and the rest of the world. With Lenin's encouragement, the Soviet government gave sustained attention to the colonial question. At the Comintern's Second Congress in 1920, communist delegates pledged to "counter the bourgeois-democratic lies that conceal the colonial and financial enslavement of the immense majority of the entire world population by a narrow majority of the richest, most advanced capitalist countries."[51] For the Soviet leader, national wars of liberation in the colonial regions had to be complemented by the extension of a Bolshevik-style socialist revolution to Europe, particularly to Germany. But by the time Lenin had been forced from the political stage by a series of ultimately fatal strokes, communist insurrections in Hungary, Bulgaria, Estonia, and Germany had fallen far short of their desired objectives. Turning a blind eye to these ominous developments, the CPSU leadership failed to adjust its internationalist dreams to the increasing odds that the Bolshevik model would remain confined to a single country for a long time to come. Stalin was the notable exception, perhaps as a result of some pragmatic political lessons he had learned as the People's Commissar on Nationalities in charge of the destruction of independent Georgia and the forcible integration into the USSR of formerly independent states like Azerbaidzhan, Ukraine, and Armenia.

Disarmingly plain in appearance, the chain of ideological claims strung together by the Secretary-General ultimately amounts to nothing less than a deadly garrote wielded by Stalin to strangle his formidable political opponents one person at a time. Keeping with Lenin's penchant for constructing socialist theory on the criticism of alleged ideological deviations from true doctrine, Stalin assembles his arguments in favor of creating socialism in Russia by blasting Trotsky's "theory of permanent revolution." Although the haughty Commissar for Military and Naval Affairs would later insist that his theoretical position had been deliberately misrepresented by his opponent, Trotsky could hardly deny that he had been a strong proponent of the view that the establishment of socialism in an industrially backward country like Russia was possible only after a proletarian victory in major European countries. Until all nations had become socialist, Trotsky had argued, revolution was a permanent condition. After all, Lenin, too, had insisted as late as 1918 that "The final victory of socialism in a single country is of course impossible."[52] Within a few months of the great leader's death, Trotsky attempted to cast himself as his logical successor by publishing a self-promoting account of the October Revolution bearing the suggestive title "Lessons of October." Casting his rivals in the worst possible light, just short of accusing them of outright treachery, the Civil War hero reiterated the necessity of communist world revolution, stating in categorical terms that Soviet Russia could not be expected to hold out against a united bourgeois Europe.[53]

Stung by Trotsky's portrayal of their political indecisiveness in the months leading up to the 1917 Revolution, both Kamenev and Zinoviev retaliated with vitriolic diatribes that failed to engage their opponent on the level of theory. Presumably, both men shared Trotsky's views on the dire prospects for socialism in isolated Russia. Conversely, Stalin refrained from entering into a personality contest with his charismatic rival, sensing that such strategy would only lead to his certain defeat. Instead, he chose to take the fight straight to the heart of Leninist ideology. Linking the Red Army leader's latest pronouncements to his earlier assertion that Soviet Russia "has not arrived, or even begun to arrive, at the creation of a socialist society," Stalin accuses his foe of proposing a "Menshevik deviation" from Lenin's authoritative theory of proletarian revolution. To make such a bold charge was a risky business, especially since Trotsky's position appeared to be extremely close to the dead leader's views on the world revolution. It was now up to the "crude fellow" to prove his rival wrong without discrediting what most members of the CPSU thought Lenin was advocating when he talked about the "world revolution."

Grasping the significance of this moment, Stalin shows considerable audacity by gambling on his ability to string together favorable quotes from Lenin's voluminous writings that would prove beyond the shadow of a doubt that the great leader believed firmly in the "extraordinary strength and capacity of the Russian proletariat" to "break through the front of capital independently."[54] This shrewd strategy of building his arguments on selective citations—held together by an interpretative narrative that exudes both confidence and authority—allowed the crafty Secretary-General not only to abjure any ambition on his part of revising Leninist doctrine but also to reject any claim to theoretical originality. Rather than imitating Trotsky's tactic of presenting himself as Lenin's equal in matters of ideology, the Georgian bureaucrat feigned modesty by pretending to merely follow in the footsteps of an unsurpassable genius. Unlike his opponent, he expected that political power would fall like a ripe apple into the lap of the person most capable of playing convincingly the secondary role of Lenin's "interpreter-in-chief."

Stalin opens the constructive part of his argument by reminding his audience of what Lenin called the "law of uneven capitalist development of imperialist states," which supposedly explained the perplexing fact that, contrary to Marx's expectations, the proletarian revolution had first occurred in an economically backward country. But the Secretary-General adds to this conventional interpretation by alleging that this law also points to the feasibility of the "victory of socialism in one country, even if that country is less developed in the capitalist sense."[55] Without offering further justifications of his assertion, Stalin embarks instead on a well-executed exercise in doctrinal hairsplitting designed to reconcile "internationalism" with "socialism in one country." Insisting that "building a complete socialist society by the efforts of our country, without help from abroad" remained a distinct *possibility*, he also emphasizes that there could be no "complete *guarantee*" for the final realization of socialism as long as the threat of foreign intervention was not eliminated by a successful world revolution.[56] Thus, Lenin's "internationalism"—as interpreted by Stalin—can only mean a firm endorsement of the building of socialism in one country while at the same time reaffirming the necessity of the world revolution which constitutes the sole guarantee for the ultimate victory of the international proletariat. But it was the Soviet Union—the only country well on its way to socialism—that held the key to the successful realization of both imperatives. Hence, Russia had to remain focused on the domestic task of building socialism while also seeking to enhance its power in the international political arena. As Stalin puts it, "For what is our country, the country 'that is building socialism,' if not the base of world revolution?"[57]

Thus, in Stalin's Russia, "socialist ideology" became even more important than it had been under Lenin. Ideology was not merely an adjunct to the political system but an absolute condition of its existence, irrespective of whether people actually believed in it or not. The basis of Stalin's communist state was entirely derived from ideology, particularly from the dictator's doctrine of "socialism in one country."[58] In addition to providing the Secretary-General with a foreign policy strategy of targeted aggression without risking the formation of a hostile foreign alliance prepared to declare war on the Soviet Union, his ideological feat of nationalizing internationalism held out more political advantages. First, it facilitated the crushing defeat of Trotsky by providing the theoretical launching pad for the potent charge that he no longer believed "in the victory of socialist construction in our country." As Stalin emphasizes, "Lack of faith in the strength and capacity of the Russian proletariat—that is what lies at the root of the theory of 'permanent revolution.' "[59] Conversely, the "struggle for building socialism" required faith in the party "as the main guiding force in the system of the dictatorship of the proletariat."[60] After the political demise of Zinoviev and his "left opposition" in the wake of Stalin's brilliant orchestration of the Fourteenth Congress of the CPSU in December 1925, faith in the Party could only mean faith in its Secretary-General. Any deviation from Stalin's doctrine—genuine or alleged—was tantamount to abandoning the path of Lenin. Much in the same way, "socialism in one country" also served as the perfect ideological justification for the Great Terror that followed the 1934 assassination of the charismatic Leningrad party boss Sergei Kirov. Ruthlessly employing his old charge of "ideological deviation," Stalin eliminated the entire top leadership of the CPSU in less than five years. What started as a massive intraparty purge projected to the West in the infamous Moscow Show Trials rapidly escalated into an inferno of violence that consumed hundreds of thousands of innocent lives in the name of combating "terrorism" and "ideological defeatism."[61]

Second, Stalin's confidence in Russia's ability to forge an independent path to socialism provided virtually unlimited ammunition for communist propaganda and agitation along increasingly patriotic lines. Hailing the Soviet Union as "the first center of socialism in the ocean of imperialist countries," the Party press endowed the "Russian proletariat and the laboring masses of the peasantry" with an aura of exceptionality rooted in their unique historical mission and their unparalleled commitment to the communist cause. By the 1930s, Stalin's "socialism in one country" had petrified into "national Bolshevism."[62] Fueled by massive Russification measures and expressed in crude nativist slogans, Soviet hyperpatriotism proclaimed the alleged superiority of the Russian national character. History textbooks introduced students to "a long line of Russian heroes" stretching from Stalin and Lenin back to the great generals of the Napoleonic era and, yes, even Tsar Peter the Great. Special praise was heaped upon Alexander Nevskii, the semi-mythical thirteenth-century defender of the Russian homeland against the "Mongol hordes." During World War II—officially referred to as the Great Patriotic War of the Soviet Union—the Supreme Commander-in-Chief routinely ended his public orders with two rousing cheers: "Long live our great motherland! Death to the German fascist invaders!"[63] Red Army soldiers and communist partisans fought bravely for "motherland, honor, freedom, and Stalin." Tellingly, the motherland was the paramount item on this list. The overwhelmingly positive reaction of the Soviet public to nationalist-Bolshevist appeals proved to be a powerful motivating force for the eventual military defeat of Hitler's invading armies.[64]

Third, the alleged necessity of building socialism in a country surrounded by economically more developed nations made it much easier for Stalin to replace the NEP in 1929 with a Five-Year Plan that mandated stringent policies of enforced agricultural collectivization and accelerated industrialization. Accusing Bukharin and his peasant-friendly "right-wing opposition" in the party of undermining their country's ability to defend itself against "foreign imperialists," the dictator demanded severe punishment for anyone criticizing his new economic vision. Peasants resisting collectivization bore the brunt of Stalin's ambitious attempts to catch up with the industrialized West in a matter of decades. Calling for "the eradication of all kulak tendencies and the elimination of the kulaks as a class," the dictator sent nearly 2 million people from all social strata into the newly unified Gulag system. Hundreds of thousands fell victim to mass executions carried out without formal trials. Millions of peasants died in devastating famines that resulted from enforced collectivization and the predatory tactics of the regime in seizing the harvests.[65] On the eve of World War II, the Soviet Union had turned into a closed totalitarian dictatorship whose destructive measures directed against its own citizens equaled those of Nazi Germany. Though seemingly opposed, these respective ideological translations of the national imaginary had much in common. The chilling totalitarian affinity between Nazism and communism found its most unexpected political expression on August 23, 1939, when Stalin, minutes after signing his infamous Nonaggression Pact with the Hitler regime, offered a toast to the health of the Führer, "beloved by the German people."[66] The protection of Stalin's political vision—socialism in one country—required a temporary accommodation with its ideological archenemy. Let us now take a closer look at the political belief system of Stalin's partner in this short-lived marriage of political convenience.

3.3. German Nazism

On the evening of November 8, 1923, the leading members of the conservative Bavarian government assembled in a large Munich beer cellar to publicly denounce the evils of Marxism. The occasion was the fifth anniversary of the German Revolution that had replaced the authoritarian regime of Kaiser Wilhelm II with the democratic Weimar Republic. Minister President Gustav Ritter von Kahr had just begun to address his fellow Bavarian citizens, when Adolf Hitler, a 34-year-old ex-corporal in the Kaiser's army and leader of the local right-wing Nazi Party—short for National Socialist German Workers' Party (NSDAP)—entered the packed hall. Flanked by two armed bodyguards and backed by the menacing barrel of a heavy machine gun that appeared at the cellar's entrance, the decorated war veteran fired a single shot into the ceiling and announced to his startled audience that the building had been surrounded by his paramilitary Brownshirts. Declaring Von Kahr's Bavarian government dissolved, he proceeded to inform the crowd that both a provisional Bavarian government and a new Reich government would soon be formed under his leadership. Hitler then forced the Minister President and two of his cabinet members into a side room where he gave them the choice of joining his coup or facing immediate execution. Having secured their predictable assent, the Nazi leader reappeared in the increasingly raucous hall and took to the podium. Praising the Minister President's enforced "support," he assured his audience that his actions were directed neither at the Bavarian police nor at the German army, but "solely at the Berlin Jew government and the criminals of November 1918." After a brief summary of his proposals for the new governments in Munich and Berlin, the failed Austrian painter ended his terse address with an emotional appeal to support the "new German Revolution." When the rapturous crowd shouted its enthusiastic approval, Hitler turned to his coconspirators in triumph, as if to reinforce his supreme leadership based on his legendary skill as a public speaker.[67]

When the Nazi leader revealed to his Munich audience the true targets of what came to be known as the Beer Hall Putsch, he put into extremist language similar sentiments harbored by a large segment of the German public. Millions of his compatriots refused to accept the fact that the Second Reich's war effort had collapsed in November 1918 as a result of devastating losses on the Western front and the ensuing decline of troop morale. Instead, they clung to right-wing conspiracy theories insinuating that the Kaiser's heroic armed forces, on their way to certain victory, had been "stabbed in the back" by unpatriotic socialists, communist strikers, and scheming Jews back on the home front. Eager to establish a Bolshevik-style dictatorship in Germany, these "traitors" bore the sole responsibility for the country's military defeat. To some extent, such insidious tales also thrived on public fears that Russian communism was rapidly spreading to the West. Moreover, most Germans had never forgotten the dreadful shock and bitter humiliation they felt on hearing the news of the Kaiser's abdication and the signing of the armistice by a parliamentarian delegation that reported to a provisional republican government headed by the Social Democrat Friedrich Ebert. Most urban residents of the vanquished Reich could still hear the sounds of gunfire and exploding shells that filled the streets when radical workers' militias clashed with the members of the Free Corps—paramilitary forces consisting mainly of ex-servicemen— and other right-wing militants. Although scores were killed or injured on both sides, the revolutionary socialists bore the brunt of the casualties. The most famous confrontation took place in January 1919 in Berlin, when the combined armed forces of the government and the nationalist militias squelched a communist uprising at the cost of 1,200 lives, most of them workers. A few days later, Karl Liebknecht and Rosa Luxemburg, the charismatic leaders of the Spartacus League, were mercilessly hunted down by renegade Free Corps troops and murdered in the most gruesome manner.

In Munich, the Revolution had taken a particularly long and bloody course. In the early November days of 1918, revolutionary workers' and soldiers' councils had sprung up across the city. After seizing power in a bloodless coup, they proclaimed the Bavarian Council Republic which collapsed only three months later when its leader, the left-wing journalist Kurt Eisner, was assassinated by a young nationalist-conservative aristocrat. Taking advantage of the resulting political chaos, communist forces headed by Max Levien and Eugen Leviné managed to establish a Bolshevik-style regime and opened communication with Lenin in Petrograd. Baffled by their tactical amateurism, the Russian leader urged them to confiscate all weapons in the city. He also counseled them to take aristocrats and wealthy members of the bourgeoisie as hostages. Within a few weeks, however, more than 35,000 Free Corps troops and regular national military units rallied outside Munich, determined to extinguish the short life of the Bavarian Soviet Republic. Hostilities opened with the summary execution of twenty revolutionary medical orderlies caught by the invaders. Local Red Army troops in the besieged city responded by putting ten of their upper-class hostages in front of a firing squad. When the news of these reprisal killings reached the advancing counterrevolutionaries, they went on a rampage. Chaos and anarchy reigned in the Bavarian capital for the next few days. Hundreds of citizens lost their lives, many of whom had not been affiliated with either side. When a new conservative government finally took over in Munich after months of strict military rule, it imposed harsh penalties on the surviving left-wing leaders while letting off the marauding Free Corps members with only the lightest of sentences.[68] The new regime then proceeded to turn the slain revolutionary leaders Kurt Eisner and Eugen Leviné into the poster boys of their large-scale propaganda campaign directed against Jewish and Bolshevik *Volksfeinde* (enemies of the people).

It was in this counterrevolutionary atmosphere thick with anti-Semitic slurs and anticommunist invectives that Hitler launched his political career as a right-wing agitator. Within months, scores of ordinary Bavarians streamed into beer halls to hear the charismatic speaker denounce "capitalist war profiteers," "Bolshevik swine," and "Jewish parasites." The only effective "solution" to the vexing "Jewish question," Hitler opined as early as September 1919, was their "removal" or "destruction" as quickly and fully as possible.[69] As we have seen, another of Hitler's favorite targets during his hours-long beer-hall diatribes were the so-called "November criminals." This slur referred not merely to the left-wing revolutionaries and striking workers of November 1918, but also to those moderate social democrats and bourgeois centrists who had committed the "treachery" of accepting the terms of the armistice. The Nazi leader conveniently stretched his slur to include the "Weimar politicians" who had signed their names to the 1919 Versailles Treaty without dwelling on the fact that they had done so only under protest. In fact, the vast majority of Germans condemned the Treaty as humiliating and unjust, particularly its controversial articles 231 and 232 obliging the Reich to accept "sole guilt" for the outbreak of the war and thus provide punitive compensation to the Allied Powers for the damage done to their civilian populations.

To make things worse, it was up to a Reparation Commission to determine—without German input—the amounts to be leveled on the vanquished nation. Other clauses stripped the Reich of 13 percent of its prewar territory; demilitarized the entire Rhineland; carved out a "Polish corridor" that isolated East Prussia; and forbade the unification of the small rump-state of German-Austria with the Reich. Finally, the Treaty ended conscription and limited the German armed forces to a maximum of 100,000 troops who were prohibited from operating tanks and heavy artillery. Most of the Second Reich's military arsenal was to be destroyed, including its formidable war fleet.[70] While some of the Treaty's 440 articles raised eyebrows even among some British and American delegates, its clauses were hardly more severe than the conditions a victorious Reich would have imposed on the defeated Allies. Indeed, the harsh terms dictated by the German victors to the Bolshevik regime at Brest-Litovsk afford a realistic glimpse into the ultimate intentions of Field Marshal Paul von Hindenburg and his second in command, General Erich Ludendorff.

Still, for most ordinary Germans, "Versailles" came to symbolize the "heinous villainy" of the French who had soiled the honor of their nation. The forced return of Alsace-Lorraine to France only augmented their sense of German victimhood. Suddenly, the glorious Prussian victory at Sedan nearly fifty years earlier appeared to have been for nought. Thus, it is hardly surprising that Hitler's blunt demands for a complete revision of the Treaty and the territorial unification of the entire German Volk struck a special chord with his Munich beer-cellar audiences, especially when combined with virulent attacks on convenient scapegoats like "Jewish-Bolsheviks" and "November criminals." Capitalizing on Hitler's mass appeal, the Nazi Party grew in less than three years from a local fringe group into a tightly-knit regional organization with a thriving propaganda machine and hundreds of aggressive Brownshirts prepared to unleash violence at a moment's notice.

By November 1923, the NSDAP and its dictatorial Führer had emerged as the vanguard force of the *völkisch* Right in the Reich, attracting to its cause such nationally recognized figures as ex-General Ludendorff. In addition, the Nazis' sudden rise to political prominence in Bavaria had been greatly aided by a political development that humiliated and enraged the German public more than anything since the signing of the Versailles Treaty. In January 1923, following the Weimar government's announcement that economic difficulties forced a postponement of its reparation payments for the second consecutive year, French troops entered the Ruhr—the Reich's premier industrial region. Prime Minister Raymond Poincaré proclaimed that his soldiers would seize and exploit various productive enterprises until the Reich's reparation obligations had been fulfilled. A passive resistance movement organized by Ruhr workers was met by the French occupiers with repressive measures, including the death penalty for saboteurs. Within months, the already precarious economic situation in Germany deteriorated to the point where hyperinflation rendered the country's paper currency virtually worthless, wiping out citizens' lifesavings in a matter of weeks and putting even the most basic consumer goods out of reach for most people.

Adding the French occupation of the Ruhr to his long list of evils besetting the German nation, Hitler pounded the Berlin government for its "shameful cowardice" in the face of such "foreign aggression." The Nazi leader also seized on the presence of Senegalese French colonial troops among the occupying forces as a potent propaganda weapon for the activation of powerful racist stereotypes of virtuous German women being raped and impregnated by "black savages."[71] Once again, the Weimar Republic found itself challenged by outbreaks of extremist violence, which took the form of revolutionary "fighting unions" waging fierce street battles with right-wing militias. Once again, communist insurgents in various parts of the country fought for the establishment of regional Soviet regimes, only to find themselves crushed by national troops that remained loyal to President Ebert. Hoping to take advantage of the political instability, Bavarian nationalist-conservative circles close to Minister President Von Kahr openly contemplated secession from the Reich and the reinstitution of the monarchy. Hitler, backed by Ludendorff and other *völkisch* extremists, also felt confident enough to launch his own bid for power. As he would later record, his decision in favor of a putsch was deeply influenced by the unexpected success of the Italian Fascist Party in 1922, when, following his threat against the Italian King to unleash thousands of his paramilitary Blackshirts, Benito Mussolini had been appointed Prime Minister as a result of the "March on Rome."[72] Although Hitler managed to garner the support of his beer-hall audience during the first few hours of his putsch, it fell apart the next day. Breaking his forced oath of allegiance, Minister President Von Kahr set his state police on the insurrectionists who were routed within hours.

Hitler's arrest and subsequent highly publicized trial resulted in little more than a slap on the wrist. Sentenced to a maximum of five years with the possibility of early parole in the ancient Bavarian fortress of Landsberg (which more closely resembled a quaint hotel than a penitentiary), the Nazi leader spent the next months of his life entertaining numerous visitors in his spacious and well-furnished prison cell. At the urging of Max Amann, the Party's business manager, Hitler began to work on his autobiography, a task that kept him preoccupied for the remainder of his short prison term. After months of heavy editing, the unwieldy manuscript—an odd mixture of racist diatribe, personal anecdotes, and Nazi movement history—was finally tweaked into publishable shape. The first volume appeared in late 1925 under its abbreviated title, *Mein Kampf: Eine Abrechnung* (*My Struggle: Settling Accounts*). The second installment bearing the subtitle *The National Socialist Movement* followed eighteen months later. Turgid, self-indulgent, and repetitive in style, the book nonetheless managed to lay out with sufficient clarity the principal ideological claims of German Nazism.

In the decades following the end of World War II, some scholars have questioned whether fascism actually amounts to a coherent political belief system, arguing instead that it should be seen as little more than a disjointed "ragbag of ideas" thrown together by politically "semi-illiterate" agitators like Hitler and Mussolini.[73] Perhaps the most incisive and balanced criticism of this sort flows from the pen of Robert Paxton who asserts in his recent study that fascism is quite unlike the three grand ideologies of modernity. Whereas the classical isms rest on a coherent philosophical system laid out in the writings of systematic thinkers, fascism—created in and for the era of mass politics—seeks to appeal "mainly to emotions by the use of ritual, carefully stage-managed ceremonies, and intensely charged rhetoric. . . . It has not been given intellectual underpinnings by any system builder, like Marx, or by any major critical intelligence, like Mill, Burke, or Tocqueville."[74]

Paxton is certainly right in highlighting fascism's philosophical lightness as well as pointing to its thick emotionalism consciously whipped up to enhance the mass appeal of the doctrine. But an ideology's low level of intellectual sophistication—however distasteful this may be in the eyes of the academic interpreter—does not make it incoherent or ineffective. As we have emphasized in this book, the codifiers of ideologies were social elites, which is not necessarily the same as elite philosophers. Once codified, the spread of ideologies always depends on the tireless efforts of dozens of gifted popularizers like August Bebel or Herbert Spencer whose respective simplifications of Marxism and classical liberalism sold hundreds of thousands of copies and thus brought the core claims of these ideologies in compressed form to a larger audience. In addition, it is somewhat disingenuous to argue that Nazism/fascism had no intellectual underpinnings. As we have seen, the ideas of first-rate thinkers like Darwin, Nietzsche, Bergson, and Sorel, to name but a few, provided fertile philosophical soil for the publications of fascist and other *völkisch* agitators. As for fascism's conscious manipulation of popular feelings, the same charge easily applies to socialism and communism. Even conservatism and liberalism are not immune to this indictment. Take, for example, Burke's *Reflections on the Revolution in France* whose tone has often been described as "raging" and "polemical," just as the stirring pathos of Rousseau's *Discourses* so fanned the feelings of Immanuel Kant that the liberal Prussian philosopher promptly forgot to take his obligatory afternoon walk through the city streets of Königsberg—a rare lapse that had his fellow-citizens shaking their heads in disbelief. And was it not raw emotion—fear of the French Revolution or enthusiasm for its principles— that fueled the flames of romantic conservatism and popular liberalism in the nineteenth century? As we noted in the Introduction, by seeking to articulate the social imaginary in accessible language that appeals to a wide audience, ideologies are quite unlike lofty political philosophy. The fact that Nazism possessed more pronounced emotional and irrational features does not invalidate its stature as a systemic worldview.[75]

But what about Paxton's final charge that fascism does not rest upon the truth of its doctrine but on the instrumentalization of its claims for the purpose of taking advantage of political circumstances? As he puts it, "Power came first, then doctrine."[76] Faced with political opportunity, all ideologies have shown a pronounced tendency to strike compromises that violate some of their principles. Millerand's decision to join a bourgeois government or Lenin's readiness to reach out to the poor peasantry represent two such examples that are not very different from Hitler's willingness to ignore some provisions of his "immutable" twenty-five point party program for the sake of power. As the Nazi leader put it himself:

The theoretician of a movement must lay down its goal, the politician strive for its fulfillment. The thinking of the one, therefore, will be determined by eternal truth, the actions of the other more by the practical reality of the moment. The greatness of the one lies in the absolute abstract soundness of his idea, that of the other in his correct attitude toward the given facts and their advantageous application; and in this the theoretician's aim must serve as his guiding star.... [T]hough human thought can apprehend truths and set up crystal-clear aims, complete fulfillment will fail due to the general imperfection and inadequacy of man.[77]

Indeed, German Nazism, however ridiculous, fanatical, and murderous its claims and however distasteful its presentation, does possess an ideational coherence and systemic structure that cannot be dismissed on account of its simplistic philosophical foundations, emotional appeals, or political opportunism. As Ian Kershaw observes, it was the very "inflexibility and quasi-messianic commitment to an 'idea,' a set of beliefs that were unalterable, simple, internally consistent and comprehensive," that infused Hitler with the strength of will and confidence that compelled his followers. His ideology, Kershaw continues, gave the dictator a "rounded explanation of the ills of Germany and the world, and how to remedy them. He held to his 'world-view' unwaveringly from the early 1920s down to his death in the bunker."[78]

What are the central ideological claims of German Nazism as they appear in Hitler's *My Struggle*? Although there are a number of possible entry points into Nazi doctrine, the most obvious one is the core concept that appears in the book's title. Struggle, for the author, represents an unalterable law forged by a stern taskmaster he usually refers to as "Nature"—occasionally also "Providence," "the Almighty," and "the eternal Creator"—for the sake of biological evolution. As Hitler emphasizes, "Struggle is always a means for improving a species' health and power of resistance and, therefore, a cause of its higher development." Convinced that armed conflict represents the most "heroic" operation of this principle in the human realm, the Nazi leader relays in glowing terms his childhood fascination with images of the Franco-Prussian War he discovered in one of his father's military books. Uplifted by the "greatest inner experience" of his youth, he became "more and more enthusiastic about everything that was in any way connected with war or, for that matter, with soldiering."[79] At some point in his adult life, however, Hitler came to believe that organized warfare represents only the tail end of a protracted Darwinian struggle based on the "most patent principles of Nature's rule: the inner segregation of the species of all living beings on this earth." In other words, "Nature's restricted form of propagation and increase" permits the "vital urge" to be fulfilled only within the same species, lest disease and infertility should result from "mating contrary to the will of Nature for a higher breeding of all life." Like so many ideological codifiers before him, the Nazi leader anchors his beliefs in "self-evident truths" readily available to even the most superficial observer "wandering about in the garden of Nature."[80]

Deploying "species" and "race" as interchangeable terms without offering an explanation, Hitler's crass vulgarization of Darwinian evolutionary theory—infused with a good dose of Schopenhauer's "will to life"—takes an even more ominous turn. Positing the "urge toward racial purity" as a universal imperative of Nature, he praises its tendency to produce a "sharp outward delimitation of the various races" and their "uniform character in themselves." "Race," for Hitler, is not rooted in language or culture, but exclusively in the blood.[81] Unlike animals, however, humans are capable of engaging in "unnatural" sex acts involving a mixing of the "weaker with stronger individuals" and "the blending of a higher with a lower race." Such mating practices can only result in offspring "patently lower" on the evolutionary scale than the "racially higher" parent. Regular acts of such "bastardization" lead, therefore, to the "defilement of the blood" of the "superior race," which radically reduces its innate capacity to prevail in the "merciless struggle for self-preservation."[82] Having established the foundation for social inequality in this "self-evident truth" of an "immutable" and "insurmountable" law of racial purity, all Hitler needs to do in order to arrive at his inflexible racial hierarchy is to supply his preferred categories. Doing so, he divides humankind into three groups: "The founders of culture, the bearers of culture, and the destroyers of culture." Unsurprisingly, only the "Aryan"—the carrier of "Nordic-German blood"—qualifies for the first tier. "Japanese" and other "Orientals" are relegated to the second category, whereas Jews are banished to the lowest tier.[83]

For our purposes, it is not necessary to describe the characteristics Hitler assigns to each group, since he follows rather closely Gobineau's previously discussed ideas about innate Aryan superiority and the servility and stagnation of the "yellow races." Moreover, Hitler's portrayal of the "Jewish race" bears striking similarity to Edouard Drumont's diatribes, especially to the claim that Aryans are doomed to clash with Jews until their total victory would lead to the utter destruction of this "pestilence." The Party leader's most notable addition to the anti-Semitic arsenal of the French journalist comes with his assertion that the inferiority of "Jewish blood" manifests itself most strikingly in the absence of a "self-sacrificing will to give one's personal labor and if necessary one's own life for others." An indispensable quality for nation-building, this spiritual impulse of *voelkischer Pflichterfüllung* (fulfillment of duty to the people of the nation) is "most strongly developed in the Aryan." Seeking to make up for this lack of "idealism," Jews have allegedly furnished two powerful tools in their own determined struggle for self-preservation: "smarts" and "individual selfishness" They wield these formidable weapons against good-natured, but not too clever Nordic-German Aryans whose culture-creating powers have provided an attractive "host-body" for the "leaching Jew." Led by "nothing but the naked egoism of the individual," Jews are incapable of creating their own culture, let alone a "nation," because their "blood" simply does not contain the qualities of individual self-sacrifice that are necessary for such a "higher" development.

This leads Hitler to conclude that Nature condemns the Jew to live as a "parasite in the body of other peoples"—a "sponger who like a noxious bacillus keeps spreading as soon as the favorable medium invites him." The mortal danger emanating from Jews is, therefore, their destructive powers that sap the host-nation of its creative energy.[84] In a short passage titled "Development of Jewry"—remarkable for its racist venom and its crudeness—Hitler launched into a bizarre history of the settlement of Jews in Germany and other parts of Europe. Blaming them for everything that went wrong in Germany from the Middle Ages to the Jewish-Bolshevik "stab in the back" in 1918, the author's indictment reaches its frenzied crescendo in a violent blanket condemnation that betrays anti-Semitic

Catholic-conservative influences: "Here he [the Jew] stops at nothing, and in his vileness he becomes so gigantic that no one need to be surprised if among our people the personification of the devil as the symbol of all evil assumes the living shape of the Jew." He concludes the section with the following assessment: "If we pass all the causes of the German collapse in review, the ultimate and most decisive remains the failure to recognize the racial problem and especially the Jewish menace."[85]

Here we finally arrive at the paramount ideological claim of Nazism: the recent decline of the German nation—caused by the Jewish contamination of the Volk's blood and culture and epitomized in the Jewish-capitalist "stock exchange bandit" and the Bolshevik follower of the "Jew Marx"—can only be reversed by the "preservation of the racial foundations of our nation."[86] Proclaiming the identity of "nation," "Volk," "race," and "blood," Hitler translates the national imaginary into the revolutionary project of creating a genuinely *völkisch* "Third Reich," starting with the necessary first step of radically nationalizing the masses."[87] Given the substantial obstacles in the way of its realization, such a monumental struggle must be set into motion by tough members of the Nazi Party vanguard who are prepared to sacrifice their individual lives for the regeneration of an organic fatherland purified of "alien blood." Moreover, the heroic soldiers in this life-and-death struggle must resort to both militant ideas and organized violence to eliminate the nation's internal and external enemies.[88] Throughout his book, Hitler emphasizes the importance of "propaganda" and "ideology" in the Nazi Party's struggle against "Jewish-Bolshevism": "The victory of an idea will be possible the sooner, the more comprehensive, propaganda has prepared people as a whole and the more exclusive, rigid, and firm the organization which carries out the fight in practice."[89]

As its corresponding political form, a regenerated nation calls for a total state that unifies the carriers of the same "master blood" regardless of existing territorial arrangements. The foreign policy of such a *völkisch* state must aim to lead the German race "from its present restricted living space to new land and soil, and hence free it from the danger of vanishing from the earth or serving others as a slave nation." The solution of the "vital question" of *Lebensraum* (living space) lay in the eastward expansion of the German Reich.[90] In order to achieve these formidable goals, the Volk must submit to the Party's "leadership principle." This means that the Führer's unparalleled devotion to his Volk must be reciprocated by his people's unconditional obedience to his orders—a claim that eventually found its public expression in the famous Nazi propaganda slogans, "One

Volk, One Reich, One Führer!" and "Führer, Give Your Orders, We Follow You!" The "leadership principle" also symbolizes the absolute dominance of the will of the organic racial community—concentrated in the person of the Führer—over the caprice of parliamentarian democracy built on arithmetical majorities of added individual self-interest. By the time Hitler finishes his autobiography, he has convinced himself of his extraordinary ability to unite the German masses behind his grand ideological vision and his pragmatic action plan: "However, the combination of theoretician, organizer, and leader in one person is the rarest thing that can be found on this earth; this combination makes the great man."[91]

When the doors of his luxurious Landsberg prison were flung open prematurely in December 1924, the paroled "great man" lost no time to prove to his compatriots that he was indeed that rare genius who would put Germany on its path to national regeneration. Two months after Hitler's release, the conservative-nationalist Bavarian Justice Minister Franz Gürtner lifted the ban on the NSDAP and its publications. Determined to pursue his vision, Hitler immediately proceeded to rebuild the Nazi Party with the help of his old comrades and new recruits like the young Joseph Göbbels, an unsuccessful novelist and literature scholar whose enthusiasm for the anti-Semitic works of Houston Stewart Chamberlain knew no bounds.

After four rather uneventful years of eking out a political living on the radical right-wing fringe that corresponded roughly with Weimar Germany's economic recovery and its apparent political consolidation, Hitler's great opportunity came with the 1929 crash of the New York Stock Exchange and the ensuing Great Depression, which reached its horrific apex in Germany between 1930 and 1932. Runaway inflation and staggering unemployment rates of 30 percent and more buoyed the electoral fortunes of the extremist parties on the left and right. But the ultimate political winner in the contest between the Communists and Nazis was Adolf Hitler. Sworn in as Reich Chancellor on January 30, 1933, he used the deliberately set fire that destroyed the Reichstag building one month later as the pretense to issue a series of authoritarian decrees that ultimately made him German dictator on March 23, 1933.

Free to pursue his domestic political enemies at will, Hitler oversaw the creation of a totalitarian state apparatus. Recently unearthed archival materials show that the Nazi regime opened its first concentration camps for political prisoners within mere weeks of Hitler's seizure of dictatorial powers. This was the beginning of a national orgy of persecution and genocide that expanded over the next twelve years into a network of ghettos, Gestapo prisons, slave labor camps, and, ultimately, extermination camps for Jews, Gypsies, and other "undesirables."[92] Much time in the previous section was spent in discussing the generally lesser-known crimes of the communist regime in Soviet Russia. Given the gruesome familiarity most readers have with the Holocaust and the other atrocities committed by the Nazis, it is not necessary to elaborate on these unspeakable crimes against humanity at great length. Suffice it to say that German Nazism amounts to the most heinous political system-ideology of modernity, responsible for the premeditated murder of millions of people, not to speak of the millions who perished as a result of its war of aggression.[93]

As he openly announced in *My Stuggle*, the Nazi leader ultimately compelled his nation toward the great conflagration that he hoped would bear out the "absolute correctness" of his *völkisch* vision. The superiority of the Aryan race was to be demonstrated in an unprecedented contest between nations. "Today Germany, tomorrow the whole world," Hitler's troops sang confidently in the fall of 1939 as they departed for the bloody battlefields of the first truly global war in human history. Ironically, however, it was precisely this bloody conflagration brought about by German Nazism—the most extremist ideological translation of the national imaginary—that would serve as an unintended catalyst for its gradual transformation.

Part II

The Global Imaginary

4

Third-World Liberationism and Other Cold War Isms: No End to Ideology

In most Western societies, the ideological controversy is dying down.

Raymond Aron (1955)

It might have been generally thought that the time had come for the world, and particularly for the Third World, to choose between the capitalist and socialist systems.... [But] the Third World ought not be content to define itself in the terms of the values which have preceded it.

Frantz Fanon (1961)

I believe that with all the dislocations we know from our experience, there also exists an extraordinary opportunity to form for the first time in history a truly global society carried on by the principle of interdependence.

Henry Kissinger (1975)

4.1. World War and the Global Imaginary

World War generated in the minds of hundreds of millions of people around the world a profound sense of rupture with the preceding era. Even the vast swath of death and destruction wrought by the Great War paled in comparison to the unfathomable levels of physical devastation left behind on three continents by the global conflagration of 1939–45. Tens of millions of soldiers and civilians had perished. As US Secretary of State Dean Acheson later noted in his memoirs, "The whole world structure and order that we had inherited from the nineteenth century was gone."[1] Aside from its historical significance as humanity's most destructive armed conflict, the World War also marked a crucial phase in the evolution of the global imaginary. To be sure, its rise occurred as a tentative and uneven process, at times surging forward only to be forced to retreat by sudden reassertions of the obstinate national imaginary. The ascent of the global *esprit général* was initially most palpable in the industrialized parts of the world, while popular movements in the developing world utilized the rallying cry for "national liberation" as a battering ram against the crumbling edifice of European colonialism. Still, the political forces in the developing world could hardly avoid situating their national struggle within the globalizing social imaginary of the Cold War era. At the same time, however, the innovative ideas of political leaders like Mahatma Gandhi, Frantz Fanon, Che Guevara, Julius Nyerere, and Kwame Nkrumah had considerable influence in shaping the ideological landscape in both the capitalist world and the communist world.

What, exactly, were the dynamics that made the World War such an important tipping point in the evolution of the global imaginary? Before we can suggest a response, however, we need to raise an even more fundamental question: how do social imaginaries change in the first place? In his recent explorations of the subject, Charles Taylor argues that new ideas and theories generated by social elites sometimes manage to seep into the dominant social imaginary: "Now it often happens that what starts out as theories held by a few people may come to infiltrate the social imaginary, first of elites perhaps, and then of the whole society."[2] But Taylor also emphasizes that the transformative power of such ideational clusters depends to a significant degree on their correspondence to their existing social contexts. Taking root in people's minds in response to experienced needs, these new ideas become applied in the expanding sphere of common action. Defining ever more sharply the contours of the changing political world, they eventually congeal into "the taken-for-granted shape of things, too obvious to mention." Thus rejecting the false dichotomy between theoretical and material forces as rival causal mechanisms, Taylor instead argues that "ideas always come in history wrapped up in practices, even if these are only discursive practices." He goes on to discuss the French Revolution as a crucial historical example when elite-engineered principles of remaking community as a modern nation gradually changed social practices among broad strata of the population. These altered practices—together with the implicit understandings they created—formed the basis for further modifications of theory, which, in turn, impacted practice and so on. Hence, as we have emphasized in previous chapters, these mutually reinforcing dynamics represent the engine driving "the profound transformation of the social imaginary in Western societies, and thus of the world in which we live."[3]

Just as the late eighteenth-century revolutions and the ensuing decades of warfare ushered in the national age, the World War served as a crucial catalyst for the birth of the global era. Destabilizing the Eurocentric system of Great Powers that had grown to maturity in the preceding epoch, the war helped to open the dominant national imaginary to penetration by new ideas and practices taking the entire globe as their frame of reference. Thus, the mid-century conflict served as a globalizing force in a number of ways.[4] First, unlike the Great War that had remained largely confined to Europe and the Mediterranean region, the World War raged as a global contest in multiple theaters stretching from the icy waters of Scandinavia to the jungles of sub-Saharan Africa, and from the green pastures of the British Isles to the volcanic islands of Japan. For a brief moment, the war even reached the Atlantic shores of the United States in the form of German submarine-conducted stealth reconnaissance missions. In the vast stretches of the Pacific, hostilities extended as far south as the Australian port of Darwin, which sustained heavy damage during Japanese air raids in 1942. The names of places that saw decisive war action—Tobruk, El Alamein, Pearl Harbor, Midway, Iwo Jima, Coral Sea, Rangoon, Imphal, Leyte, Chungking, Port Moresby, Kursk, Stalingrad, or Hiroshima—were etched into the minds of hundreds of millions who realized that the fate of their own nations was sealed in far-distant locations whose names they could hardly pronounce.

Second, military success depended more than ever on the effective formation of transnational alliances. Take, for example, the prolonged siege of the German-held Italian fortress of Monte Cassino. On February 14, 1944, an Allied infantry attack on the former monastery involved Americans of various ethnic backgrounds, Eastern European volunteers, New Zealand Maoris, Nepalese Gurkhas, and members of various Indian ethnic groups.[5] Similarly, the German High Command was forced to extend its search for allies to far-distant corners of the earth. It must have taken the racist leaders of the Third Reich some time to digest the obvious lesson that the ultimate success of their European operations depended on the ability of their Japanese brothers-in-arms—supposedly belonging to an "inferior race" of mere "culture-bearers"—to vanquish the American forces on the other side of the globe.

Third, the ultimate defeat of the Axis powers and the discovery of their unspeakable crimes against civilians and "undesirables" of all kinds took a heavy toll on the central claims of their political belief systems. In the postwar era, it became close to impossible for any ideology—old or new—to build a mass-following on an explicitly racist translation of the national imaginary. In fact, the term "nationalism" was now laden with ominous meanings that conjured up haunting images of raving dictators in military uniforms and emaciated corpses piled up in the ghastly extermination camps of Eastern Europe. The American public's growing unease with racist political belief systems, together with the desegregation of the military, was a major factor in the demise of the Jim Crow system in the South. Even the brutal South African apartheid state eventually collapsed under the combined weight of unfavorable world opinion and stringent international economic sanctions. Although the ideological link between race and nation continued to operate in various regional and local settings, it had lost much of its former appeal by the end of the century.

Fourth, the three major Allied war conferences of Teheran (1943), Bretton Woods (1944), and Yalta (1945) laid the foundation of a global political and economic order that divided the planet into expansive "spheres of influence" cutting across national borders. In the sleepy New England town of Bretton Woods, the major economic powers of the West led by the United States jettisoned the protectionist policies of the interwar period and struck a compromise that combined international economic integration with national policy independence. Their strong commitment to the expansion of trade and economic cooperation reflected their shared belief in the effectiveness of global commercial interdependence as a bulwark against another devastating economic crisis or a new world war. The successful establishment of binding rules on international economic activities resulted in the creation of a stable currency exchange system in which the value of participating currencies was pegged to the American dollar worth one thirty-fifth of an ounce of gold. Bretton Woods also set the institutional foundations for the creation of three new international economic organizations. The International Monetary Fund (IMF) was established to administer the global monetary system. The International Bank for Reconstruction and Development, later known as the World Bank, provided loans for Europe's postwar reconstruction (in the late 1950s, however, its purpose was expanded to fund major industrial projects in the developing world). And the General Agreement on Tariffs and Trade (GATT) became the first global trade organization charged with fashioning and enforcing multilateral trade agreements (in 1995, the World Trade Organization (WTO) emerged as its successor). The creation of these institutions served as clear evidence for the growing impact of global designs on the national imaginary.

Finally, many of the technological innovations that would contribute to the late twentieth-century compression of time and space were the direct result of war-related activities. An abbreviated list of these inventions includes airplanes powered by jet engines; guided missiles like the German V-1 "flying bomb" and the V-2 rocket; basic radar and sonar systems; digital electronic machines like Harvard University's Mark I computer, used by the US Navy for gunnery and ballistic calculations; the microwave-generating magnetron; synthetic rubber; supersized ships made of welded steel; streamlined production lines; and so on. Even the Internet—the most celebrated hallmark of the global age—originated in secret US war communication projects that underwent further development in the Cold War era in response to pathbreaking Soviet satellite technology.

The atomic bomb, of course, was both the most spectacular and terrifying of the war-related technologies. Nothing did more to convince people of the linked fate of geographically and politically separated nations than the nuclear obliteration of two Japanese cities and nearly 200,000 of their inhabitants, most of them civilians. "Hiroshima has shaken the whole world," a disingenuous Stalin confided to his inner circle immediately before ordering his top scientists to catch up with the Americans. US President Harry Truman put the implications of nuclear globality in stark terms: "[T]he human animal and his emotions change not much from age to age. He must change now or he faces absolute and complete destruction and maybe the insect age or an atmosphereless planet will succeed him."[6] But the full global impact of the nuclear arms race did not reveal itself until the 1950s with the successful detonation of hydrogen bombs. Operating on the principles of atomic fusion, these devices were hundreds of times more powerful than the bombs that devastated Hiroshima and Nagasaki. Despite these weapons' potential for mass destruction, the quite realistic prospect of nuclear war between the United States and the Soviet Union nonetheless prevailed, revealing the magnitude of the rupture with traditional conceptions of "international" conflict. Thermonuclear warfare would spell not only the end of humanity but also the annihilation of nearly all forms of life on earth. More than anything, it was this recurring nightmare of total planetary destruction that forced people around the world to think beyond the nation in terms that captured the new reality of global interdependence. The scope of "high-consequence risks"—those manufactured by humans as a result of their intervention into the conditions of social life and nature—had been dramatically expanded by the atomic bomb. No longer contained by the geography of the national age, these manufactured risks had become globalized.[7]

4.2. The Globalization of the Cold War and the Emergence of the Three-World Order

The 1945 conferences in Yalta and Potsdam laid the foundations for a new geopolitical world order based on diametrically opposed political belief systems that competed for influence on the rest of the world. As the doomed German dictator had prophesied during his last days in the Berlin bunker, "The laws of both history and geography will compel these two Great Powers [the United States and Soviet Russia] to a trial of strength, either militarily or in the fields of economics and ideology."[8] Their wartime marriage of convenience in shambles at the conclusion of hostilities, the two superpowers seemed to be heading for certain confrontation. However, they could no longer afford to act in accordance with Carl von Clausewitz's early nineteenth-century dictum that war was the continuation of political activity by other means. Gone was the old certainty that armed conflict would always lead to victory for some nations and defeat for others. The impossibility of fighting each other militarily without risking mutual destruction—a frightening scenario eventually known by its fitting acronym, MAD ("Mutually Assured Destruction")—left the superpowers with only two options, both of which were implemented with great regularity throughout the Cold War. First, the United States and the Soviet Union might choose to engage in *limited* warfare, either directly or through dependent third parties. Naturally, direct military confrontation was a risky business, for it harbored the danger of escalation and ultimate nuclear confrontation. Accordingly, the antagonists sought to avoid this option, though they came dangerously close to pulling the nuclear trigger, if only briefly, during the Korean War and the 1962 Cuban Missile Crisis. Fortunately, both Moscow and Washington blinked and instead continued to exercise their safer second option of engaging in limited warfare by proxy, in the process transforming the newly emerging nations of the global South into the volatile flash points of the Cold War.

Second, in their insatiable hunger for greater power, security, and prestige, the superpowers could exercise the option of complementing indirect warfare with an all-out ideological contest. Realizing that the likelihood of changing the political beliefs and values of the other side was close to zero, the antagonists directed their struggle for hearts and minds primarily toward those people whose political imagination was not yet fully captured by either capitalist liberalism or collectivist communism. United in their rejection of old-fashioned European colonialism, Moscow and Washington offered the developing world competing paths to modernity rooted in the same Enlightenment ideals of science and rationality. Having supposedly "worked" in their respective national contexts, Russian communism and American liberalism were seen by their codifiers as eminently exportable to the rest of the world. Thus seeking to globalize their respective ideologies, the superpowers ended up globalizing the Cold War, with each side utterly convinced that the superiority of its worldview would ultimately reveal itself in the "development" and "progress" of its adoptive nation. As Cold War historian Odd Arne Westad notes, "Locked in conflict over the very concept of European modernity—to which both states regarded themselves as successors—Washington and Moscow needed to change the world in order to prove the universal applicability of their ideologies, and the elites of the newly independent states proved fertile ground for their competition."[9] Hence, it would be a grave mistake to limit the role of ideology in the Cold War to that of a superficial mask hiding more profound material interests. Ideology functioned as a crucial factor in an epic contest that was just as much about showcasing the global applicability of liberal or communist ideas and values as it was about economics or geopolitics: "Ideas, values, and belief systems were at the heart of the struggle that defined the second half of the twentieth century."[10]

Ironically, the globalization of the Cold War added to the growing problems of the competing grand ideologies. The harder the superpowers tried to prove the Truth of their ideological claims—sometimes at the price of military intervention—the greater the resistance generated in the form of "new ideologies" that emerged in both the West and the South. Given that American liberalism and Russian communism represented context-sensitive translations of the national imaginary, they struggled to make their ideas and values stick in an increasingly global environment. On the one hand, each superpower encouraged recipient countries to copy its ideology. On the other hand, however, they bristled when client states like Guatemala or Egypt chose to adapt those borrowed ideologies to their national contexts in rather idiosyncratic ways. Consequently, the globalizing dynamics of the Cold War fueled *both* the globalization of the European idea of sovereign nation-states (as reflected in the "United

Nations" model) *and* the affirmation of a postwar conceptual and geo-graphical order that cut across national borders and divided the globe into three related, yet separate, "worlds": a liberal-capitalist First World led by the United States; a collectivist-communist Second World presided over by the Soviet Union; and a formally nonaligned Third World lacking a dominant center.[11]

Predictably, this seemingly contradictory picture of independent and formally equal nation-states existing within communities of value that transcended the familiar national frame of reference is precisely what one would expect in the transformational period leading from the national to the global imaginary. People's identity as "nationals" began to inter-mingle with their new sense of belonging to one of these three worlds. National affiliation and national integration were no longer the sole markers of communal existence. Terms like "democracy," "capitalism," "communism," and "socialism" served as shorthand for geographical and political systems composed of "nation-states" that were nonetheless alleged to converge around a common set of ideological claims regardless of national differences.

The Kremlin, for example, continued its interwar Comintern strategy of portraying its brand of Marxism-Leninism as the only valid ideological formula for all "socialist" countries. But the ideological hegemony of the Soviet Union was openly challenged by Mao Zedong in the late 1950s. Recognizing that the Chinese peasantry possessed a much stronger revo-lutionary potential than the thin urban working class, Mao broke with Leninist principles by holding to his firm belief in the "spontaneous" and "proletarian" instincts of the rural masses. He went far beyond the revolutionary voluntarism of the Soviet founder by pushing the role of subjective forces in history to the point of arguing for their ability to alter the economic base: "In certain conditions, such aspects as the relations of production, theory and the superstructure in turn manifest themselves in the principal and decisive role." Mao's unshakable belief in the power of "correct ideas" translated into the publication of millions of copies of *Quotations from Chairman Mao Zedong*. Waved in the air by his enthusiastic followers, the famous Little Red Book became the ubiquitous symbol of the Chinese Cultural Revolution in the 1960s. As the Great Leader told the crowds, "The proletariat... must meet head-on every challenge of the bourgeoisie in the ideological field and use the new ideas, culture, customs and habits of the proletariat to change the mental outlook of the whole of society."[12] Shattering the Soviet monopoly on communism, the influence of Maoism extended from the European "New Left"—particularly among

French thinkers like Louis Althusser and Michel Foucault who pushed Marxist theory into a poststructuralist direction—to revolutionary Third-World leaders like Kim Il-Song, Ho Chi Minh, Fidel Castro, and Che Guevara.

Many of these leaders—including Yugoslavia's Marshall Tito who pursued a socialist path independent of the Kremlin—met at the 1955 Bandung Conference in an impressive international display of Third-World solidarity. Calling for the end of colonial rule in all its manifestations, representatives of twenty-nine African and Asian nations vowed to strengthen their cultural and economic ties. Committed to the articulation of a common set of political principles based on their neutrality in the Cold War and a socialist path to modernity independent of the Soviet Union, they hoped to give ideological coherence to what six years later became the Movement of Non-Aligned Countries.[13] In his welcoming speech at the Bandung Conference, Indonesian President Sukarno impressed on the minds of the delegates that the fortunes of the developing world depended, first and foremost, on ideological unity: "I hope it [the conference] will give evidence of the fact that we Asian and African leaders understand that Asia and Africa can prosper only when they are united, and that even the safety of the World at large cannot be safeguarded without a united Asia-Africa."[14] Eleven years later, Fidel Castro hosted the Tricontinental Conference of the Peoples of Africa, Asia, and Latin America in Havana. The size of this gathering even surpassed the Bandung Conference, attracting representatives from the entire non-Western world in an impressive display of an anti-imperialist Third-World liberationism that was particularly critical of the United States. Although many of the delegates represented countries receiving material support from the Soviet Union, they nonetheless made strenuous efforts to signal their ideological independence from both Russia and China. Unavoidably, the attempt to stretch old radical formulas to fit the new vision of "Tricontinentalism" resulted in serious theoretical strains and contradictions. Even the speeches of charismatic leaders like Che Guevara were marred by confusing calls for a "true proletarian internationalism" to be fought by subaltern heroes prepared "to die under the flag of Vietnam, of Venezuela, of Guatemala, of Laos, of Guinea, of Colombia, of Brazil.... "[15]

The rising global imaginary called for more suitable ideological articulations, which began to emerge in rudimentary form in the 1960s. Flowing across national borders more easily as a result of fledgling global communication technologies, these "new ideologies" undermined the dominant thesis that ideology had come to an end in the West and frightened the stagnant communist regimes in Russia and Eastern Europe. The Kremlin responded forcefully with increased repression and citizen surveillance, whereas Maoist China resorted to a state-engineered Cultural Revolution that threatened to spin out of control. In the Third World, the codifiers of national liberationism continued to build their ideological alternatives to Western capitalism and Soviet communism as conceptual mixtures of various socialist ideals anchored in their powerful assertion of multiple civilizations. But the humanist visions of figures like Mahatma Gandhi, Frantz Fanon, or Che Guevara often conflicted with their pragmatic imperatives of nation-making. Despite these inherent tensions, their political imagination provided vital nourishment for the evolution of the so-called new ideologies in the West. Let us turn to a more detailed examination of these ideological innovations in the Third and First Worlds.

4.3. Third-World Liberationisms: Gandhism and Fanonism

By the end of the tumultuous 1960s, nearly fifty Third-World "nations" with a population surpassing a quarter of the world's inhabitants had won political independence from their former European and American colonial masters. Their struggle against Western imperialism—aptly defined by the Chinese nationalist leader Sun Yat-Sen as "the policy of aggression against other countries by means of political force"—had begun in earnest with the 1905 surprising defeat of the Russian Empire by Japan.[16] Even Westernized elites like young Mohandas Gandhi, known in his Anglophile circle of friends for his bravura renditions of "God Save the King," began to question the cultural assumptions of European liberalism as a result of the Japanese victory. Praising the Japanese soldiers for their acts of bravery and self-sacrifice, the Indian pacifist highlighted the significance of such "oriental" virtues in his own philosophy of nonviolence.

As we noted in Chapter 3, the Great War represented another early milestone in the process of decolonization. The horrific bloodletting in Europe fatally undermined the pretense of rational and moral superiority that stood at the core of what Michael Adas has called the European "civilizing mission ideology." Formulations of this discourse of domination varied widely from colonial administrators who stressed the internal pacification and political order that European colonization imposed upon "backward peoples" suffering from incessant warfare and despotic rule to those missionaries and reformers who saw religious conversion and education as the centerpieces of the Western civilization effort.[17] Encapsulated in John Stuart Mill's claim that liberty had no application whatsoever to "backward races," the civilizing mission ideology thrived on numerous assertions of difference between colonizers and colonized. Universalistic ideals of liberalism were inscribed with specific cultural practices anchored in contingent notions of history, civilization, and nationhood. Translating the national imaginary in this fashion allowed British liberals like Mill not only to present themselves as members of a "mature society," but also provided them with a seemingly benign justification for their exclusionary practices toward the colonial Other. But the heavy blows inflicted by the Empire of Japan on the Western imperialist powers in the World War further strengthened nativist criticisms of the European civilizing mission discourse. As Frank Furedi suggests, "Many Africans, Asians and Caribbeans were delighted by the spectacle of a colored nation dishing it out to Europeans."[18] In the immediate aftermath of the war, anti-imperialist forces received further support from the superpowers whose denouncement of the old European colonial arrangements served as a necessary preamble to their ideological competition for the Third World.

But European nations were reluctant to let go of their prized possessions. In most cases, it took colonial subjects decades to shake off their imperialist yoke. Although the regional patterns of the decolonization process varied considerably, the various iterations of Third-World liberationism contained similar ideological claims that mixed their socialist and humanist ideas with the assertion that "civilization" was hardly a singular European achievement. As Prasenjit Duara notes, the discourse of alternative civilizations was developed over several decades by figures like Mahatma Gandhi, Rabindranath Tagore, Liang Qichao, Gu Hongming, Lamine Senghor, Aimé Césaire, Kwame Nkrumah, and many others.[19] Advancing the fiction of inclusive "nations" existing within political boundaries haphazardly drawn by the colonial powers, these voices were nonetheless forced to fit their nationalist program into the existing framework of the three-world order.[20] What were the major ideological claims of these Third-World liberationisms? What political means were considered to be most suitable in the struggle against colonialism? To answer these questions, let us examine the ideological perspectives of two of the most influential codifiers of Third-World liberationism: Mahatma Gandhi (1869–1948) and Frantz Fanon (1925–61).

Gandhi's nonviolent liberationism emerged in the first half of the twentieth century in response to the oppressive British colonial system in South Africa and India. Although the internalization of European knowledge and its normative claims were instrumental for the young Indian lawyer's formation as a colonial subject, this process never led to total conformity. As he awakened to the plight of Indian immigrants in his adopted South Africa, Gandhi began to realize how the liberal construction of cultural difference according to the European civilizing mission discourse legitimized colonial practices that imposed on Asians the inferior identity of second-class citizens and subjected them to frequent racial slights, threats, beatings, and other forms of discrimination. The violence of British colonialism in South Africa was structurally embedded in a vast network of norms and rules which, through the meticulous regulation, dissection, and reallocation of time and space, imbued "Indianness" with essential qualities and definitive traits. Assigning proper names and authoritative meanings to all phenomena, authoritative colonial discourses employed invidious notions of difference to validate elaborate cultural, racial, and religious classification schemes that reified the sharp boundaries separating the colonizer from the colonized.

Pejorative terms such as "coolie" signified the immigrant Indians' particular location within the parameters of linear time and physical, psychological, symbolic, and discursive space set by South African whites. To be Indian meant, among other things, to partake in a particular historical record assembled by Europeans; to belong to an assigned ethnic category; to speak an identifiable language or dialect; to be affiliated with a classified religion; to live in a physical place named by the colonizers; and to follow customs and traditions duly registered by colonial authorities. On the level of daily experience, it meant that Indians were expected to know their inferior place in the colonial system and to validate this knowledge through public reenactments of submissive behaviors like removing one's turban in courts of law. Among the many obligatory performances expected from Indians were the acceptable ways of addressing Europeans; appropriate gestures and looks; correct manners of dress; and, of course, the strict adherence to a long list of forbidden acts and excluded spaces. Thus, Indian identity in South Africa was the indelibly marked result of technologies of rule that incessantly reenacted ideological claims of oriental cultural inferiority, thereby making humiliation and low self-esteem a permanent feature of Indianness.

Stung by continuous racist insults, Gandhi finally shook off his political passivity and began to confront the physical and epistemic violence embedded in the harsh technologies of European colonial rule. His political method combined the legal redress of grievances with nonviolent public protests.[21] But the conceptual weight of the method of *satyagraha* ("truth-force") rested on his alternative conception of an "Indian civiliza-tion" rooted in spiritual and moral concerns rather than in Western con-ceptions of material progress. The best starting point for the exploration of Gandhi's perspective on Indian civilization is his eighty-page monograph *Hind Swaraj* ("Indian Self-Rule"), completed in 1909 upon his return from a disillusioning political trip to London. Written as a dialogue between two fictional characters—a newspaper "Editor" representing Gandhism and a radical "Reader" modeled after the political views of violent Indian nationalists like V. D. Savarkar—the booklet defends Gandhi's claim that "ancient Indian civilization has little to learn from the modern."[22] At one point in the dialogue, the Reader asks the Editor to justify his blanket condemnation of Western civilization: "If [modern] civilization is a dis-ease, and if it has attacked the English nation, why has she been able to take India, and why is she able to retain it?" The response comes without hesitation: "The English have not taken India; we have given it to them. They are not in India because of their strength, but because we keep them."[23] In other words, Gandhi insists that most Indians have accepted colonial rule for purely materialistic reasons: "[W]e keep the English in India for our base self-interest. We like their commerce, they please us by their subtle methods, and get what they want from us. To blame them for this is to perpetuate their power."[24]

This charge of materialist corruption dressed up as the rational embrace of material progress anchors the first central ideological claim of Gandhism: the political objective of Indian home rule can only be achieved through a rigorous program of moral reformation that restores the nation to its spiritual health and ethical integrity. As Partha Chatterjee points out, the Mahatma's entire political project of nonviolent national liberation must be understood as predicated upon his commitment to identify, address, and rectify moral failure on the part of colonized Indians.[25] Although he bemoans their wholesale adoption of Western civilization, Gandhi himself constructs his vision of an alternative civil-ization within a historiographical framework developed by European Ori-entalists, particularly their linear model of India's decline from a classical Golden Age to its present "degenerate" and "stagnant" condition. Calling for a reversal of this trend, the Indian leader believes that the successful recovery of India's "authentic values" depends upon its people's ability to access the "eternally valid" moral resources of their ancestors. Drawing on deep symbolic resources contained in the language and imagery of a Golden Age, Gandhi infuses his idea of India's ancient civilization with socialist ideas his Marxists contemporaries derided as "utopian" and "primitive." Still, Gandhian socialism cannot be separated from his moral vision of a spiritual civilization sustained by a communal people whose selfless character sets natural limits to the physical indulgences that come with material progress: "They [ancient Indians] saw that happiness was largely a mental condition.... Observing all this, our ancestors dissuaded us from luxuries and pleasures."[26]

Rejecting large cities as "snares and useless encumbrances" corrupting people's "natural sense" of simplicity and reciprocity, Gandhi conjures up the agrarian-socialist utopia of self-sufficient "village communities." His vision resembles the belief of Russian Populists in their country's special path to an idyllic peasant socialism based on an idealized model of the traditional Russian village commune. Presented as paragons of social cooperation and harmony, such self-contained communities constitute the basic building blocs of Gandhi's socialist model of Indian nationhood. Like his Russian counterparts, the Mahatma manages to convince himself that twentieth-century villagers could revive traditional ways of forming intimate face-to-face relationships. For Gandhi, mutual trust represents a timeless virtue that allows political and economic decisions to be made collectively in direct-democratic fashion.[27] He urges his compatriots to follow their own occupations and trades without engaging in much competition and by embracing the same basic technologies of production utilized by their ancestors. Finally, he invokes India's time-tested educational system that rejects abstract schooling in the sciences in favor of practical skills and moral "character-building." By cultivating *swadeshi* ("home manufacture" or economic "self-reliance"), Indians would learn to resist the corrupting influence of the colonial powers and achieve genuine self-rule. Unsurprisingly, Gandhi decontests *swaraj* or "true home rule" not primarily as political independence, but as "observance of morality" for the purpose of attaining "mastery over mind and passions."[28] In other words, political liberation represents but the inevitable consequence of more important processes of psychological and moral emancipation from the ideological prison of the Western civilizing mission discourse.

Moreover, by emphasizing that the Third World's struggle for national liberation ought to be rooted in *satyagraha*, Gandhi firmly rejects violence as a suitable means for political change. Unlike the Russian Populists who fought Tsarist despotism with innovative forms of violence such as bombings and guerilla warfare, the Indian leader draws his political inspiration from his core concepts of *ahimsa* ("not harming" or "nonviolence") and *satyagraha*. For Gandhi, the exercise of violence for the purpose of achieving political independence was self-defeating for three reasons. First, the colonized lacked access to and training in the advanced war technologies of their oppressors. Still, it cannot be stressed enough that the Mahatma's notion of *ahimsa* represents not merely a political tactic or a prudent means toward an end, but a moral way of life grounded in a metaphysical-religious view about the nature of reality. Reading Indian traditions of nonviolence through a lens colored by his Western education, he decontests *ahimsa* as a mode of being and action consistent with a provisional "truth" that points to the unity of all beings. Gandhi identifies two principal expressions of nonviolence: "In its negative form, it [nonviolence] means not injuring any living being, whether by body or mind. I may not therefore hurt the person of a wrong-doer, or bear any ill will to him and so cause him mental suffering.... In its positive form, *ahimsa* means the largest love, the greatest charity."[29]

Second, Gandhian liberationism disputes the basic assumption inherent in Western political discourses that the nature of power lies in its capacity to unleash violence, and, consequently, that the exercise of political power inevitably involves employing violent means of coercion. In this respect, Dennis Dalton makes an important point when he argues that "soul-power" would be a better translation for *satyagraha* than "truth-force" or "soul-force," since force is usually associated with violence.[30] After all, it was precisely this supposedly natural connection between power and violence that Gandhi challenged in his assertion that *satyagraha* represented power "born of Truth and Love or nonviolence."[31] For the Mahatma, then, the infliction of violence on another person presumed society's ability to pass ultimate judgment in terms of right and wrong. But since there was never absolute certainty as to the absolute truth of an opinion—including Gandhi's own perspective—there could be no fundamental right or even competence to punish: "In the application of *satyagraha*, I discovered in the earliest stages that pursuit of Truth did not admit of violence being inflicted on one's opponent, but that he must be weaned from error by patience and sympathy. For what appears to be Truth to one may appear false to the other."[32]

Third, Gandhi holds that even violence used against the colonial oppressor merely imitates the morally bankrupt methods of a materialist European civilization based on "brute force." Undermining the British Empire's moral and political authority, the Indian leader suggests that it was never in a position to ascertain at what point a particular colony would achieve a sufficiently high level of development to be permitted to rule itself. He seeks to bolster this claim by arguing that India possesses a special relationship to the practice of *ahimsa*. Moving moral considerations once again to the core of his exposition, the Mahatma insists that any civilization worth the name ought to respect the correspondence of political means and moral ends: "...I wish only to show that only fair means can produce fair results, and that, at least in the majority of cases, if not, indeed, in all, the force of love and pity is infinitely greater than the force of arms. There is harm in the exercise of brute force, never in that of pity."[33] In their immoral reliance on violence, modern Europeans stand accused of having failed to grasp the significance of *ahimsa* as a superior truth-force. Ancient Indians, on the other hand, built their civilization on the nonviolent principles of self-sacrifice and passive resistance. Praising the imaginary lives of the subcontinent's communal peasants, Gandhi insists that faint traces of these virtuous practices can still be detected in colonial India: "The fact is that, in India, the nation at large has generally used passive resistance in all departments of life. We cease to co-operate with our rulers when they displease us. This is passive resistance [*satyagraha*].... Real home rule is possible only where passive resistance is the guiding force of the people. Any other rule is foreign rule."[34]

At first glance, Gandhi's call for the moral regeneration of the Indian nation appears to be an idyllic socialist translation of the modern national imaginary that had been exported to the South by the colonial powers. But, as we noted above, the formulation of national liberationisms culminated in a three-world order increasingly oriented toward a global frame of reference. This mounting tension between the bubbling national consciousness in the Third World and the strengthening of the global imaginary found its expression in the writings of virtually all anticolonial thinkers. Although he was assassinated at the outset of the Cold War era, Gandhi was no exception. Throughout his life, he struggled to reconcile his nonviolent struggle for Indian *swaraj* with his sympathies for a "world federation" based on nonviolence and beyond race and color.[35] Describing himself both as a "nationalist" whose "nationalism includes the well-being of the whole world" and a "cosmopolitan" whose mission was to "unite the world," the Mahatma believed that his vision of a nonviolent Indian nationalism was perfectly compatible with a "commonwealth of all world states."[36] At the same time, he emphasized that a genuine global society would only emerge after the successful completion of national liberation struggles in the Third World. Thus, Gandhi saw the process of nation-making as a necessary step toward the realization of a global order:

In my opinion, it is impossible for one to be internationalist without being a nationalist. Internationalism is possible only when nationalism becomes a fact, i.e., when people belonging to different countries have organized themselves and are able to act as one man. It is not nationalism that is evil, it is the narrowness, selfishness, exclusiveness which is the bane of modern nations which is evil.... Indian nationalism has, I hope, struck a different path. It wants to organize itself and find full self-expression for the benefit and service of humanity at large. Anyway there is no uncertainty about my patriotism or nationalism. God having cast my lot in the midst of the people of India, I should be untrue to my Maker if I failed to serve them.[37]

There can be no doubt as to the remarkable *global* legacy of Gandhism. In the First World, its major ideological claims served as powerful catalysts for the formation and development of the "new ideologies" in the 1960s and 1970s. As we shall see shortly, Martin Luther King anchored his struggle against racial discrimination in the ideas and method of his Indian role model. Arne Naess, the Norwegian father of "deep ecology," wrote his doctoral dissertation on Gandhian philosophy and its applicability to global environmentalism. Petra Kelly, cofounder of the German Green Party and active participant in the American civil rights movement, made sure that Gandhian nonviolence was enshrined as one of the "four pillars" of the Party's official platform. Feminist activists like Barbara Deming embraced Gandhian nonviolent strategies in their influential campaigns for world peace during the 1970s and 1980s. In the Second World, dissidents like Vaclav Havel and Lech Walesa openly acknowledged their debt to Gandhian ideas and tactics as they mounted their nonviolent challenge to communism in the 1980s. Likewise, Chinese students occupying Beijing's Tiananmen Square from April to June 1989 based their determined struggle for democracy on the Mahatma's principles of *ahimsa* and *satyagraha*. In the Third World, Gandhism inspired major popular forms of resistance to authoritarian governments like those organized by the Mothers of the Plaza de Mayo in Argentina in the 1970s, the 1980s People's Power Movement in the Philippines, the 1987–9 Palestinian Intifada in the Israel-occupied territories of the West Bank and Gaza, the ongoing Burmese Pro-Democracy Movement led by Nobel-Prize winner Aung San Suu Kyi, and the Ogoni People's struggle for human rights and civil society in Nigeria in the 1990s, to name but a few.[38]

Gandhian liberationism also dominated the political imagination in Africa during the early postwar period. Political leaders from diverse cultural backgrounds, such as Egypt's Gamal Nasser, Ghana's Kwame Nkrumah, and Zambia's Kenneth Kaunda, embraced the ideas and tactics of the Great Soul. Nkrumah, in particular, countered British colonialism with his creative program of Positive Action that included "legitimate political action, newspaper and educational campaigns and, as a last resort, the constitutional application of strikes, boycotts and noncooperation based on the principle of non-violence, as used by Gandhi in India."[39] In the early 1960s, however, Gandhi's nonviolent liberationism came under sustained attack from African and Asian critics who called for the use of reciprocal violence to dislodge entrenched white settler regimes like those in South Africa and Algeria. Even Nelson Mandela, initially committed to Gandhism, changed his approach in the aftermath of the 1960 Sharpeville massacre, "Government violence can do only one thing and that is to breed counter-violence."[40]

Perhaps the most eloquent and passionate proponent of such counterviolence was the French-Caribbean psychiatrist and journalist Frantz Fanon. Representing the militant National Liberation Front (FLN) of his adopted Algeria at the 1958 All-Africa Peoples Conference in Accra, he resolutely rejected Nkrumah's nonviolent model of Positive Action. His brilliant address to the conference delegates, destined to turn into the opening chapter of his book *The Wretched of the Earth*, posited the psychological and political necessity of violence in the struggle against the European colonial system of oppression: "National liberation, national renaissance, the restoration of nationhood to people, commonwealth: whatever may be the headings used or the new formulas introduced, decolonization is always a violent phenomenon."[41] Indeed, Fanon's literary masterpiece, completed only weeks before his premature death, is predicated on the ideological claim that violence serves as the "cleansing force" for the "veritable creation of new men" in the Third World: "It [violence] frees the native from his inferiority complex and from his despair and inaction; it makes him fearless and restores his self-respect.... Illuminated by violence, the consciousness of the people rebels against any pacification."[42] Thus, the Algerian psychiatrist draws particular attention to the pernicious psychological effects of the colonial system on subjugated populations. As Robert Young notes, Fanon builds his model of anticolonial liberationism on both psychological redemption and black empowerment. These ideals were first articulated in the 1920s and 1930s by Fanon's early mentor Aimé Césaire, the Caribbean founder of the cultural *négritude* movement, and by Marcus Garvey, the charismatic American leader of the Universal Negro Improvement Association.[43]

The author of *The Wretched of the Earth* paints a Manichean picture of colonialism as a "world cut in two." The colonizers' zone of respect, prosperity, and order contrasts sharply with the colonized space of discrimination, exploitation, and oppression. As the author asserts, no conciliation is possible, "for of the two terms, one is superfluous." Fanon reminds his readers time and again that it was the European colonizers who first brought "violence into the home and into the mind of the native." Hence, they should not be surprised to reap exactly what they sowed. He emphasizes that the compartmentalized world of colonialism cannot be made whole by pacifists like Gandhi, because nonviolence suggests compromise where none can be had. Representing "violence in its natural state," the colonial system "will only yield when confronted with greater violence." Hence, it must be dismantled by "a murderous and decisive struggle between the two protagonists." Fanon shows great confidence in the power of the colonized masses—composed for the most part of largely illiterate peasants. But although he endows them with superior "intuition" for "absolute violence," Fanon concedes that they face two gigantic hurdles on their path to national liberation. First, they must find the strength to withstand the furies of retaliatory violence unleashed by their European adversaries at the first sign of rebellion. Second, they must ignore the reformist siren calls of their native middle-class leaders. After all, the bourgeois sympathies for a "nonviolent strategy of liberation" expose not only souls deeply imprinted with "the essential qualities of the West" but also betray elitist fears of a radical, bottom-up decolonization process in which "the last shall be first."[44]

Consciously stretching his revolutionary Marxist perspective to the point of replacing "class" with "race" as the master concept in his analysis, Fanon insists that Western imperialism is about much more than just capitalist exploitation. Racist denigration and exclusion lie at the very heart of a system that valorizes "whiteness" as the inherent foundation of any "civilization" worth the name while relegating "blackness" to the realm of a "primitive tribalism" rooted in animalistic drives and uncontrolled sexuality. Fanon's first book, *Black Skin, White Masks*, offers a dazzling account of how the constant objectification and animalization of the colonized feeds a "psycho-existential complex," that is, a socially produced but internalized sense of inferiority.[45] But it is precisely the white settlers' projection of colonized otherness as "bestiality bereft of all humanity" or "absolute evil" that discloses their deep-seated fears of the native. Indeed, the colonizers' anxieties are reflected in their preoccupation with security.

In *The Wretched of the Earth*, Fanon picks up this theme, urging his native brothers to play on the colonizers' insecurities by "pulling out a knife" whenever they hear pretentious speeches about Western culture.

Overall, then, decolonization by means of violence constitutes, for Fanon, a necessary act of existential empowerment that unifies the colonized "on a national, sometimes a racial, basis." Their common exercise of violence binds the people together as a whole, since "each individual forms a violent link in the great chain, a part of the great organism of violence which has surged upward in reaction to the settler's violence in the beginning. The groups recognize each other and the future of the nation is already indivisible." Unlike Gandhi's moral vision of regenerating the nation by means of a nonviolent "truth-force," the Algerian thinker seeks to forge national identity in the Third World by prescribing generous doses of amoral violence. After all, it is the Manichean character of the colonial world that determines the content of morality in purely oppositional terms: "[T]he good is quite simply that which is evil for 'them.'" Fanon defines "truth" in similarly instrumental fashion as the "property of the national cause." After all, it "is that which hurries the break-up of the colonialist regime; it is that which promotes the emergence of the nation; it is all that protects the natives, and ruins the foreigners. In this colonialist context there is no truthful behavior.... "[46]

Given Fanon and Gandhi's conflicting responses to the question of the most suitable political means in the struggle against colonialism, many commentators have put them into opposing ideological camps. Indeed, their disparate views on the role of violence in the decolonization process seem to justify the introduction of two ideal types of Third-World liberationism. And yet, we must not ignore the considerable ideational overlap that exists between Gandhism and Fanonism: a common emphasis on the subjective dimension of colonialism; sympathies for some form of "socialism" based on the needs of the impoverished rural masses; and the insistence on the multiplicity of civilizations. But for the purpose of our discussion, their most significant ideological commonality can be found in their struggle to reconcile their political visions of national liberation with the rising global imaginary. Like the Mahatma, Fanon emphasizes the importance of regaining a sense of community in areas where social life was destroyed by the European colonial presence. Nationhood— even if only claimed by the representatives of the people—provides the community with a national identity, which, in turn, contributes to the restoration of their damaged sense of selfhood. Diffused to the masses, national consciousness allows them to take their destiny into their own hands. Because Algerians had begun to consider themselves as sovereign in spite of the continued French colonial presence, the country was "virtually independent."[47] Like Gandhi, Fanon was convinced that the striving for national existence and the strengthening of national consciousness through the process of decolonization would ultimately force the oppressor to vacate the land, thus bringing political independence as a result of a previous act of psychological liberation.

Fanon insists that the "national period" could not be skipped in the global South only because the region's "development" was limping behind the First World. In fact, he considers the establishment of independent nations in the Third World "the most urgent thing today." At the same time, however, he leaves no doubt that "the building of the nation is of necessity accompanied by the discovery and encouragement of universalizing values.... It is at the heart of national consciousness that international consciousness lives and grows."[48] Groping for a way to articulate the emergence of the global consciousness from its national shell, Fanon ends up reiterating Gandhi's claim that genuine humanist values must be realized first on the level of the nation before they can be spread throughout the whole of humankind. As for the concrete political and ideological manifestation of the global, the Caribbean thinker remains rather vague. In concluding *The Wretched of the Earth*, he speaks only in very general terms about a "new humanism" of global reach.[49] Born of the national liberation struggles in the Third World, such humanism would transcend both Anglo-American liberalism and Soviet communism in its ability to bring "the problem of mankind to an infinitely higher plane." Echoing Gandhi's belief in India's special mission to unite the world, Fanon assigns to the Third World the task of advancing humanity step by step without committing the grave error of regurgitating the central claims of established European ideologies:

It is a question of the Third World starting a new history, a history which will have regard to the sometimes prodigious theses which Europe has put forward, but which will also not forget Europe's crimes, of which the most horrible was committed in the heart of man, and consisted of the pathological tearing apart of his functions and the crumbling away of his unity. And in the framework of the collectivity there were the differentiations, the stratification, and the bloodthirsty tensions fed by classes; and finally, on the immense scale of humanity, there were racial hatreds, slavery, exploitation, and above all the bloodless genocide which consisted in the setting aside of fifteen thousand millions of men.... For Europe, for ourselves, and for humanity, comrades, we must turn over a new leaf, we must work out new concepts, and try to set afoot a new man.[50]

Fanon's death from leukemia in 1961 at the age of 36 prevented him from working out these "new concepts"—presumably in the form of a more concrete articulation of the rising global imaginary. This task of "reintroducing mankind into the world, the whole world" was left to the intellectual heirs of Fanonism—those voices around the globe who, like the inspiring Caribbean thinker, envisioned a world liberated from the triple scourge of poverty, race prejudice, and war.

4.4. The End of Ideology in the First World?

In 1955, with the decolonization process and the Cold War in full swing, an obscure Scandinavian political scientist published a short article that amounted to the opening salvo in what came to be known in the West as the "end-of-ideology debate."[51] Within a short period, prominent academics and journalists on both sides of the Atlantic came to echo the Swedish scholar's thesis. The grand political belief systems had lost their previous "grandeur and power," Herbert Tingsten proclaimed, and the result was an unprecedented ideological consensus characterized by the absence of "metaphysical and speculative ideas."[52] Focusing on the postwar Swedish political system as an illustration of this overarching trend, Tingsten noted that the world's "successful democracies" were showing a clear tendency toward a "leveling—both ideologically and in fact—which entails the growth of the fund of common purpose and the shrinkage of the margin for conflicts, particularly fundamental conflicts." Postwar politics in the First World reflected a broad agreement among major parties—even on previously divisive issues like national defense, the status of church and religion, public policy and taxation, and government intervention into the economic sphere. Politicians of all stripes eagerly presented themselves as levelheaded problem solvers with nothing but contempt for anything that smacked of "ideological" utopias. Regardless of their different party labels, they equally emphasized "their patriotism, their feeling for democracy, their progressiveness and their striving for social reform." Hence, Tingsten concluded, "Liberalism in the old sense is dead, both among the Conservatives and in the Liberal Party; Social Democratic thinking has lost nearly all its traits of doctrinaire Marxism."[53]

Attributing this wholesale "liquidation of the great ideological controversies" to people's postwar disenchantment with the "extremes and follies" of communism and fascism, the Swedish scholar suggested that "common sense" and "pragmatism" were the creative forces behind the building of a common Western "community of values" based on a "kind of unconscious compromise" that incorporated conservative, liberal, and social democratic elements. But such a "commonly accepted program" was clearly hostile to both early twentieth-century liberalism and Marxist socialism. "The essential point is that through the acceptance of the programme the importance of general ideas has been so greatly reduced, that—without falling prey to illusions about a clear difference between means and ends—one can speak of a movement from politics to administration, from principles to technique."[54] Although Tingsten expressed passing nostalgia for the lost "vitality nurtured on impassioned battles of ideas," he unabashedly celebrated the new conciliatory climate permeating Western democracies: "We cannot wish for vitality at the expense of stability." Although he hinted at some negative consequences of ideology's disappearance, such as the growth of the administrative state, the mechanization of politics, and the decline of civic engagement, Tingsten ultimately shrugged off those shortcomings as temporary ailments easily curable by political reforms designed to enhance democratic participation.[55]

Five years later, Harvard sociologist Daniel Bell offered a similar assessment of the American political landscape. Bearing the suggestive title *The End of Ideology: On the Exhaustion of Political Ideas in the Fifties*, his book became an instant best seller exemplifying the political imagination of the First World in the late 1950s.[56] Bell not only reassured his readers that fascist totalitarianism had been vanquished for good but also postulated the "utter exhaustion" of Marxist socialism and classical liberalism. Built on what he saw as "speculative claims" like the "inevitability of history" or the "self-regulating market," these grand political belief systems had lost their power to inspire people hit hard by the misery of the Great Depression and the devastation of the world war. Convinced that these calamities had been brought about by the excesses of "ideology," Bell argued that Westerners had finally abandoned their simplistic beliefs in nineteenth-century schemes that projected illusive visions of human perfection and social harmony—be it the classless society of Marxism or the laissez-faire paradise of liberalism. Hence, the Harvard scholar arrived at his famous conclusion: "[I]deology, which once was a road to action, has come to be a dead end."[57] Although he acknowledged that communism still posed a formidable military threat, Bell nonetheless postulated that its core concepts no longer inspired the working class in the First World. Likewise, he insisted that the emancipatory message of Third-World liberationism was far too parochial, naive, and anachronistic to appeal to Western audiences.

Bell's account relied on a critical conception of ideology as utopian, distorting, emotionally laden, extremist, dogmatic, and irrational. Linking ideology to totalitarianism, he used these terms interchangeably throughout his book. Like his Swedish colleague, Bell showed much appreciation for the alleged cessation of major ideological battles in the West. The pragmatic "class compromise" underpinning the modern welfare state and its "mixed economy" held out the promise of enduring political stability and social security. Bell and his colleague Seymour Martin Lipset even suggested that the remaining problems of modern democracies were, in principle, solvable by levelheaded reformers endowed with the virtues of administrative efficiency, technical expertise, and scientific objectivity: "The only issues are whether the metal workers should get a nickel more an hour, the price of milk should be raised, or old-age pensions extended."[58] Nevertheless, Bell intuited that social reformism might not offer "a younger generation the outlet for 'self-expression' and 'self-definition' that it wants." With no personal experience of the ideological clashes of the interwar period and bored by their state-administered societies, young people could be tempted to recharge their dispassionate intellectual environment by drawing on the "apocalyptic and chiliastic visions" of the past.[59]

In spite of their passing concerns with the possible social consequences of political boredom, the transatlantic participants of the end-of-ideology debate believed firmly in the dawning of a new Golden Age in the West. Its longevity, of course, depended on the durability of the underlying ideological compromise, which required the further cultivation of the existing First-World "community of values." Bell aptly summarized its virtues: "In the Western world, there is today a rough consensus among intellectuals on political issues: the acceptance of a Welfare State; the desirability of decentralized power; a system of mixed economy and of political pluralism."[60] Accepting the moral and political leadership of the United States, the West would remain strongly opposed to communism while seeking to enhance its appeal in the developing world. Safeguarding the socioeconomic aspects of the ideological consensus meant for Bell and his colleagues honoring the postwar commitment to socialize capitalism without abandoning market principles. A "well-defined" list of such "principles for action" included the achievement of prosperity through enhanced economic production; the maintenance of a high and stable level of employment; the avoidance of serious inflation; the creation of educational opportunities for all; the assurance of a decent standard of living for all, especially for the young, the aged, and the sick; and, finally, the state's assumption of responsibility for the attainment of these goals.[61]

As illustrated in Chapter 2, the late nineteenth-century antecedents of such postwar welfarism—a loose amalgamation of liberal and social democratic political ideas attached to the core concept of the welfare state—can be found in the reformist schemes of British New Liberals and their social democratic contemporaries in Imperial Germany. While disagreeing on the ultimate goal of social reformism, both camps emphasized that the state had a positive duty to promote the welfare of all of its members.[62] Modern welfarism with its dual commitment to political democracy and the state-directed regulation of capitalism emerged in the 1930s as an alternative to fascism and communism in industrialized nations that included Sweden, Belgium, France, the United States, Canada, Australia, and New Zealand.

Its theoretical justification—the return to a high and stable level of employment by means of countercyclical fiscal and monetary policies—can be found in John Maynard Keynes' writings, particularly his *The General Theory of Employment, Interest, and Money* (1936). Although contemporary economic historians still argue about the actual influence of Keynesianism on public policy during the 1930s, there remains little doubt that the ideological consensus celebrated by Bell and his colleagues two decades later rested to a significant extent on the British thinker's prescriptions. Convinced that the old laissez-faire model was dangerously out of step with the conditions of advanced capitalism, Keynes had launched a frontal attack on the ideological foundations of classical liberalism as early as the 1920s: "It is *not* true that individuals possess a prescriptive 'natural liberty' in their economic activities.... The world is *not* so governed from above that private and social interest always coincide.... Nor is it true that self-interest generally *is* enlightened...."[63] As the Great Slump persisted during the 1930s, Keynes' ferocious indictment of old-style capitalism as an "unintelligent" and "decadent" system lacking both in virtue and in beauty sounded like an apt characterization. Unable to find their way out of mass unemployment, industrial democracies had failed to "deliver the goods."[64]

Keynes savored his role as capitalism's savior while lambasting the closed economic nationalism of Nazi Germany and the Soviet Union. Arguing that classical liberalism's focus on reviving production was misplaced in national economies suffering from chronic underconsumption, he suggested that consumption drove production—and not the other way around. Thus he insisted that the road to economic recovery had to start with the stimulation of demand by enhancing the purchasing power of the middle class and the industrial proletariat. Since Keynes held that chronically depressed economies were incapable of righting themselves if left to their own devices, he assigned to national governments the crucial task of slaying the dragon of mass unemployment. Working people would stimulate demand and private investment would resume. The vicious cycle of low economic expectations leading to low investment and low demand would be broken by countercyclical fiscal policies based on public jobs and heavy public spending. Even in the bleakest of economic times, Keynes suggested, national governments could procure the necessary funds through a combination of massive borrowing and progressive taxation schemes. Once the goal of full employment had been achieved, the inflationary tendencies caused by increased money supply were to be combated by countercyclical monetary measures such as the raising of interest rates.

A bold thinker with a strong pragmatic streak, Keynes recognized that his plan for saving modern capitalism forced democratic governments to adopt interventionist economic policies with a decidedly socialistic flavor:

I conceive, therefore, that a somewhat comprehensive socialisation of investment will prove the only means of securing an approximation to full employment; though this need not exclude all manner of compromises and devices by which public authority will co-operate with private initiative. But beyond this no obvious case is made out for a system of State Socialism which would embrace most of the economic life of the community.[65]

His lifelong aversion to "state socialism" notwithstanding, Keynes offered a theoretical justification for a mixed economy that provided a powerful macroeconomic rationale for the ideological codifiers of mid-century welfarism in the First World. Put into practice most spectacularly in Britain by the postwar Labor government of Prime Minister Clement Attlee, this innovative mixture of central planning, nationalization of key industries, and regulatory measures ushered in three decades of economic prosperity and political stability—the First World's Golden Age of "managed capitalism."[66] During this period, employers were generally willing to pay relatively high wages as long as putting spending money into the hands of consumers did not eat too deeply into their profits or investments. In exchange for maintaining labor peace and rising levels of productivity, workers received higher wages and important social protections.[67] Reaching the zenith of its popularity in the early 1960s, the modern welfare state offered its citizens unparalleled social security benefits "from cradle to grave," including universal health care, generous unemployment assistance, free or low-cost public education, and generous old-age pensions.

Indeed, the broad ideological appeal of welfarism went beyond the mere provision of social services by the state. T. H. Marshall, one of its most eloquent proponents, noted perceptively that the growth of social welfare had led to a significant expansion of conventional ideas of citizenship. Concepts of "civil" or "political rights" located at the core of liberal definitions had been complemented by the idea of "social rights." Indeed, citizenship in modern industrialized nations now included "the right to share to the full in the social heritage and to live the life of a civilized being according to the standards prevailing in a society."[68] Although the nation-state still constituted the primary conceptual and geographical container of postwar welfarism in the West, the nearly universal acceptance of Keynesian principles had reduced the importance of the national imaginary and its associated political belief systems—hence Bell's claim that ideology had come to an end.

4.5. First-World Liberationisms: The New Left

Ironically, the First-World "community of values" postulated by Herbert Tingsten began to show signs of serious strain as early as 1955—the very year his article was published. The demise of the political-cultural consensus was most obvious in the nation that saw itself as the political and moral polestar of the "Free World." Although the Swedish scholar had skipped over relevant ideological developments in the Third World, he briefly referred to the "color question" in the United States as a "dark spot" in the overall "bright picture" of ideological consensus. But Tingsten and his colleagues were hardly prepared for the dramatic cultural and political impact of the American Civil Rights movement both at home and on the rest of the world.[69] At the same time, the leaders of this powerful movement owed much of their ideational inspiration to the liberationist voices in the decolonizing world. Mobilizing millions of people around the globe against deep-seated practices of racial segregation and discrimination, black liberationism in the United States came in two principal versions that mimicked their ideological predecessors in the Third World.

The first version, championed by the Reverend Martin Luther King, Jr., and his associates in the Southern Christian Leadership Conference (SCLC), drew on a combination of Mahatma Gandhi's philosophy of nonviolence, politically engaged forms of Protestantism such as the late nineteenth-century social gospel tradition, and liberal progressivism anchored in Enlightenment ideals of social equality, human dignity, and natural rights. Condemning the persistence of racism in America, King suggests in his famous *Letter from Birmingham City Jail* (1963) that the existence of social injustice anywhere represents a threat to justice everywhere. Hence, any decent human being bore a moral responsibility to support efforts underway in the American South to force state governments to dismantle the racist Jim Crow system of the post-Reconstruction era. As early as during the 1955 Montgomery bus boycott, the young pastor insisted that his followers adhere to the "four essential steps" formulated by Gandhi in his nonviolent struggle against British colonialism: the collection of evidence to document existing injustices; good-faith negotiations with authorities to achieve a satisfactory settlement; moral purification in preparation for the struggle; and direct political action ranging from mass protests to coordinated acts of civil disobedience. Rejecting his white opponents' charge that nonviolent direct action was deliberately designed to provoke retaliatory violence, King defended Gandhi's method of *satyagraha* as a moral device to confront deeply embedded forms of racial hatred and bigotry. In his eloquent "I have a Dream Speech," the civil rights leader stepped up his criticism of white America for having defaulted on its liberal "promissory note" insofar as citizens of color were concerned. Despite his profound disappointment, King refused to abandon his integrationist vision: "I have a dream that one day on the red hills of Georgia, sons of former slaves and sons of former slave-owners will be able to sit down together at the table of brotherhood."[70] Invoking the image of a "beloved community" that would protect the inalienable human rights and the pursuit of happiness of all its members, King gradually expanded his vision beyond America's political borders in the form of a powerful plea for transnational solidarity. Pointing to the "interrelated structure of reality," King adhered to a global frame of reference: "If we are to realize the American dream we must cultivate this world perspective."[71]

The second version of American black liberationism owed much to the theories of pan-African leaders like W. E. B. Du Bois, George Padmore, C. L. R. James, Marcus Garvey, Tiémoho Garan Kouyaté, Kwame Nkrumah, Jomo Kenyatta, Julius Nyerere, Aimé Césaire, and Lamine and Léopold Senghor. It entered the political arena in the United States full force in the mid-1960s with the founding of the Black Panther Party in California and the launching of the Black Power movement by former supporters of King's nonviolent integrationism like Student Nonviolent Coordinating Committee (SNCC) chair Stokely Carmichael and Floyd McKissick, national director of the Congress of Racial Equality (CORE). Frustrated by what they considered the systemic limits of electoral and institutional strategies of conventional American interest-group politics, young black activists around the country vented their disillusionment with the "emptiness of traditional liberalism."[72] Gradually, they began to stake out a radical politics of black separatism and cultural exclusivity which they saw as a more effective vehicle for enhancing black people's power and psychological strength.

The ideas of black nationalists like Malcolm X were at the center of this new vision. A former leader in Elijah Muhammad's militant Black Muslim organization, Malcolm X characterized the nonviolent integrationism of King's SCLC as a philosophy supporting "the white man's tactics for keeping his foot on the black man's neck." For the youthful master orator, the solution to his country's race problem was not the "turn-the-other-cheek stuff" popularized by "ignorant Negro preachers," but the propagation of black supremacy and his community's rejection of an inherently racist white society.[73] Malcolm X's separatist alternative to King's integrationism became the ideological foundation of a militant brand of black liberationism that bore the ideological fingerprints of Fanonism: "Revolution is bloody, revolution is hostile, revolution knows no compromise, revolution overturns and destroys everything that gets in its way."[74] Shortly before his assassination in February 1965, however, Malcolm X's seemingly unyielding position underwent significant moderation as a result of his transformative pilgrimage to Mecca and his traumatic break with the Black Muslim organization. Seeking strong ties to Third-World liberation movements, his newly founded Organization of Afro-American Unity began to gravitate toward more integrationist language by emphasizing the importance of universal human rights and global justice.[75]

In spite of their considerable differences, King and Malcolm X gradually expanded their frame of reference from the national to the global stage. Both men stepped up their criticism of the moral and political leadership exerted by the United States around the world. A discerning observer of ideological Cold War dynamics in the Third World, Malcolm X unleashed his verbal broadsides against "the earth's number-one hypocrite" long before King dared to go public with his condemnation of the American war effort in Vietnam.[76] Once he had taken this step, however, the Baptist minister began to distance himself from liberal reformism without abandoning his Gandhian principles of nonviolence. Calling the United States the "greatest purveyor of violence in the world today," he accused the Johnson administration of testing its weapon arsenals on the peasants of Vietnam.[77] King's "revolution of values" envisioned a fundamental reconstruction of social relations on the global level. Deeply skeptical of Marxism-Leninism, the civil rights leader argued instead that revolutionary change on a global scale had to start with a profound reorientation of American foreign policy. Declaring his solidarity with "ordinary folks" in Southeast Asia, King considered his antiwar stance part of a worldwide ethical struggle against American neo-imperialism in the Third World. But his moral outrage did not stop with those war-related denouncements of his government. After condemning First-World countries for refusing to take a firmer stand against the apartheid regime in South Africa, King chastised multinational corporations for showing little regard for the well-being of people in the global South.[78]

By 1968, the status of the United States as the political and moral leader of the First World had come under severe attack not only by determined African-American Civil Rights activists and increasing numbers of Vietnam War protesters but also by a broad phalanx of antisystemic voices of a "New Left" that had sprung up across the First World. The political upheavals of this remarkable year seemed to bear out their radical prediction that the forces of the establishment were losing their grip on power. Social revolution in the West no longer seemed to be a utopian dream but a real possibility reflected on the ground by powerful left-wing movements. As 23-year-old radical student leader Daniel Cohn-Bendit put it, "Our objective is now to overthrow the regime."[79] The surprising Tet Offensive launched by the Vietcong in the waning days of January and the March massacre of hundreds of civilians in the Vietnamese hamlet of My Lai revealed not only the vulnerability and brutality of the American military juggernaut but also made a mockery of American democratic values.

The assassination of Martin Luther King in April 1968 triggered large-scale race riots in major American cities resulting in dozens of violent deaths, thousands of injuries, and considerable property damage. Three weeks after King's murder, students at Columbia University began their occupation of five university buildings that ended a week later with a brutal New York police offensive and the arrest of hundreds of youths. The assassination of Senator Robert Kennedy in June deepened young people's alienation from the "system" not only in the United States but throughout the First World. During the long summer, legions of disaffected students and striking workers pushed France to the brink of paralysis. The slogan "All Power to the Imagination" graced Parisian buildings, signaling the demonstrators' conscious intention to question deep-seated normative notions and images underpinning daily routines and commonsense social repertoires. Protesters in Italy, Spain, West Germany, Canada, Japan, and the United States followed the French example and disrupted "business as usual" for months. The tidal wave of youth and workers' protests spilled into the post-Stalinist Second World where Czechoslovakian students called for "socialism with a human face" and workers demanded self-management from the newly installed Communist Party leadership headed by the reform-minded Alexander Dubcek.[80] But the Prague Spring came to a traumatic end in August with the invasion of nearly half a million Soviet-bloc troops. This ruthless execution of the Brezhnev Doctrine was designed to send a clear message to the West that there was no place for ideological experimentation in the Second World.

The summer of 1968 also brought large-scale demonstrations to the Third World. In Mexico City, hundreds of thousands of students and workers marched peacefully chanting radical Che Guevara slogans when they were violently attacked by the police. Hundreds of protesters died in these clashes. Further to the North, the Democratic Party Convention in Chicago spawned a bloody spectacle when more than 20,000 law enforcement officers indiscriminately clubbed hundreds of street demonstrators in full view of television cameras. In September, scores of outraged feminist activists descended on Atlantic City to protest the commercial exploitation of female bodies at the Miss America pageant. Toward the end of this tumultuous year marking the end of his political career, President Lyndon Johnson offered his fellow citizens a sobering assessment: "Americans, looking back on 1968, may be more inclined to ask God's mercy and guidance than to offer him thanks for his blessings."[81]

No doubt, 1968 and its aftermath saw the substantial expansion of traditional social movement activity to students, feminists, ethnic minorities, religious minorities, gays and lesbians, environmentalists, indigenous people, poor people, animal rights activists, and other groups claiming marginalization or discrimination. Academics and journalists began to refer to these collectivities and their associated ideational orientations as the "new social movements" and the "new ideologies."[82] Pervading the First-World political discourse by the late 1970s, these new political ideas were said to fan the flames of a left-wing "cultural revolution" that shattered the illusion of a consensual community of values. But what, exactly, was new about these social movements and their ideas?

Some observers point to a left-leaning humanism sensitive to cultural issues and sympathetic to unorthodox lifestyles. Unlike the prewar old left that embraced Marxist class-based categories, the New Left coalesced around ideological positions opposed to racial, political, economic, and patriarchal exploitation. It rejected centralized and bureaucratic models of political power while committing to forms of freedom and liberation that went far beyond purely material concerns. Expressing a fondness for participatory democracy anchored in ideals of individual agency, autonomy, and equality, the New Left emphasized direct political action and endorsed "spontaneous" desires and personal behaviors that ran afoul of established social norms and conventions.[83] There is little doubt that American and European activists who considered themselves part of the New Left did, indeed, subscribe to such forms of "humanist socialism" that were often shot through with pronounced libertarian or anarchist streaks. It is also fair to say that most members of the New Left fancied themselves the creators of a "radical culture."[84] But to call their ideological claims new runs the risk of ignoring similar positions previously held by the leading figures of French existentialism and the German-American Institute for Social Research during the 1930s and 1940s. The considerable ideational overlap that exists between these earlier currents and the New Left goes a long way in explaining the wild popularity of critical theorists like Herbert Marcuse with such radical student organizations as the Students for a Democratic Society in the United States or the *Sozialistischer Deutscher Studentenbund*.

If the New Left's embrace of cultural humanism falls short of supporting the thesis of the novelty of its associated political beliefs, then what about its focus on "identity" and "difference"? As American sociologist Craig Calhoun observes, however, identity-based demands for political accommodation and cultural recognition hardly qualify as new features of modern social movements. Similar claims stood at the center of nineteenth-century mobilizations on behalf of ethnic minorities, women, religious minorities, and industrial workers. It appears, therefore, that identity-based demands have been part of all major social movement activities during the last 200 years. According to Calhoun, "The proliferation of 'new social movements' is normal to modernity and not in need of special explanation...."[85] Even if we assume that Calhoun overstates his case to some extent, it is hard to quarrel with his contention that identity and difference make rather unconvincing candidates for ideological novelty.

It seems that we are left with only one more possibility, namely, the newness of the issues themselves. But, as we have seen in the case of the Civil Rights Movement, Martin Luther King's impassioned critique of racial inequality and discrimination has deep political and ideational roots in American history and culture. The same applies to the women's movement. For example, Betty Friedan's pathbreaking *The Feminist Mystique* (1963)—often hailed as the founding text of feminism—did not invent a new ideology *ex nihilo*. Her brilliant deconstruction of the pervasive patriarchal norm of the "happy housewife heroine" surely helped to politicize millions of mostly middle-class white American women and contributed significantly to the 1966 formation of the National Organization for Women (NOW). Still, as Friedan readily conceded, her work was built on the efforts of first-wave women's advocates like Elizabeth Cady Stanton, Susan B. Anthony, and Margaret Sanger.[86] By focusing their criticism on the gendered division between the "political" and the "private," Friedan and her fellow second-wave feminists did, however, expand the long-standing issue of women's oppression into previously uncharted territory. In this qualified sense, then, one can, in fact, speak of a new feminism. By the late 1970s, the ideological perspectives and political agendas of these second-wave feminists included traditional liberal demands for equal rights, socialist attacks on sex-based forms of economic inequality, and radical rejections of institutionalized heterosexuality and violence against women.

The same logic applies to the new environmentalism of the 1960s and 1970s that eventually broadened into various philosophical schools ranging from reform-minded conservationism to radical "deep ecology" and "eco-socialism."[87] Contrary to the myth still propagated in some quarters today, Rachel Carson's runaway 1962 best seller *Silent Spring* did not invent from scratch a novel set of ideological claims geared toward the protection of the environment. Instead, the author advances her main arguments by consciously drawing on the cumulative insights of a long line of biologists and conservationists that stretches back to the late nineteenth century. And yet, Carson's luminous indictment of the devastating effects of synthetic pesticides and insecticides on human health and the planet's biosphere did much to inspire a young generation of ecological activists. Redoubling their predecessors' efforts, they responded to Carson's challenge of developing imaginative new approaches "to the problem of sharing our earth with other creatures. . . . "[88]

Does this mean that the novelty of the new social movements and their political ideas consists of little more than updating old issues, reassembling various ideas, and expanding familiar concerns into new directions? Not quite, for it is possible to identify at least two entirely new dimensions. Let us start with the youth factor. Representing the heart and soul of the 1960s movements, students and young people coined the appropriate slogan, "Don't trust anybody over thirty!" The unprecedented representation of this age group in social movements cannot be explained solely as the inevitable effect of the postwar baby boom. In addition, the postwar socioeconomic stability celebrated by Bell and his colleagues made secondary and higher education a realistic and affordable option for increasing numbers of young people. Between 1960 and 1980, university enrollment in the United States and most European countries tripled and quadrupled.[89] The emerging youth culture expressed its antiestablishment sentiments in film, music, fashion, sexual attitudes, and, of course, in its passionate embrace of radical left-wing political ideas. Intense intergenerational tensions only stoked the passions of young people. As Eric Hobsbawm has emphasized, the novelty of the 1960s youth culture was epitomized in the new status of the adolescent as a self-conscious actor, increasingly recognized as an independent adult by the political system and by the captains of advanced industrial capitalism eager to expand the market for their consumer goods.[90]

The other genuine novelty of the "new ideologies" relates to their broad reach beyond the national and regional boundaries of the three-world order. Their global appeal was perhaps most clearly demonstrated in the worldwide eruption of nearly 200 major student demonstrations from 1968 to 1970.[91] Many observers began to realize that any attempt to make sense of these social movements exclusively within a national framework was bound to miss the global interconnectedness of these ideas and their worldwide political impact. As George Katsiaficas points out, "The global oppositional forces converged in a pattern of mutual amplification: 'The whole world was watching,' and with each act of the unfolding drama, whole new strata of social forces entered the arena of history, until finally a global contest was created."[92] Even some of the former end-of-ideology warriors began to change their views. Edward Shils, for example, conceded that "The turbulence of student radicalism now has the appearance of being worldwide.... [T]here is a spontaneous and unorganized, or at best an informal, unity of sympathy of the student movement which forms a bridge across national boundaries. In 1968, student radical movements seemed to be synchronized among different countries and uniform in content and technique."[93]

The new social movements' global appeal and their ideological uniformity corresponded to the rising global imaginary. The sensitivity shown by young people to the entire planet as an interconnected political stage made their ideas a globalizing force in its own right. Indeed, its genuine novelty lay not merely in their ability to revise and add to the political vision of the traditional left, but, more importantly, in its fledgling attempts to translate the global imaginary into a unified political agenda. At the same time, however, these "new ideologies" lacked the ideational density and sophistication of mature ideologies. We will explore in Chapter 5 how and when this maturation process actually took place.

4.6. In the Long Shadow of Hayekism: The New Right

As the New Left was taking its first tentative steps toward translating the ascending global imaginary into concrete political programs, the ideas and beliefs of the conventional right, too, underwent significant transformation as a result of the gradual demise of the Keynesian socioeconomic consensus. This process started in earnest in 1971 when private investors and governments around the world sought to unload most of their dollar reserves for a fixed gold value before a widely expected devaluation of the American currency. Unwilling to defend the dollar by raising interest rates and cutting spending—and risk a recession only a year before a national election—President Richard Nixon sacrificed the dollar–gold convertibility that constituted the cornerstone of the time-tested Bretton Woods system. The ensuing decline of the dollar delivered both the desired US trade surplus and a temporary drop in unemployment, thus contributing to Nixon's 1972 triumph at the polls by a margin wider than that of any of his predecessors in the twentieth century. But, as political economist Jeffry Frieden notes in his landmark history of global capitalism, Nixon's pursuit of domestic objectives at the expense of America's international obligations came at a high price: the dissolution of Keynes' Bretton Woods system that had successfully blended international economic integration with national independence and the market with the welfare state.[94] The sudden elimination of the exchange rate constraint allowed governments to supercharge their economies. Prices in the United States shot up by 40 percent between 1970 and 1973, and by a staggering 70 percent between 1972 and 1973 in

Britain. Inflation ran amok in the First World—an ominous development that spiraled totally out of control when the Organization of Petroleum Exporting Countries (OPEC) quadrupled its oil prices in the aftermath of the 1973 Yom Kippur War between Israel and its Arab neighbors.[95]

Unable to cope with the economic fallout of the Oil Shock, the industrial world plunged into its severest recession since the 1930s. The Keynesian model of countercyclical measures was rendered powerless by what US economist Paul Samuelson christened "stagflation"—the simultaneous occurrence of high inflation and rising unemployment. By the end of 1974, the American stock market had shed about half of its 1972 value. Industrial output in the First World had fallen by more than 10 percent, and the unemployment rate had exploded to levels deemed unacceptable by financial experts accustomed to decades of economic stability and growth.[96] Another round of OPEC oil price boosts in 1979 sounded the final death knell to the Golden Age of managed capitalism. Increasingly unwilling to sustain their costly social services in times of enduring economic crisis, governments began to listen closely to previously marginalized supply-side economists like Milton Friedman and his colleagues of the "Chicago School" who called for drastic anti-inflationary measures and rigid fiscal discipline, even at the risk of driving up unemployment.

The point of no return came in the fall of 1979 when incoming US Federal Reserve Chair Paul Volcker attacked inflation by raising interest rates to nearly 20 percent and kept them high for almost three years. Other industrialized nations had little choice but fall in line. Some, like Britain under Margaret Thatcher's incoming Conservative government, did so enthusiastically. By the mid-1980s, inflation had been brought under control in most Western countries, but only at the cost of keeping unemployment at elevated levels. Moreover, budget deficits were ballooning as a result of increased military spending and new supply-side policies of austerity that included deep cuts in top-tax rates; the reduction of welfare programs; the curbing of trade-union power; the privatization of state-owned enterprises; the deregulation of the economy; the liberalization of trade; the reduction of government controls on cross-border investment; and the regional and global integration of national economies. The nearly universal adoption of at least some parts of this comprehensive public policy package in the First World reflected the growing power of a broad set of ideological claims centered on this D[regulation]-L[iberalization]-P[rivatization] agenda. By the 1980s, it became generally known as "neoliberalism," or, after its most prominent political proponents, "Thatcherism" and "Reaganism."[97]

This ideational D-L-P cluster formed the seed out of which the new ideology of market globalism would grow to maturity in the 1990s. Its most influential architects were the Austro-British economist and social philosopher Friedrich August Hayek and his American protégé Milton Friedman. A determined but rather obscure critic of Keynesian economic theory during his tenure as professor of economics at the London School of Economics from 1931 to 1950, Hayek achieved instant fame in 1944 with the publication of his trenchant critique of socialist collectivism, *The Road to Serfdom*. A smashing best seller in the United States and Britain, the book anticipated the First World's postwar turn toward the welfare state. The main objective of Hayek's polemic was to warn its readership against the "danger of totalitarianism raised by central planning." According to the author, even such laudable economic goals as the reduction of unemployment cannot justify the government's subversion of the "spontaneous social order" generated by competing individuals who pursue their own vision of the good in a free-market economy. As the author puts it, "[I]ndividual freedom cannot be reconciled with the supremacy of one single purpose to which the whole society must be entirely and permanently subordinated." For Hayek, economic freedom is not a secondary principle subordinated to political liberty and confined to the narrow sphere of material production, but a profoundly political and moral force that shapes all other aspects of a free and open society. Thus, he arrives at his central ideological claim: "Freedom to order our own conduct in the sphere where material circumstances force a choice upon us, and responsibility for the arrangement of our own life according to our own conscience, is the air in which alone moral sense grows and in which moral values are daily re-created in the free decision of the individual."[98]

Hayek then proceeds to subsume communism, socialism, Nazism, fascism, and even social democracy under his master category of "collectivism." In his view, all of these ideologies share the same totalitarian impulse to embrace central economic planning. Concepts like the "common good," "social justice," or the "welfare state" are nothing but a "hodgepodge of ill-assembled and often inconsistent ideas" serving as a convenient mask for organized group interests. They provide ideological legitimacy for collectivists of all kinds who limit the economic freedom of the individual entrepreneur and thus undermine political liberty in general. A great believer in the free market's spontaneous ability to function as a self-regulating and knowledge-generating engine of human freedom and ingenuity, Hayek considers most forms of state intervention in the economy as ominous milestones on the "road to serfdom" leading to new forms of government-engineered despotism.[99] Still, as he makes abundantly clear both in *The Road to Serfdom* and in his more philosophical later studies, the "dogmatic laissez-faire attitude" of classical liberals does not represent an acceptable solution. In fact, he insists that the "general principles of a liberal order" can only be realized by "purging traditional liberal theory of certain accidental accretions" and by "facing up to some real problems which an oversimplified liberalism has shirked."[100]

Consequently, Hayek assigns to the state the crucial task of designing and safeguarding a legal system that would "preserve competition and make it operate as beneficially as possible." His core concept of liberty— decontested negatively as a condition "in which a man is not subject to coercion by the arbitrary will of another or others"—becomes linked to the notion of "legality."[101] In turn, Hayek defines the "rule of law" as the "known rules of the game" according to which the "individual is free to pursue his personal ends and desires, certain that the powers of government will not be used deliberately to frustrate his efforts."[102] As one of his sympathetic biographers has suggested, Hayek's preferred social order is not necessarily one in which the state has been shrunk to insignificance, but one where governments maximize competition, support economic competition and private property, and provide for the free exchange of goods and services on the basis of voluntary contracts impartially enforced by law.[103]

Its attempted revival of liberal economic ideals without endorsing nineteenth-century laissez-faire conceptions makes Hayekism difficult to categorize.[104] In fact, what provides it with such a suitable platform for the evolution of market globalism is its peculiar mixture of liberal and conservative ideological claims. Some commentators have referred to this ideational eclecticism as "libertarianism"—a label for which Hayek showed very little enthusiasm. An enthusiastic proponent of the power of ideas in history who thought of himself as a "liberal," the Nobel-Prize-winning economist nonetheless strays time and again into conservative territory by emphasizing the limits of human knowledge and the pivotal role of ignorance in public affairs. Clearly at odds with the rationalist constructivism of the Enlightenment tradition, Hayek's reactive attitude of confining the role of reason to the evaluation of existing social practices clearly smacks of conservatism: "Human reason can neither predict nor deliberately shape its own future. Its advances consist in finding where it has been wrong."[105] The Austrian thinker also betrays a clear conservative preference for social change occurring slowly in accordance with the existing traditions of Western societies. Indeed, he considers the "spontaneous order" emerging from free economic activity a natural development while criticizing public policies based on "rational design."[106] Finally, he tempers his spirited defense of negative liberty and individual economic entrepreneurship with a good dose of conservative elitism. As Michael Freeden observes, Hayek's idea of progress is "conceptually tied to inequality, being spurred on by those who moved fastest, and, although accompanied by a process of catching up by the rest, it would be undermined by undue leveling and redistribution." Such elitism, Freeden insists, "is not to be found in the prominent types of modern liberalism."[107]

But the incorporation of conservative concepts into Hayekism does not represent the only case of creative conceptual cannibalism. Surprisingly, there is strong evidence for the conscious absorption of some socialist elements. In an essay addressed to the members of the Mont Pelerin Society (MPS)—an anticollectivist, free-market think tank Hayek founded in 1947 together with Milton Friedman, Walter Eucken, Jacques Rueff, and other like-minded individuals—he explicitly compares the intellectual task of the newly established organization to that of avant-garde socialist "think tanks" like the British Fabian Society at the turn of the century.[108] Admiring their "intense intellectual effort" to draw up a theoretical program of social development that would gain the support of powerful political and social elites, Hayek suggests that his organization ought to imitate the socialists' attempt to paint a compelling "picture of a future at which they were aiming, and a set of general principles to decisions on particular issues." However, his unexpected fascination with socialism extends from mere strategic considerations to issues of ideological substance as well. In a strikingly militant passage, he praises socialists for their "courage to be utopian," adding that the MPS should formulate the mirror image of a "liberal utopia" based on the principles of free trade, individualism, and economic freedom. The popularity of the mixed economy and the welfare state would ultimately be undermined by a utopian "appeal to imagination" that gave no thought whatsoever to its feasibility in the near future. Indeed, Hayek's utopian proclivities are hardly indistinguishable from those of the French student protestors who, in 1968, proclaimed their faith in the "power of imagination." In fact, the Austrian economist displays the same militant spirit by insisting that the main purpose of the MPS was "to kindle an interest in—an understanding of—the great principles of social organization of the conditions of individual liberty as we have not known it in our life-time . . . We must raise and train an army of fighters for freedom."[109]

Most importantly, Hayekism shares with the "new ideologies" of the left a remarkable sensitivity to the rising global imaginary. Already in *The Road to Serfdom*, the author shows considerable fondness for the universalistic "idea of the world at last finding peace through the absorption of the separate states in large federated groups and ultimately perhaps in one single federation. . . ."[110] After the creation of the MPS, Hayek moved from a fairly conventional liberal sympathy for regional cooperation and internationalism to a conceptual framework centered on the entire planet as interconnected space for intellectuals engaged in the spread of liberty and free markets around the world. An ideological movement without borders, the MPS issued a "Statement of Aims" which called on "liberals around the world" to work for the creation of an "international order conducive to the safeguarding of peace and liberty, and permitting the establishment of harmonious international economic relations."[111] Committed to the vision of a single, self-regulating global free market, Hayek suggests that modern capitalism requires the weakening of traditional bonds of solidarity—a "revolution in consciousness" hostile to the anachronistic concepts of "foreigners" and "strangers." Elaborating on this theme, the aging economist drew up plans for the denationalization of money that would allow people around the world to choose the most stable currency as the global means of exchange.[112]

The global orientation of Hayekism and its ingenious ideological mixture contributed greatly to its increasing popularity in the 1970s and 1980s. Still, its growing political influence cannot be explained exclusively in terms of its ideational appeal or the global influence of the MPS. Providing a crucial opening for Hayekism, the stagflation of the 1970s seemed to confirm the susceptibility of Western mixed economies to those structural problems its opponents had described decades earlier. Indeed, sudden crises in the political and economic environment open up opportunities for new ideas to penetrate the dominant social imaginary. New ideologies never develop in isolation from the political arena. As Monica Prasad notes in her analysis of the rise of neoliberalism in the First World, the policy implementation of ideological commitments is significantly constrained by political factors such as entrepreneurial politicians in search of issues that resonate with public opinion. But even institutionalist critics of ideational causation like Prasad concede that the ideological claims formulated by neoliberals like Hayek and Friedman clearly provided inspiration and guidance to Thatcherism and Reaganism.[113] No doubt, the national context still played an important role. Deregulatory measures were at the heart of American neoliberalism, whereas privatization initiatives like the sale of Telecom and public housing units quickly rose to the top of Prime Minister Thatcher's agenda. In both the United States and the UK, however, the development of the free market and the emasculation of trade unions stood at the center of New Right thinking. In both countries, newly formed alliances between business leaders and previously marginalized right-wing academics carefully copied Hayek's "socialist" strategy of encouraging well-endowed think tanks to persuade political elites to abandon welfarism. This was not an easy task given that even traditional conservatives like Richard Nixon had proudly proclaimed their Keynesian sympathies as recently as the early 1970s. Political standard bearers of the New Right like Margaret Thatcher and Ronald Reagan would have never imbibed Hayekian ideas without the expanding activities of well-endowed think tanks such as the Institute of Economic Affairs, the Centre for Policy Studies, the Hoover Institution, the Heritage Foundation, the American Enterprise Institute, or the Cato Institute. These corporate-funded institutions proliferated in the First World during the 1970s. Mobilizing the advertising industry and educational business associations, they promoted the peculiar Hayekian combination of global free-market liberalism, elitist conservatism, and militant socialist utopianism variously known as "neoliberalism," "neoconservatism," or "free-market fundamentalism."[114]

These designations invite the conclusion that Hayekism recharged and rearranged various ideas of the political right for the post-Keynesian First World of the 1980s. The leading voices of the New Right expressed enthusiasm for free markets, a clear preference for traditional values over rationalist designs, and an aggressive stance against communism reflected in a muscular foreign policy. As we shall see, even "neoconservatives" like Irving Kristol and Norman Podhoretz who regarded themselves as the defenders of traditional family values threatened by runaway consumerism offered at least "two cheers" for Hayekian turbo-capitalism. Indeed, they called on business to organize, "think politically," and save Western civilization and the cause of freedom.[115] But it took the dissolution of the three-world order for these various neoisms of the New Right to mature into the comprehensive ideology of market globalism.

5

Market Globalism and Justice Globalism in the Roaring Nineties

For now, I like the feeling of being home in a lot of places. I like the feeling that there are lots of places where I belong, that are familiar.... That's kind of nice. That you belong all over the world rather than a little part. You're proud of the world, not just of your neighborhood. Proud to be part of it. It's not like you're saying, "Go Bronx." It's "Go World."

Esther Dyson, CEO, Internet Corp.
for Assigned Names and Numbers (2000)

Today we must embrace the inexorable logic of globalization—that everything from the strength of our economy to the safety of our cities, to the health of our people, depends on events not only within our borders, but half a world away.

Bill Clinton (1999)

I believe that it is particularly important for both journalists, who are charged with explaining the world, and strategists, who are responsible for shaping it, to think like globalists.

Thomas L. Friedman (1999)

The priority task is to counterpose a deepening process of global democracy and of planetary-scale cultural change to worldwide neoliberal disorder.

Candido Grzybowski, World Social
Forum Cofounder (1995)

5.1. The Demise of the Second World: The End of History?

For many years following the final break between Moscow and Beijing in 1960, the Second World wore two principal ideological faces: Chinese communism according to Chairman Mao Zedong and the post-Stalinist versions of Russian communism adopted by the Soviet leaders Nikita Khrushchev, Leonid Brezhnev, Yuri Andropov, and Konstantin Chernenko. By the mid-1970s, the decline of American influence in the wake of Vietnam and Watergate and the crisis of the modern European welfare state fueled a growing sense that the communist world, despite its internal tensions, was poised to claim victory in the ideological war for hearts and minds in the global South. Ho Chi Minh's armies had just forced the most powerful military force on the planet to retreat. The former Portuguese colonies in sub-Saharan Africa appeared to have been captured by communist regimes. In 1979, the USSR invaded Afghanistan to prevent the fall of the newly established socialist People's Democratic Republic. Latin America, too, witnessed the installation of yet another revolutionary Marxist-Leninist regime in Nicaragua with close ties to Cuba and the Soviet Union. Even in the heart of Europe, charismatic Euro-communists offered a new vision for the democratic Left while the radical members of the Italian Red Brigades and the German Baader-Meinhof Gang preferred to spread their ideological message through shocking acts of violence and assassination.

Oddly enough, the first signs of the profound crisis that would ultimately overwhelm the Second World appeared during the seemingly triumphant 1970s. It was in this decade that the orthodox Stalinist and Maoist assumption of cultivating socialism in one country—while fomenting revolution in developing world—became ideologically unsustainable. Let us take, for example, the routine meeting of the Central Committee of the Chinese Communist Party (CCP) convened in Beijing in December 1978. Today, students of political history remember this Third Plenary Session as the first in a series of high-level CCP gatherings that transformed China's closed command economy into an open-door "socialist market economy with Chinese characteristics." In less than two decades, even state-owned enterprises would be restructured into capitalist shareholding companies chasing business opportunities around the world. Indeed, the gradual opening of China's national economic space to the capitalist First World appeared to be the central story in an astonishing process of reform that produced over thirty years of staggering annual GDP growth rates of nearly 10 percent, soaring trade surpluses, and rising living standards for large portions of the population.[1] But the modernization of the country through global economic integration and market reforms required more than just economic decision-making. First and foremost, the opening of China depended on shedding an ideological straitjacket that allowed the centralized state to run the economy strictly according to the Chairman's whims. At the time of his death in 1976, many ordinary Chinese had already paid the ultimate price for submitting to Mao's vision. Devastating famines had followed the Great Leap Forward in the 1950s and the political persecutions of the Great Proletarian Cultural Revolution in the late 1960s had killed or incarcerated millions. With the regime's crimes of the past still casting dark shadows in the 1970s, the pragmatic reorientation of China toward the market and the rest of the world was impossible without a fundamental ideological reformulation of orthodox "Mao Zedong Thought." As we know today from recently released documents, an epic battle of ideas preceded the crucial period of reformist policymaking between 1978 and 1992.[2]

The aging Deng Xiaoping emerged as the unlikely architect of the restructured ideological edifice. A tough political survivor who had been stripped of influential party posts twice during the Cultural Revolution on charges of being a "revisionist" and "capitalist roader," Deng took advantage of the period of political instability following the arrest of the ultra-Maoist Gang of Four shortly after the Great Leader's death. Engineering his full rehabilitation behind the scenes with the support of a pragmatic Old Guard that had lost much of its power during the Cultural Revolution, Deng moved cautiously but resolutely against his Maoist opponents. At the top of his list were the leaders of the dominant "Two Whatevers" faction, aptly named after a slogan attributed to Mao's handpicked successor Hua Guofeng: "We will resolutely uphold whatever policy decisions Chairman Mao made, and unswervingly follow whatever instructions Chairman Mao gave."[3] Determined to put an end to the old ways, Deng spearheaded a nationwide campaign to "emancipate the mind, unite, and look ahead." Just as Stalin had portrayed his version of socialism in one country as the essence of Leninism, Deng presented his revisionist ideas as a return to Maoism's "true meaning." At the core of his vision stood a four-character slogan the Great Leader had coined in 1942 for the Central Party School at Yan'an: *shi shi qiu shi*—"seek truth from facts" or, more fully, "arrive at truth by verifying the facts."[4]

Linking this rather general and ambiguous statement to the findings of a critical report on the weaknesses of the Chinese economy authored by the new revisionist Head of the Chinese Academy of Sciences, Deng proceeded to rally the Old Guard behind his plan to flood the Party press with "Maoist" arguments for economic and political reform. Indeed, the sly capitalist roader carefully prefaced his version of Maoism with the solemn pledge to defend to the death what he considered to be the "three essences" of Mao Zedong Thought: truth verified by facts, full trust in the people, and the promotion of socialist democracy. Some commentators have argued that Deng deliberately designed his strategy to de-ideologize China by portraying his drive toward a capitalist economy as being beyond politics.[5] In spite of its obvious pragmatic undertones, however, Dengism was hardly devoid of ideology. Rather, it represented a genuine search for an alternative model of state-socialism-plus-market to be evaluated primarily in terms of measurable economic progress and political stability. Within months, the rising leader's Mind Emancipation Campaign produced the desired results, thus ensconcing Dengism as the ideological umbrella under which the comprehensive economic reform package was ultimately endorsed at the Third Plenary Session. The Party's main resolutions included the abandonment of Mao's doctrine of "continual class struggle" in favor of economic construction and modernization "based on facts"; the gradual devolution of economic and political power to local and regional bodies without compromising the CCP's principle of democratic centralism; and the gradual, state-controlled opening up to the world for the express purpose of "learning advanced management and new technologies from foreign countries."[6] The communist state remained the crucial institution with the sole power to legalize new forms of enterprise, revise the way in which prices were set, supervise imports and foreign direct investment, and permit local firms to export.[7]

Having successfully invoked the doctrinal authority of the late Chairman, Deng moved quickly to sweep away what remained of the crumbling Two Whatevers faction, demoting Hua Guofeng to increasingly insignificant posts. The transformation of Mao Zedong Thought into Deng Xiaoping Theory reflected the disillusionment of the Old Guard with an anachronistic ideology unable to cope with intensifying global interdependence, enduring economic stagnation, and the decline of the Party's political legitimacy. Deng's ideological reorientation, aimed at the rehabilitation of the CCP by means of economic restructuring and political reform, appeared to work for more than a decade. But the Tiananmen protests of 1989 brought to the fore the fundamental contradiction at the core of Dengism: how can the Party extend market reforms without jeopardizing its hold on political power? The government's response to

Tiananmen was severe political repression, followed by a radical backlash that lasted until 1992. The regime managed to avoid a Soviet-style collapse of the political system, but failed to remove the underlying contradiction. By the time of Deng's death in 1997, the CCP's quest for political legitimacy by means of global economic integration had led to the adoption of what David Harvey calls "neoliberalism with Chinese characteristics"—an unstable mixture of market-globalist claims with the authoritarian-nationalist imperatives of the centralized one-party state.[8]

A careful consideration of the ideological dynamics in post-Mao China suggests, therefore, that the demise of the Second World did not simply appear *ex nihilo* in the Soviet Union with the rise of Mikhail Gorbachev. Rather, the new Secretary General's ideological reformulation of Russian communism in terms of *perestroika* (economic and political restructuring) and *glasnost* (openness about public affairs in every sphere of life) followed closely the example set by Deng and his revisionist comrades. In fact, the Soviet leader conceded in his memoirs that his ideas "were similar to Deng Xiaoping's reform methods in China."[9]

Like Mao's China, the Soviet Union under Andropov and Chernenko was overwhelmed by systemic problems of economic stagnation, perennial shortages of essential consumer goods, staggering waste, bureaucratic inefficiency, and the Party's declining political legitimacy. This crisis reached new heights by the time Gorbachev took over the reins of power from the geriatric CPSU elites. Like Deng, the energetic new Soviet leader launched his plan for the structural reorganization of the economy at a routine Plenary Session in 1985 which paved the way for the historic adoption of the *perestroika* policies at the Twenty-Seventh Party Congress in 1986. Following the Chinese example, Gorbachev engaged in a process of ideological reformulation that promised Soviet citizens the "acceleration of scientific, technological, and economic progress" by means of returning to the "core characteristics" of true Marxism-Leninism: "The essence of *perestroika* lies in the fact that *it unites socialism with democracy* and revives the Leninist concept of socialist construction both in theory and in practice."[10]

Unlike their Chinese counterparts, however, Gorbachev and his reformist faction were far less in control of the pace and extent of *perestroika* since its feasibility remained much more bound to the external dynamics of the Cold War. Most importantly, the accelerating arms race with the United States and the disastrous war in Afghanistan against American-sponsored Islamist *mujahideen* devoured nearly 40 percent of the Soviet Union's entire national budget. Its sprawling military–industrial complex was unquestionably the main culprit respon-sible for rapidly dropping incomes and declining living standards. Hence, it had to be shrunk. It was, most likely, out of his deep recognition that "we can't go on living like this" that Gorbachev, formerly his Party's chief ideologist, preceded his reforms with a call for "New Political Thinking."[11]

Appearing in the subtitle of his international best seller, *Perestroika*, New Thinking referred not only to the theoretical basis of Russia's eco-nomic reforms. Convinced that history was entering into a global era where domestic politics and international affairs were inextricably linked, Gorbachev emphasized that both the Soviet Union and the whole world needed restructuring.[12] Anchored in the acknowledgment of "global interdependence," New Thinking became the indispensable prerequisite for the possible resolution of "global issues" that threatened people regardless of their national and regional loyalties: the escalating nuclear arms race, the destruction of the environment, the need for alterna-tive sources of energy, and the combating of poverty, hunger, and new diseases.[13] In a nutshell, Gorbachev's global vision rested squarely on the premise that humanity's very survival depended on people's ability to move beyond antiquated ideological preoccupations with class or nation: "The backbone of the new way of thinking is the recognition of the priority of human values.... We—all mankind—are in the same boat and we can sink or swim only together." Although he reaffirmed that every nation retained its right to choose its path of social development, the Soviet leader insisted that the time had come to develop a global model of "human security." At its core would be the superpowers' renouncement of their "imperialist desire" to reshape the world according to their own patterns: "That era has receded or, at least, is receding into the past." In the area of Soviet foreign policy, New Thinking received its most spec-tacular expression in the replacement of the old Brezhnev Doctrine with Gorbachev's assurances that the formerly dominated countries in Europe and the developing world were now free to forge their own destinies. The Soviet government promised to end its participation in the ideological struggle for their hearts and minds: "We have no intention whatsoever of converting everyone to Marxism.... [I]t is high time to recognize that the Third World nations have the right to be their own bosses."[14]

It is tempting to interpret, as some observers have done, Gorbachev's remarkable articulation of the rising global imaginary as a largely self-serving and propagandistic effort aimed at saving a crumbling Soviet Empire. According to this interpretation, New Thinking was but a ruse designed to dupe the United States into accepting a drastic arms reduction scheme that would allow Gorbachev to put the budget savings into his domestic *perestroika* reforms, thus restoring the "Evil Empire" to its former glory. No doubt, the combination of instrumental calculations of national interest and ideological maneuvering has made for good bedfellows throughout modern history. But in the transitional politics of late 1980s' Russia, it does not tell the whole story. Gorbachev's dogged pursuit of *perestroika* reflects, on a microcosmic level, the intensifying eruptions of the global within the national. Refusing to remain captive to his predecessor's Old Thinking that saw autarkic nations competing with each other in a zero-sum power game, the Soviet leader articulated his political goals in stark globalist terms. His revolution from above represented a concerted effort to move beyond the central claims of Stalin's socialism in one country: the doctrine of international class struggle, one-party rule, bureaucratic centralism, the command economy, Great Russian chauvinism, national security based on military advantage, and the political straightjacket of a "brotherly union" forced upon the non-Russian Soviet republics. For a long time, Gorbachev managed to convince himself and most of his inner circle that New Thinking could serve as the ideological framework for the renewal of Marxism-Leninism, or, at the very least, as a transition toward European social democracy. Ultimately, however, he recognized the limitations of translating the rising global imaginary into an ideological framework that wore the indelible imprints of a political belief system giving voice to the national that was gradually losing its rationale in a globalizing world. The following brief exchange between the Secretary General and the skeptical Politburo member Yegor Ligachev is symptomatic of Gorbachev's attention to global issues even at the risk of compromising Soviet power interests:

Ligachev: We don't reject universal human values, but you just can't throw out class interests.

Gorbachev: Yes, but I am speaking about the priority of universal human values. This doesn't mean that we are negating class, group, national and other interests. However, it is clear that they will become meaningless if we fail to join together to prevent nuclear war. What importance will interests be in this case, or even classes? Everything will go up in smoke....[15]

During his final years at the helm of the disintegrating Soviet state, in particular, Gorbachev bloodied his nose time and again in his stubborn attempts to break through what he referred to as the Party's "wall of hardened dogma." He also vastly underestimated the staying power of the national imaginary in Soviet republics suddenly confronted with the possibility of independence. Members of the old guard like the 1991 coup leaders General Dmitry Yazov and Vice President Gennady Yanayev as well as many pro-Russia radicals around Boris Yeltsin still viewed politics largely in the traditional way—through the prism of the national interests—whereas the beleaguered President built his political vision on the new reality of global interests. The ultimate success of Yeltsin's faction testifies to the fact that the rising global imaginary was a long way from overpowering national sentiments stirred up by domestic upheavals and the accelerating pace of globalization in the 1990s.

Moreover, Gorbachev found himself battling the same fundamental contradiction between reformism and political authoritarianism that exploded in Deng's face at Tiananmen Square. Unlike his less scrupulous Chinese comrade, however, Mikhail Sergeyevich stuck with his political reforms, hoping, as he put it dramatically for the last time in his televised 1991 Farewell Address to the Soviet Citizens, that postcommunist Russia would "become a major stronghold for the reorganization of modern civilization on the basis of peaceful democratic principles."[16] No doubt, there are significant differences separating the two towering figures presiding over the demise of the Second World. Yet, both men took the first steps toward articulating the rising global imaginary in concrete political terms. Deng settled on a market globalism that coexisted uncomfortably with the idea of "Chinese characteristics," while Gorbachev favored a justice globalism anchored in his conviction "that our country and the world need new thinking, a new global understanding, a new interpretation of the ideas of progress, humanism, and justice.... "[17]

Thus, the Cold War ended some forty-five years after Stalin and Truman first locked horns over the new geopolitical realities emerging from the defeat of German Nazism and Japanese militarism. The predictability of the Three World Order was giving way to a vaguely defined New World Order, most notable for the glaring absence of any serious countervailing forces to American power. This unique moment of "unipolarity," however, hardly translated into world harmony. Although the Iron Curtain had lifted in Europe, the planet remained divided along both cultural and economic lines as the prosperous Northern Hemisphere continued to dominate an impoverished global South. Nevertheless, the old ideological divisions of the Cold War appeared to be destined for the dustbin of history. Given the sudden and quite unexpected passing of communism, it was perhaps unavoidable that triumphant voices in the North began to peddle a new version of Daniel Bell's "end-of-ideology" thesis. In a seminal 1989 article he later expanded into a best-selling book, Francis Fukuyama, the then Deputy Director of the US State Department's policy-planning unit, proclaimed the "end of history"—defined in Hegelian-idealist terms as the "triumph of the West, of the Western *idea*." Given the "total exhaustion" of all systematic alternatives to Western liberalism, he argued, the logical end point of humanity's ideological evolution was nothing less than "the universalization of Western liberal democracy as the final form of human government."[18]

Fukuyama's triumphant vision of a de-ideologized world overlapped only partially with the arguments offered three decades earlier by the likes of Bell and Tingsten. While concurring with their assertion of the irrevocable demise of Marxist socialism, Fukuyama rejected their belief in the inexorable convergence between capitalism and socialism. In addition, he objected to Bell's view of free-market liberalism as antiquated nineteenth-century utopianism built on Enlightenment illusions of rationality and prosperity. Elated by the death of Marxism-Leninism, Fukuyama convinced himself and many others that the last barrier to the realization of the free-market model envisioned by Hayek and Friedman had been overcome. "Political and economic liberalism" was taking its rightful place as a universal doctrine on the *global* stage devoid of any competitors. His only regret was the prospect of history turning into a boring succession of mundane events such as the "endless solving of technological problems" and the "satisfaction of sophisticated consumer demands."[19]

In a series of essays and interviews published during the 1990s, Fukuyama expanded on his original vision, arguing that the spread of consumerism to all corners of the earth would prove to be both unstoppable and irreversible. Reflected in the globalizing nexus of free-market dynamics and powerful new technologies, norms and values anchored in the Western liberal tradition would ultimately underwrite the cultural makeup of the New World Order. As Hegel had predicted, the United States had taken over as the world's unchallenged leader; hence it was "inevitable that Americanization will accompany globalization." At the same time, however, he conceded that the "unabashed victory of economic and political liberalism" had so far only occurred in the realm of ideas or human consciousness while remaining "as yet incomplete in the real or material world."[20]

The implications of this admission were ambiguous. On the one hand, it seemed that the global spread of free-market liberalism was a historical necessity "determined by the progressive nature of scientific knowledge and its embodiment in technology." But on the other, it appeared that the material completion of history had to be spearheaded by the world's sole remaining superpower. In the end, Fukuyama leaned toward a translation of the rising global imaginary into ideological claims that endowed the universalization of "Western democracy" with absolute finality to which people could no longer pose viable alternatives. The inevitable "common marketization of international relations" left no room for ideological competitors like Islamism or nationalism. Political religions, according to Fukuyama, lacked universal significance, while the narrow nationalistic visions lacked a comprehensive agenda for the organization of socioeconomic relations on a global scale.[21] By the end of the Roaring Nineties, Fukuyama had taken his place as an influential ideologue—in the non-pejorative sense—among a growing chorus of social elites around the world whose articulation of the rising global imaginary revolved around the new buzzword "globalization." But what, exactly, did they mean by globalization?

5.2. The "Objectivity" of Globalization

Although the origin of the term can be traced back to the early 1960s, it was not until the 1980s and 1990s that it emerged as a pivotal signifier in public debates relating to the expansion and intensification of social relations across world-space and world-time. As Nayan Chanda observes, "globalization" surfaced as a buzzword because the tangibility and visibility of globally interrelated life called for a single word naming this interconnectedness. His analysis of some 8,000 newspapers, magazines, and reports worldwide attests to the tremendous acceleration of the frequency with which "globalization" was used. From a mere 2 in 1981, the number of items mentioning the term grew to 57,235 in 2001.[22] The comet-like appearance and proliferation of the concept not only reflected the "factual" compression of time and space but also testified to the thickening of a global consciousness—the global imaginary—whose intuitions of the world as a single place were spread through the Herculean labors of various ideological codifiers. Most of these earliest coiners of "globalization" were academics, business elites, and public figures linking the term to material and empirical processes of growing economic and technological interdependence.[23] As we discussed, Mikhail Gorbachev appears to have been one of the first major political leaders who connected the necessity for a new political thinking to globalization, understood as "objective processes [that] are making our complex and diverse world more and more interrelated and interdependent."[24] His assumption that these powerful new dynamics "out there" called for conceptual readjustments "in here" makes sense in the context of dominant scientific narratives that explained social change in terms of measurable effects produced by material forces.

Like his contemporaries all over the world, Gorbachev was particularly impressed with the scope and accelerated pace of technological innovation during the 1980s and 1990s. Scores of academic books and articles written during these two decades connect globalization to novel information and communication technologies (ICTs), such as electronic mass media (Cable TV, Interactive TV, Digital TV, Direct Broadcast Satellite systems), computers and digital consumer electronics (PCs, the Internet and the World Wide Web, DVDs, laser printers), and telephone and satellite technologies (broadband networks, wireless telephone and data services, pagers, advanced fax machines, personal digital assistants, videoconferencing). Related technologies hailed as major contributors to globalization included vastly improved optical fibers, commercial silicon microchips whose capacities doubled every eighteen months, standardized bar codes, networked cash machines, and faster and more efficient means of transportation like the containerization of cargo that allowed for the smooth transference of consumer goods from ship to truck or train. As we discussed in Chapter 4, many of these innovations originated in the military–industrial sector, or, at the very least, received further refinement as a result of war-related applications. The spectacular deployment of martial technologies by the Coalition Forces during the 1991 Gulf War, for example, raised the public's awareness of an ongoing "Revolution in Military Affairs" (RMA). Pentagon officials attributed the fundamentally altered conduct of military operations to such devices as handheld global positioning systems (GPS) that interacted with radar-guided long-range precision missiles and "smart bombs."[25] A few years later, GIS technology found its way into luxury cars equipped with computer-assisted navigation devices that guided drivers through the sprawling suburbs of the world's multiplying megacities.

Another obvious playground for the digital revolution was the vastly expanded commercial space of free-market capitalism. ICTs provided the technical means for what came to be known as the "globalization of markets." This influential association of terms appeared for the first time in 1983 in the title of a seminal article penned by a prominent Harvard marketing professor for the *Harvard Business Review*.[26] The tremendous impact of Theodore Levitt's essay is perhaps best illustrated by the fact that American globalization guru Thomas Friedman adopted one of its subheadings as the title for his 2005 runaway best seller, *The World Is Flat*.[27] Levitt's arguments laid the foundation for the dominant decontestation of globalization as a techno-economic process destined to give birth to a "global market for standardized consumer products on a previously unimagined scale of magnitude." But his supposedly neutral description of empirical trends was inseparable from his ideological prescriptions. For example, he insisted that multinational companies had to transform themselves into global corporations capable of operating in a more cost-effective way by standardizing their products. The necessary elimination of costly adjustments to various national markets depended on the swift adoption of a "global approach," that is, the willingness of CEOs to think and act "as if the world were one large market—ignoring superficial regional and national differences... It [the global corporation] sells the same things in the same way everywhere."[28] Levitt's article spawned hundreds of similar pieces convincing the world's leading companies to "go global." The advertising industry, in particular, set about creating "global brands" by means of global commercial campaigns. One of these early examples for the new practice of attaching the words "world" and "global" to every conceivable commodity or service is the British Airways' slogan "the world's favorite airline" unleashed on "global customers" by the advertising giant Saatchi and Saatchi whose founder had been one of Ted Levitt's most fervent disciples.[29] We will return to an extended analysis of market globalism in Section 5.3; but for now let us make a mental note of the discursive link between globalization and the notion of standardized global markets fueled by the ICT revolution.

Although Levitt's new market thinking and Gorbachev's new political thinking emerged in very different social and geographical contexts, they shared a common understanding of globalization as an objective process forcing people to expand their mental-geographical horizons. My emphasis on the ideological constitution of globalization, however, is not meant to suggest that the compression of time and space did not manifest itself in "objective" ways. After all, it is hard to quarrel with the factuality of increased flows of capital and technology in the 1980s and 1990s that stimulated worldwide exchanges of goods and services. There occurred, indeed, an explosion of the total value of world trade from $57 billion in 1947 to an astonishing $6 trillion in the late 1990s. Total foreign direct investment shot up to nearly $250 billion in the mid-1990s. Taking advantage of the demise of the Second World, markets of all sorts extended their reach around the globe. Huge transnational corporations (TNCs), powerful international economic institutions, and large regional trading systems like the European Union or NAFTA emerged as the major building blocs of what came to be known as the "New Economy." The globalization of trade went hand in hand with the liberalization of financial transactions. Its key components included the deregulation of interest rates, the removal of credit controls, and the privatization of government-owned banks and financial institutions. The globalization of financial trading allowed for increased mobility among different segments of the financial industry, with fewer restrictions on capital flows and greater global investment opportunities. The world's major stock markets chased each other around the clock. After the temporary hiccup caused by Wall Street's crash in October 1987, the new global financial infrastructure accelerated in the late 1980s with the gradual deregulation of capital and securities markets in Europe, the Americas, East Asia, Australia, and New Zealand. Soon thereafter, Southeast Asian countries, India, and several African nations followed suit, driving the number of financial transactions to levels unimaginable only a decade earlier.

Similarly, the number of TNCs skyrocketed from 7,000 in 1970 to nearly 50,000 in 2000. Enterprises like General Motors, Wal-Mart, Exxon-Mobil, Mitsubishi, and Siemens belonged to the 200 largest TNCs accounting for over half of the world's industrial output. Rivaling nation-states in their economic power, these corporations controlled much of the world's investment capital, technology, and access to international markets. During the 1990s, transnational companies consolidated their operations in an increasingly deregulated global labor market. The availability of cheap labor, resources, and favorable production conditions in the global South enhanced corporate mobility and profitability. Accounting for over 70 percent of world trade, TNCs boosted their foreign direct investments by ~15 percent annually during the 1990s. Their ability to disperse manufacturing processes into discrete phases carried out in many different locations around the world reflected a seismic shift toward global production. Such transnational production networks allowed companies like Wal-Mart, General Motors, and Volkswagen to produce, distribute, and market their products on a global scale while bypassing nationally based trade unions and other workers' organizations. Nike, for example, subcontracted all of its goods production to 75,000 workers in China, South Korea, Malaysia, Taiwan, and Thailand. In the course of the Roaring Nineties, therefore, the buzzword "globalization" became associated with a flood of related terms such as "outsourcing" and "offshore production."

Naturally, the dominant discourse of globalization as a set of objective techno-economic processes spilled into the political arena where it provoked speculation that state sovereignty was being weakened by global economic integration, the growing impact of inter- and nongovernmental organizations, and the new possibilities for regional and global governance. Was the rapid deterritorialization of politics and law the inevitable by-product of ever-increasing flows of capital, people, and technology across national borders? Were regional and global forms of governance like the "United States of Europe" or the "world-state" inevitable? Was the modern nation-state, as one hyperglobalist put it, a "dinosaur waiting to die"? Obviously, the vigor and passion with which these questions were discussed around the world attested to the destabilization of a national imaginary based on the arbitrary division of the globe into "national" and "foreign" spaces. Captivated by a powerful narrative that emphasized the objective dimensions of globalization, commentators on both ends of the political spectrum suggested that politics was being rendered impotent by an unstoppable techno-economic juggernaut freed of the conceptual and geographical chains of the past. Following in Hayek's ideational footsteps, market globalists thrived in this atmosphere, assigning to economic exchange an inner logic superior to politics and projecting an image of a "borderless world" in which governments ought to serve as superconductors for global capitalism.[30]

Largely missing in this avalanche of popular and academic depictions of globalization as an objective set of techno-economic processes was the recognition of how this deeply ideological articulation of the rising global imaginary supported the material instantiation of the phenomenon itself.[31] Just as technology and markets contributed to the compression of time and space, so did particular ideas and narratives about globalization shape the material designs for the "global marketplace." Still, we must bear in mind that the ICT revolution was never fated to interlink with global markets in ways that forced people everywhere to adapt to what Ted Levitt reified as the "new commercial reality." Neither was the seamless globality of cyberspace—mediated by the World Wide Web—destined to serve as the proliferating nervous system of the global marketplace. The commercialization of the Internet and the incredible speed with which it became a medium for global commerce depended not just on the expansion of existing technological infrastructure but also on the ideological-metaphorical production of the "global Internet economy."[32] Worldwide techno-economic networks grew largely in a manner and a direction described *and* prescribed by influential market globalists. To be sure, the objectification of globalization as a set of empirical processes open to quantitative manipulation has its intellectual virtues—as long as we acknowledge the lived interconnectedness of materiality and discursive practices. Such an *analytical* distinction between globalization as an objective phenomenon and globalism as an ideology actually helps draw attention to globalization's *discursive* dimension. The existence of these narratives suggests that globalization is not merely an objective process but also a plethora of stories and metaphors—told, retold, and performed countless times—that define, describe, and analyze that very process. Disseminating these competing accounts of globalization, various social groups seek to endow their core concepts with norms, values, and meanings that not only legitimate and advance their interests but also shape the personal and collective identities of billions of people. In the Roaring Nineties, market globalism circulated the globe as the dominant story of an evolving world order said to relate less and less to the old meanings associated with the national imaginary.[33]

5.3. The Morphology of Market Globalism

Among these countless codifiers of market globalism, *New York Times* syndicated columnist Thomas L. Friedman stands out not only because of the enormous impact of his writings or his personal relationships with political and economic elites on all five continents but also for his ability to speak to his millions of readers in easily digestible sound bites that bring conceptual order to the threatening complexity and unevenness of our integrating world. For all of these reasons, we will examine the morphology of market globalism by focusing on his arguments, bearing in mind that myriads of similar claims saturated the global public sphere in the 1990s.[34]

As I have argued elsewhere, the articulation of the rising global imaginary as market globalism fell mainly to global social elites composed of corporate managers, executives of large TNCs, corporate lobbyists, high-level military officers, journalists and public-relations specialists, intellectuals writing to large audiences, state bureaucrats, and politicians.[35] As James Mittelman has pointed out, numerous institutions bundle market globalism and globalization, seeking to universalize the core ideas. In addition to the WTO, the IMF, and the World Bank, these diverse institutions include the media, the lecture circuit, schools, and universities, with business faculty being key to developing and disseminating market-globalist claims: "MBA programs serve as vital mechanisms in the transnational spread of distinctive combinations of values and hence for the emergence of a common ideological framework among policymakers in diverse countries. Indeed, many MBA-toting ministers and senior bureaucrats around the world have been trained in neoclassical economics at leading universities in the United States."[36] These combined efforts to harness the economistic vision of Hayekism to the buzzword "globalization" allowed market globalism to acquire a substantive morphology within a short period of time.

Friedman presents his ideological claims in systematic fashion in *The Lexus and the Olive Tree: Understanding Globalization* (1999), his international best seller lionized by scores of reviewers as the "official narrative of globalization." Francis Fukuyama, for example, hails the expanded paperback edition as "A powerful volume that comes as close as anything we now have to a definition of the real character of the new world order."[37] So what, then, is the "real character of the new world order"? For Friedman, it boils down to "The One Big Thing" people should focus on: "I believe that if you want to understand the post–Cold War world you have to start by understanding that a new international system has succeeded it—globalization." Taking the entire globe as his frame of reference, the author proceeds by juxtaposing "division" as the central aspect of the Cold War system with "integration" as the overarching feature of the globalization system. This fundamental dichotomy underlies his frequent challenges to the legitimating discourses of the national imaginary: "The world has become an increasingly interwoven place, and today, whether you are a company or a country, your threats and opportunities increasingly derive from who you are connected to." For Friedman, globalization is both a new phase in the unfolding of modernity and an objective, interconnected "system." Possessing an all-encompassing structure and logic, the rules of the globalization system "today directly or indirectly influence the politics, environment, geopolitics and economics of virtually every country in the world." Serving as a leading metaphor for the "greased" and "turbo-charged globalization system," the "Lexus" defies the limitations of time and space much in the same manner as globalization "shrinks the world from a size 'medium' to a size 'small.' "[38]

Citing a 1998 full-page advertisement run by the global investment firm Merrill Lynch in major American newspapers, Friedman declares November 9, 1989—the day the Berlin Wall fell—as the "birthday" of the globalization system. For the journalist, three statements made in the advertisement best characterize the dynamics underpinning the 10-year-old global age: the auspicious "liberalization of markets" following the collapse of the "walled-off world"; the "spread of free markets and democracy around the world permitting more people everywhere to turn their aspirations into achievements"; and the awesome power of technology—"properly harnessed and liberally distributed"—to "erase not just geographical borders but also human ones."[39] These assertions serve as the ideological foundation for the principal decontestation chains Friedman weaves together in his book. First, he argues that globalization is primarily about the ICT-fueled liberalization and global integration of markets. The increased flow of goods, services, and people across conventional national boundaries enervates nation-states while invigorating global corporations and a few "super-empowered individuals." Second, he insists that globalization, in the long run, will benefit everyone. On balance, it generates prosperity and spreads democratic principles that provide for greater political stability in the world. Third, he sees the liberalization and global integration of markets inextricably intertwined with the global diffusion of American values, consumer goods, and lifestyles. Although the world is becoming increasingly "Americanized," these values are hardly unalterable entities tied to a political territory called the United States. Universal in their appeal and application, they can be absorbed and modified by any culture in the world without necessarily destroying its distinctiveness. Let us now explore how Friedman's translation of the global imaginary relies on the projection of these three central ideological claims.

The first decontestation chain is clearly crucial for it attempts to persuade readers that the New World Order amounts to nothing less than a fundamentally new system of globalization powered by objective techno-economic forces:

[Globalization] is the inexorable integration of markets, nation-states, and technologies to a degree never witnessed before—in a way that is enabling individuals, corporations and nation-states to reach around the world farther, faster, deeper, and cheaper than ever before, and in a way that is enabling the world to reach into individuals, corporations, and nation-states farther, faster, deeper, and cheaper than ever before.[40]

"Market" represents *the* core concept in Friedman's decontestation of "globalization," and he leaves no doubt as to what he has in mind: "But the relevant market today is the planet Earth and the global integration of technology, finance, trade, and information in a way that is influencing wages, interest rates, living standards, culture, job opportunities, wars and weather patterns all over the world."[41] Notice also how Friedman's adjective "inexorable" adds conceptual weight to his definition by suggesting that the liberalization and global integration of markets is an inevitable and perhaps even irreversible process. Social elites in the South like Manuel Villar, the Philippines Speaker of the House of Representatives, appeared to agree with Friedman: "Of course, we cannot simply wish away the process of globalization. It is a reality of a modern world. The process is irreversible."[42] But isn't the belief in the inevitability of globalization a poor fit for a market globalism rooted in Hayekian principles? After all, throughout the twentieth century, liberals and conservatives of all stripes and shades criticized Marxism for its devaluation of the power of ideas and other noneconomic factors. In particular, they attacked Marx and Engels' materialist conception of history as a deterministic doctrine that predicted the demise of capitalism in the name of economic inevitability. So, why would influential market globalists like Friedman link their projected path of globalization to such an economistic narrative of historical inexorability?

There are a number of good political reasons for why market globalists would put an "alien" socialist idea in close proximity to their core concepts. Regardless of how the early twentieth-century leaders of German Social Democracy really felt about the alleged "inevitability" of socialism, most of them cherished the tremendous political potency of determinism. August Bebel, as we noted, considered the belief in the inevitable coming of socialism a key element in the successful organization of the German proletariat. Likewise, the presentation of globalization as some sort of natural force, like an earthquake or gravity, makes it easier for globalists to convince people that they must adapt to the "discipline of the market" if they are to survive and prosper. Thus, the notion of inexorably integrating markets functions as a suppressant to dissenting discourses. Public policy based on economic inevitability appears to be above politics; elites simply carry out what is ordained by the logic of globalization. Resistance would be unnatural, irrational, and ineffective. Market globalists' dangerous gamble of adopting seemingly incompatible concepts drawn from socialism has the potential to produce an immense political payoff.

Moreover, the belief in globalization's inexorability facilitates the political project of engineering free markets. When, in the early 1980s, Margaret Thatcher famously pronounced that there are no more alternatives to Hayekism, she sought to forestall a possible return to Keynesian welfarism. In fact, she accused those who still dared to pose ideological alternatives of foolishly relying on anachronistic, socialist fantasies that betrayed their inability to cope with empirical reality.[43] By the late

1990s, market globalists like Thomas Friedman relied on the same strategy to declare that people had no choice but to adjust to the inevitability of globalization. The tasks of government were to be limited to the protection of private property, the delivery of basic social services, and the integration of national economies in a single global market. Like Thatcher and Reagan, Friedman was prepared to defend the use of governmental power to weaken or eliminate public policies and institutions resisting the market imperative. Like Hayek, he supported the creation of national and international legal norms that would preserve competition and make it operate as beneficially as possible. For all of these reasons, the idea of inevitability served as a powerful ideological justification for the engineering of free markets by neoliberal national governments and international economic institutions like the IMF and the World Bank—a process fiercely condemned by justice globalists who opposed Friedman's version as "globalization from above."

Friedman routinely interweaves explanations of globalization with ideological prescriptions. Attached to the Hayekian ideal of the self-regulating market as the heart of the evolving global order, he advocates the restructuring of public enterprises and the privatization of key industrial sectors, including energy, transportation, utilities, and communication: "Globalization means the spread of free-market capitalism to virtually every country in the world. Therefore, globalization also has its own set of economic rules—rules that evolve around opening, deregulating and privatizing your economy, in order to make it more competitive and attractive to foreign investment." In the postcommunist global age, he asserts, virtually every country in the world has access to the same ideological "software," making the creation of a single global market a foregone conclusion.[44] Friedman also activates another Hayekian ideal— the notion of a spontaneous order emerging from free economic activity— to present globalization as a leaderless and impartial process. To illustrate this point, he imagines himself engaged in a spirited debate with the Prime Minister of Malaysia who had reprimanded Western powers for allegedly manipulating markets and currencies during the 1997–8 Asian crisis in order to destroy the vibrant economies of their oversees competitors. Friedman tells his readers how he would respond to Mahatir Mohamad's accusation:

Ah, excuse me, Mahatir, but what planet are you living on? You talk about participating in globalization as if it were a choice you had. Globalization isn't a choice. It's a reality. There is just one global market today, and the only way you can grow at the speed your people want to grow is by tapping into the global stock and bond markets, by seeking out multinationals to invest in your country and by selling into the global trading system what your factories produce. And the most basic truth about globalization is this: *No one is in charge.*[45]

This globalist rendition of Hayek's spontaneous, self-regulating market order buttresses Friedman's larger argument that globalization does not reflect the arbitrary agenda of a particular social class or group. In other words, globalists merely carry out the unalterable imperatives of a transcendental force much larger than narrow partisan interests. People are not in charge of globalization; markets and technology are. Enter the "Golden Straitjacket," Friedman's rather revealing metaphor for the defining political-economic framework of the globalization system. First stitched together by Thatcher and Reagan in the early 1980s, he explains, the Golden Straightjacket took the world by storm in the early 1990s, forcing every single country in the world to adopt the same Hayekian principles:

[M]aking the private sector the primary engine of its economic growth, maintaining a low rate of inflation and price stability, shrinking the size of its state bureaucracy, maintaining as close to a balanced budget as possible, if not a surplus, eliminating and lowering tariffs on imported goods, removing restrictions on foreign investment, getting rid of quotas and domestic monopolies, increasing exports, privatizing state-owned industries and utilities, deregulating capital markets, making its currency convertible, opening its industries, deregulating its economy to promote as much domestic competition as possible, eliminating government corruption, subsidies and kickbacks as much as possible, opening its banking and telecommunications systems to private ownership and competition and allowing its citizens to choose from an array of competing pension options and foreign-run pension and mutual funds. When you stitch all of these pieces together you have the Golden Straitjacket.[46]

The image of the "Golden Straitjacket" comes together with the "Electronic Herd," another memorable metaphor for the "global marketplace." Friedman describes "the herd" as "often anonymous stock, bond and currency traders and multinational investors, connected by screens and networks.... The herd knows only its own rules. But the rules of the herd are pretty consistent—they are the rules of the Golden Straitjacket."[47] In order to succeed in the global age, countries must don the Golden Straitjacket in order to please the Electronic Herd:

The Electronic Herd loves the Golden Straitjacket, because it embodies all the liberal, free-market rules the herd wants to see in a country. Those countries that put on the Golden Straitjacket are rewarded by the herd with investment capital. Those that don't want to put it on are disciplined by the herd—either by the herd avoiding or withdrawing its money from that country.[48]

Friedman's ideal of the leaderless market—embodied in a global Electronic Herd playing by Golden Straitjacket rules that override those of the old nation-state order—seems to take for granted that the market-globalist project of liberalizing and integrating markets around the world was sustained by asymmetrical power relations.

Backed by the powerful global North, international economic institutions like the WTO, the IMF, and the World Bank enjoyed in the 1980s and 1990s the privileged position of making and enforcing the rules of the global economy. In return for supplying much needed loans to developing countries, they pressured debtor countries in the global South and the former Second World to put on the Golden Straitjacket. Dubbed the "Washington Consensus," these policies aimed at reforming the internal economic mechanisms of debtor countries in the developing world so that they would be in a better position to repay their incurred debts. For incensed justice globalists, the draconian terms of these neoliberal policies spelled out a new form of colonialism. To refer to this program as the Washington Consensus was no coincidence, for the United States was the most dominant economic power on earth. Its stock market capitalization hovered around 50 percent of the world total. The views of Wall Street and Silicon Valley commanded the attention of the Electronic Herd. The actions of the Federal Reserve chairman or the US Treasury influenced markets from Singapore to Buenos Aires. National banks from Japan to Germany called in American investment firms like Goldman Sachs, Merrill Lynch, or McKinsey & Company to reorganize their management structures and streamline operations.[49] The largest global corporations were headquartered in America and the US government controlled the IMF and the World Bank. One of the principal aims of the Economic Security Council set up by President Bill Clinton in 1993 was to open Asian "target countries" to American trade and finance.

This does not mean, however, that the United States was in complete control of the global economic system. But its disproportionate influence on a globalization system defined in techno-economic terms forced market globalists like Friedman into a number of ideological inconsistencies. On the one hand, he tried to minimize the impression that the United

States was the main shaper of globalization. The image of a leaderless, anonymous Electronic Herd following universal market rules certainly helped in this effort. On the other hand, however, he spoke in glowing terms about the benign global leadership exerted by the United States, suggesting that there was, after all, a captain at the helm of the global ship:

The Golden Straitjacket was made in America and Great Britain. The Electronic Herd is led by American Wall Street Bulls. The most powerful agent pressuring other countries to open their markets for free trade and free investments is Uncle Sam, and America's global armed forces keep these markets and sea lanes open for this era of globalization, just as the British navy did for the era of globalization in the nineteenth century.[50]

A few pages later, the *New York Times* journalist chooses even more explicit language when referring to the American military–industrial complex: "Indeed, McDonald's cannot flourish without McDonnell Douglas, the designer of the U.S. Air Force F-15. And the hidden fist that keeps the world safe for Silicon Valley's technologies to flourish is called the U.S. Army, Air Force, Navy and Marine Corps. And these fighting forces and institutions are paid for by American taxpayer dollars."[51] This, of course, sounds like an open admission that historical necessity and the invisible hand of a leaderless Electronic Herd must rely at times on the not-so-hidden fist of US military power to advance the liberalization and global integration of markets. We shall return to this issue again in Chapter 6 where we shall examine the turn toward imperial globalism after the terrorist attacks of September 11, 2001. For the moment, let us simply note that Friedman oscillated between the ideological claim that nobody was in charge of globalization and the admission that America was in control (or that it should be).

The market globalists' fondness for American global power and influence cannot be reduced to its military dimension. The prospect of American-style capitalism serving as the economic engine of a globalization system born of the demise of the Second World excited many elites around the world. The promise of economic prosperity and liberal democracy for the world's 6 billion people frequently translated into the ideological claim that globalization was a beneficial economic and political process destined to ease the tensions and bridge the divisions of the national age. The promotion of liberal democracy through globalization, in particular, represents a theme Friedman returns to time and again. Already in the early chapters of *The Lexus and the Olive Tree*, the author links his explanation for the transformation of the Cold War order to democratizing tendencies that allegedly inhere in new technologies like the Internet and the demise of the Bretton Woods system in the early 1970s. Friedman speaks of "three democratizations"—technology, finance, and information—as powerful leveling forces breaking down the walls around which the citizens of the old nation-states system communicate, invest, and learn about each other. Enabling the "world to come together as a single, integrated, open plain," these dynamics intensified with the extension of the Electronic Herd's reach around the world, ultimately forcing all nations to integrate into a single global system dominated by the United States.[52]

Friedman refers to these democratization processes as a "revolution from beyond [the nation-state]," or "globalution," by which he means the bloodless imposition of "business practices and disciplines" on every country in the world by the rules of the market. Products of a liberal-democratic Western sphere, these practices and disciplines include financial transparency, "generally accepted" accounting principles and business standards, low levels of corruption, a free press, and the unimpeded creation of bond and stock markets around the world. Demanding stability, predictability, transparency, and the ability to transfer and protect private property as the precondition for investment, the Electronic Herd will intensify pressures for political democratization.[53] Friedman uses the example of Indonesian strongman Suharto's fall from power in 1998 as an example for globalution. And yet, only a few pages later, he concedes that integrating market forces might not only dispose of dictators but also undermine democracy by making people's elected representatives carry out the mandates of an unelected Electronic Herd. Friedman's previous invocation of a spontaneous, impersonal market logic that puts nobody (or perhaps the United States) in charge of globalization now comes back to haunt him. Scrambling to iron out this ideological inconsistency, he arrives at a rather vague conclusion: "Clearly, one of the biggest challenges for political theory in this globalization era is how to give citizens a sense that they can exercise their will, not only over their own governments, but over at least some of the global forces shaping their lives."[54]

The ideological claim that globalization furthers the spread of democracy in the world is rhetorically anchored in the usage of "free markets" and "democracy" as synonymous terms. Persistently affirmed as common sense, the equivalence of these concepts went largely unchallenged in the mainstream discourse of the 1990s. Francis Fukuyama, for example, argued that there existed a clear correlation between a country's level of economic development and successful democracy. While globalization and capital development did not automatically produce democracies, "the level of economic development resulting from globalization is conducive to the creation of complex civil societies with a powerful middle class. It is this class and societal structure that facilitates democracy."[55] But the assumed affinity between democracy and free markets hinges on a definition of democracy that emphasizes formal procedures such as voting at the expense of the direct participation of broad majorities in political and economic decision-making. This thin definition of democracy differs from "popular democracy" in that the latter posits democracy as both a process and a means to an end—a tool for devolving political and economic power from the hands of elite minorities to the masses. "Low-intensity" or "formal" market democracy, on the other hand, limits democratic participation to voting in elections, thus making it easier for the elected to govern effectively, that is with a minimum of popular inputs.[56] The promotion of low-intensity democracy provides market globalists with an opportunity to advance their economistic vision in a language that ostensibly supports the "democratization" of the world. Articulating the ideological position of justice globalists, Benjamin Barber suggests that the thinning of democracy resulting from the rapid globalization of markets should be tackled by a commensurable globalization of political and civic institutions that are committed to "thick," participatory forms of democracy: "The democratic world is out of control because the instruments of benign control—democratic governing institutions— simply do not exist in the international setting, where markets in currency, labor, and goods run like engines without governors. Happily, the rising internationalism of transnational institutions and social movements promises a measure of countervailing power in the international arena. . . . "[57]

Friedman's vision of a globalizing American-style business culture contributing to creation of the political conditions for a more democratic world order relates closely to his third ideological claim: the benign globalization of American culture. Before we embark on our analysis of this decontestation chain, let us remind ourselves that the theme of my book is the transformation of the ideological landscape as a result of a shifting mode of understanding community and people's place in it. This complex process has been unfolding since at least the mid-twentieth century in the form of a gradual superimposition of images and metaphors of the global on the conventional national imaginary.[58] As the national background gets layered over, chunks of the global paint sometimes fall off or stick only partially to the recalcitrant surface, creating quite a checkered picture. Hence, the transformation of the national imaginary is a slow and messy business, hardly a matter of either national or global, but of both national *and* global. Both formations will continue to coexist uneasily for the next decades. What makes ideological codifiers like Friedman "globalists," however, is their ideological orientation toward the world as a single, interdependent place that commands more attention than the nation-state. But making the globalization system their frame of reference does not mean that the national imaginary no longer exerts a significant influence—especially on Americans who take great pride in their nation's unchallenged post–Cold War hegemony. For Friedman, one way to square the circle was to treat the United States as "the world's great geopolitical shaper"—with the shaky proviso that "it would be too much to say that the United States is in charge of globalization."[59] He seems to suggest that, culturally speaking, globalization is actually Americanization, that is, the global diffusion of American values, consumer goods, and lifestyles. This perspective had gained steam throughout the 1990s, but it had also received its fair share of criticism from justice globalists who shuddered at the "McDonaldization" or "McWorldization" of the planet's diverse cultures.[60]

Friedman, however, does not see much harm in the global spread of Big Macs, iMacs, or Mickey Mouse. Cultural homogenization has happened many times before in world history, he observes, except this time around it was occurring on a global rather than a regional or national scale. As he puts it dispassionately, "weak cultures" might indeed get "wiped out like any species that cannot adapt to changes in its environment" while "stronger cultures" would adapt to and assimilate those aspects of globalization that aided their growth and diversity without allowing themselves to be overwhelmed by "alien" elements. For Friedman, Americanization does not mean that those "adapters" had to swallow hook, line and sinker all aspects and manifestations of American culture without making some modifications. Healthy forms of cultural adaptation—or "glocalization"— are those in which the receiving culture would "absorb influences that naturally fit into and can enrich that culture."[61] As many justice globalists pointed out, however, Friedman's argument begged the question of how one would distinguish definitively between enriching and alien cultural influences. Normative judgments of this sort lie notoriously in the eye of the beholder. And it is precisely deep disagreements over such norms and values—and who should be entitled to speak for whom—that make for culture wars between and within communities.

The Lexus and the Olive Tree closes fittingly with an unapologetic paean to America and its unique role in the globalizing world: "And that's why America, at its best, is not just a country. It's a spiritual value and role model. . . . And that's why I believe so strongly that for globalization to be sustainable America must be at its best—today, tomorrow, all the time. It not only can be, it must be, a beacon for the whole world."[62] Fukuyama concurs, claiming that globalization stands for the irreversible Americanization of the world: "I think it has to be Americanization because, in some respects, America is the most advanced capitalist society in the world today, and so its institutions represent the logical development of market forces. Therefore, if market forces are what drive globalization, it is inevitable that Americanization will accompany globalization."[63]

Influential codifiers of market globalism like Friedman and Fukuyama proved indispensable in the process of increasing the conceptual density and sophistication of the ideational cluster we referred to in Chapter 4 as Hayekism. They constructed multiple decontestation chains capable of responding to a wide array of salient political questions. They extracted chunks of conventional ideologies like conservatism and socialism and then rearranged or combined them with new ideas, most importantly, with the key concept "globalization." Putting expanding conceptions of community, time, and space into accessible language, these ideological decontestation chains strengthened market globalism's appeal to broader segments of the population, thus enhancing its political potency. Its principal claims challenged conventional notions of sovereign nation-states serving as the natural containers of community coexisting with similar containers in an international order. Instead, Friedman and other codifiers focused on the translation of the rising global imaginary in terms of a single, worldwide free market in goods, services, and capital. Although market globalists still found themselves under the influence of the national, they suggested that nation-states were threatened by an underlying techno-economic logic of globalization. But in the long run, the emerging global order would allow people everywhere to enjoy the benefits of free-market capitalism and democracy. Nations had little choice but to embrace the objective process of globalization and accept its inevitable consequences.

This articulation of the global imaginary as the inexorable global integration of leaderless markets fueled by the ICT revolution and spreading American (Western) culture provoked different responses. By the end of the Roaring Nineties, not just privileged elites but also large segments of the population in both the North and the South had, perhaps reluctantly, accepted the core claims of market globalism, thus internalizing its norms. A comprehensive poll conducted in 2004 in nineteen countries on four continents found that 55 percent of respondents believed that globalization was "positive" for them and their families, while only 25 percent responded negatively (20% remained unsure). Surprisingly, a good number of similar polls suggest that popular support for globalization appeared to be especially high in developing countries.[64] The articulation of the rising global imaginary in market-globalist terms had congealed into a strong discourse that presented its ideological prescriptions as objective descriptions of a globalizing world. Their constant repetition, public recitation, and performance contributed to the material production of what they named globalization.[65]

5.4. Toward Porto Alegre: The Genesis of Justice Globalism

While sharing Francis Fukuyama's conviction that the triumph of liberalism and free-market capitalism was the most effective way to organize societies globally, Thomas Friedman remained rather skeptical with regard to the alleged finality of this triumph. Indeed, he acknowledges a powerful "backlash against globalization" generated by those "brutalized or left behind." His metaphor for people's attachments to their traditional identities is the olive tree. According to Friedman, the relentless drive of homogenizing and standardizing market forces to turn the whole world into a hi-tech consumerist landscape has irreversibly destabilized these familiar feelings of belonging. Yet, writing in 1999, the *New York Times* columnist still hoped that the ongoing wrestling match between the Lexus and the olive tree might end in a draw—a "healthy balance" between the radiating warmth of "home" and the coldness of doing what it takes to thrive economically in the globalization system. Although he recognized the seriousness of the contest between the contending yet mutually engendering forces of the Lexus and the olive tree, Friedman concurred, surprisingly, with Fukuyama's prediction of a "de-ideologized world." The backlash against globalization was "unlikely to develop a coherent alternative ideology," he concluded, because "the backlash itself involved so many disparate groups—as evidenced by the coalition of protectionist labor unionists, environmentalists, anti-sweatshop protestors, save-the-turtles activists. . . . who came together in December 1999 to protest globalization at the Seattle WTO summit." Showing little ideological imagination beyond their simplistic message of "STOP," these groups have been lashing out at globalization without offering a "sustainable economic alternative."[66]

What are we to make of Friedman's assertions? Had the "disparate coalition of antiglobalization forces," indeed, shown little ideological imagination? Were its members really "antiglobalization"? Were there no more possible ideological alternatives to market globalism? Let us try to find answers to these questions by exploring, for the remainder of this chapter, the formation and morphology of the ideational cluster associated with those alliances which, by the end of the 1990s, began to refer to themselves as the "global justice movement" (GJM). We will proceed with our analysis in the same manner as our examination of market globalism, that is, by focusing primarily on the writings of one influential codifier. Before we examine the core arguments of the American-born, French author and citizen-activist Susan George, however, let us first consider some contextual factors that contributed to the formation of justice globalism.

Resistance to what members of the GJM increasingly referred to as "neoliberal globalization" was mounting during the Roaring Nineties in reaction to the perceived disastrous global impact of the Right's Deregulation-Liberalization-Privatization agenda. As we discussed earlier, the left–right distinction originated in the revolutionary French National Assembly and remained a reliable marker of fundamental ideological differences for two centuries. With the collapse of the Soviet Union and the market-oriented reforms in China, the relevance of this distinction for the New World Order was increasingly questioned in public discourse. Their self-confidence battered by the electoral triumphs of the New Right in Europe and the United States, some prominent leftists joined the chorus of critics. Acknowledging the terminal crisis of socialism in both its Marxist-Leninist and Keynesian social-democratic manifestations, they argued that the distinction between left and right had lost its meaning, except, perhaps, in the practical context of party politics. Calling for the construction of a "posttraditional" progressivism "beyond left and right," they sought to reframe the left project in terms of Tony Blair's "New Labor" or Gerhard Schröder's "Neue Mitte" (New Center).[67] Other members of the left, however, disagreed vociferously with such a "turn to the right." Instead, prominent radical democrats like Norberto Bobbio offered a spirited defense of the continued relevance of the left–right cleavage for the post–Cold War era. Reminding his audience that the line dividing the left and the right had always shifted with changing historical circumstances, the influential Italian thinker argued that the core value of the political left was its commitment to *social justice*, which he decontested as the "reduction of *social inequalities*" such as power, wealth, gender, and educational opportunity. The political Right, on the other hand, had been far more reluctant to support egalitarian policies.[68] In a world that abounded with social inequalities, the ideal of social justice remained firmly implanted on the ideological firmament as a reliable polestar marking an enduring political distinction.

Bobbio presented his thesis in the mid-1990s in his enormously successful *Left & Right*, a short monograph that sold hundreds of thousands of copies in Europe and the United States, in addition to piling up translations into the world's major languages. The book's vigorous defense of the left–right cleavage and its lucid presentation of social justice and equality as the perennial core values of the left appealed to both dispirited labor circles attached to the traditional socialist ideal of class solidarity and a more eclectic New Left concerned with issues of racism, sexism, militarism, environmental degradation, and the North–South divide. But rather than searching for new ways of integrating social justice and equality into a national framework, progressives around the world began to discuss the continued relevance of these ideals in explicitly global terms. Academics like Martha Nussbaum or David Held, for example, envisioned a "new cosmopolitanism" anchored in "the worthy moral ideals of justice and equality."[69] Indeed, an analysis of more than 6,000 international news sources shows that the values of global justice and solidarity with people beyond one's own national borders became widely diffused during the Roaring Nineties. References to "global citizenship," for example, increased by an annual average of 35 percent between 1991 and 2000. Scores of universities and schools around the world drafted new mission statements in favor of "moral cosmopolitanism". New educational programs emphasized the importance of preparing students of all ages for global citizenship, which required the proper "understanding of the forces that affect cross-cultural connections" as well as a moral "commitment to a global community based on human interdependence, equality, and justice."[70]

Social activists around the world began to engage in what social movement expert Sidney Tarrow calls "global framing," that is, a flexible form of "global thinking" that connects local or national grievances to the larger context of global justice, global inequalities, or world peace. Tarrow argues that most of these activists could be characterized as "rooted cosmopolitans," because they remained embedded in their domestic environments while at the same time developing a global consciousness as a result of vastly enhanced contacts to like-minded individuals and organizations across national borders.[71] Indeed, the forging of global attitudes inside and alongside the national identities by social activists was one particular manifestation of the eruption of the global imaginary within the national. In addition to articulating their particular concerns and demands within a global framework, the members of this New-New Left increasingly engaged in "multi-issue framing"—the ability to grasp how certain issues like environmental protection or the struggle against AIDS related to other issues such as patriarchy, race, or the debt burden of the global South.[72] The organizational result of both global framing and multi-issue framing was a broader and more eclectic GJM that began to cohere ideologically through its opposition to market globalism.

Most of the movement's leaders would later point to a number of events that had a galvanizing impact on the ideological formation of justice globalism. On January 1, 1994, the day NAFTA took effect, a relatively small group of guerillas calling themselves the Zapatista Army of National Liberation (EZLN) launched an uprising in their native province of Chiapas in Southern Mexico. Drawing on the beliefs and values of Che Guevara, Emiliano Zapata, indigenous Mayan culture, and Catholic Liberation Theology, the Zapatistas stitched together an interpretive framework that presented their rebellion as an act of popular resistance against their government's free-trade policies. Engaging in effective global framing, their leader Subcomandante Marcos announced to the world that the local struggle in Chiapas was of global significance: "[W]e will make a collective network of all our particular struggles and resistances. An intercontinental network of resistance against neoliberalism, an intercontinental network of resistance for humanity."[73] Keeping their promise, the Zapatistas managed to get their message out to other progressive forces around the world. Their efforts culminated in the 1996 First Intercontinental Meeting for Humanity and Against Neoliberalism held in the jungles of Chiapas and attended by more than 4,000 participants from nearly thirty countries. The conference set into motion further initiatives that sensitized millions of people to the suffering of poor peasants in the global South caused by market-globalist policies. Indeed, the creation of the global "Zapatista solidarity network" served as a model for dozens of other alliances that vowed to challenge neoliberal globalization "from below."

Another significant catalyst in the formation of the GJM and its corresponding ideology was the devastating Asian economic crisis of 1997.

A few years earlier, the governments of Thailand, Indonesia, Malaysia, South Korea, and the Philippines had gradually abandoned their control over the domestic movement of capital in order to attract foreign direct investment. Intent on creating a stable monetary environment, they raised domestic interest rates and linked their national currency to the value of the US dollar. The ensuing influx of foreign investments translated into soaring stock and real estate markets all over Southeast Asia. However, by 1997, many investors realized that prices had become inflated far beyond their actual value. They panicked and withdrew a total of $105 billion from these countries within days, forcing governments in the region to abandon the dollar peg. Unable to halt the ensuing free fall of their currencies, those governments used up nearly all of their foreign exchange reserves. As a result, economic output fell, unemployment increased, and wages plummeted. Foreign banks and creditors reacted by declining new credit applications and refusing to extend existing loans. By the end of 1997, the entire region found itself in the throes of a financial crisis that threatened to wreak havoc on the global economy. Disaster was narrowly averted by a combination of international bailout packages and the immediate sale of Southeast Asian commercial assets to foreign corporate investors at rock-bottom prices. In addition to wrecking the regional economy for years to come, the crisis also caused serious ideological damage: power elites and ordinary citizens alike had been treated to an ominous preview of what a world run on unfettered market-globalist principles might look like.

Finally, the formation of the ideational cluster associated with the GJM owed much to a spectacular series of strikes that hit France in 1995 and 1998. Protesting government policies that had driven up unemployment while reducing social services, the striking workers and public employees received tremendous support from these New-New Left networks. Lasting alliances between unions and environmentalists were forged and many new multi-issue coalitions were born. One of these novel organizational networks was the *Association pour une taxation des transactions financiers pour l'aide aux citoyen* (Association for the Taxation of Financial Transactions for the Aid of Citizens, ATTAC). Founded by academics and intellectuals associated with *Le Monde Diplomatique*—a multilingual leftist monthly with a global circulation of over 1 million copies—ATTAC began to draft comprehensive proposals for the elimination of offshore corporate tax havens, the blanket forgiveness of developing countries' debts, and the radical restructuring of the major international economic institutions, including the IMF and the WTO. But its core demand was the leveling of a "Tobin Tax," named after its inventor, the Nobel Prize-winning economist James Tobin, on international short-term financial transactions, with proceeds going to the global South. If introduced globally, a tax from 0.1 to 0.25 percent on these transactions might have raised up to $250 billion. Within a few years, ATTAC grew into an impressive global network with tens of thousands of members and autonomous branches in more than fifty countries. From its very inception in 1998, ATTAC was an important voice in the fight against "neoliberal globalization." It played an instrumental role in defeating the Multilateral Agreement on Investment (MAI), an international investment legislation proposal negotiated in secret among G-7 members that favored TNCs and global investors. Together with Brazilian and Asian global justice networks, ATTAC also served as a vital catalyst in the 2001 creation of the World Social Forum (WSF) in Porto Alegre, Brazil. By the mid-2000s, the WSF had become a central organizing space and ideological site for tens of thousands of justice globalists who delighted in their annual counter-summit to the January meeting of the market-globalist World Economic Forum (WEF) in the exclusive Swiss ski resort of Davos.[74]

Refusing to accept orthodox Marxist categories as the common ideological denominator of all left politics, global justice organizations like ATTAC formed responsive nodes in a decentralized, nonhierarchical, and transnational "network of networks." The ideological coherence and political dominance of market globalism allowed the various groups belonging to the GJM to pull together even more closely, in the process sharing organizational know-how, strategy, and ideas. Embedded in their national framework without being confined to it, this pluralistic "movement of movements" learned to take advantage of the ICT-mediated flow of goods, services, and ideas that their opponents associated with the "inevitable" globalization of markets. Gradually, prominent movement activists like Susan George, Naomi Klein, and Walden Bello articulated a set of principles guiding the GJM's interactions with international institutions, states, and other private and public organizations. Academic observers like Mary Kaldor analyzed the birth of a global civil society—"groups, networks and movements which comprise the mechanisms through which individuals negotiate and renegotiate social contracts or political bargains on a global level."[75] Cultivating ever closer contacts with members of distant cultures, these transnational activists traversed geographical space as well as cyberspace in search for new ways to put their ideals of global justice, equality, diversity, and pluralism into practice. Although the GJM of the 1990s incorporated most of the issues dear to the new social movements of the 1960s and 1970s, it rearranged and rearticulated the New Left concerns around the core concept of "globalization."

The wild popularity of the Zapatistas, the horrors of the East Asia economic crisis, the challenge of the French mass strikes, and the depth of the Russian currency crisis combined in the second half of the Roaring Nineties to send shock waves around the globe. For the New-New Left, these events were signs of encouragement after nearly two decades of political drought, while the market-globalist Right found itself caught off guard at the unfamiliar sight of crisis. George Soros, a world-famous currency speculator-turned-philanthropist, was among the first market globalists to raise his influential voice against the "prevailing ideology of market fundamentalism." Pointing to the "inherent instability of global markets," the sobered billionaire scolded his former ideological allies for their continued pursuit of economic self-interest that strengthened the "supremacy of market values" over "all political and social values."[76] Other prominent defectors followed suit, openly supporting Soros' demand that market globalism ought to be subjected to serious reform—without, however, questioning the underlying logic of globalizing capitalism.[77] The potent combination of spectacular market failures and elite criticism created larger discursive and political openings for the fledgling GJM which had become confident enough to call upon its mass membership to participate in contentious counter-summits held at official international meetings of high-profile market-globalist institutions like the IMF, the World Bank, the G-7 (after 1998, the G-8), the WEF, or the WTO.

A clear indication of an impending, large-scale confrontation between the forces of market globalism and its challengers on the left came in June 1999, when various labor, human rights, and environmental groups organized global protests, known as J18, to coincide with the G-8 Economic Summit in Cologne, Germany. Financial districts of cities in North America and Europe were subjected to well-orchestrated direct actions that included large street demonstrations, as well as to more than 10,000 cyber-attacks perpetrated by sophisticated hackers against the computer systems of large corporations. In London, a march of 2,000 protesters turned violent, causing dozens of injuries and significant property damage. The coming out party of the GJM took place six months later when about 50,000 people took part in the anti-WTO protests in Seattle.[78] In spite of the predominance of North American participants, there was also a significant international presence from 135 countries. Celebrity activists like José Bové, the French sheep farmer who had famously trashed a McDonald's outlet in his country, marched shoulder to shoulder with poor Indian farmers and leaders of the Philippines peasant movement. Motivated by slogans such as "our world is not for sale," and "no globalization without participation," this eclectic alliance of justice globalists included, among others, consumer activists, labor activists, students demonstrating against sweatshops, environmentalists, opponents of genetically modified foods, animal rights activists, religious advocates of debt relief for developing countries, pacifists and nonviolent direct action proponents, feminists, and human rights activists. This impressive crowd rallied against the WTO because of its market-globalist position on agriculture, multilateral investments, and intellectual property rights. Representing more than 700 networked organizations and groups, the GJM displayed its global reach not only in its membership but also in its balanced list of public speakers drawn from both the North and the South.

In the end, the demonstrators were forcibly dispersed by police forces in menacing riot gear who launched tear gas cans into the crowds—including people who sat peacefully on the streets and pavements. The police employed batons, rubber bullets, and pepper spray stingers against demonstrators, some of whom had resorted to physical violence. According to various estimates, however, there were only perhaps 200 protesters who, refusing to honor the organizers' pledge of nonviolence, went about smashing storefronts and turning over garbage cans. Most of these youths belonged to the Black Bloc, an American-based anarchist organization opposed to free-market capitalism and centralized state power of any kind. Wearing dark hoods and black jackboots, they damaged stores and offices of firms alleged to engage in extremely callous business practices. For example, Fidelity Investments was hit for maintaining high stakes in Occidental Petroleum, the oil company most responsible for violence against indigenous people in Colombia. GAP outlets were targeted for relying on sweatshop labor in Asia. Ultimately, the Battle of Seattle derailed the WTO meeting's agenda, forcing delegates to leave the meeting without any concrete results. Moreover, the GJM managed to broadcast its ideas and beliefs to millions of people around the world. In spite of mostly unfavorable mainstream media coverage, Seattle became a global symbol for the arrival of a new left—a foundational event that established the GJM as a permanent actor on the stage of world politics.[79]

In the months following the anti-WTO protests in Seattle, similar large-scale demonstrations against neoliberal globalization took place in rapid succession all over the world. In February 2000, for example, the annual meeting of the WEF was targeted by thousands of international protesters denouncing the ideological vision and policy recommendations of their adversaries. Having transformed itself from a small international body concerned with management issues into a dynamic political forum, the WEF attracted to its annual meeting hundreds of the world's most powerful business executives and political leaders. It also generated dozens of publications, including a yearly index measuring the economic competitiveness of all the world's countries. Davos provided unparalleled opportunities for market globalist elites to streamline their views and policies. Employing their Seattle strategy, transnational activists clashed with police forces in the streets of the town. A year later, Swiss authorities announced their determination to prevent a repetition of such "embarrassing events" by trying to keep protesters out of Davos. In what turned into the country's largest security operation since World War II, Swiss border units refused entry to thousands of people—often merely on the suspicion that these individuals might be participating in anti-WEF demonstrations. Police and military units set up dozens of roadblocks on all streets leading to the Alpine village. They also halted train services, and placed thousands of police and military troops on alert. In spite of these drastic measures, however, demonstrators and police confronted each other in Davos and Zurich. Yet, though the ensuing street battles led to dozens of injuries and hundreds of arrests, most of these protests remained nonviolent.

Perhaps the most dramatic of what Thomas Friedman and the mainstream media dubbed "antiglobalization protests" occurred at the August 2001 G-8 Summit in Genoa, where the Italian government employed a contingent of over 16,000 police and military troops to "guarantee the safety" of the delegates. As world leaders were feasting on sea bass and champagne aboard a luxury liner safely anchored in the city's harbor, dozens of demonstrators and police were injured in violent confrontations. Twenty-three-year-old Carlo Giuliani, one of hundreds of thousands of protesters taking to the streets of the Mediterranean port city, was shot to death by police. The reaction from most attending politicians was predictable, with French President Jacques Chirac wondering what was prompting so many people to turn up in the streets. The general tenor of the comments was to focus on the actions of a relatively small group of violent anarchist and right-wing extremists. Prime Minister Silvio Berlusconi and President George W. Bush, for example, argued that both violent and nonviolent protesters were spoilers who subscribed to "deplorable policies that lock poor people into poverty."[80] Countering these accusations, Italian Green Party politicians later claimed that their government had used infiltrators and provocateurs to cement the public image of violent cobblestone-throwing radicals, thereby manufacturing the justification for extreme police reactions. There were even reports of police collusion with radical right-wing organizations. In the end, the Italian parliament approved a report absolving the police of wrongdoing during the Genoa G-8 Summit.

Categorically opposed to the use of violence in the movement's struggle against market globalism, Susan George participated in most of these demonstrations as a key organizer and featured speaker. Her widely read articles and books soon earned her the reputation as the GJM's premier "idea person."[81] A prolific writer-activist with deep roots in the anti-Vietnam movement and various 1970s Third-World development initiatives, including the campaign to end world hunger, George today holds key offices in prominent transnational justice networks, including ATTAC, the WSF, the Amsterdam-based Transnational Institute, and Greenpeace International. In 1999, she published *The Lugano Report*, a biting satire that attacked the economic and ideological foundations of the New World Order. The book centers on a fictional report purported to have been penned by a group of international economists in response to an unnamed commission's directive to search for the best way to preserve and maintain a free-market, globalized capitalist system in the twenty-first century. A few years later, George presented the main principles, values, and demands of the GJM in exceptionally clear and condensed language in a monograph employing the official slogan of the WSF in its title: *Another World Is Possible If. . . .*[82]

The author opens her book with a spirited rebuttal of the common accusation made by Friedman and other market globalists that justice globalists are reflexively and unthinkingly "antiglobalization." Conversely, she reminds her readers that those who refer to themselves collectively as the GJM strongly object to the rather insulting label "anti," preferring instead the less loaded prefixes "alter" or "counter." As she emphasizes, "The movement is not 'anti' but internationalist and deeply engaged with the world as a whole and the fate of everyone who shares the planet. It also has plenty of concrete proposals to offer, making it easily more 'pro-globalization' than its adversaries." What unites people who feel themselves part of the movement, she insists, is their belief that another world is possible and that today's pressing social problems "can no longer be solved individually, locally, or even nationally."[83] George's emphatic embrace of the global imaginary, however, begs a whole series of questions. Who, exactly, are those "people who feel themselves part of the movement"? How do they express their global collective identity? What do they mean by "globalization"? What do they mean by "another world"? What are some of those "concrete proposals" that make justice globalists allegedly more "pro-globalization" than their opponents? Our search for answers on the basis of key textual passages should allow us to gauge whether the ideational cluster associated with the GJM did, indeed, acquire a sufficiently dense morphology to count as a mature ideology. Our examination should also help us to evaluate the viability of Friedman's claim that the "disparate" nature of the "anti-globalization coalition" prevented the formulation of a coherent ideological alternative to market globalism.

In response to the question regarding the movement's collective identity, let us consider two 2001 WSF documents that bear George's intellectual fingerprints: the Charter of Principles and the Call for Mobilization, approved and adopted by the main networks that make up the WSF Organizing Committee. Both documents invoke a global "we" defined as "social forces from around the world" and "organizations and movements of civil society from all the countries in the world" that are committed to "building a planetary society directed toward fruitful relationships among humankind and between it and the Earth." These general declarations of global subjectivity are then further specified in a sentence referring to "women and men, farmers, workers, unemployed, professionals, students, blacks, and indigenous peoples, coming from the South and from the North."[84] Thus, the movement's affirmation of a "global we" becomes tied to its irreducible plurality and diversity. In his careful analysis of five similar documents authored by transnational networks that belong to different sectors of the GJM, Donatella della Porta also underlines the construction of a global collective self respectful of differences of views and cultural and political traditions: "[M]ultifacetedness becomes an intrinsic element of the movement's collective identity, so intrinsic that it becomes implicit...."[85] Likewise, scholar-activists Michael Hardt and Antonio Negri, the authors of the international best seller *Empire*, emphasize the process of "finding what is common in our differences and expanding that commonality while our differences proliferate."[86] And so it appears that market-globalists like Friedman disregard, intentionally or not, two crucial and easily available self-definitions of their opponents. First, by pushing the image of a "disparate anti-globalization crowd," they fail to acknowledge the explicit globalist orientation of the GJM, including its construction of a *global* "we" anchored in values of pluralism and diversity. Second, Friedman's assertion that the movement's heterogeneity is responsible for its allegedly lacking ideological imagination offers no explanation as to why diversity *necessarily* prevents the formation of an alternative political belief system. Thus, he presents as a statement of fact what is little more than conjecture.

As to the question of the GJM's decontestation of globalization, George seems to envision an "engagement in the world as a whole" that is fundamentally different from or contrary to the "inevitable" integration of markets along Hayekian lines. To get a better grasp of her alternative understanding of globalization, she suggests, people must first recognize that the term has already been deeply imbued with ideas and values that "best serve the interests of people who profit from the present economic, social, and political arrangements." Portraying market globalists as members of an elite network that hides their power interests behind the promise of universal benefits, George attacks Friedman's claim that "nobody is in charge of globalization." In so doing, she uses ideology in the Marxist sense of dominant social elites producing a distorted and inverted image of reality that becomes internalized by the subordinate classes as "false consciousness." Ignoring the unavoidably ideological (in the neutral sense) character of her perspective, George arrives at the following conclusion:

Since we seem to be stuck with the word, however, it's helpful to put one or several adjectives in front of globalization so that its real nature is better defined. People who are fighting against its harmful effects often speak of "corporate-led," "finance-driven" or "neo-liberal" globalization. In the United States, some also call it "neo-conservative" globalization.[87]

As this discursive maneuver reveals, the author attempts to arrive at the "real" meaning of globalization *indirectly* by means of uncovering the more primary economic dynamics underlying the capitalist distortion. Hence, she uses "globalization" as a signifier that contains both a negative and a positive meaning. The former seeks to capture the distorted market-globalist articulation of the global imaginary. George's insistence on putting the qualifiers "finance-driven" or "corporate-led" in front of the term represents, therefore, an act of discursive resistance to the dominant narrative. The positive meaning of globalization refers to the possibility of an undistorted translation of the global imaginary in the interest of all humanity, not just for the benefit of a powerful few.

Thus, readers find themselves in the midst of an ideological struggle over the meaning of "globalization," with each side accusing the other of distorting reality. Market globalists consider their opponents "biased" and "antiglobal," whereas justice globalists condemn the "corporate-led" agenda of their adversaries. Both camps, however, fight their battle of ideas primarily on economic terrain, hoping to vanquish the enemy with relevant economic "facts" and the statistics that bear out the "truth" of their position while revealing the "falsehood" of the other side. Consequently, George insists time and again that "corporate-led" or "finance-driven" globalization is an "accurate" description of "capitalism's most recent phase which it entered roughly around 1980." She then proceeds to attack the ideological claims of market globalism as both "incorrect" and "unjust." Let us consider the following textual passage: "Corporations, financial-market operators, and governments aligned with their interests... promise more and better jobs to come, but in order to deserve them labor markets must become more 'flexible'—the code word for giving up the gains of the past century concerning wages, working conditions, benefits, holidays, fair hiring and firing practices, health insurance and social protection." Here is another one: "In fact, neoliberal globalization and human welfare, are, at bottom, enemies." And one more: "Over the past two decades, the situation of the planet and its inhabitants has dramatically worsened.... These two decades correspond roughly to the acceleration and spread of globalization (as we'll call it from now on, with the neo-liberal, corporate-led, finance-driven qualifiers understood)." Such claims are usually followed by a flood of supporting "hard evidence," in this case various statistics taken from the United Nations Development Program's (UNDP) *Human Development Report 2002* that show widening economic inequalities within most nations as well as between the global North and South.[88] Likewise, two recent surveys of up to ninety-five countries published by critical World Bank economists conclude that greater openness to trade has helped the upper strata of society to raise their income while lowering the earnings of the poorest 40 percent of the population. Needless to say, the market-globalist camp presents equally impressive numbers "proving" the beneficial economic effects of free trade and other forms of economic globalization. Almost nobody, however, takes issue with two grim statistics. First, since 1985, the share of the world's population living in poverty has declined, but the absolute number of people living in poverty has risen by 100 million to 1.6 billion. Second, the economic benefits of globalization have bypassed an entire continent. Between 1981 and 2001, the proportion of Africans living below the international poverty lines *increased* from 42 to 47 percent.[89]

At the core of George's extensive critique of market globalism lies her unshakable conviction that the liberalization and global integration of markets lead to greater social inequalities, environmental destruction, the escalation of global conflicts and violence, the weakening of participatory forms of democracy, the proliferation of self-interest and consumerism, and the further marginalization of the powerless around the world. Hence, she assigns the GJM two fundamental tasks. The first is ideological, reflected in concerted efforts to undermine "the premises and ideological framework" of the "reigning neoliberal worldview" by constructing and disseminating an alternative translation of the global imaginary based on the core principles of the WSF: equality, social justice, diversity, democracy, nonviolence, solidarity, ecological sustainability, and planetary citizenship. The second is political, manifested in the attempt to realize these principles by means of mass mobilizations and nonviolent direct action targeting the core structures of market globalism: international economic institutions like the WTO and the IMF, TNCs and affiliated NGOs, large industry federations and lobbies, the mainstream corporate media, and the "present United States government."[90]

Although George reaffirms the GJM's commitment to fight capitalism, she rejects Marxism's radical antimarket rhetoric: "The issue as I see it is not to abolish markets. . . . Trying to ban markets would rather be like banning rain. One can, however, enforce strict limitations on what is and is not governed by market rules and make sure that everyone can participate in exchange." The author also shows no hesitation to dispense with Marx's agent of social change—the international working class—as "more wishful thinking than reality." Scientific socialism's revolutionary expectation of the inevitable collapse of capitalism strikes her as a "global accident" unlikely to occur. Neither is such a doomsday scenario to be cheerfully contemplated for it would entail "massive unemployment, wiped-out savings, pensions and insurance; societal breakdown, looting, crime, misery, scapegoating and repression, most certainly followed by fascism, or at the very least, military takeovers." George ends her extended criticism of Old Left thinking with a ferocious broadside against the "totalitarian systems" of "state-socialism." In her view, the gulags and killing fields of the Soviet Union, Mao's China, and other purportedly revolutionary Third-World regimes belie their supposed humanist ideals. But the New Left does not fare well either in George's hard-nosed approach to changing the world. For example, she counters the New Age slogan of "personal transformation" as the prequisite for "enlightened" political action with Kant's famous statement of unavoidable human fallibility—the "crooked timber of humanity, from which no straight thing was ever made." While acknowledging the far-reaching cultural and social effects of the 1960s, she reminds readers that the New Left's political and ideational framework was not strong enough to withstand the "neo-liberal onslaught of the Reagan-Thatcher years."[91]

Obviously, George's vision is neither about reviving a moribund Marxism nor about a return to the good old days of 1968. Although justice globalism contains elements of Gandhian Third-World liberationism and traditional European social democracy, it goes beyond these Cold War ideational clusters in several respects—most importantly in its ability to bring together a large number of New Left concerns around a more pronounced orientation toward the globe as a single, interconnected arena for political action. As the WSF slogan suggests, "Another *World* is possible." One example of its strong global focus is the movement's publicity campaign to highlight the negative consequences of deregulated global capitalism on the planet's environmental health. Indeed, in the first decade of the new century, the issue of global climate change has advanced to the forefront of public discourse around the world, on a par with global terrorism and warfare.

The second half of George's book lays out in some detail concrete proposals offered by justice globalists in support of their vision. The programmatic core of these demands is a "global Marshall Plan" that would create more political space for people around the world to determine what kind of social arrangements they want: "Another world has to begin with a new, worldwide Keynesian-type programme of taxation and redistribution, exactly as it took off at the national level in the now-rich countries a century or so ago." The author envisions the necessary funds for this global regulatory framework to come from the profits of TNCs and financial markets—hence ATTAC's campaign for the introduction of the global Tobin Tax. Other proposals include the cancellation of poor countries' debts; the closing of offshore financial centers offering tax havens for wealthy individuals and corporations; the ratification and implementation of stringent global environmental agreements; the implementation of a more equitable global development agenda; the establishment of a new world development institution financed largely by the global North and administered largely by the global South; establishment of international labor protection standards, perhaps as clauses of a profoundly reformed WTO; greater transparency and accountability provided to citizens by national governments and global economic institutions;

making all governance of globalization explicitly gender sensitive; the transformation of free trade into fair trade; and a binding commitment to nonviolent direct action as the sole vehicle of social and political change.[92]

In some respects, perhaps all of these proposals might turn out to be flawed or naïve. But we must remember that a perfect theoretical design and easy applicability are not the decisive criteria for what makes, or does not make, an ideology. Comprehensive political belief systems composed of patterned ideas and claims to truth, ideologies always contain logical inconsistencies and utopian yearnings. Our brief analysis of relevant texts suggests, therefore, that the oppositional ideational cluster Thomas Friedman deemed "incoherent" developed during the Roaring Nineties into a comprehensive ideology offering an alternative translation of the rising global imaginary. Key figures of the GJM like Susan George constructed ideological claims that challenged the principal decontestation chains of their dominant competitors. For justice globalists, globalization is *not* about the inevitable liberalization and global integration of markets, but about the global regulation of markets. "Finance-driven" globalization is *not* a benign, leaderless market dynamic that generates prosperity or democracy for all. Rather, it is controlled by small but powerful global elites who benefit from the subordination of billions to the unjust and inegalitarian imperatives of free-market capitalism. "Corporate-led" globalization is *not* inevitable, but, as massive alter-globalization demonstrations around the globe have shown, it can be resisted by transnational alliances and networks committed to building "another world." Finally, the global diffusion of American values, consumer goods, and lifestyles is *not* inherent in globalization. Rather, the Americanization of the planet serves the interests of market globalists in the United States and their allies around the world eager to universalize American-style capitalism and consumerism. In support of this claim, Susan George devotes a full chapter of her book to a critique of the "American model," particularly in its post–9/11 "imperialist" manifestation.[93]

However, our textual reading suggests that Friedman is right about justice globalists' desire to put an immediate "STOP" to neoliberal globalization. But to call their alternative vision a simplistic and incoherent "backlash against globalization" belittles the impressive ideological imagination of his opponents without engaging in a sustained analysis of their political ideas and beliefs. Indeed, Friedman's pronouncements about the quality of thinking exhibited by the "coalition of protectionist labor unionists, environmentalists, anti-sweatshop protestors, save-the-turtles activists" are themselves value-laden salvos in the ongoing battle between market globalism and its challenger. Moreover, the contrarian nature of justice globalism does not necessarily inveigh against its possible status as a mature ideology. As Michael Freeden suggests, in order to acquire a more substantive morphology, any evolving cluster of political ideas must accomplish two difficult tasks. First, it must appropriate, rearrange, and incorporate suitable chunks of older established ideologies. Second, it must contest and reconceptualize the primary decontestation chains embedded in contending political belief systems.[94] As we have seen, justice globalists accomplish the first task by selectively appropriating elements of democratic socialism and liberalism. After being welded together with the core issues of the Cold War new ideologies, the resulting ideational structure receives coherence and definition when it is linked, in inverted fashion, to the main ideological claims of its dominant competitor. By the end of the Roaring Nineties, the evolving ideational cluster of the New-New Left had thickened sufficiently into a comprehensive set of decontestation chains that translated the rising global imaginary as the new ideology of "justice globalism." Let us now see whether the challengers of market globalism on the political right managed to present their ideological claims in similarly coherent fashion.

6

Jihadist Globalism versus Imperial Globalism: The Great Ideological Struggle of the Twenty-First Century?

The war we fight today is more than a military conflict; it is the decisive ideological struggle of the twenty-first century. On one side are those who believe in the values of freedom and moderation—the right of all people to speak, and worship, and live in liberty. On the other side are those driven by the values of tyranny and extremism—the right of a self-appointed few to impose their fanatical views on the all the rest.... They're successors to Fascists, to Nazis, to Communists, and other totalitarians of the twentieth century.

George W. Bush (2006)

The current Zionist-Crusader campaign against the *umma* is the most dangerous and rabid ever, since it threatens the entire *umma*, its religion, and presence. Did Bush not say that it is a Crusader War? Did he not say that the war will continue for many years and target 60 states? Is the Islamic world not around 60 states? Do you not realize this? Did they not say that they want to change the region's ideology, which vents hatred against the Americans? What they mean is Islam and its peak.

Osama Bin Laden (2004)

One World, One Dream.

Official Slogan of the Beijing Olympic Games (2008)

6.1. Globalism and Populism

Although justice globalists made up the vast majority of those millions who protested worldwide against "corporate-led globalization," they were not the only political camp opposed to it. Patrick Buchanan, for example, an American TV commentator and three-time presidential candidate, emerged in the 1990s as a prominent right-wing champion of economic and cultural isolationism. Urging "the American people" to "put their country first," Buchanan enthusiastically threw his support behind the anti-WTO demonstrators in Seattle.[1] Similarly, hard-nosed soldiers of the extreme racist right, like Illinois-based World Church of the Creator founder Matt Hale, encouraged their followers to come to the Pacific Northwest and "throw a monkey wrench into the gears of the enemy's machine." Even the American neo-Nazi group, National Alliance, took part in the Battle of Seattle. White supremacist leader Louis Beam, too, praised the demonstrators, claiming that the "police state goons" who come down on them were paid by international capital to protect "the slimy corporate interests of 'free trade' at the expense of free people." Thus, amid a sea of signs bearing justice-globalist slogans, one could find occasional posters denouncing the "Jewish Media Plus Big Capital" or the "UN-sponsored New World Order."[2] As the Roaring Nineties drew to a close, market globalism had become the principal target not only for justice globalists but also for a growing number of national-populists.[3]

Deriving from the Latin *populus*—"the people"—populism has been associated with a variety of phenomena including "an ideology," "a social movement," "a strategy of political mobilization," "a political outlook," "a mentality," "a political syndrome," and "an emotional appeal."[4] But none of these definitions has achieved universal acceptance. Margaret Canovan, perhaps the world's foremost authority on the subject, reminds us that the meaning of populism varies from context to context, thus demanding different kinds of analysis.[5] Others have argued that populism and democracy refer to virtually synonymous "modes of articulation" that divide the social into two camps: "power and the underdog."[6] Still, even a cursory perusal of modern political history reveals that populists have been reluctant to endorse the rules of representative democracy. In fact, their hostility to representative politics could be seen as one of populism's most prominent features.[7] In addition, the fundamental democratic notion of political power residing in the people can be made to fit the temperaments of both radical egalitarians in favor of people's direct, unmediated rule and staunch authoritarians claiming to speak and act on behalf of the entire *populus*. Juan Peron or Hugo Chavez, for example, portrayed their repeated violations of basic constitutional liberties as necessary measures to carry out "the will of the people" against the power interests of corrupt social elites. Seizing upon emotionally charged issues that are modified or even disavowed according to changing political conditions, populists have been called political chameleons that routinely change their colors in searching for prey. To be sure, populism is not the only political discourse that thrives on passions, but, perhaps more than others, it relies on an extra emotional ingredient to attract normally apolitical people to its vision of society's great renewal.[8] Although populism cuts across the ideological spectrum, its latest manifestations have been skewed toward the right. Indeed, the alleged concern of contemporary national-populists with the "corrupt party system" or the "liberal media" mixes all too easily with the fondness of right-wing authoritarians for paternalist policies, their aversion to participatory and critical debate, pluralism, compromise between conflicting interests, and their hostility toward the political agenda of feminists, gays and lesbians, and multiculturalists.[9]

In spite of its rhetorical power, populism lacks the developed ideational structure that enables comprehensive political belief systems to translate the largely prereflexive social imaginary into concrete political terms and programs. As Paul Taggart points out, its "empty heart" is responsible for both its ideational weakness and its potential ubiquity.[10] Incapable of standing on its own ideological feet, populism attaches itself to various host vessels in the form of a "persistent yet mutable style of political rhetoric."[11] Populists perform at least four mutually reinforcing rhetorical maneuvers with great regularity. The first involves the construction of unbridgeable political differences. Fond of airtight Manichean divisions between Good and Evil, populists divide the population into the vast majority of ordinary people ("us") and a small but powerful elite ("them"). The people are idealized as decent, good-natured folk susceptible to the corrupt machinations of the privileged few. Thus, they require protection and guidance from a personalized leader or a dedicated vanguard of moral warriors fighting "intellectuals," "capitalists," "speculators," "politicians," "city-dwellers," "Jews," "international financiers," and other "enemies of the people." Domestic political elites are frequently taken to task for allowing "our community" to be infiltrated by immigrants, guest-workers, ethnic minorities, or foreign radicals—allegedly for material gain and other self-serving reasons. Hence, "the Establishment" stands for corruption, abuse of power, parasitism, arbitrariness, and treachery, whereas the people radiate honesty, purity, piety, resourcefulness, resilience, quiet wisdom, willingness to play by the rules, attachment to tradition, and hard work.

Second, populists attack their enemies from a moralistic high ground rather than facing them on a political level playing field. Reluctant to form traditional political parties, they spark short-lived movements against moral corruption and the alleged abuse of power. Couched in absolutist terms, the battle is never just about political and cultural differences but over fundamental moral disagreements. Casting themselves as the defenders of the people's collective traditions, populists blame an ominous "them" for the alleged moral decay of the community. Keen to awaken "the common man" from his perilous slumber, they construct emotional charges armored in deep-seated stereotypes and prejudices. As Chip Berlet observes, such techniques include demonizing, scapegoating, and the spinning of conspiracy tales. And yet, in the end it is the victim who stands accused of hatching some insidious plot against the people while the scapegoater is valorized as a paragon of virtue for sounding the alarm.[12]

Pat Buchanan, for example, routinely demonizes his country's "liberal advocates of multiculturalism" for opening the doors to millions of legal and illegal immigrants. In his view, trade with other nations should be reevaluated on the basis of common-sense criteria that reflect the interests of ordinary people: US sovereignty, the protection of the nation's vital economic interests, and ordinary people's standard of living. During the acrimonious 2007 public debate over immigration reform in the United States, Buchanan accused Latinos of Mexican extraction of promoting the cultural and political *reconquista* of the US Southwest. He insisted that most of "them" lacked a passionate attachment to the core of America— its land, people, its past, its heroes, literature, language, traditions, culture, and customs.[13] Such a retroactive construction of a homogenous heartland based on an idealized picture of the past represents a common theme in populist narratives.[14] Moreover, populist moralism lends itself to the easy incorporation of religious and mystical themes that resonate particularly well with conservative or anti-intellectual audiences. Still, the evocation of faith and tradition does not necessarily result in an endorsement of the religious establishment. As we shall see in our ensuing ideological analysis of jihadist globalism, religiously inspired populist rhetoric often favors militant sectarianism. Apocalyptic narratives and millennial visions, generally downplayed in mainstream religions, loom large in such discourses.[15]

The third rhetorical maneuver routinely performed by populists involves the evocation of an extreme crisis which requires an immediate and forceful response. Usually directed to segments of the population most threatened by the forces of modernization, such appeals thrive on the alleged discrepancy between the idealized values of the heartland and existing political practices.[16] The American People's Party, for example, emerged in the 1890s as an unstable alliance of small indebted farmers; urban workers hit by inflation; prohibitionist and moral crusaders outraged by the cultural decay of society; currency reformers opposed to Big Money; and various socialist revolutionaries railing against the power of finance capital. Built on intense emotions of fear and resentment, this short-lived political coalition demanded governmental protection from the economic and cultural consequences of advancing industrial capitalism. At the Party's founding rally in St. Louis, speaker after speaker evoked the specter of extreme crisis gripping the country: "We meet in the midst of a nation brought to the verge of moral, political, and material ruin."[17]

Likewise, today's populists focus on the challenges and dislocations brought about by globalization to appeal to those segments of the population most in danger of losing their status in the conventional social hierarchies of the nation-state. Responding to people's growing sense of fragmentation and alienation, national-populists present themselves to "globalization losers" as strong leaders capable of halting the erosion of conventional social bonds and familiar cultural environments. Lending an authoritarian voice to their audiences' longing for the receding world of cultural uniformity, moral certainty, and national parochialism, they refuse to rethink community in light of the rising global imaginary. Their critique of market globalism is reactionary in that it seeks to retain the national at any cost. Thus, they are quite unlike early nineteenth-century conservatives. As we have seen, even ultraroyalists like Maistre and Bonald recognized the need to correspond constructively to the new imperatives and aspirations contained in the rising national imaginary. Likewise, radical French conservatives like Drumont employed a populist style of rhetoric that helped articulate the dominant social imaginary of their time in extremist anti-Semitic terms. Conversely, contemporary national-populists, stuck in the declining background understanding, fail to provide their audiences with an alternative globalist vision.

Finally, populists imagine the people as a homogenous unit welded together by a common will, a single interest, an ancestral heartland, shared cultural and religious traditions, and national unity. However, the common "we" applies only to those persons deemed to belong to the nation. The presumed identity of "our" people-nation—often conveyed in explicitly racist terminology—allows populists to fuel and exploit existing hostilities against those whose very existence threatens their essentialist myth of homogeneity.[18] This long-standing populist projection of community as homogenous nation has led various commentators to draw the conclusion that "Populism was (and remains) inevitably nationalist."[19] Indeed, national-populist narratives still represent potent modes of political communication capable of mobilizing millions. One need not look much further than France's Jean-Marie Le Pen, Austria's Jörg Haider, Holland's late Pim Fortuyn, Switzerland's Christoph Blocher, Italy's Umberto Bossi, Australia's Pauline Hanson, New Zealand's Winston Peters, or America's Patrick Buchanan. Moreover, by definition, all forms of populism remain inescapably tied to some conceptualization of the people. Nevertheless, there is no compelling reason for why the concept should *always* and *necessarily* refer to a *national* community. As we noted previously, the more holistic imaginings of "the people" offered by justice globalists clearly transcend the national framework. The same is true for jihadist globalists like Osama Bin Laden who incorporate into their militant version of political Islam a populist style of rhetoric that decontests "the people" as the *umma* of *tawhid*—the *global* Islamic community of believers in the one and only God. Unlike national populism, however, this religiously inspired style of populist rhetoric merged with political Islam to create a comprehensive ideology capable of translating the rising global imaginary into concrete political terms and programs. Today, jihadist globalism represents market globalism's most formidable ideological challenger from the political Right.

6.2. Defending the *Umma* Against the Judeo–Crusader Alliance: Al-Qaeda's Jihadist Globalism

"The American people," the idealized subject of national-populists like Patrick Buchanan or CNN anchor Lou Dobbs, reacted to the al-Qaeda terror strikes of 9/11 with a mixture of horror and disbelief. Over time, their shock gave way to anger, fear, and a keen sense of vulnerability to a complex dynamic of political violence linking the local with the global. "Why do they hate us so much?" was the most frequently asked question attributed by the mainstream media to the American people. Associating globalization primarily with economic interdependencies, many Americans were surprisingly ignorant about their nation's political and cultural impact on the rest of the world, particularly the Islamic world. Several public intellectuals, however, had sounded the alarm long before 9/11. One of them was Chalmers Johnson, a seasoned American political scientist with past connections to the CIA, who appropriated the long-standing intelligence term "Blowback" as the central metaphor for his discerning analysis of the unintended costs and consequences of America's globalizing military infrastructure.[20]

It is not difficult to identify as early as the mid-1990s some of the principal answers given by Islamist militants as to why they hated the United States and its allies so much that they would plan and execute high-profile attacks on civilian targets. These operations got underway in earnest in 1993 with the bombing of the World Trade Center in Manhattan, masterminded by Ramzi Yousef, a Pakistani militant with associative links to a jihadist organization eventually to be known as "al-Qaeda" ("the Base," "the Foundation"). The magnitude of Yousef's attack prompted FBI investigators to assemble elaborate profiles of hundreds of similar "Middle Eastern extremists... working together to further the cause of radical Islam."[21] As Jason Burke notes in his riveting account of al-Qaeda, a permanent association of this term with Osama Bin Laden's transnational network was only made after the 1993 detention of an Islamist militant at New York's JFK airport who was found in possession of a terrorist training manual entitled "al-Qaeda."[22]

But the origins of al-Qaeda can be traced back to the *Maktab al-Khidamat* (MAK; "Office of Services"), a Pakistan-based support organization for Arab *mujahideen* fighting invading Soviet troops in Afghanistan. Set up in 1980 by Bin Laden and his Palestinian teacher and mentor Abdullah Azzam, MAK received sizeable contributions from the government of Saudi Arabia as well as from private donors from other Islamic countries. It also enjoyed the protection of Pakistan's Inter-Services Intelligence agency intent on replacing, with CIA support, the communist puppet regime in Kabul with an Islamist government friendly to Pakistan. Thus, al-Qaeda and other radical Islamist groups operating at the time in this region should be seen as creatures of the Cold War who eventually outlived the purpose assigned to them by their benefactors. Left without much support after the withdrawal of the Soviet troops in 1989, the multinational coalition of Arab–Afghani fighters found itself put out of business by its own success. Stranded in a country devastated by decades of continual warfare, the victorious *mujahideen* lacked a clear sense of purpose or mission.

As can be gleaned from the burgeoning literature on the subject, the term "Islamism" has been used in many different ways by both Muslim and non-Muslim scholars to refer to various "movements" and "ideologies" dedicated to the revival of Islam and its full political realization.

Related terms currently in circulation include "political Islam," "Islamic fundamentalism," "Islamist purism," and "Islamofascism."[23] Our focus on al-Qaeda's jihadist globalism is neither meant to downplay the diversity of ideational currents within Islamism nor to present their brand as its most representative or authentic manifestation. Rather, our interest in Bin Laden's doctrine dovetails with a number of issues pertinent to our subject. First, it acknowledges the tremendous political and ideological influence of jihadist globalism around the world. Second, it highlights the rise of new political ideologies resulting from the ongoing deterritorialization of Islam. Third, it recognizes the most successful ideological attempt yet to articulate the rising global imaginary around the core concepts of *umma*, *jihad* (armed or unarmed "struggle" against unbelief purely for the sake of God and his *umma*), and *tawhid* (the absolute unity of God). However, before we embark on our analysis of the central ideological claims assembled in the writings of al-Qaeda's two principal leaders, it is necessary to consider some relevant biographical matters.

Osama Bin Laden was born in 1957 the seventeenth son of Muhammed Bin Laden, a migrant laborer from Yemen who created a multibillion dollar construction empire in his adopted Saudi Arabia. Osama's early experiments with libertarian Western lifestyles ended abruptly when he encountered political Islam in classes taught by Abdullah Azzam and Muhammad Qutb at King Abd al-Aziz University in Jeddah. After earning a graduate degree in business administration, the ambitious young man proved his managerial talent during a short stint in his father's corporation. But his professional successes were soon trumped by his fervent religious vocation, expressed in his support of Arab *mujahideen* in their struggle against the Soviet-backed Afghan regime. Acquiring extensive skill in setting up guerilla training camps and planning military operations, Bin Laden saw battle on several occasions and quickly acquired a stellar reputation for his martial valor. Euphoric at the Soviet withdrawal from Afghanistan but bitterly disappointed by the waning support of the United States and Arab countries, Bin Laden returned to Riyadh in 1990 as a popular hero, his close ties to the Saudi regime still intact.

At the time, Saddam Hussein's occupation of Kuwait was threatening the balance of power in the Middle East. To counter the threat, the House of Saud invited half a million "infidels"—American and other foreign troops—into their country, ostensibly for a short period of time and solely for protective purposes. To ensure religious legitimacy for its decision, the government then pressured the Saudi *ulema* (learned interpreters of the sacred texts) to approve of the open-ended presence of foreign troops in the Land of the Two Holy Sanctuaries (Mecca and Medina). The scholars complied, ultimately even granting permission for Muslims to join the US-led Operation Desert Storm against Iraq.

Stung by the royal families' rejection of his proposal to organize thousands of Arab–Afghan veterans, and outraged by their enlistment of foreign infidels in defense of the kingdom against a possible Iraqi attack, Bin Laden severed all ties with the Saudi regime. Like tens of thousands of angry religious dissenters, Bin Laden, too, denounced these acts of "religious heresy" and "moral corruption" and openly accused the rulers of selling out to the West. The Saudi government immediately responded to these accusations with political repression, arresting several opposition leaders and shutting down their organizations. Bin Laden and his closest associates fled to Sudan where the sympathetic Islamist government of Hassan al-Turabi offered them political exile and the opportunity to create dozens of new training camps for militants. Stripped of his Saudi citizenship in 1994, Bin Laden forged a lasting alliance with Ayman al-Zawahiri, the charismatic leader of the radical Egyptian group Islamic Jihad. This partnership would eventually lead to the formation of the World Islamic Front with main branches in Pakistan and Bangladesh and an unknown number of affiliated cells around the world.

Forced to leave Sudan in 1996 as a result of mounting US pressure on the Turabi regime, Bin Laden and his entourage returned to Afghanistan where they entered into an uneasy relationship with the Taliban. In the same year, the forces of Mullah Omar managed to capture Kabul. Imposing a strict version of *shari'a* (God-given, Islamic law) on the Afghan population, the Taliban based its rule on the "true tenets of Islam" alleged to have been realized in the world only once before by the seventh-century *salaf* (pious predecessors) who led the *umma* for three generations following the death of the Prophet. By the end of the 1990s, Bin Laden had openly pledged allegiance to the Taliban, most likely in exchange for the regime's willingness to shelter his organization from US retaliation following the devastating 1998 al-Qaeda bombings of the American embassies in Kenya and Tanzania. To show his gratitude to his hosts, Bin Laden referred to the Taliban leader Mullah Omar as the Commander of the Faithful—one of the honorific titles of the *caliph*, the Islamic ruler of both the religious and civil spheres. Since this designation was deprived of its last bearer in 1924 when the modernist Turkish leader Kemal Ataturk replaced the Ottoman Caliphate with a secular nation-state, Bin Laden's fondness for it signifies nothing less than his rejection of eight decades of Islamic modernism—both in its nationalist and socialist garbs—as well as his affirmation of Taliban-ruled Afghanistan as the nucleus of a global Caliphate destined to halt the long decline of the Islamic world and the corresponding ascendancy of the West. His anti-Western convictions notwithstanding, Bin Laden never hesitated to use modern technology to communicate his message.

As Bruce Lawrence notes, the bulk of Osama bin Laden's writings and public addresses emerged in the context of a virtual world moving from print to the Internet and from wired to wireless communication. Largely scriptural in mode, the Sheikh's "messages to the world" are deliberately designed for the new global media. They appear on video- and audiotapes, Web sites, and handwritten letters scanned onto computer disks and delivered to Arabic-language news outlets, including the influential Qatari satellite television network al-Jazeera. Bin Laden conveys his ideological claims in carefully crafted language that draws on the five traditional types of Muslim public discourse: the declaration, the juridical degree, the lecture, the written reminder, and the epistle. Disdainful of ghost-written tracts of the kind supplied by professional speechwriters to many politicians, he produces eloquent pieces of Arabic prose that speak in the "authentic, compelling voice of a visionary, with what can only be called a powerful lyricism."[24] Bin Laden's writings over the last fifteen years amount to a coherent doctrine appealing to millions of Muslims. His post–9/11 messages, in particular, contain specific instructions to the faithful on how to resist the advances of the American Empire, the "New Rome."

The ideological edifice of jihadist globalism rests on the populist evocation of an exceptional crisis: the *umma* has been subjected to an unprecedented wave of attacks on its territories, values, and economic resources. Although he blames the global "Judeo–Crusader alliance," Bin Laden considers its assault on Islam to be the expression of an evil much larger than that represented by particular nation-states or imperialist alliances.[25] At the same time, however, he and his lieutenants insist that the forces of "global unbelief" are led by specific individuals like President Bush or by concrete "hegemonic organizations of universal infidelity" such as the United States and the United Nations.[26] In their view, the collapse of the Soviet Empire—attributed directly to the efforts of the Arab-Afghan *mujahideen*—has made America even more haughty and imperialistic:

[I]t has started to see itself as the Master of this world and established what it calls the new world order. . . . The U.S. today, as a result of this arrogance, has set a double standard, calling whoever goes against its injustice a terrorist. It wants to occupy our countries, steal our resources, install collaborators to rule us with man-made laws, and wants us to agree on all these issues. If we refuse to do so, it will say we are terrorists.[27]

Bin Laden cites as evidence for such "Satanic acts of aggression" the open-ended presence of American troops on the Arabian peninsula, the ongoing Israeli oppression of the Palestinian people, the 1993 American operations against Muslim warlords in Somalia, the Western indifference to the slaughter of thousands of Bosnian Muslims during the 1991–5 Yugoslav Civil War, and the economic sanctions imposed by the West on Iraq after the first Gulf War, which contributed to the death of countless innocent civilians. Indebted to the discursive legacy of Third-World liberationism, the Sheikh considers these immoral and imperialist acts inflicted by Western powers on the *umma* but the latest crimes in a series of humiliations that can be traced back to the Great Powers' division of the Ottoman Empire after the Great War and post–World War II establishment of the Jewish state in Palestine. But what makes today's "attacking enemies and corrupters of religion and the world" even more dangerous than the medieval Christian crusaders or the thirteenth-century Mongol conquerors of the mighty Abbasid Empire is their all-out "campaign against the Muslim world in its entirety, aiming to get rid of Islam itself."[28] Rather than supporting the *umma* at this critical point in history when the Judeo–Crusader alliance has "violated her honor, shed her blood, and occupied her sanctuaries," Saudi Arabia and other Islamic countries have colluded with the infidel enemy. Abandoning the *umma* in her hour of need, these "apostate rulers" have desecrated the true religion of God's messenger and thereby lost their political legitimacy. Likewise, Islamic scholars and clerics who lent their learned voices to the defense of these "defeatist Arab tyrannies" deserve to be treated as "cowardly heretics" and "traitors to the faith."

In populist fashion, Bin Laden directs his first public letter intended for a wider audience against the appointed head of Saudi Arabia's collaborationist *ulema*. In addition to accusing the Mufti of spiritual corruption, he also objects to his alleged willingness to turn a blind eye to the moral decay of modern Islamic societies, most visibly reflected in their toleration of practices of usury expressly prohibited in the Qur'ān. The letter also laments the *ulema's* unwillingness to resort to more drastic measures to prevent the further intrusion of Western values at the expense of Muslim principles. In several poignant passages, Bin Laden identifies as the worst feature of the present age of *jahiliyya* (ignorance, pagan idolatry) "the degree of degradation and corruption to which our Islamic *umma* has sunk."[29] But what, precisely, does Bin Laden mean by "*umma*"? After all, this core concept, together with *jihad* and *tawhid*, serves as the ideational anchor of his political belief system. In the Sheikh's major writings, one finds ample textual evidence for his populist understanding of *umma*.[30] As Mohammed Bamyeh notes, the concept of the "Islamic community" has functioned historically as an equivalent of the Western idea of "the people," empowered to set limits to the tyrannical tendencies of governing elites.[31] Drawing on this traditional understanding of the *umma*, Bin Laden nonetheless departs from Western variants of populism by emphasizing that political authority can never rest on popular sovereignty, for political rule is not the exclusive property of the people. Rather, the righteous *umma* exercises political power in the name of God only, thus building its political institutions on the foundation of Islamic sovereignty.[32] Since God's authority transcends all political borders and any humanly designed lines of demarcation, the *umma* supersedes not only ancient tribal solidarities and traditional kinship structures but also, most importantly, modern Western conceptions of community rooted in the national imaginary. To be sure, contemporary Muslims carry national passports, but their primary solidarity must lie with the *umma*, a community that encompasses the entire globe: "You know, we are linked to all of the Islamic world, whether that be Yemen, Pakistan, or wherever. We are part of one unified *umma*. . . ."[33]

This central idea of "the people of the Qur'an" having been commanded by God to safeguard His sovereignty and to resist the sinful influences of despots, heretics, and infidels usurping God's ultimate sovereignty, received its most radical modern interpretation in the writings of the Egyptian political Islamist Sayyid Qutb, the older brother of Bin Laden's influential teacher at al-Aziz University. Taking as his point of departure the Islamic doctrine of *tawhid*, Qutb argued that all worldly power belongs to the one and only Lord of the Worlds whose single, unchanging will is revealed in the Qur'ān. Unconditional submission to His will entails the responsibility of every member of the *umma* to prevent the domination of humans over humans, which violates the absolute authority of Allah. According to Qutb, the highest purpose of human existence is "to establish the Sovereignty and Authority of God on earth, to establish the true system revealed by God for addressing the human life; to exterminate all the Satanic forces and their ways of life, to abolish the lordship of man over other human beings."[34]

Having failed to repel the corrupting influences of Islam's internal and external enemies, today's *umma* has fallen into the equivalent of the pre-Islamic pagan age of *jahiliyya* characterized by rampant materialism and the rebellion of unbelief against the sovereignty of God on earth. Qutb even suggests that with the disappearance of proper political governance according to *shari'a*, the *umma* itself had ceased to exist in its "true" form. If only ordinary Muslims somehow could be shown the seriousness of their predicament, they might renew their faith and cleanse Islamic culture of its debasing accretions. The final goal of such an Islamic revival would be the restoration of the *umma* to its original moral purity under a new *salaf*. As Mary Habeck notes, Qutb's seemingly premodern inclinations actually contain strong modernist influences that turn political Islam into "a sort of liberation ideology, designed to end oppression by human institutions and man-made laws and to return God to his rightful place as unconditional ruler of the world."[35]

Qutb's version of political Islam greatly influenced al-Qaeda's understanding of the *umma* as a single global community of believers united in their belief in the one and only God. As Bin Laden emphasizes, "We are the children of an Islamic Nation, with the Prophet Muhammad as its leader; our Lord is one, our prophet is one, our direction of prayer is one, we are one *umma*, and our Book is one."[36] Expressing a populist yearning for strong leaders who set things right by fighting corrupt elites and returning power back to the "Muslim masses," al-Zawahiri shares his leader's vision of how to restore the *umma* to its earlier glory.[37] In their view, the process of regeneration must start with a small but dedicated vanguard willing to sacrifice their lives as martyrs to the holy cause of awakening the people to their religious duties—not just in traditionally Islamic countries, but wherever members of the *umma* yearn for the establishment of God's rule on earth. With a third of the world's Muslims living today as minorities in non-Islamic societies, Bin Laden regards the restoration of the *umma* as no longer a local, national, or even regional event. Rather, it requires a concerted *global* effort spearheaded by a jihadist vanguard operating in various localities around the world. Al-Qaeda's desired Islamization of modernity takes place in global space emancipated from the confining territoriality of "Egypt" or the "Middle East" that used to constitute the political framework of religious nationalists fighting modern secular regimes in the twentieth century. As Olivier Roy observes, "The Muslim *umma* (or community) no longer has anything to do with a territorial entity. It has to be thought of in abstract and imaginary terms."[38]

Although al-Qaeda embraces the Manichean dualism of a "clash of civilizations" between its imagined global *umma* and global *kufr*, its globalism transcends clear-cut civilizational fault lines. Its desire for the restoration of a transnational *umma* attests to the globalization and Westernization of the Muslim world just as much as it reflects the Islamization of the West. Constructed in the ideational interregnum between the national and the global, jihadist-globalist claims still retain potent metaphors that resonate with people's national or even tribal solidarities.[39] Nevertheless, al-Qaeda's focus is firmly on the global as its leaders successfully redirected militant Islamism's struggle from the traditional "Near Enemy" (secular-nationalist Middle Eastern regimes) to the "Far Enemy" (the globalizing West). This remarkable discursive and strategic shift reflects the destabilization of the national imaginary. By the early 1990s, nationally based Islamist groups were losing steam, partly as a result of their inability to mobilize their respective communities around national concerns, and partly because they were subjected to more effective counterstrategies devised by secular-nationalist regimes.[40] Hence, Bin Laden and al-Zawahiri urged their followers to take the war against Islam's enemies global. Al-Qaeda's simple ideological imperative—rebuild a unified global *umma* through global *jihad* against global *kufr*—resonated with the dynamics of a globalizing world. It held a special appeal for Muslim youths between the ages of 15 and 25 who lived for sustained periods of time in the individualized and decultured environments of Westernized Islam (or an Islamized West).[41] As Roy reminds us, this second wave of al-Qaeda recruits, responsible for the most spectacular terrorist operations between 9/11 and the London bombings of 7/7 (2005), were products of a westernized Islam. Most of them resided in Europe or North America and had few or no links to traditional Middle Eastern political parties. Their affinity for al-Qaeda's transnational *umma* and its rigid religious code divorced from traditional cultural contexts made them prime candidates for recruitment. These young men followed in the footsteps of al-Qaeda's first-wavers in Afghanistan who developed their ideological outlook among a multinational band of idealistic *mujahideen*.[42]

If the restored, purified *umma*—imagined to exist in global space that transcended particular national or tribal identities—was the final goal of populist-jihadist globalism, then *jihad* surely served as its principal means. For our purposes, it is not necessary to engage in long scholastic debates about the many meanings and "correct" applications of *jihad*. Nor do we need to excavate its long history in the Islamic world. It suffices to note that jihadist globalists like Bin Laden and al-Zawahiri endorse both "offensive" and "defensive" versions of *jihad*.[43] Their decontestation of this core concept draws heavily on interpretations offered by Azzam and Qutb, for whom *jihad* represents a divinely imposed *fard 'ayn* (individual obligation) on a par with the nonnegotiable duties of prayer and fasting. Likewise, Bin Laden celebrates *jihad* as the "peak" or "pinnacle" of Islam, emphasizing time and again that armed struggle against global *kufr* is "obligatory today on our entire *umma*, for our *umma* will stand in sin until her sons, her money, and her energies provide what it takes to establish a *jihad* that repels the evil of the infidels from harming all the Muslims in Palestine and elsewhere."[44] For al-Qaeda, *jihad* represents the sole path toward the noble goal of returning the *umma* to "her religion and correct beliefs"—not just because the venerable way of *da'wa* (preaching, admonishing) has failed to reform the treacherous Muslim elites or convert the hostile crusaders, but, most importantly, because Islam is "the religion of *jihad* in the way of God so that God's word and religion reign supreme." Moreover, jihadist globalists are not choosy about the means of struggle: anything that might weaken the infidels suffices. Such tactics include large-scale terrorist attacks, suicide bombings, and the public killing of hostages: "To kill the Americans and their allies—civilians and military—is an individual duty incumbent upon every Muslim in all countries. . . . "[45]

For Osama Bin Laden, *jihad* and *umma* are important manifestations of the revealed truth of *tawhid*, the oneness of God and His creation. As we have seen, it demands that Islamic sovereignty must be established on earth in the form of a Caliphate without national borders or internal divisions. This totalistic vision of a divinely ordained world system of governance whose timeless legal code covers all aspects of social life has prompted many commentators to condemn jihadist Islamism as a particularly aggressive form of totalitarianism that poses a serious challenge to cultural pluralism and secular democracy.[46] Responding to this charge, the al-Qaeda leadership has turned the tables on its critics. Pointing to the long legacy of Western aggression against the *umma*, Bin Laden tends to portray his organization's attacks as retaliatory measures designed to respond in kind to the oppression and murder of thousands of Muslims by the "Judeo–Crusader Alliance." The leaders of al-Qaeda never hesitate to include as legitimate targets of their strikes those Muslims deemed to be "apostates" and "handmaidens" of the infidel enemy. In their view, such actions of treachery have put such Muslim "hypocrites" outside of the *umma*.[47]

In the end, jihadist globalists fall back on a Manichean dualism that divides the world into two antagonistic camps: "One side is the global Crusader alliance with the Zionist Jews, led by America, Britain, and Israel, and the other side is the Islamic world." For Bin Laden and al-Zawahiri, reconciliation violates the Islamic imperatives of unconditional loyalty to the *umma* and absolute enmity to the non-Muslim world: "The Lord Almighty has commanded us to hate the infidels and reject their love. For they hate us and begrudge us our religion, wishing that we abandon it." Consequently, al-Qaeda's message to Muslims all over the world is to nurture "this doctrine in their hearts" and release their hatred on Americans, Jews, and Christians: "This [hatred] is a part of our belief and our religion."[48] In an impassioned post–9/11 letter, Bin Laden offers a detailed refutation of the notion that Islam should be a religion of moderation or balance. In his view, "[I]t is, in fact, part of our religion to impose our particular beliefs on others.... And the West's notions that Islam is a religion of *jihad* and enmity toward the religions of the infidels and the infidels themselves is an accurate and true depiction." He also considers the UN-sponsored call for a dialogue among civilizations nothing but an "infidel notion" rooted in the "loathsome principles" of a secular West advocating an "un-Islamic" separation of religion and the state.[49]

His extremist rhetoric notwithstanding, Bin Laden never loses sight of the fact that jihadist globalists are fighting a steep uphill battle against the forces of market globalism. For example, he discusses in much detail the ability of "American media imperialism" to "seduce the Muslim world" with its consumerist messages. He also makes frequent references to a "continuing and biased campaign" waged against jihadist globalism by the corporate media—"especially Hollywood"—for the purpose of misrepresenting Islam and hiding the "failures of the Western democratic system."[50] The al-Qaeda leader leaves little doubt that what he considers to be the "worst civilization witnessed in the history of mankind" must be fought for its "debased materialism" and "immoral culture" as much as for its blatant imperialism. He repeatedly accuses the United States of trying to "change the region's ideology" through the imposition of Western-style democracy and the "Americanization of our culture."[51] And yet, even against seemingly overwhelming odds, Bin Laden and al-Zawahiri express their confidence in the ultimate triumph of *jihad* over American Empire. The destruction of New York's "immense materialistic towers by nineteen young men" serves as an especially powerful symbol for the alleged waning global appeal of "Western civilization backed by

America."[52] 9/11 assumes great significance in al-Qaeda's *jihad* insofar as the successful terror attack offers the faithful clear proof that "this destructive, usurious global economy that America uses, together with its military force, to impose unbelief and humiliation on poor people, can easily collapse. Those blessed strikes in New York and other places forced it [America] to acknowledge the loss of more than a trillion dollars, by the grace of God Almighty."[53] Gloating over the staggering financial toll of the terrorist attacks on the global economy, Bin Laden offers a chilling cost–benefit analysis of jihadist strategy:

[A]l-Qaeda spent $500,000 on the September 11 attacks, while America lost more than $500 billion, at the lowest estimate, in the event and its aftermath. That makes a million American dollars for every al-Qaeda dollar, by the grace of God Almighty. This is in addition to the fact that it lost an enormous number of jobs— and as for the federal deficit, it made record losses, estimated over a trillion dollars. Still more serious for America was the fact that the *mujahideen* forced Bush to resort to an emergency budget in order to continue fighting in Afghanistan and Iraq. This shows the success of our plan to bleed America to the point of bankruptcy, with God's will.[54]

This passage is part of a videotaped address aired around the world only a few days before American voters went to the polls on November 3, 2004. Bin Laden ends his speech with a warning to the American people that their security is their own responsibility, not that of corrupt Democrat or Republican political elites. Thus, the Sheikh managed to inject himself into a national electoral contest as the self-appointed leader of the global *umma*. Articulating the rising global imaginary as a set of political claims, jihadist globalism appeared on the TV screens of a global audience as the world's chief critic of American democracy. As Faisal Devji notes, Osama Bin Laden's brand of political Islam projected no national ambitions, for it was as global as the West itself, both being intertwined and even internal to each other: "This is why Bin Laden's calls for the United States to leave the Muslim world do not entail the return to a cold-war geopolitics of détente, but are conceived rather in terms of a global reciprocity on equal terms."[55]

Another videotaped message delivered by the al-Qaeda leader in September 2007 unleashed further verbal broadsides against the "corrupt American political system." He linked the Bush administration's involvement in Iraq to transnational corporate interests that held the American people hostage to their all-out scramble for war-related profits. Osama Bin Laden's critique shows a remarkable resemblance to Pat Buchanan's populist tirades against corporate elites. Indeed, the Sheikh charges "the capitalist system" with seeking "to turn the entire world into a fiefdom of the major corporations under the label of 'globalization'...." However, unlike Buchanan's defensive attempt to hold on to a social imaginary that has seen better days, Bin Laden's vision contains an ideological alternative that, despite its chilling content, imagines community in unambiguously global terms.[56]

6.3. Imperial Globalism

Soon after 9/11, intellectual elites around the world began to wonder whether the al-Qaeda attacks marked the beginning of the end of globalization. In their view, the dark side of intensifying global interdependence had revealed itself in the United States' unexpected vulnerability to large-scale terrorist strikes carried out by nineteen jihadist hijackers armed with little more than box cutters and a spotty knowledge of how to fly commercial airliners. Impressed by the massive outbursts of patriotic sentiment that gripped the United States in the aftermath of 9/11, some commentators went so far as to predict the impending "collapse of globalism" followed by a worldwide resurgence of nationalism.[57] Enhanced surveillance and draconian security measures put in place in many countries appeared to bolster arguments in favor of the inevitable hardening of national lines of demarcation. American economist Robert J. Samuelson, a moderate advocate of market globalism, reminded the readers of his popular *Newsweek* column that previous globalization processes had been halted and even reversed by similarly traumatic events such as the 1914 assassination of the Austrian Archduke Franz Ferdinand in Sarajevo. If such a relatively minor act of terrorism had pushed Europe into the nationalist nightmare of the Great War, then the al-Qaeda attacks surely possessed the potential of sparking an even larger conflagration.[58]

As we shall see, however, market globalism did not expire on September 11, 2001. Although its basic ideational architecture remained intact, some of its core claims underwent modification in the hands of "neoconservatives" in the Bush administration who turned their militaristic vision of "democratic globalism" and "Pax Americana" into official American foreign policy.[59] Strictly speaking, of course, the United States did not constitute an "empire." But one could make a reasonable case for the persistence of American imperialism as a continuous and largely informal process that started with the seventeenth-century expansionist settlement of the North American continent and periodically assumed more coercive expressions. Perhaps the most obvious of these formal imperialist chapters in US history was the annexation of the Hawaiian Islands, Guam, parts of Samoa, the Philippines, and Puerto Rico in the 1890s. A century later, however, the United States no longer exerted direct dominion or formal rule over conquered peoples under its sovereign authority. And yet, the country had emerged from the Cold War as a new kind of empire of vast wealth, peerless military power, and global cultural reach. Its economy accounted for almost one-third of the world's output, and its military expenditures exceeded those of the next twenty nations combined. Its films, music, food, sports, and technological products flooded the planet. American investments in research and development reached nearly 40 percent of the world's spending on scientific innovation. No doubt, America had become a "hyperpower" that considered the entire world its geopolitical sphere of influence. After 9/11, it found itself in the historically unprecedented position of enforcing its own idea of global order—even in unilateral fashion if it so desired. American foreign policy expert Max Boot expressed such sentiments in the pages of the neoconservative *Weekly Standard* when he argued that only a muscular United States willing to accept its imperial status was up to the necessary task of stabilizing a world unsettled by the actions of jihadist terrorists eager to get their hands on weapons of mass destruction. For Boot, the new environment of global insecurity presented nothing less than a clear-cut "case for American Empire."[60]

"Imperial globalism" might, therefore, be an apt characterization of this neoconservative inclination to shape the globe in its own image by military means. As Martin Shaw notes, "It is clearly plausible to define the Bush administration's kind of globalism as 'imperial' in character."[61] But let us recall from our earlier discussion that neoconservativism and neoliberalism were hardly ideological opposites. Sprouted from the rich soil of 1970s' Hayekism, they represent two variations on the basic market-globalist theme. On the major issues of economic globalization, their ideological differences were negligible. Neoconservatives pushed the liberalization and global integration of markets just as hard as neoliberals, but they were more inclined to combine their economic laissez-faire attitude with intrusive government action for the regulation of the ordinary citizenry in the name of public security and traditional values. In the waning months of George H. W. Bush's one-term presidency, neoconservative hawks in his administration were linking their demands for a more assertive and expansive use of US military power to the claim that their country's promotion of globalization furthered the spread of freedom and democracy around the world. Their unilateralist vision for American "benevolent global hegemony" was sketched out in the 1992 Defense Planning Guidance document, drafted by the then Undersecretary of Defense Paul Wolfowitz. The plan called for an unprecedented military build-up for the express purpose of deterring any potential competitors—even America's traditional Western European allies—from "even aspiring to a larger regional or global role."[62]

This imperative served as the strategic foundation of a more philosophical statement of principles issued in 1997 by the Project for a New American Century (PNAC), a newly founded neoconservative think tank that included such political and intellectual heavyweights as Dick Cheney, Donald Rumsfeld, Paul Wolfowitz, Richard Perle, Robert Kagan, Norman Podhoretz, and William Kristol. Recanting his neoconservative heresy in the aftermath of the Bush administration's conduct of the Global War on Terror, Francis Fukuyama, another cosigner of the PNAC platform, offered an apt summary of its ideological principles: the belief that the internal character of political regimes matters; the conviction that American foreign policy must reflect the deepest values of democratic societies, and that American power has been and could be used for moral purposes; the notion that the United States needs to remain engaged in international affairs, and, as the world's dominant power, it has a special responsibility for global security; a fervent belief in free markets and free trade coupled with a strong distrust of "social engineering projects"; and strong skepticism about the legitimacy and effectiveness of international law and institutions to achieve global security.[63] After 9/11, the PNAC's credo of preventing the rise of a global competitor was complemented by the idea that America reserved its right to strike any nation, organization, or network deemed to impede "freedom's cause" at any time. Known as the Bush Doctrine, this preemption clause found its official expression in the 2001 *Quadrennial Defense Review*, the 2002 *Nuclear Posture Review*, and, most importantly, the 2002 *National Security Strategy of the United States of America* (updated 2006). The core principle of the PNAC now stood at the center of American national security: "It is time to reaffirm the essential role of American military strength. We must build and maintain our defenses beyond challenge."[64]

But market globalism's imperial turn did not start with the al-Qaeda attacks and the ensuing dominance of neoconservatives in the Bush administration. As we have seen, even Thomas Friedman conceded that America's "soft power"—its culture, political ideals, and policies—depended on its not-so-hidden "iron fist" of globally stationed troops whose military might keeps the world's markets and trade routes "safe" for corporate globalization. Toward the end of its second term, the Clinton administration encountered serious challenges to this market-globalist vision of the world. As a result, it began to oscillate between its long-standing soft-power approach of persuading others to want what it wanted and a new hard-power strategy of breaking down resistance by forcing others to comply with America's wishes.[65] Between 1998 and 2000, President Clinton authorized the NATO-led war against Serbia as well as extensive bombing raids on Iraq without bothering to obtain approval from the UN Security Council. Critics charged that such unilateral interventions violated nothing less than the Charter's core principle: the inviolable sovereignty of each member nation. Moreover, the increasingly hawkish American president backed extraordinary "security measures" against justice-globalist protesters in the United States and abroad that included hi-tech surveillance and the massive use of police force. He even tightened his soft-power outlook on world trade and global commerce. In his best-selling account of the Roaring Nineties, Joseph Stiglitz provides striking examples of his country's increasingly hard-powered economic agenda, citing the government's growing willingness to support coercive measures devised by transnational drug companies for their operations in the global South. Clinton's former economic adviser did not mince words: "America's international political economy was driven by a whole variety of special interests which saw the opportunity to use its increasing global dominance to force other countries to open their markets to its goods on its terms. The U.S. government was seizing the opportunities afforded by the new post–Cold War world, but in a narrow way, benefiting particular financial and corporate interests."[66]

However, the existence of such imperial threads of continuity between the late Clinton and the early Bush administrations should not detract from the fact that America's new hard-power approach added an entirely new dimension in the aftermath of 9/11 when the glove came off, exposing the iron fist of an irate Empire. Declaring a Global War on Terror in "defense of liberty, democracy and free markets," George W. Bush abandoned the mild isolationist rhetoric of "compassionate conservatism" he had espoused for a short period during the 2000 election campaign and reverted to his hard-line neoconservatism—a perspective he shared with the likes of Cheney, Rumsfeld, and Wolfowitz. Failing to take advantage of the remarkably pro-American global sentiments expressed in the September 12 "We are all Americans now" headlines of French newspapers and the solidarity vigil staged by thousands of Iranian youths in downtown Tehran, the Bush administration escalated its unilateralism and indifference to the interests of others. Allies were informed rather than consulted. "Regime change" in Iraq was a foregone conclusion. The world's population was neatly divided into those standing "with us" and those who were "against us." The "enemy" label was slapped onto any foreign country or organization that did not display an unconditional willingness to carry out the will of the forces of light. Indeed, the American government seemed to suffer from what Robert Jay Lifton referred to as "superpower syndrome"—a medical metaphor pointing to an aberrant collective mindset projecting dangerous fantasies of apocalyptic confrontation and cosmic control.[67]

Its militaristic inclinations notwithstanding, the Bush administration constructed its imperial globalism within the established framework of market globalism. Its new National Security Strategy (NSS) continued to hold out the promise of "a new era of global economic growth through free markets and free trade." Dedicated to the vigorous promotion of "economic freedom beyond America's shores," NSS reaffirmed in unambiguous terms the importance of opening the entire world to "commerce and investment." Given the centrality of its preemption clause, it is easy to overlook the document's unwavering commitment to market-globalist policies. For example, NSS underscores the government's determination to use its "economic engagement with other countries" to "secure the benefits" of deregulatory measures, business investment and entrepreneurial activity, tax cuts, "sound" fiscal polices that enhance business activity, and free trade. For the Bush administration, the lessons of history were crystal clear: market economies, not command-and-control systems choked by the heavy hand of government, represented the best way to promote prosperity and reduce poverty in the world. Policies that "further strengthen market incentives and market institutions" were not only good for America but also "relevant for all economies—industrialized countries, emerging markets, and the developing world." Rearranging the ideological claims of market globalism around the new core concept of security, NSS proclaims "free markets and free trade" the "key priorities of our national security strategy."[68]

This post–9/11 emphasis on America's global security agenda required additional ideological modifications of market globalism. For one, there was no longer any need to hold on to the shaky ideological claim that nobody was in charge of globalization. Although rhetorical echoes of the "leaderless market" still reverberated in corporate circles, imperial globalists promoted their idea that global security and stable world markets depended on the United States—that "indispensable nation"—wielding its power. Almost overnight, the "free market" was stripped of its miraculous self-regulating powers. Arguing that the United States had an obligation to ensure that the global integration of markets was not hampered by "ideological extremists" at both ends of the political spectrum, President Bush delighted in the glorification of American global leadership: "Today, humanity holds in its hands the opportunity to further freedom's triumph over all these [terrorist] foes. The United States welcomes our [sic] responsibility to lead in this great mission." The assertion that the United States was now in charge of globalization was usually made in conjunction with the familiar market-globalist claim of the democratic benefits accruing from the liberalization and global integration of markets. For example, Bush's *New York Times* op-ed piece published at the first anniversary of 9/11 contains the following passage: "As we preserve the peace, America also has an opportunity to extend the benefits of freedom and progress to nations that lack them. We seek a peace where repression, resentment and poverty are replaced with the hope of democracy, development, free markets and free trade."[69] A year later, the President reiterated his government's unwavering "commitment to the global expansion of democracy," which represented one of the pillars of America's "peace and security vision for the world." The same claim takes center stage in Bush's 2005 Inaugural Address: "The best hope for peace in our world is the expansion of freedom in all the world.... So it is the policy of the United States to seek and support the growth of democratic movements and institutions in every nation and culture, with the ultimate goal of ending tyranny in our world."[70]

It is easy to see how the notion of "securing freedom" by means of an American-led drive for global democratization facilitated the integration of the military objectives of the Global War on Terror into the larger market-globalist discourse. As international law expert Richard Falk notes, imperial globalism "combines ideas of American dominance associated with economic globalization, that were prevalent before September 11, with more militarist ideas associated with the anti-terrorist climate of the early 21st century.... While not abandoning the ideological precepts of neoliberal globalization, the Bush administration places its intense free market advocacy beneath the security blanket that includes suspect advice to other governments to devote their resources to non-military activities." Cultural theorist William Thornton concurs: "Empire keeps all the major features of globalization, plus one: it stands ready to enforce market privileges the old-fashioned way. . . . Emphatically, however, power economics did not surrender the field to resurgent power politics. Rather the two joined forces in the common cause of Empire."[71]

Another important consequence of Bush's assumption of responsibility for globalization and the democratization of the world was the addition of a new claim to the ideological arsenal of imperial globalism: globalization requires a Global War on Terror. Power elites around the world put forward this contention on countless occasions and in numerous contexts. Let us consider three versions of presenting American-led perpetual warfare as the necessary bodyguard of corporate-led globalization. The first comes from neoconservative veteran Robert Mcfarlane, President Reagan's former National Security Adviser. Shortly after the US military's opening "shock and awe" Iraq campaign in March 2003, Mcfarlane, now the chairman of a Washington-based energy corporation, teamed up with Michael Bleyzer, CEO of an international equity fund management company, to write a revealing op-ed piece for the *Wall Street Journal*. Bearing the suggestive title, "Taking Iraq Private," the article praises the military operations in Iraq as an "indispensable tool" for establishing security and stability in the region. According to the imperial-globalist duo, the Global War on Terror prepared the ground for the profitable enterprise of "building the basic institutions that make democracy possible."[72]

In the second version, pondering how a "Global American Empire" should "manage an unruly world" after 9/11, Robert Kaplan, an award-winning journalist and influential Pentagon insider, quickly settles on the claim that globalization requires a Global War on Terror. Arguing that free markets cannot spread without military power, the best-selling author advises the Bush administration to adopt the pagan warrior ethos of second-century Rome, which he distills into "ten rules" for the expansion of American Empire. These include fast-track naturalization for foreign-born soldiers fighting for the Empire; training special forces to be "lethal killers one moment and humanitarians the next"; using the military to promote democracy; preventing military missions from being compromised by diplomacy; establishing the resolve to "fight on every front," including the willingness to strike potential enemies preemptively on limited evidence; dealing with the media "more strictly"; and cracking down on internal dissent, targeting justice-globalists and antiwar demonstrators in particular.[73] Similarly, Norman Podhoretz, foreign policy adviser to Republican Presidential candidate Rudy Giuliani, calls for the escalation of the US-led Global War on Terror into a full-blown "World War IV" (apparently, "World War III" ended in the defeat of the Soviet Union). Podhoretz surveys a post–9/11 landscape teeming with "enemies" of all kinds, the two principal ones being "Islamofascism" and misguided Western leftist intellectuals critical of the US operations in Iraq. For the patriarch of American neoconservatism, only a "tough" and "unforgiving" approach of the kind adopted by the Bush administration might eventually succeed in "draining the swamps" of terrorism and political treachery, thus ensuring the full globalization of liberal democracy and free markets.[74]

The third, and perhaps most original, version of the new imperial-globalist claim that globalization requires a Global War on Terror flows from the pen of Thomas P. M. Barnett, managing director of a global security firm and former professor of military strategy at the US Naval War College. A former Assistant for Strategic Futures in the Pentagon's Office of Force Transformations, the Harvard-educated strategist provided regular briefings to Secretary of Defense Rumsfeld and the intelligence community. He also interacted regularly with thousands of high-ranking officers from all branches of the US armed forces. *The Pentagon's New Map*, Barnett's best-selling reexamination of American national security, links the author's military expertise to his long-standing interests in economic globalization.[75] The book presents a straightforward thesis: in the global age, America's national security is inextricably bound up with the continued global integration of markets and increasing flows of trade, capital, ideas, and people across national borders. Since 9/11, it has become abundantly clear that the one-sided identification of globalization with an "economic rule set" must be complemented by an understanding of globalization as a "security rule set" mandating the destruction of transnational terrorist networks and all states harboring them.

For Barnett, both of these rule sets are normatively anchored in the universal values of individual freedom, democracy, multiculturalism, and free markets. At the same time, however, these norms are also uniquely American, for they found their political expression for the first time in human history in the eighteenth-century American experiment of an expanding democratic union of *united states*.[76] In a daring conflation of national interest with global interest that runs counter to the Cold-War mindset of the US defense establishment, Barnett presents America as "globalization's ideological wellspring" destined to bring to the world nothing less than what its citizens already enjoy today: "the individual pursuit of happiness within free markets protected from destabilizing strife by the rule of law." For the strategist, American interests are by definition global interests precisely because the country is built on universal ideals of freedom and democracy and not restricted to narrow ethnic or national identities. As the world's first truly multinational union, the United States is globalization incarnate. Moreover, the universal values at the heart of its constitution allow the American government to judge the rest of the world in universal terms of right and wrong, good and evil: "What gives America the right [to render these judgments] is the fact that we are globalization's godfather, its source code, its original model." And so it appears that by human design and historical destiny, the United States serves as the evolutionary engine of a multicultural world-system that ascends toward ever higher levels of connectivity, rule-bound behavior, wealth, security, and happiness. Although Barnett considers this course likely, he disavows historical determinism by conceding that there are no guarantees. Clearly, al-Qaeda and other "anti-globalization forces" committed to "a sort of permanent civilizational apartheid" are capable of derailing the globalization of individualism, democracy, and free markets. Thus, 9/11 marks a critical juncture in human history where America, globalization's source code, is called upon to guide the rest of the world toward the noble goals of "universal inclusiveness" and "global peace." Its Herculean task is to "make globalization truly global"—by any means necessary.[77]

This is, of course, where the new claim of globalization requiring a Global War on Terror comes in. In order to defeat the enemies of global interdependence, the Pentagon must devise a new strategy that, once and for all, abandons antiquated "inter-national thinking." National security in the twenty-first century must be reimagined in global terms as the ruthless destruction of all forces of disconnectedness and the nurturing of the "networks of political and security connectivity commensurate with the mutually assured dependence that now exists among all states that are deeply integrated with the growing global economy." In short, the Pentagon's new global strategy requires a new map—both in a cognitive and geographical sense—that divides the globe into three distinct regions. Unlike the three-world order of the Cold War, however, the entire world is now fair game for US military operations.

Barnett calls the first region on the Pentagon's new map the "Functioning Core," defined as "globalization thick with network connectivity, financial transactions, liberal media flows, and collective security." Featuring stable democratic governments, transparency, rising standards of living, and more deaths by suicide than by murder, the Core is made up of North America, most of Europe, Australia, New Zealand, a small part of Latin America, and with significant reservations, possible "new core" countries like India and China. Conversely, he refers to areas where "globalization is thinning or just plain absent" as the "Non-Integrating Gap." This region is plagued by repressive political regimes, handcuffed markets, mass murder, and widespread poverty and disease. For Barnett, the Gap provides a dangerous breeding ground for "global terrorists" and other "forces of disconnectedness" opposed to the "economic and security rule sets we call globalization." This region includes the Caribbean Rim, virtually all of Africa, the Balkans, the Caucasus, parts of Central Asia, the Middle East, and parts of Southeast Asia. Along the Gap's "bloody boundaries," the military strategist locates "Seam States" such as Mexico, Brazil, South Africa, Morocco, Algeria, Greece, Turkey, Pakistan, Thailand, Malaysia, the Philippines, and Indonesia. Lacking the Core's high levels of connectivity and security, these countries are the logical entry point for terrorists plotting their attacks.[78]

Despite its horrific toll, Barnett considers 9/11 a necessary "wake-up call" that forced the United States to make a long-term military commitment to "export security" to the Gap. The Core has no choice but to treat the entire Gap region as a "strategic threat environment." Inaction or a premature retreat from Iraq and Afghanistan would jeopardize the fledgling world order based on America's universal values. For Barnett, the imperative for the Global War on Terror is rooted in the "underlying reality" of a "military–market nexus"—the dependence of "the merchant culture of the business world" on the military's "warrior culture":

I express this interrelationship [of the military and the market] in the form of a "ten commandments of globalization": (1) Look for resources and ye shall find, but.... (2) No stability, no markets; (3) No growth, no stability; (4) No resources, no growth; (5) No infrastructure, no resources; (6) No money, no infrastructure; (7) No rules, no money; (8) No security, no rules; (9) No Leviathan [American military force], no security; and (10) No (American) will, no Leviathan. Understanding the military-market link is not just good business, it is good national security strategy.[79]

Ultimately, Barnett proposes a "global transaction strategy" built on three basic principles. First, the United States must increase the Core's "immune system capabilities" by responding quickly and efficiently to 9/11-like "system perturbations." Second, it must pressure the Seam States to "firewall the Core from the Gap's worst exports," namely, terror, drugs, and pandemics. Finally, America must remain firmly committed to a Global War on Terror and its overriding objective of "shrinking the Gap." There can be no compromise or vacillation. Globalization's enemies must be eliminated and the Gap region must be integrated into the Core. As

Barnett emphasizes, "I believe it is absolutely essential that this country lead the global war on terrorism, because I fear what will happen to our world if the forces of disconnectedness are allowed to prevail—to perturb the system at will."[80]

Needless to say, there are a number of problematic assumptions and omissions in Barnett's construction of imperial globalism. Three of its most troubling features are the author's inability to recognize al-Qaeda's jihadism as a globalist ideology; his uncritical perspective on American history; and his unreflective equation of "American values" with "universal values." As I have pointed out elsewhere, Barnett's third assumption also lies at the heart of the Bush administration's post–9/11 public diplomacy initiatives, which have done much to fuel anti-American sentiments around the world.[81] A testimony to Barnett's "military–market nexus," the newly created office of Undersecretary of State for Public Diplomacy and Public Affairs unleashed a Madison Avenue-style advertisement campaign of "branding American values" on the Middle East. Since its official launch in 2002, however, evidence has been mounting that the intended "end-users" of "Brand USA" in the Gap region are not buying. In fact, world opinion polls conducted between 2002 and 2007 actually point to intensifying anti-American sentiments. This trend appears to be strongly related to the perceived discrepancy between America's proclamation of freedom and democracy and its actual policies in the Middle East and elsewhere.[82]

However, Barnett's construction of imperial globalism perfectly illustrates why 9/11 should not be read as leading to a "collapse of globalism" and the resurgence of the national imaginary. Rejecting dualistic notions of national security that place the global outside the national, the Pentagon strategist masterfully harnesses the language of American exceptionalism to his globalist vision. Pro-immigration and fiercely opposed to isolationism, he articulates the rising global imaginary in terms that would make national-populists like Buchanan cringe: "Globalization is this country's gift to history—the most perfectly flawed projection of the American Dream onto the global landscape.... In short, *we the people* needs to become *we the planet*."[83] Barnett may be an imperialist, but his communal orientation is decidedly globalist. His ideological leanings suggest that the post–9/11 era has been a fertile ground for the hardpowering of market globalism into a doctrine that unites the twin goals of globalizing markets and American global hegemony—all in the name of "we the planet." If globalization represents a long-term historical trend toward greater worldwide interconnectedness, then the current imperial episode should be seen as part of this trend: American empire inhabits globalization.[84]

Thus, we are led to conclude that the adaptation of market globalism to American Empire constitutes neither a retreat nor a defeat of the global imaginary. Rather, it is just another moment in the destabilization of the national that affects all geographical scales. The apparent reassertion of the national in the form of millions of flag-waving Americans who believe in the exceptional greatness and goodness of their country occurs squarely within the parameters of the rising globalist imaginary. Market globalism's love affair with American Empire is hardly a sign of its ideological incoherence or political weakness, but a reflection of its growing flexibility and responsiveness to a new set of political issues. Like all mature political belief systems, market globalism has begun to bear the marks of an ideational family, broad enough to contain both the economistic prototype of the Roaring Nineties and its more imperialist post–9/11 permutation. This ideological broadening of market globalism is also reflected in the rapid conversion of scores of neoliberals to at least a moderate version of what Michael Ignatieff calls "Empire Lite."[85] The militaristic display at the 2004 Democratic Convention in Boston, for example, showed that despite persisting differences with the Bush administration that deepened further after the Democratic takeover of Congress in 2006, prominent neoliberals like John Kerry and Hillary Rodham Clinton were warming up to some form of imperial globalism, including the President's unilateralist dogma that the United States does not "ask anybody's permission" in pursuit of its enemies. Even Thomas Friedman accepted the new claim that globalization requires a Global War on Terror, adding that the "epic struggle" against jihadist globalism was being waged by both military and ideological means: "We're fighting to defeat an ideology: religious totalitarianism.... The opposite of religious totalitarianism is an ideology of pluralism ...."[86] Strong words, indeed, for the American globalization guru who had only two years earlier insisted that the backlash against the globalizing economy was unlikely to produce a coherent alternative ideology.

6.4. The Return of Religion?

There is yet one more adaptation that market globalism underwent in the wake of 9/11: the incorporation of religious and moralistic features that mirrored, to some extent, the jihadist discourse of al-Qaeda. Like their adversaries, imperial globalists saw the Global War on Terror as a necessary and righteous campaign against incorrigible evildoers. As George W. Bush put it, "Our responsibility to history is clear: to answer these attacks [of 9/11] and rid the world of evil."[87] Time and again, the American President emphasized that the ongoing "global war of uncertain duration" should be seen as the "decisive ideological struggle of our time." And, like his jihadist adversaries, he used "ideology" in ways that blurred conventional distinctions between political and religious belief systems. For example, he argued that al-Qaeda's "totalitarian ideology" was not grounded in "secular philosophy but in the perversion of a proud religion. Its content may be different from the ideologies of the last century, but its means are similar: intolerance, murder, terror, enslavement, and repression." On the other hand, Bush linked his own belief system to a noble "freedom agenda" intended by its divine Author for all of humanity: "We believe that freedom is a gift from almighty God, beyond any power on earth to take away."[88] Although his public pronouncements consistently disparaged the notion of an all-out war against Islam as well as the thesis of an inevitable clash of civilizations, they teemed with religious references and expressions of faith. The President's much criticized characterization of the Global War on Terror as a "crusade," for example, may have been an ignorant gaffe, but it nonetheless revealed his religious conviction that the "ideological struggle between freedom and terror" represented an epic confrontation between the forces of Good led by America and the unremitting Evil of radical Islamism.

The extension of the Global War on Terror into Iraq further intensified the administration's tendency to mix the determinist language of market globalism with belligerent pronouncements promising ultimate victory. Just as the Soviet "Evil Empire" had eventually succumbed to the forces of the "New Jerusalem," the jihadists' attempt to build a "radical Islamic Empire" would meet inevitable defeat. The same fate awaited the rogue states that constituted the President's famous "Axis of Evil." As Princeton ethicist Peter Singer has pointed out, Bush's tendency to see the world through religious Manichean lenses was evident in his speeches. Hundreds of times, he employed "evil" as a noun—a "thing" or a "force" with a real existence apart from the brutal and selfish acts of which human beings are capable. Singer concludes that Bush's narrow judgmental views eschew critical reflection in favor of moralistic intuitions expressed in the fundamentalist language of apocalyptic Christianity.[89]

The President's belief in the faith-based "moral clarity" of his message is shared by several key members of his administration who also consider the creation of a global American imperium as part of God's plan. In 2003, Vice President Dick Cheney sent out a Christmas card to friends and supporters that read: "And if a sparrow cannot fall to the ground without His notice, is it probable that an empire can rise without His aid?"[90] Formal and informal prayer meetings and Bible study sessions among White House staffers take place regularly. Since the emergence of Christian fundamentalists as the dominant constituency of the Republican Party in the 1990s, critical observers have pointed to an internal power shift toward the more radical end of the spectrum. Political commentator Kevin Phillips speaks of "theocons" enforcing "theological correctness"—a tendency he regards as the mirror image of the "political correctness" displayed by secular liberals in discussing minority groups, women's rights, and environmental issues.[91] Former *New York Times* foreign correspondent Chris Hedges takes this argument a step further by referring to the radical members of the Christian Right who dream of extending their "Christian nation" into a global Christian empire as "American Fascists." Out of nearly seventy million American evangelicals, Hedges estimates the size of this "militant core" as constituting around twenty million, or 7 percent of the US population. But his research on the expanding activities of this radical movement suggests that its political potency far exceeds its numbers. He closes his chilling study with an impassioned warning: "The radical Christian Right calls for exclusion, cruelty and intolerance in the name of God. Its members do not commit evil for evil's sake. They commit evil to make a better world. To attain this better world, they believe, some must suffer and be silenced, and at the end of time all those who oppose them must be destroyed."[92] Indeed, jihadism is hardly confined to Islam.

To be sure, the convergence of religion and ideology in the dawning global age appears to be a broader phenomenon that extends beyond Christian fundamentalists, jihadists, or imperial globalists. It is also happening in the justice-globalist camp. Ever since the Global War on Terror and global climate change became key issues on a par with the global economy, justice globalism has absorbed heavy doses of spiritual and religious thought from affiliated environmentalists and peace activists. Are we witnessing a reversal of the powerful secularization dynamic that served two centuries as the midwife of ideology? If so, does the rising global imaginary create more favorable conditions for the mixing of political and religious belief systems?

In recent years, there has been a growing chorus of critics who argue that students of political ideology have indulged for far too long in an overly secularized approach to their subject. Mainstream studies of political belief systems are said to reify a spurious religion–ideology divide, paying inadequate attention to the fact that religious beliefs and political ideas have always been intermingled. Reflecting on the post–9/11 explosion of interest in "political theology," one critic has recently asserted that "Intellectual complacency, nursed by implicit faith in the inevitability of secularization, has blinded us to the persistence of political theology and its manifest power to shape human life at any moment."[93] Another concludes his discerning inquiry into the legitimacy of political religion as a concept with the suggestion that "the concept of 'political religion' is, for the time being, a necessary if somewhat ill-defined conceptual category.... It reminds us that religion does not allow itself to be easily banished from society, and that, where it is tried, it returns in unpredictable and perverted forms."[94]

Emilio Gentile—a leading proponent of the currently fashionable view that totalitarian ideologies like fascism, Nazism, or communism are best explained as political phenomena that assume the features of religion—adds his voice to the chorus with his discussion of the "sacralization of politics," which allegedly occurred in the modern era after the political realm had gained its independence from traditional religion. According to this Italian historian, the religious impulse continued to exert its power on those modern systems of meanings that came to be known as political ideologies: "By taking over the religious dimension and acquiring a sacred nature, politics went so far as to claim for itself the prerogative to determine the meaning and fundamental aim of existence for individuals and the collectivity, at least on earth."[95] Much in the same vein, the prominent political thinker John Gray has recently argued that the most influential secular ideologies of the modern period were actually shaped by repressed religion. His recent book represents an extreme version of the alleged primacy of religious ideas: "Modern politics is a chapter in the history of religion.... The Enlightenment ideologies of the past centuries were very largely spilt theology." For Gray, the rise of al-Qaeda's jihadist globalism and Bush's imperial globalism merely marks the return of "apocalyptic religion" as a major force in global politics.[96]

One of the unfortunate outcomes of this timely and necessary discussion has been the proliferation of concepts invented to shed light on the intensifying ideology–religion nexus. As one learns very quickly by following the scholarly debates raging in various academic journals devoted to the subject, "political religion" should not be confused with "civil religion." "Religious politics" is not necessarily the same as "secular religion." The "sacralization of politics" is alleged to differ from the "politicization of religion."[97] Since it would require another book to enter into the subtleties of these debates, let us end this study with a brief reflection on the possible reasons for the convergence of ideology and religion that draws on the main arguments presented here.

Six chapters ago, we started our discussion of ideology with a detailed account of Destutt de Tracy's attempt to establish a "science of ideas" without appeal to divine revelation or metaphysical speculation. Separating reflection about human affairs from theological conjecture about the other world, such a science would yield truths applicable to politics and society. Henceforth, the metaphysical claims to transcendental Truth generated by established religion would be, at best, a private matter. Although Napoleon Bonaparte and Karl Marx linked *idéologie* to the misty realm of metaphysics, false consciousness, and religion, the emerging grand political belief systems of the national age remained true to Tracy's conception of ideology as secular ideational systems serving the larger cause of human betterment by rejecting or at least curtailing religious faiths. As we emphasized in the early chapters of this book, however, there never existed in politics impenetrable walls separating ideology from religion, the secular from the sacred, or the church from government. Struggling to escape the womb of theology and establish alternative ideational systems trading in certitudes, the elite codifiers of all ideologies—even conservatives after a slow start—were forced to devise multiple strategies for the containment of religion, including co-option, absorption, and imitation.

Most of all, however, ideologies sought to keep a healthy distance from religion in order to fulfill their primary function of articulating a political agenda for the secular, *national* community. Citizens' freedom *of* religion was predicated on the liberal imperative of freedom *from* religion. During the last two centuries, therefore, the national imaginary and its political articulations served as a curb, or a lid, on religion that kept it from regaining its prerevolutionary dominance. To be sure, the religious never simply faded away as some hubristic "ideologues" had predicted. But it was curtailed, checked, reined in, and, in some cases, driven underground by the national. With the rise of the global imaginary, however, the national and its political translations have become destabilized. As a result, the curb on religion is being eased, allowing it to spill into ideology more than at any other time in recent memory. Hence, we should not be surprised at the convergence of ideology and religion in an era when the national imaginary is weakening. Moreover, as any attentive student of history knows, Empire and religion have always been fond of each other as both harbor global aspirations. At the very least, they have shown greater affinity for each other than the nation and religion. Assuming that the current phase of globalization is, indeed, one characterized by the "great ideological struggle" between imperial globalism and jihadist globalism, then one would expect religion to play a much more prominent role than in the national age.

We can, therefore, respond to our two questions probing the possible return of religion in the affirmative. We are, indeed, witnessing a weakening, if not a reversal, of the powerful secularization dynamic of the last centuries as a result of the decline of the national. And, yes, the rising global imaginary has been creating more favorable conditions for the convergence of political and religious belief systems. It is unlikely that secularity in the West will disappear any time soon, but the religious will give it a run for its money, forcing previously unimagined forms of accommodation and compromise. In short, the rising global imaginary will continue to create favorable conditions for "religious ideologies" or "ideological religions." Consequently, we ought to treat religious ideas and beliefs as an increasingly integral part of the three competing globalisms that translate the rising global imaginary into concrete political agendas. Increasingly, the common frame of reference will be the "global community" although national, and even tribal, imaginings of human association will remain with us for a long time to come.

6.5. Concluding Remarks

Philosopher Nelson Goodman once noted, "Worldmaking as we know it always starts from worlds already at hand; the making is a remaking."[98] The world already at hand has been erected on the foundation of the national imaginary. Its continued impact is apparent in the enduring power of the organizing logic of the national over crucial aspects of social life. While globalization remains in full swing after 9/11 and the ensuing Global War on Terror, it remains a partial and conditional dynamic. But it would be foolish to deny that globalization—the expansion and intensification of social relations across world-space and world-time—has unsettled the geographical and conceptual territoriality of the national. Loosening the grip of traditional time–space constraints on billions of people, the global appears in a largely immaterial economy mediated by the digital communication and information of our network society.[99] It has empowered individuals who enjoy access to the myriad nodes and nerves of the global matrix while consigning the excluded to the postmodern equivalent of the Dark Ages.

As the eruptions of the global continue to sear the national, they not only change the world's economic infrastructure but also transform our sense of self, identity, and belonging. For example, as late as the 1980s, jet travel was considered a special occasion that triggered anticipatory excitement for days. Today, boarding a transcontinental airliner has become a mundane marker of people's increased mobility—thanks to new security measures an increasingly bothersome event as commonplace as train rides in the late nineteenth century. The same applies to multiple geographical and social attachments like dual and regional citizenships. Individuals from various socio-economic backgrounds who consider themselves to be at home in more than one country are no longer perceived as rare curiosities. The number of such "place polygamists" has skyrocketed in the last few decades.[100] Until recently, most people spent their entire working lives in the nation-state of their birth. But the generation born between 2000 and 2020 will find it rather common to pursue its professional careers in multiple locations around the world.

Even Americans, reared in a self-referential cultural environment that visitors from abroad often experience as stifling parochialism, can no longer isolate themselves from the intrusion of the global imaginary. It springs to life with a click of the mouse or a cursory glance at wall-mounted HDTV screens showing in real-time US troops battling a multinational force of Islamist "insurgents" half a world away. But it is not technology in the abstract that builds and energizes the global imaginary. The local concreteness of the global stares us in the face as the Cuban-Chinese restaurant around the corner or the Eurasian fusion café next door. These hybrid culinary establishments are serving us up a daily taste of a global stew that is slowly thickening but still needs plenty of stirring.

The national is slowly losing its grip on people's minds, but the global has not yet ascended to the commanding heights once occupied by its predecessor. It erupts in fits and false starts, offering observers confusing spectacles of social fragmentation and integration that cut across old geographical hierarchies in unpredictable patterns.[101] Consider, for example, the arduous processes of regional economic and political integration that are limping along on all continents. And yet, expanding formations like the European Union—however chronic their internal tensions—have become far more integrated than most observers predicted only a decade ago. The short duration and unevenness of today's globalization dynamics make it impossible to paint a clear picture of the New World Order. But the first rays of the rising global imaginary have provided enough light to capture the contours of a profoundly altered ideological landscape.

Notes

Preface

1. Eric Hobsbawm, *The Age of Extremes: A History of the World, 1914–1991* (New York: Vintage, 1996), p. 287.
2. See, for example, Michael Mandelbaum, *The Ideas that Conquered the World: Peace, Democracy and Free Markets in the Twenty-First Century* (Washington, DC: Public Affairs, 2002).
3. For a masterful treatment of the multiscalarity of globalization, see Saskia Sassen's pioneering work on the subject. Her most recent study is *A Sociology of Globalization* (New York: W. W. Norton, 2007).
4. John B. Thompson, *Ideology and Modern Culture: Critical Social Theory and the Era of Mass Communication* (Stanford, CA: Stanford University Press, 1990); Michael Freeden, *Ideologies and Political Theory* (Oxford: Oxford University Press, 1996), and Michael Freeden, ed., *Reassessing Political Ideologies: The Durability of Dissent* (London: Routledge, 2001); and John Schwarzmantel, *The Age of Ideology: Political Ideologies from the American Revolution to Postmodern Times* (London: Macmillan Press, 1998).
5. See, for example, Leon P. Barat, *Political Ideologies: Their Origins and Impact*, 8th edn. (Upper Saddle River, NJ: Prentice Hall, 2003); Matthew Festenstein and Michael Kenny, eds., *Political Ideologies: A Reader and Guide* (Oxford, UK: Oxford University Press, 2005); Andrew Heywood, *Political Ideologies: An Introduction*, 3rd edn. (Houndmills, UK and New York: Palgrave Macmillan, 2003); and Lyman Tower Sargent, *Contemporary Political Ideologies: A Comparative Analysis*, 12th edn. (Belmont, CA: Wadsworth, 2003).

Introduction

1. Hannah Arendt, "Ideology and Terror: A Novel Form of Government," *The Review of Politics* 15 (July 1953), p. 315.
2. Giovanni Sartori, "Politics, Ideology and Belief Systems," *American Political Science Review* 63 (1969), p. 411. Though shorn of its Cold War rhetoric, the ideology/science binary still dominates in social science literature. See, for example, Graham C. Kinloch and Raj P. Mohan, eds., *Ideology and the Social Sciences* (Westport, CT: Greenwood Press, 2000), pp. 12–13. For an enlightening

discussion of ideology in the US academy, see David McLellan, *Ideology*, 2nd edn. (Minneapolis: University of Minnesota Press, 1995), chapter 5.

3. See, for example, Anthony Downs, *An Economic Theory of Democracy* (New York: Harper & Row, 1957). For a more detailed discussion of behaviorist notions of ideology, see Gayil Talshir, "The Objects of Ideology: Historical Transformations and the Changing Role of the Analyst," *History of Political Thought* XXVI.3 (Autumn 2005), p. 539.

4. Francis Fukuyama, "The End of History?" *National Interest* 16 (Summer 1989), p. 4.

5. Francois Furet, *The Passing of an Illusion: The Idea of Communism in the Twentieth Century* (Chicago: University of Chicago Press, 2000).

6. George W. Bush, "Address to Joint Session of Congress and Americans," September 20, 2001, in J. W. Edwards and Louis de Rose, *United We Stand: A Message for All Americans* (Ann Arbor, MI: Mundus), p. 13.

7. George W. Bush cited in Thom Shanker and Jim Rutenberg, "President Wants to Increase Size of Armed Forces," *The New York Times* (December 20, 2006).

8. See Sudhir Hazareesingh, *Political Traditions in Modern France* (New York: Oxford University Press, 1994), p. 13.

9. John B. Thompson, *Studies in the Theory of Ideology* (Berkeley, CA: University of California Press, 1984), pp. 3–4; and *Ideology and Modern Culture*, pp. 53–4.

10. Louis Althusser, *For Marx* (London: Allen Lane, 1969), p. 232.

11. Michael Freeden, "Confronting the Chimera of a 'Post-Ideological' Age," *Critical Review of International and Social Political Philosophy* 8.2 (June 2005), p. 262.

12. See Manfred B. Steger, *Globalism: Market Ideology Meets Terrorism*, 2nd edn. (Lanham, MD: Rowman & Littlefield, 2005).

13. Michael Freeden, *Ideology: A Very Short Introduction* (Oxford: Oxford University Press, 2003), pp. 54–5. See also Michael Freeden, *Ideologies and Political Theory* (Oxford: Oxford University Press, 1996). My own thinking on ideology is greatly indebted to Freeden's pioneering efforts. The ideological function of "fixing" the process of signification around certain meanings was discussed as early as the 1970s by the French linguist Michel Pecheux and intellectuals associated with the French semiotic journal *Tel Quel*. See Terry Eagleton, *Ideology: An Introduction* (London: Verso, 1991), pp. 195–7.

14. Harold D. Lasswell, *Politics: Who Gets What, When and How* (New York: Meridian Books, 1958).

15. For a useful summary of the main functions of ideology, see Paul Ricoeur, *Lectures on Ideology and Utopia* (New York: Columbia University Press, 1986). A short summary of Ricoeur's arguments can be found in Steger, *Globalism*, pp. 7–8.

16. The existing differences between "fascism" and "Nazism" highlight the crucial role played by the national context. Some writers regard "anarchism" as an ideology in its own right, but I consider its various currents too

closely intertwined with either liberalism or socialism. Communism and fascism/Nazism, too, contain important ties to socialism and conservatism, but their morphologies strike me as more distinct than anarchism. In addition, the historical impact of communism and fascism/Nazism has been more significant.

17. Charles Taylor, *Modern Social Imaginaries* (Durham and London: Duke University Press, 2004), pp. 2, 23–6; and *A Secular Age* (Cambridge, MA: The Belknap Press of Harvard University Press, 2007), chapter 4. As employed throughout this book, my key twin concepts of the "national" and "global" imaginary draw on relevant arguments presented in the works of Charles Taylor, Benedict Anderson, Pierre Bourdieu, and Arjun Appadurai.

18. Pierre Bourdieu, *The Logic of Practice* (Stanford, CA: Stanford University Press, 1990), pp. 54–5. See also Hubert Dreyfus, *Being in the World* (Cambridge, MA: MIT Press, 1991) and John Searle, *The Construction of Social Reality* (New York: Free Press, 1995).

19. This propensity of social imaginaries to give birth to ideologies that serve primarily on the level of "fantasies" constructing political subjects has been emphasized by Slavoj Zizek, *Mapping Ideology* (London: Verso, 1994), pp. 1–33; and *Iraq: The Borrowed Kettle* (London: Verso, 2004).

20. On the useful notion of historical "tipping points" as particular combinations of dynamics and resources that can usher in a new organizing logic, see Saskia Sassen, *Territory, Authority, Rights: From Medieval to Global Assemblages* (Princeton, NJ: Princeton University Press, 2006), chapter 4, and pp. 404–5.

21. William E. Connolly, *Political Theory and Modernity* (Cambridge: Basil Blackwell, 1988), pp. 2–3.

22. Jürgen Habermas, *The Philosophical Discourse of Modernity* (Cambridge, MA: MIT Press, 1987), p. 7.

23. Eric Hobsbawm, *Nations and Nationalism since 1780* (Cambridge, UK: Cambridge University Press, 1992), p. 14.

24. Anthony Smith, *Nationalism and Modernism: A Critical Survey of Recent Theories of Nations and Nationalism* (London and New York: Routledge, 1998), p. 1.

25. Tom Nairn, "Make for the Boondocks," *London Review of Books* (May 5, 2005), p. 13.

26. Benedict Anderson, *Imagined Communities: Reflections on the Origin and Spread of Nationalism*, rev. edn. (London: Verso, 1991), pp. 4–5; Clifford Geertz, "Ideology as Cultural System," in *The Interpretation of Cultures* (New York: Basic Books, 1973), pp. 193–233; Louis Dumont, *German Ideology: From France to Germany and Back* (Chicago: University of Chicago Press, 1994), p. vii; and Michael Freeden, "Is Nationalism a Distinct Ideology?" *Political Studies* 46 (1998), pp. 748–65.

27. See Ernest Renan, "What Is a Nation," in Omar Dahbour and Micheline Ishay, eds., *The Nationalism Reader* (Atlantic Highlands, NJ: Humanities Press, 1995), pp. 143–55; and Julia Kristeva, *Nations Without Nationalism* (New York:

Columbia University Press, 1993), p. 57. For a discussion of "national consciousness" as "secularized religion," see George L. Moss, *The Nationalization of the Masses: Political Symbolism and Mass Movements in Germany from the Napoleonic Wars through the Third Reich* (New York: Howard Fertig, 1975), p. 2.

28. See Liah Greenfeld, *Nationalisms: Five Roads to Modernity* (Cambridge: Harvard University Press, 1992); and *The Spirit of Capitalism: Nationalism and Economic Growth* (Cambridge: Harvard University Press, 2001).

29. Liah Greenfeld, "Is Modernity Possible without Nationalism?" in Michel Seymour, ed., *The Fate of the Nation-State* (Montreal: McGill-Queen's University Press, 2004), p. 40.

30. Anderson, *Imagined Communities*, pp. 6–7.

31. See also Ulrich Beck, *Power in the Global Age: A New Global Political Economy* (Cambridge, UK: Polity Press, 2005), p. xii.

32. Craig Calhoun argues that such nationalist "essentialism" represents one of the guiding assumptions in modern thinking on matters of personal and collective identity. See Craig Calhoun, *Nationalism* (Minneapolis: University of Minnesota Press, 1997), pp. 18–20.

33. Arjun Appadurai, *Fear of Small Numbers: An Essay on the Geography of Anger* (Durham and London: Duke University Press, 2006), p. 3.

34. Michael Billig makes a similar point when he argues that "normalized" nationalism tends to operate mindlessly, that is, below the level of conscious awareness. See *Banal Nationalism* (London: Sage, 1995).

35. See ibid. pp. 6–7. See also Martin Albrow, *The Global Age: State and Society Beyond Modernity* (Stanford, CA: Stanford University Press, 1997); and Beck, *Power in the Global Age*. Albrow's epochal theory postulates the "end of modernity," whereas Beck argues for a seismic shift from a "first modernity" to a "second modernity."

36. See Roland Robertson, *Globalization: Social Theory and Global Culture* (Thousand Oaks, CA: Sage, 1992), p. 6. For similar arguments, see Albrow, *The Global Age*; Ulrich Beck, *What Is Globalization?* (Cambridge: Polity Press, 2000), and *Power in the Global Age*; John Urry, *Global Complexity* (Cambridge, UK: Polity Press, 2003); Ulf Hannerz, *The Transnational Connection* (London: Routledge, 1996); and Malcolm Waters, *Globalization* (London: Routledge, 1995).

37. See Anthony Elliott and Charles Lemert, *The New Individualism: The Emotional Costs of Globalization* (London: Routledge, 2006), p. 90.

38. Sassen, *Territory, Authority, Rights*, p. 402.

39. For a helpful discussion of "disaggregating states" in the global age, see Anne-Marie Slaughter, *A New World Order* (Princeton: Princeton University Press, 2004).

40. See Andrew C. Gould, *Origins of Liberal Dominance: State, Church, and Party in Nineteenth-Century Europe* (Ann Arbor, MI: University of Michigan Press, 1999), p. 2; John Gray, *Liberalism*, 2nd edn. (Minneapolis, MN: University

of Minnesota Press, 1995), p. xi; and Irene Collins, *Liberalism in Nineteenth-Century Europe* (London: The Historical Association, 1957), p. 3.

41. On the persistence of "zombie categories," see Beck, *Power in the Global Age*, p. xi.

42. For extreme versions of this claim, see Kenichi Ohmae, *The End of the Nation-State: The Rise of Regional Economies* (New York: Free Press, 1995); and Jean-Marie Guehenno, *The End of the Nation-State* (Minneapolis, MN: University of Minnesota Press, 1995).

43. Ulf Hedetoft and Mette Hjort, eds., *The Postnational Self: Belonging and Identity* (Minneapolis: University of Minnesota Press, 2002), p. xv.

Chapter 1

1. See Otto Dann, "Introduction," in Otto Dann and John Dinwiddy, eds., *Nationalism in the Age of the French Revolution* (London: Hambledon Press, 1988), p. 11.

2. See Stephen Toulmin, *Cosmopolis: The Hidden Agenda of Modernity* (Chicago: University of Chicago Press, 1990), pp. 96–7.

3. See William Doyle, *The Ancien Régime*, 2nd edn. (Houndmills, UK: Palgrave Macmillan, 2001), p. 4.

4. Pierre Manent, *An Intellectual History of Liberalism* (Princeton, NJ: Princeton University Press, 1995), p. 10.

5. See, for example, Thompson, *Ideology and Modern Culture*, p. 77.

6. My account accepts the central thesis of Martin S. Staum, *Minerva's Message: Stabilizing the French Revolution* (Montreal, CAN: McGill-Queen's University Press, 1996). For an accessible summary of the revolutionary events, see William Doyle, *The French Revolution: A Very Short Introduction* (Oxford: Oxford University Press, 2001). For a longer academic treatment, see Nigel Aston, *The French Revolution 1789–1804: Authority, Liberty and the Search for Stability* (Houndmills, UK: Palgrave Macmillan, 2004).

7. Nicholas Atkin and Frank Tallett, "Introduction," in *The Right in France: From Revolution to Le Pen*, 2nd edn. (London: I. B. Tauris, 2003), p. 4.

8. Staum, *Minerva's Message*, pp. 3–4.

9. Pierre Daunou cited in ibid. p. 37. See also Emmet Kennedy, *A Philosophe in the Age of Revolution: Destutt de Tracy and the Origins of "Ideology"* (Philadelphia, PA: The American Philosophical Society, 1978), pp. 39–44.

10. Staum, *Minerva's Message*, p. 4.

11. Kennedy, *A Philosophe in the Age of Revolution*, p. 5.

12. Destutt de Tracy cited in ibid. p. 12.

13. Thomas Jefferson, "Prospectus," in Count Destutt Tracy, *A Treatise on Political Economy: To Which Is Prefixed a Supplement to a Preceding Work on the Understanding of Elements of Ideology*, translated and edited by Thomas Jefferson (New York: Augustus Kelley Publishers, 1970 [1817]), p. v.

14. Destutt de Tracy cited in Kennedy, *A Philosophe in the Age of Revolution*, pp. 15–16.

15. Brian William Head, *Ideology and Social Science: Destutt de Tracy and French Liberalism* (Dordrecht, Holland: Martinus Nijhoff Publishers, 1985), p. 7.

16. Destutt de Tracy cited in Kennedy, *A Philosophe in the Age of Revolution*, pp. 18–20.

17. For a concise summary of these speeches, see Cheryl B. Welch, *Liberty and Utility: The French Idéologues and the Transformation of Liberalism* (New York: Columbia University Press, 1984), pp. 20–3.

18. Kennedy, *A Philosophe in the Age of Revolution*, p. 30.

19. Ibid. pp. 31–6.

20. Destutt de Tracy cited in Head, *Ideology and Social Science*, pp. 10, 36.

21. Kennedy, *A Philosophe in the Age of Revolution*, pp. 36–7.

22. Ibid. p. 37.

23. In eighteenth-century language, the term "positive" meant "exact" or "scientific." Influenced by Tracy's work, Auguste Comte based his "positivistic" model of modern social science on "ideology." See Kennedy, *A Philosophe in the Age of Revolution*, pp. 337–9.

24. Destutt de Tracy cited in Head, *Ideology and Social Science*, p. 26.

25. Destutt de Tracy, *A Treatise on Political Economy*, pp. 2–3.

26. Destutt de Tracy cited in Head, *Ideology and Social Science*, p. 27.

27. For a detailed account of the role of memory and language in Tracy's ideology, see Welch, *Liberty and Utility*, pp. 59–69; Head, *Ideology and Social Science*, chapters 2 and 3; and Kennedy, *A Philosophe in the Age of Revolution*, chapter 2.

28. For a discussion of the critical ideological function of "decontestation," see the Introduction of this study. See also Freeden, *Ideology*, pp. 54–5.

29. Destutt de Tracy cited in Head, *Ideology and Social Science*, p. 10.

30. Destutt de Tracy cited in Kennedy, *A Philosophe in the Age of Revolution*, pp. 46, 48.

31. Destutt de Tracy cited in ibid. p. 64, and Head, *Ideology and Social Sciences*, p. 60.

32. For a more detailed account of the Chateaubriand-Tracy controversy, see Joseph F. Byrnes, "Chateaubriand and Destutt de Tracy: Defining Religious and Secular Polarities in France at the Beginning of the Nineteenth Century," *Church History* 60.3 (September 1991), pp. 316–30.

33. For a list of the names of the "ideologists" affiliated with the Institute, see Staum, *Minerva's Message*, pp. 232–5.

34. Destutt de Tracy cited in Emmet Kennedy, " 'Ideology' from Destutt de Tracy to Marx," *Journal of the History of Ideas* 40.3 (July–September 1979), p. 355.

35. Napoleon Bonaparte cited in Kennedy, *A Philosophe in the Age of Revolution*, p. 76. This section on Bonaparte has greatly benefited from the discussions offered in ibid., chapter 3, and Welch, *Liberty and Utility*, chapter 1.

36. Martyn Lyons, *Napoleon Bonaparte and the Legacy of the French Revolution* (London: Macmillan, 1994), p. 24.

37. Kennedy, ' "Ideology' from Destutt de Tracy to Marx," p. 358.

38. Kennedy, *A* Philosophe *in the Age of Revolution*, p. 82.

39. Maine de Biran cited in Kennedy, ' "Ideology' from Destutt de Tracy to Marx," pp. 357–8.

40. Napoleon Bonaparte cited in ibid. p. 359.

41. See Michael Broers, "The First Napoleonic Regime, 1799–1815: The Origins of the Positivist Right or the Zenith of Jacobinism?" in Atkin and Tallett, eds., *The Right in France*, p. 30.

42. See Kennedy, " 'Ideology' from Destutt de Tracy to Marx," p. 363.

43. Napoleon Bonaparte cited in Kennedy, *A* Philosophe *in the Age of Revolution*, p. 215.

44. Letter of John Adams to Thomas Jefferson, December 16, 1816, in Lester J Cappon, ed., *The Adams-Jefferson Letters: The Complete Correspondence between Thomas Jefferson and Abigail and John Adams* (Chapel Hill, NC: University of North Carolina Press, 1959), vol. II, pp. 500–1. See also Lawrence S. Kaplan, "Jefferson's Foreign Policy and Napoleon's Ideologues," *The William and Mary Quarterly* 19.3 (July 1962), pp. 344–59.

45. John Stuart Mill, "Coleridge," in Gertrude Himmelfarb, ed., *Essays on Politics and Culture* (New York: Anchor Books, 1963), p. 132.

46. Karl Marx, *Das Kapital: Kritik der politischen Oekonomie*, vols. 1 and 2 (Berlin: Dietz Verlag, 1975–6), pp. 677, 484. All Marx and Engels translations from the original German are by the author.

47. The two best assessments of the Marx–Engels intellectual partnership are Terrell Carver, *Marx & Engels: The Intellectual Relationship* (Bloomington, IN: Indiana University Press, 1983); and Max Adler, *Marx und Engels als Denker* (Frankfurt: Makol Verlag, 1972 [1908; 1920]).

48. This is the subtitle of *The German Ideology*.

49. Karl Marx and Friedrich Engels, *Werke*, vol. 3 (Berlin: Dietz Verlag, 1978), p. vi.

50. For the best available translation of the text (with a valuable introduction by the editor), see Terrell Carver, ed., "Rough Notes, formerly known as 'I. Feuerbach', drawn from 'the German ideology' manuscripts by Karl Marx, Friedrich Engels and Joseph Weydemeyer: New English Translation from a new German Text," unpublished manuscript, 2007. I thank Professor Carver for sharing his important translation with me.

51. Marx and Engels, *Werke*, vol. 3, pp. 18–25.

52. Ibid. pp. 26–7.

53. Ibid.

54. Ibid. pp. 46–7.

55. Ibid. p. 7.

56. Ibid. p. 20.

57. Leszek Kolakowski, *Main Currents of Marxism: 1—The Founders* (Oxford: Oxford University Press, 1978), p. 176.

58. Marx and Engels, *Werke*, vol. 3, pp. 38, 46–7. For an informative discussion of the role of ideas in Marxist theory, see Philip J. Kain, "Marx's Theory of Ideas," *History and Theory* 20.4 (December 1981), pp. 357–78.

59. Karl Marx and Friedrich Engels, *Werke*, vol. 39 (Berlin: Dietz Verlag, 1976), p. 96.

60. Eduard Bernstein, *The Preconditions of Socialism*, ed. Henry Tudor (Cambridge, UK: Cambridge University Press, 1993), p. 200.

61. Marx and Engels, *Werke*, vol. 3, pp. 14.

62. Karl Marx and Friedrich Engels, *Werke*, vol. 1 (Berlin: Dietz Verlag, 1978), p. 404. See Oscar J. Hammen, "The Young Marx Revisited," *Journal of the History of Ideas* 31.1 (January–March 1970), p. 114. For various views on the "national question" in Marx and Engels, see, for example, Ian Cummins, *Marx, Engels, and National Movements* (New York: St. Martin's Press, 1980); Ephraim Nimni, *Marxism and Nationalism: Theoretical Origins of a Political Crisis* (London: Pluto, 1991); John Schwarzmantel, *Socialism and the Idea of the Nation* (London: Harvester Wheatsheaf, 1991); and Michael Forman, *Nationalism and the International Labor Movement: The Idea of the Nation in Socialist and Anarchist Theory* (University Park, PA: Pennsylvania State University Press, 1998).

Chapter 2

1. See Margaret Canovan, *Nationhood and Political Theory* (Cheltenham, UK: Edward Elgar, 1996), p. 13; and "Sleeping Dogs, Prowling Cats, and Soaring Doves: Three Paradoxes of Nationhood," in Seymour, ed., *The Fate of the Nation-State*, pp. 19–37.

2. Alan S. Kahan, *Liberalism in Nineteenth-Century Europe: The Political Culture of Limited Suffrage* (New York: Palgrave Macmillan, 2003), p. 9.

3. See Mosse, *The Nationalization of the Masses*, pp. 2–4. See also Mark Goldie, "Ideology," in Terence Ball, James Farr, and Russell Hanson, eds., *Political Innovation and Conceptual Change* (Cambridge, UK: Cambridge University Press, 1989), p. 274; and Manent, *An Intellectual History of Liberalism*.

4. Simón Bolívar cited in David Bushnell and Neill Macaulay, *The Emergence of Latin America in the Nineteenth Century* (New York: Oxford University Press, 1994), p. 25.

5. See Eric J. Evans, *Political Parties in Britain 1783–1867* (London: Methuen, 1985), p. 15.

6. Ibid. pp. 12–16; and J. R. Jennings, "Conceptions of England and Its Constitution in Nineteenth-Century Political Thought," *The Historical Journal* 29.1 (1986), pp. 65–85.

7. Eduard Bernstein, *The Preconditions of Socialism*, ed. Henry Tudor (Cambridge, UK: Cambridge University Press, 1993), pp. 147–8. For a biography of Bernstein,

see my *The Quest for Evolutionary Socialism: Eduard Bernstein and Social Democracy* (Cambridge, UK: Cambridge University Press, 1997).

8. Orhan Pamuk, "In Defence of the Ideal Reader," *The Age* (October 21, 2006), p. A2.

9. See Hobsbawm, *Nations and Nationalisms since 1780*, p. 24; and Billig, *Banal Nationalism*.

10. Gray, *Liberalism*, p. 13. For the influence of Lockean ideas on American liberalism, see Louis Hartz, *The Liberal Tradition in America: An Interpretation of American Political Thought since the Revolution* (New York: Harcourt Brace & Company, 1991).

11. Freeden, *Ideologies and Political Theory*, pp. 141–2.

12. Charles Tilly, *Social Movements, 1768–2004* (Boulder, CO: Paradigm Publishers, 2004), p. 7.

13. Ibid. pp. 29–30.

14. Richard Cobden cited in Evans, *Political Parties in Britain*, p. 43.

15. Kahan, *Liberalism in Nineteenth-Century Europe*, p. 21.

16. Ibid. p. 24.

17. Richard Bellamy, "Introduction," in Richard Bellamy, ed., *Victorian Liberalism: Nineteenth-Century Political Thought and Practice* (London: Routledge, 1990), p. 2. See also Richard Bellamy, *Liberalism and Modern Society: A Historical Argument* (University Park, PA: Pennsylvania State University Press, 1992), Introduction and chapter 1.

18. See, for example, ibid. p. 22; Freeden, *Ideologies and Political Theory*, pp. 143–4; J. G. Merquior, *Liberalism Old & New* (Boston: Twayne Publishers, 1991), p. 59; Peter Berkowitz, *Virtue and the Making of Modern Liberalism* (Princeton, NJ: Princeton University Press, 1999), p. 134; and Sheldon S. Wolin, *Politics and Vision*, exp. ed. (Princeton: Princeton University Press, 2004), pp. 312–13.

19. Freeden, *Ideologies and Political Theory*, pp. 144–68; and Michael Freeden, "The Family of Liberalisms: A Morphological Analysis," in James Meadowcroft, ed., *The Liberal Tradition: Contemporary Reappraisals* (Cheltenham, UK: Edward Elgar, 1996), pp. 14–39.

20. See, for example, Robert Paul Wolff, *The Poverty of Liberalism* (Boston: Beacon Press, 1968); and Mary Ann Glendon, *Rights Talk: The Impoverishment of Political Discourse* (New York: Free Press, 1990). For a vigorous contestation of these interpretations, see Karen Zivi, "Cultivating Character: John Stuart Mill and the Subject of Rights," *American Journal of Political Science* 50.1 (January 2006), pp. 49–61.

21. John Stuart Mill, *On Liberty* (New York, Macmillan, 1987), p. 3.

22. Ibid. p. 5.

23. Ibid. p. 69.

24. Ibid. p. 13.

25. Ibid. pp. 13–14.

26. John Robson, "Civilization and Culture as Moral Concepts," in John Skorupski, ed., *The Cambridge Companion to Mill* (Cambridge, UK: Cambridge University Press, 1998), pp. 356–7.

27. John Stuart Mill, "Coleridge," in Gertrude Himmelfarb, ed., *Essays in Politics and Culture* (New York: Anchor Books, 1963), pp. 138.

28. Samuel Smiles, *Self-Help, with Illustrations of Conduct and Perseverance* (London, 1925), p. 3.

29. John Stuart Mill, "Representative Government," in *Utilitarianism, Liberty, Representative Government* (London: Dent, 1910), p. 361.

30. James Mill cited in Bellamy, *Liberalism and Modern Society*, pp. 10–11.

31. John Stuart Mill, "Civilization," in Gertrude Himmelfarb, ed., *Essays in Politics and Culture* (New York: Anchor Books, 1963), p. 63.

32. As Margaret Canovan argues lucidly, this tendency still lives on in current political philosophy and democratic theory. See *Nationhood and Political Theory*, p. 126.

33. See Andrew Vincent, *Nationalism & Particularity* (Cambridge, UK: Cambridge University Press, 1992), p. 97.

34. T. H. Green, "On the Different Senses of 'Freedom' as Applied to Will and the Moral Progress of Man," in Paul Harris and John Morrow, eds., *Lectures on the Principles of Political Obligation and Other Writings* (Cambridge, UK: Cambridge University Press, 1986), p. 256.

35. L. T. Hobhouse, "Irish Nationalism and Liberal Principle," in James Meadowcroft, ed., *Liberalism and Other Writings* (Cambridge, UK: Cambridge University Press, 1994), pp. 166–70.

36. Tilly, *Social Movements*, p. 39.

37. Adolphe Thiers cited in D. L. L. Parry and Pierre Girard, *France since 1800: Squaring the Hexagon* (Oxford: Oxford University Press, 2002), p. 71.

38. Hobsbawm, *The Age of Revolution*, pp. 245–7; and Jan-Werner Mueller, "Comprehending Conservatism: A New Framework for Analysis," *Journal of Political Ideologies* 11.3 (October 2006), p. 364.

39. *Le Conservateur* (5.10.1818) cited in Jerry Z. Muller, ed., *Conservatism: An Anthology of Social and Political Thought from David Hume to the Present* (Princeton, NJ: Princeton University Press, 1997), p. 26.

40. See Jerry Muller, "Introduction," in ibid. pp. 25–6. See also John Weiss, *Conservatism in Europe* (New York: Harcourt Brace Jovanovich, 1977).

41. See René Rémond, *La Droite en France* (Paris: Aubier, 1963). See also J. S. McCelland, ed., *The French Right from de Maistre to Maurras* (London: Jonathan Cape, 1970); Atkin and Tallet, *The Right in France*; Peter Davies, *The Extreme Right in France, 1789 to the Present* (London: Routledge, 2002).

42. See Zeev Sternhell, *Neither Left nor Right: Fascist Ideology in France* (Berkeley: University of California Press, 1986), pp. 25–6; and *The Birth of Fascist Ideology* (Princeton, NJ: Princeton University Press, 1994).

43. For a detailed discussion of conservative core concepts and claims, see Freeden, *Ideologies and Political Theory*, chapter 8; Robert Nisbet, *Conservatism* (Milton Keynes, UK: Open University Press, 1986); Albert O. Hirschman, *The Rhetoric of Reaction: Perversity Futility Jeopardy* (Cambridge, MA: Harvard University Press, 1991); and Roger Scruton, *The Meaning of Conservatism*, 3rd rev. edn. (Houndmills, UK: Palgrave Macmillan, 2001).

44. See Davies, *The Extreme Right in France*, pp. 32–3.

45. Joseph de Maistre, *Considerations on France*, trans. Richard A. Lebrun (Montreal: McGill-Queen's University Press, 1974), p. 31.

46. Ibid. p. 97.

47. Ibid. pp. 71, 120.

48. Ibid. p. 47.

49. Joseph de Maistre, "Two Extracts from the *Study of Sovereignty*," in McClelland, ed., *The French Right*, p. 46.

50. Ibid. pp. 44–7.

51. See Davies, *The Extreme Right in France*, p. 32.

52. J. L. Talmon, *The Myth of the Nation and the Vision of Revolution: The Origins of Ideological Polarisation in the Twentieth Century* (Berkeley: University of California Press, 1981), p. 539.

53. Joseph de Maistre, "Extract from the Seventh of the *St. Petersburg Dialogues*," in McClelland, ed., *The French Right*, p. 53.

54. D. K. Cohen, "The Vicomte de Bonald's Critique of Industrialism," *The Journal of Modern History* 41.4 (December 1969), p. 479.

55. Merquior, *Liberalism Old and New*, pp. 68–98.

56. See Jeremy Jennings, "Doctrinaires and Syndicalists: Representation, Parties and Democracy in France," *Journal of Political Ideologies* 11.3 (October 2006), p. 274; and Aurelian Craiutu, *Liberalism under Siege: The Political Thought of the French Doctrinaires* (Lanham, MD: Lexingron Books, 2003).

57. See Michael D. Biddiss, "Introduction," in Arthur de Gobineau, *Selected Political Writings*, ed. Michael D. Biddiss (London: Jonathan Cape, 1970), p. 31. See also Michael D. Biddis, *Father of Racist Ideology: The Social and Political Thought of Count Gobineau* (London: Weidenfeld & Nicolson, 1970).

58. Gobineau, *Selected Political Writings*, p. 41.

59. Ibid. pp. 134–40, 155, 175–6.

60. George M. Fredrickson, *Racism: A Short History* (Carleton, VIC: Scribe Publications, 2002), pp. 32–3.

61. See ibid. pp. 52–68. See also Ivan Hannaford, *Race: The History of an Idea in the West* (Baltimore, MD: Johns Hopkins University Press, 1996).

62. Ibid. p. 68.

63. Fredrickson, *Racism*, p. 170.

64. Ibid. pp. 60.

65. Ibid. p. 164.

66. Ibid. pp. 163–4.

67. See Hobsbawm, *The Age of Revolution*, pp. 290–1; *The Age of Capital*, pp. 259–69.

68. Niall Ferguson, *The War of the World: Twentieth-Century Conflict and the Descent of the West* (New York: Penguin Press, 2006), pp. 20–4.

69. See Walter Laqueur, *Black Hundred: The Rise of the Extreme Right in Russia* (New York: HarperCollins, 1994), p. 34.

70. See Richard J. Evans, *The Coming of the Third Reich* (London: Penguin Books, 2003), pp. 32–3.

71. Ibid. p. 33. See also Biddiss, "Introduction," in Gobineau, ed., *Selected Political Writings*, p. 30.

72. For the role of the media in the dissemination of radical conservative ideology in the wake of the Dreyfus Affair, see Nancy Fitch, "Mass Culture, Mass Parliamentary Politics, and Modern Anti-Semitism: The Dreyfus Affair in Rural France," *American Historical Review* (February 1992), pp. 55–95.

73. See ibid. and R. D. Anderson, *France 1870–1914: Politics and Society* (London: Routledge & Kegan Paul, 1977), p. 116.

74. Edouard Drumont, "Extract from the First Volume of *La France Juive*," in McClelland, ed., *The French Right*, pp. 90–2.

75. Ibid. pp. 95–6, 106.

76. Ibid. pp. 98, 102, 105, 109.

77. Maurice Barrès, "Excerpt from *Scènes et Doctrines du Nationalisme*," in McClelland, ed., *The French Right*, p. 184.

78. Ibid. p. 192.

79. Ibid. pp. 162, 184, 164.

80. Ibid. p. 187.

81. See Peter Pulzer, *Germany, 1870–1945: Politics, State Formation, and War* (Oxford, UK: Oxford University Press, 1997), p. 4; and Michael Stuermer, *The German Empire, 1870–1918* (New York: The Modern Library, 2000), p. 15.

82. Susanne Miller and Heinrich Potthoff, *A History of German Social Democracy: From 1848 to the Present*, trans. J. A. Underwood (Lexington Spa, UK: Berg, 1986), p. 8.

83. Ibid. p. 15.

84. Circular of GGBW (18 September 1848), cited in ibid. pp. 15–16.

85. See Edgar Feuchtwanger, *Imperial Germany 1850–1918* (London: Routledge, 2001), pp. 2–3.

86. August Bebel, *My Life* (Chicago: University of Chicago Press, 1913), pp. 44–5.

87. Ferdinand Lassalle cited in Eduard Bernstein, *Ferdinand Lassalle as a Social Reformer* (New York: Charles Scribner's Sons, 1893), p. 128. The most comprehensive biography of Ferdinand Lassalle remains Hermann Oncken, *Lassalle: Zwischen Marx und Bismarck* (Stuttgart: W. Kohlhammer, 1966 [1904]).

88. Ferdinand Lassalle to Gustav Lewy (March 9, 1863), cited in David Footman, *Ferdinand Lassalle: Romantic Revolutionary* (New Haven: Yale University Press, 1947), p. 164.

89. Ferdinand Lassalle, "Open Reply Letter," in Eduard Bernstein, ed., *Ferdinand Lassalle's Gesammelte Reden und Schriften*, 3 vols. (New York: Wolff and Hoehne, 1883), vol. I, pp. 27, 56–7; my translation.

90. Ibid. p. 50.

91. Ferdinand Lassalle, "The Workers' Program," in ibid. p. 263.

92. Bismarck quoted in Footman, *Ferdinand Lassalle*, p. 175.

93. Karl Kautsky, *Das Erfurter Program: In seinem grundsaetzlichen Teil erlaeutert* (Berlin: Verlag J. H. W. Dietz Nachfolger, 1974 [1922]), p. 234; my translation.

94. Friedrich Engels, "Vorwort zur ersten deutschen Auflage," in Karl Marx and Friedrich Engels, eds., *Werke*, vol. 19 (Berlin: Dietz Verlag, 1969), p. 187; and Friedrich Engels, "Ergaenzung der Vorbemerkung von 1870 zu 'der Deutsche Bauernkrieg,'" in Karl Marx and Friedrich Engels, eds., *Werke*, vol. 18 (Berlin: Dietz Verlag, 1969), p. 516; my translation.

95. August Bebel cited in Miller and Potthoff, *A History of German Social Democracy*, p. 57.

96. Joshua Moravchik, *Heaven on Earth: The Rise and Fall of Socialism* (San Francisco: Encounter Books, 2002), p. 128.

97. Gary P. Steenson, *"Not One Man! Not One Penny!" German Social Democracy, 1863–1914* (Pittsburgh: University of Pittsburgh Press, 1981), p. 234.

Chapter 3

1. Eric Hobsbawm, *The Age of Extremes: A History of the World, 1914–1991* (New York: Pantheon, 1994), pp. 109–11; and *The Age of Empire: 1875–1914* (New York: Pantheon Books, 1987). My brief account of the chief dynamics characterizing the opening decades of the twentieth century offered at the outset of this chapter is greatly indebted to Hobsbawm's insights.

2. Robert C. Young, *Postcolonialism: An Historical Introduction* (Malden, MA: Blackwell Publishing, 2001), p. 27. See also Barbara Bush, *Imperialism and Postcolonialism* (Harlow, UK: Pearson, 2006), pp. 45–7.

3. Michael Adas, "Contested Hegemony: The Great War and the Afro-Asian Assault on the Civilizing Mission Ideology," in Prasenjit Duara, ed., *Decolonization: Perspectives from now and then* (London: Routledge, 2004), p. 78.

4. See Odd Arne Westad, *The Global Cold War: Third World Interventions and the Making of Our Times* (Cambridge: Cambridge University Press, 2005), pp. 73–9.

5. Young, *Postcolonialism*, p. 117.

6. See, for example, Robert Gilpin, *The Challenge of Global Capitalism: The World Economy in the 21st Century* (Princeton: Princeton University Press, 2000); Jeffrey A. Frieden, *Global Capitalism: Its Fall and Rise in the Twentieth Century* (New York: W. W. Norton, 2006); and Daniel Cohen, *Globalization and Its Enemies* (Cambridge, MA: MIT Press, 2006).

7. Eric Hobsbawm, *On the Edge of the New Century*, with Antonio Polito (New York: New Press, 2000), p. 64.

8. Hobsbawm, *The Age of Empire*, p. 49.

9. The most famous of these explanations is the "Heckscher-Ohlin trade theory," named after two Swedish economists who developed a new way of understanding different nations' involvement in international trade. See Frieden, *Global Capitalism*, pp. 77–9.

10. Hobhouse, *Liberalism*, pp. 81–4.

11. For a detailed discussion of the decline of the Liberal Party in Britain, see David Powell, *British Politics, 1910–35: The Crisis of the Party System* (London: Routledge, 2004); Michael Freeden, *Liberalism Divided: A Study in British Political Thought 1914–1939* (Oxford: Clarendon Press, 1986); and Peter Clarke, *Liberals and Social Democrats* (Cambridge: Cambridge University Press, 1978).

12. Gustave Le Bon, *Psychologie des foules* (Paris: Alcan, 1895), p. 3.

13. Evans, *The Coming of the Third Reich*, p. 35.

14. See also Michael Mann, *Fascists* (Cambridge: Cambridge University Press, 2004), p. 2.

15. John Lukacs, *Democracy and Populism: Fear & Hatred* (New Haven: Yale University Press, 2005), p. 36.

16. See Benjamin Lieberman, *Terrible Fate: Ethnic Cleansing in the Making of Modern Europe* (Chicago: Ivan R. Dee, 2006).

17. E. Berth cited in Sternhell, *Neither Right nor Left*, pp. 57–8.

18. T. Maulnier cited in Sternhell, *Neither Right nor Left*, p. 12.

19. See Freeden, *Liberalism Divided*, p. 331.

20. Eduard Bernstein, *The Preconditions of Socialism* (Cambridge, UK: Cambridge University Press, 1993), p. 146. See also Steger, *The Quest for Evolutionary Socialism*, chapters 4 and 5.

21. See also Sternhell, *Neither Right nor Left*, pp. 1–2.

22. As Hans Buchheim points out, by November 1929 the *London Times* had picked up the term to give expression to the "reaction against parliamentarianism in favor of a 'totalitarian' or unitary state whether Fascist or Communist." See Hans Buchheim, *Totalitarian Rule: Its Nature and Characteristics* (Middletown, CT: Wesleyan University Press, 1967), p. 11.

23. Some essays representative of these approaches appear in Carl J. Friedrich, ed., *Totalitarianism* (Cambridge, MA: Harvard University Press, 1954). They are also discussed in Buchheim, *Totalitarian Rule*; and in Carl J. Friedrich, Michael Curtis, and Benjamin R. Barber, *Totalitarianism in Perspective: Three Views* (New York: Praeger, 1969).

24. Jeane J. Kirkpatrick cited in Odd Arne Westad, *The Global Cold War: Third World Interventions and the Making of Our Times* (Cambridge: Cambridge University Press, 2005), p. 358.

25. In my view, the label "totalitarianism" also applies to Chinese communism under Mao and to Pol Pot's genocidal regime in Cambodia.

26. Richard Pipes, *The Formation of the Soviet Union: Communism and Nationalism 1917–1923* (Cambridge, MA: Harvard University Press, 1964), pp. 1–3.

27. See Peter Waldron, *The End of Imperial Russia, 1855–1917* (New York: St. Martin's Press, 1997), p. 2.

28. David Brandenburger, *National Bolshevism: Stalinist Mass Culture and the Formation of Modern Russian National Identity, 1931–1956* (Cambridge, MA: Harvard University Press, 2002), chapter 1.

29. See Laqueur, *Black Hundred*; Sarah Davies, *Popular Opinion in Stalin's Russia: Terror, Propaganda, and Dissent, 1933–1941* (Cambridge: 1997), pp. 88–9; and John B. Dunlop, *The Faces of Contemporary Russian Nationalism* (Princeton: Princeton University Press, 1983), pp. 3–4. For a readable account of the origins and history of the *Protocols*, see Stephen Eric Bronner, *A Rumor about the Jews: Reflections on Antisemitism and the Protocols of the Learned Elders of Zion* (New York: St. Martin's Press, 2000).

30. See Leszek Kolakowski, *Main Currents of Marxism: Its Origins, Growth and Dissolution, Vol. 2: The Golden Age* (Oxford: Oxford University Press, 1978), pp. 398–400.

31. For an excellent interpretation of Lenin's and Stalin's theories of nationality, see Foreman, *Nationalism and the International Labor Movement*, chapters 2 and 3.

32. V. I. Lenin, *What Is to Be Done?* in *The Lenin Anthology*, ed. Robert C. Tucker (New York: W. W. Norton, 1975), p. 85.

33. Tucker, "Introduction: Lenin and Revolution," in ibid. pp. xxvii, xxxi. For a comprehensive treatment of the revolutionary tradition in modern Russian thought, see Andrzej Walicki, *A History of Russian Thought: From the Enlightenment to Marxism* (Stanford: Stanford University Press, 1979).

34. V. I. Lenin, *What Is to Be Done?* in *The Lenin Anthology*, ed. Tucker, pp. 20, 22. Italics in the original.

35. Ibid. pp. 112–14.

36. See Tucker, "Introduction: Lenin and Revolution," in ibid. pp. xliii.

37. Lenin, *What Is to Be Done?* in *The Lenin Anthology*, ed. Tucker, pp. 21–4.

38. Ibid. p. 20.

39. Ibid. p. 49.

40. Ibid. pp. 24–5.

41. For an accessible account of the Russian revolution, see Richard Pipes, *A Concise History of the Russian Revolution* (New York: Vintage, 1995).

42. Karl Marx and Friedrich Engels, "Manifest der Kommunistischen Partei," in *MEW*, vol. 4, p. 472. Translation by the author.

43. Lenin, *What Is to Be Done?* in *The Lenin Anthology*, ed. Tucker, pp. 27–31.

44. Ibid. pp. 52, 51, 55, 56, 92–3, 68, 74.

45. Leon Trotsky, *The Defence of Terrorism: A Reply to Kautsky* (London: G. Allen & Unwin, 1921), p. 122.

46. Kolakowski, *Main Currents of Marxism*, vol. 2, pp. 516–17. See also Peter Kenez, *A History of the Soviet Union from the Beginning to the End*, 2nd edn. (New York: Cambridge University Press, 2006), p. 104.

47. Lenin cited in Nicolas Werth, "A State against Its People: Violence, Repression, and Terror in the Soviet Union," in Stéphane Courtois, Nicolas Werth, Jean-Louis Panné, Andrzej Paczkowski, Karel Bartosek, Jean-Louis Margolin, eds., *The Black Book of Communism: Crimes, Terror, Repression* (Cambridge, MA: Harvard University Press, 1999), p. 79.

48. For an extensive account of these events that contains the relevant citations, see ibid. pp. 35–131.

49. Ibid. p. 130.

50. See "The Foundations of Leninism" and "The October Revolution and the Tactics of the Russian Communists," in J. V. Stalin, ed., *Works*, vol. 6 [1924] (Moscow: Foreign Languages Publishing House, 1953); and "Concerning Questions of Leninism," in J. V. Stalin, ed., *Works*, vol. 8 [1926] (Moscow: Foreign Languages Publishing House, 1954). For Bukharin's role in the formulation of "socialism in one country," see Stephen F. Cohen, *Bukharin and the Bolshevik Revolution* (New York: Oxford University Press, 1980).

51. See John Riddell, ed., *The Communist International in Lenin's Time. Workers of the World and Oppressed People, Unite! Proceedings and Documents of the Second Congress, 1920*, 2 vols. (New York: Pathfinder, 1991), vol 1, p. 284.

52. V. I. Lenin, *Collected Works*, vol. 26 (Moscow: Progress Publisher, 1972), p. 470.

53. The most riveting account of the protracted struggle for power following Lenin's death remains E. H. Carr's *Socialism in One Country: 1924–1926*, 2 vols. (London: Macmillan, 1958–9).

54. Stalin, "The October Revolution and the Tactics of the Russian Communists," pp. 396, 415.

55. Ibid. pp. 387–93.

56. Ibid. p. 391. The italics are mine.

57. Stalin, "Concerning Questions of Leninism," pp. 79, 66–7.

58. Leszek Kolakowski, *Main Currents of Marxism, Vol. 3: The Breakdown* (Oxford: Oxford University Press, 1978), p. 90.

59. Stalin, "The October Revolution and the Tactics of the Russian Communists," p. 395; and "Concerning Questions of Leninism," pp. 69, 78–9.

60. Ibid. pp. 36–7.

61. See Melanie Ilic, ed., *Stalin's Terror Revisited* (Houndmills, UK: Palgrave Macmillan, 2006).

62. For the rise of Russocentric discourse and imagery in the 1930s and 1940s, see Brandenberger, *National Bolshevism*; Sheila Fitzpatrick, *Everyday Stalinism: Ordinary Life in Extraordinary Times: Soviet Russia in the 1930s* (New York: Oxford University Press, 1999); John B. Dunlop, *The Faces of Contemporary Russian Nationalism* (Princeton: Princeton University Press, 1983), chapter 1; and Carr, *Socialism in One Country*, pp. 47–52.

63. J. Stalin, *On the Great Patriotic War of the Soviet Union* (Moscow: Foreign Languages Publishing House, 1944).

64. See, for example, Kenez, *A History of the Soviet Union from the Beginning to the End*, pp. 137–54.

65. Courtois et al., *The Black Book of Communism*, pp. 206–7.

66. Stalin cited in Kenez, *A History of the Soviet Union from the Beginning to the End*, p. 131.

67. See, Ian Kershaw, *Hitler 1889–1945, Vol. 1: Hubris* (London: Penguin, 2001), pp. 206–7; Martin Gilbert, *A History of the Twentieth Century Vol 1: 1900–1933* (London: HarperCollins, 1997), pp. 657–8; and Evans, *The Coming of the Third Reich*, pp. 193–4.

68. Ibid. p. 160; and Gilbert, *A History of the Twentieth Century*, pp. 542–4.

69. Evans, *The Coming of the Third Reich*, p. 169; and Kershaw, *Hitler*, p. 151.

70. Gilbert, *A History of the Twentieth Century*, pp. 549–56.

71. Evans, *The Coming of the Third Reich*, pp. 186–7.

72. For the history and ideological development of Italian fascism and its impact on German Nazism, see, for example, F. L. Carsten, *The Rise of Fascism* (Berkeley, CA: University of California Press, 1967); Ernst Nolte, *Three Faces of Fascism: Action Francaise, Italian Fascism, National Socialism* (New York: Mentor Books, 1969); and Emilio Gentile, *The Origins of Fascist Ideology: 1918–1925* (New York: Enigma Books, 2005).

73. See, for example, Karl Dietrich Bracher, *The German Dictatorship* (Harmondsworth: Penguin, 1971); Martin Brozat, *Hitler and the Collapse of Weimar Germany* (Leamington Spa: Berg, 1987); Detlev Peukert, *Inside Nazi Germany: Conformity, Opposition, and Racism in Everyday Life* (London: Penguin, 1989); R. J. B. Bosworth, *Mussolini* (London: Arnold, 2002); and Michael Burleigh, *The Third Reich: A New History* (New York: Hill and Wang, 2001).

74. Robert O. Paxton, *The Anatomy of Fascism* (New York: Vintage, 2004), p. 16.

75. Given the great variety of "fascisms," there has been much discussion in the relevant literature as to whether they all fit under a common generic term. As I have argued in this book, any modern "ism" ought to be considered within its specific national context. However, this is not to say that Italian fascism and German Nazism do not share a good number of core concepts they decontest in similar ways. In this sense, then, attempts to identify "ideological families" serve a useful analytical purpose—as long as the desire to come up with an "ideological minimum" does not detract from crucial contextual matters.

76. Paxton, *The Anatomy of Fascism*, p. 17.

77. Adolf Hitler, *Mein Kampf*, trans. Ralph Manheim (Boston: Houghton Mifflin, 1971), pp. 210. See also ibid. pp. 380–1, 580–1.

78. Kershaw, *Hitler*, pp. xxviii, 243. Today, most scholars converge on the view that fascist ideology must be taken seriously on its own terms. See, for example, Mann, *Fascists*; Evans, *The Coming of the Third Reich*; George L. Mosse, *The Crisis of German Ideology: Intellectual Origins of the Third Reich* (New York: Schocken Books, 1981); Stanley G. Payne, *A History of Fascism: 1914–1945* (Madison: University of Wisconsin Press, 1995); Roger Griffin, ed., *Fascism*

(Oxford: Oxford University Press, 1995); Walter Laqueur, *Fascism: Past, Present, Future* (Oxford: Oxford University Press, 1996); Mark Neocleous, *Fascism* (Minneapolis: University of Minnesota Press, 1997); Roger Eatwell, *Fascism: A History* London: Pimlico, 2003); and Richard Griffiths, *Fascism* (London: Continuum, 2005).

79. Hitler, *Mein Kampf*, pp. 6, 285.
80. Ibid. p. 285.
81. Ibid. p. 312.
82. Ibid. pp. 285–6.
83. Ibid. pp. 287–308.
84. Ibid. pp. 300–5.
85. Ibid. pp. 324, 327.
86. Ibid. p. 327.
87. Ibid. pp. 338, 389, 392–4, 440.
88. In this sense, I concur with Daniel Jonah Goldhagen's thesis that the Holocaust is unthinkable without the central role played by what he calls an "eliminationist anti-Semitism" in Nazi Germany. Still, as the genocidal history of the twentieth century shows, the existence of such "eliminationist" mind-sets outside the borders of Germany belies the notion of German exceptionality. See Daniel Jonah Goldhagen, *Hitler's Willing Executioners: Ordinary Germans and the Holocaust* (New York: Vintage Books, 1996). The apt title of Lucy Davidowicz's seminal book on the Holocaust reflects the intimate connection between the metaphors of "war" and "struggle" in German Nazism: *The War Against the Jews, 1933–1945* (New York: Bantam, 1975).
89. Hitler, *Mein Kampf*, p. 582. For Hitler's view on various propaganda techniques, including his low opinion of the masses, see ibid. pp. 176–86.
90. Ibid. pp. 646–54.
91. Ibid. 580–1.
92. The Associated Press, "Archive Sheds Light on Nazi Death Camps," in *The New York Times* (December 23, 2006).
93. As might be expected, the literature on this subject is enormous. In addition to those books already cited above, let me mention four more studies: Saul Friedlaender, *Nazi Germany and the Jews, Vol. 1: The Years of Persecution* (London: Weidenfeld & Nicolson, 1997); Peter Longerith, *Politik der Vernichtung: Eine Gesamtdarstellung der nationalsozialistischen Judenverfolgung* (Munich: Beck, 1998); Goetz Aly, *Nazi Population Policy and the Murder of the European Jews* (New York: Oxford University Press, 1999); and Deborah Dwork and Robert Jan Van Pelt, *Holocaust: A History* (New York: W. W. Norton, 2003).

Chapter 4

1. Dean Acheson cited in Robert J. McMahon, *The Cold War: A Very Short Introduction* (Oxford: Oxford University Press, 2003), p. 3. For a readable account of the

profound sense of rupture produced by World War II, see Thomas G. Paterson, *On Every Front: The Making and Unmaking of the Cold War*, rev. 2nd edn. (New York: R. S. Means Co, 1992), chapter 1.

2. Taylor, *A Secular Age*, p. 172.

3. Ibid. p. 176; and Taylor, *Modern Social Imaginaries*, pp. 29–33.

4. For an insightful discussion of the generally neglected function of warfare as a globalizing process, see Tarak Barkawi, *Globalization and War* (Lanham, MD: Rowman & Littlefield, 2006).

5. Martin Gilbert, *A History of the Twentieth Century: The Concise Edition of the Acclaimed World History* (New York: HarperCollins, 2002), pp. 294–5.

6. Stalin cited in John Lewis Geddis, *The Cold War: A New History* (New York: Penguin Press, 2005), p. 26.

7. For an informative history of nuclear weapons, see Joseph Siracusa, *Nuclear Weapons: A Very Short Introduction* (Oxford: Oxford University Press, 2008). For the concept of "manufactured risk," see Ulrich Beck, *Risk Society: Toward a New Modernity* (London: Sage, 1992); and Anthony Giddens, *Beyond Left and Right: The Future of Radical Politics* (Stanford, CA: Stanford University Press, 1994), pp. 4, 78–80.

8. Adolf Hitler cited in Ferguson, *The War of the World*, p. 591.

9. Westad, *The Global Cold War*, p. 4.

10. Jussi Hanhimaki and Odd Arne Westad, eds., *The Cold War: A History in Documents and Eyewitness Accounts* (Oxford: Oxford University Press, 2003), p. xii.

11. See Michael Denning, *Culture in the Age of Three Worlds* (London: Verso, 2004). Invented by a French journalist in the early 1950s, the notion of a "Third World" was predicated on the existence of a "First World" and a "Second World." The rapid spread of this terminology in the public discourse points to the growing power of a social imaginary increasingly envisioning community in regional and global terms. In this chapter, I employ the term "Third World" in a nonhierarchical, nonpejorative sense as one of three geographical markers of ideological Cold War dynamics.

12. Mao Zedong, *Mao Papers. Anthology and Bibliography*, ed. Jerome Ch'en (Oxford: Oxford University Press, 1970), p. 118; *Selected Works of Mao Tse-Tung*, 5 vols. (Peking: Foreign Languages Press, 1965), vol. 1, p. 336; and *Quotations from Chairman Mao Tse-Tung*, ed. Stuart R. Schram (New York: Praeger, 1968). For expositions of Mao's political thought, see, for example, Stuart R. Schram, *The Political Thought of Mao Tse-Tung* (New York: Praeger, 1969); Kolakowski, *Main Currents of Marxism*, vol. 3, pp. 494–522; and Chenshan Tian, *Chinese Dialectics: From Yijing to Marxism* (Lanham, MD: Lexington Books, 2005), chapter 7.

13. Young, *Postcolonialism*, pp. 191–2.

14. "President Sukarno Speaks at Bandung, 1955," in Hanhimaki and Westad, *The Cold War*, p. 350.

15. Ernesto Che Guevara, *Guerilla Warfare* (Lincoln, NE: University of Nebraska Press, 1998), p. 172.
16. Sun Yat-Sen, "The Three Principles of the People," in Duara, ed., *Decolonization*, p. 22.
17. Michael Adas, "Contesting Hegemony: The Great War and the Afro-Asian Assault on the Civilizing Mission Ideology," *Journal of World History* 15.1 (2004), p. 31.
18. Frank Fueredi, *Colonial Wars and the Politics of Third World Nationalism* (London: I. B. Tauris, 1994), p. 27.
19. Prasenjit Duara, "Introduction: The Decolonization of Asia and Africa in the Twentieth Century," in Duara, ed., *Decolonization*, pp. 8–12; and "The Discourse of Civilization and Decolonization," *Journal of World History* 15.1 (2004), p. 3.
20. See Westad, *The Global Cold War*, p. 94.
21. For a discussion of Gandhi's conflict between ethical principles and political expediency, see Manfred B. Steger, *Gandhi's Dilemma: Nonviolent Principles and Nationalist Power* (New York: St. Martin's Press, 2000).
22. Mohandas K. Gandhi, *Hind Swaraj and Other Writings*, ed. Anthony J. Parel (Cambridge, UK: Cambridge University Press, 1997), p. 121.
23. Ibid. p. 39.
24. Ibid. p. 41.
25. Partha Chatterjee, *Nationalist Thought and the Colonial World: A Derivative Discourse?* (Minneapolis, MN: University of Minnesota Press, 1993), p. 85.
26. Gandhi, *Hind Swaraj and Other Writings*, p. 68.
27. Gandhi's hopes of restoring the *panchayat*, an "ancient" form of governance with a five-member assembly elected by the villagers, owe much to Henry Maine's idealized notion of "village republics" based upon prior writings of German romantics and Victorian liberals. Gandhi cites Maine's and Wilson's respective studies on the subject as early as the 1890s. See Mahatma Gandhi, *The Collected Works of Mahatma Gandhi (CWMG)*, 100 vols. (New Delhi: Publications Division, Ministry of Information and Broadcasting, Government of India, 1958–1994), vol. 1, pp. 129–30 [1894]; 269–70 [1895].
28. Gandhi, *Hind Swaraj and Other Writings*, pp. 67, 69, 70.
29. Mahatma Gandhi, *The Moral and Political Writings of Mahatma Gandhi*, ed. Raghavan Iyer, 3 vols. (Oxford: Clarendon Press, 1986–7), vol. 2, p. 212 [1916].
30. Dennis Dalton, *Mahatma Gandhi: Nonviolent Power in Action* (New York: Columbia University Press, 1993), p. 201.
31. Gandhi, *CWMG*, vol. 29, p. 92.
32. M. K. Gandhi, *Young India* (March 23, 1921), in *CWMG*, vol. 19, p. 466. For a discussion of Gandhi's perspective on truth and political power, see Manfred B. Steger, "Searching for *Satya* through *Ahimsa*: Mahatma Gandhi's Challenge to Western Discourses of Power," *Constellations: An International Journal of Critical and Democratic Theory* 13.3 (September 2006), pp. 332–53.

33. Gandhi, *Hind Swaraj and Other Writings*, p. 84.

34. Ibid. pp. 95–6.

35. Gandhi offered his clearest expression of his belief in world unity at the Asian Relations Conference in Delhi (April 1, 1947). See Rashmi-Sudha Puri, *Gandhi on War and Peace* New York: Praeger, 1987), pp. 201–2.

36. Ibid. p. 200.

37. *CWMG*, vol. 27, pp. 255–6 [1925].

38. For a detailed account of the influence of Gandhi's ideas on these nonviolent social movements, see Stephen Zunes, Lester R. Kurtz, and Sarah Beth Asher, *Nonviolent Social Movements: A Geographical Perspective* (Malden, MA: Blackwell, 1999); Peter Ackerman and Jack Duvall, *A Force More Powerful: A Century of Nonviolent Conflict* (New York: Palgrave, 2000); and David Hardiman, *Gandhi in His Time and Ours: The Global Legacy of His Ideas* (New York: Columbia University Press, 2003).

39. Kwame Nkrumah, *The Autobiography of Kwame Nkrumah* (Edinburgh: T. Nelson, 1957), p. 92.

40. Nelson Mandela quoted in Young, *Postcolonialism*, p. 249.

41. Frantz Fanon, *The Wretched of the Earth*, with a Preface by Jean-Paul Sartre (New York: Grove Press, 1963), p. 35.

42. Ibid. pp. 36, 94.

43. Young, *Postcolonialism*, pp. 265–75.

44. Fanon, *The Wretched of the Earth*, pp. 36–9, 46–7, 61, 84–5.

45. Frantz Fanon, *Black Skin, White Masks* (New York: Grove Press, 1967), p. 12.

46. Fanon, *The Wretched of the Earth*, pp. 42–3, 46, 50, 93.

47. Frantz Fanon, *A Dying Colonialism* (New York: Grove Press, 1965), p. 28.

48. Fanon, *The Wretched of the Earth*, pp. 247–8.

49. Ibid. pp. 311–16. For a concise interpretation of Fanon's "new humanism," see Robert Bernasconi, "Casting the Slough: Fanon's New Humanism for a New Humanity," in Lewis R. Gordon, T. Denean Sharpley-Whiting, and Reneé T. White, eds., *Fanon: A Critical Reader* (Oxford: Blackwell, 1996), pp. 113–21.

50. Fanon, *The Wretched of the Earth*, pp. 314–16.

51. It seems that the phrase "end of ideology" first appeared in an essay on socialism and ethics penned by Albert Camus in 1946 for a French newspaper. Another early use of the concept occurs in a 1951 article authored by H. Stuart Hughes, a Harvard sociologist. See Russell Jacoby, *The End of Utopia: Politics and Culture in an Age of Apathy* (New York: Basic Books, 1999), pp. 3–4. Some of the most prominent participants in this decade-long end-of-ideology debate include Daniel Bell, Seymour Martin Lipset, Raymond Aron, Edward Shils, and Irving Kristol. For a representative sample of their contributions, see Chaim I. Waxman, ed., *The End of Ideology Debate* (New York: Funk & Wagnalls, 1968).

52. Herbert Tingsten, "Stability and Vitality in Swedish Democracy," *Political Quarterly* 26 (1955), pp. 140–51.

53. Tingsten, "Stability and Vitality in Swedish Democracy," pp. 145–6.

54. Ibid. p. 147.

55. Ibid. pp. 149–51.

56. Daniel Bell, *The End of Ideology: On the Exhaustion of Political Ideas in the Fifties* (Glencoe, IL: Free Press, 1960).

57. Ibid. p. 370.

58. Seymour Martin Lipset, *Political Man: The Social Bases of Politics* (Garden City, NY: Anchor, 1963), p. 442.

59. Bell, *The End of Ideology*, pp. 374–5.

60. Ibid. p. 373.

61. Tingsten, "Stability and Vitality in Swedish Democracy," pp. 146–7.

62. For a concise and enlightening account of the emergence of the welfare state in the first half of the twentieth century, see Michael Freeden, "The Coming of the Welfare State," in Terrence Ball and Richard Bellamy, eds., *The Cambridge History of Twentieth-Century Political Thought* (Cambridge: Cambridge University Press, 2003), pp. 7–44; and David Gladstone, *The Twentieth-Century Welfare State* (New York: St. Martin's Press, 1999).

63. John Maynard Keynes, "The End of Laissez Faire," in D. E. Moggridge, ed., *The Collected Writings*, 30 vols. (London: Macmillan, 1971–89), vol. IX, pp. 287–8.

64. John Maynard Keynes cited in Frieden, *Global Capitalism*, p. 229.

65. John Maynard Keynes, "The General Theory of Employment, Interest, and Money," in *The Collected Writings*, vol. VII, p. 378.

66. See Hobsbawm, *The Age of Extremes*, Part II; and Edward Luttwak, *Turbo-Capitalism: Winners and Losers in the Global Economy* (New York: HarperCollins, 2000), pp. 27–36.

67. John Ehrenberg, *Servants of Wealth: The Right's Assault on Economic Justice* (Lanham, MD: Rowman & Littlefield, 2006), p. 5.

68. T. H. Marshall, *Class, Citizenship, and Social Development* (Garden City, NY: Doubleday, 1965), p. 78.

69. Tingsten, "Stability and Vitality in Swedish Democracy," p. 146.

70. Martin Luther King, Jr., "I Have a Dream," in James M. Washington, ed., *A Testament of Hope: The Essential Writings and Speeches of Martin Luther King, Jr.* (New York: HarperCollins, 1991), p. 219. See also ibid., "Letter from Birmingham City Jail," pp. 289–302. For treatments of King's philosophy of nonviolence, see John J. Ansbro, *Martin Luther King, Jr.: The Making of a Mind* (Maryknoll, NY: Orbis, 1984); James A. Colaiaco, *Martin Luther King Jr.: Apostle of Militant Nonviolence* (New York: St. Martin's Press, 1993); Greg Moses, *Revolution of Conscience: Martin Luther King, Jr., and the Philosophy of Nonviolence* (New York: Guilford Press, 1997); and Manfred B. Steger, *Judging Nonviolence: The Dispute between Realists & Idealists* (New York: Routledge, 2003), pp. 77–90.

71. King, *A Testament of Hope*, p. 210.

72. David Garrow, *Bearing the Cross: Martin Luther King, Jr., and the Southern Christian Leadership Conference* (New York: Vintage, 1986), p. 351.

73. Malcolm X cited in Stephen B. Oates, *Let the Trumpet Sound: The Life of Martin Luther King, Jr.* (New York: New American Library, 1982), p. 252.
74. Malcolm X, *Malcolm X Speaks*, ed. George Breitman (New York: Pathfinder, 1965), p. 9.
75. Ibid. p. 34.
76. Ibid. p. 35.
77. King cited in Ansbro, *Martin Luther King, Jr.*, p. 253.
78. Martin Luther King, Jr., *Where Do We Go from Here: Chaos or Community?* (New York: Harper & Row, 1967), pp. 174–5.
79. Daniel Cohn-Bedit cited in Tilly, *Social Movements*, p. 69.
80. For a comprehensive analysis of the events and ideas during the "Prague Spring," see H. Gordon Skilling, *Czechoslovakia's Interrupted Revolution* (Princeton, NJ: Princeton University Press, 1976); Alexander Dubcek, *Hope Dies Last: The Autobiography of Alexander Dubcek*, ed. and trans. Jiri Hochman (New York: Kodansha International, 1993); and Tony Judt, *Postwar: A History of Europe Since 1945* (London: Penguin, 2005), chapter xiii.
81. Lyndon B. Johnson, "1968 Thanksgiving Proclamation," cited in George Katsiaficas, *The Imagination of the New Left: A Global Analysis of 1968* (Boston: South End Press, 1987), p. 4.
82. See, for example, Tilly, *Social Movements*; Sidney Tarrow, *Power in Movement*, 2nd edn. (Cambridge: Cambridge University Press, 1998); and Christine A. Kelly, *Tangled Up in Red, White, and Blue: New Social Movements in America* (Lanham, MD: Rowman & Littlefield, 2001).
83. Some of these characteristics are described and celebrated by Katsiaficas, *The Imagination of the New Left*, pp. 22–7. For a more guarded perspective, see Stephen Eric Bronner, *Moments of Decision: Political History and the Crisis of Radicalism* (New York: Routledge, 1992), chapter 5. For a critical account, see Richard J. Ellis, *The Dark Side of the Left: Illiberal Egalitarianism in America* (Lawrence, KS: University Press of Kansas, 1998), chapters 4–6.
84. See, for example, Robin Archer et al., eds., *Out of Apathy: Voices of the New Left Thirty Years On* (London: Verso, 1989), p. 8.
85. Craig Calhoun, "'New Social Movements' of the Early Nineteenth-Century," in Mark Traugott, ed., *Repertoires and Cycles of Collective Action* (Durham, NC: Duke University Press, 1995), p. 205. See also Kelly, *Tangled Up in Red, White, and Blue*, p. 39.
86. Betty Friedan, *The Feminist Mystique* (New York: W. W. Norton, 1963), pp. 82–95.
87. For a comprehensive and systematic survey of the main theoretical currents within "ecologism," see Robin Eckersley, *Environmentalism and Political Theory: Toward an Ecocentric Approach* (London: UCL Press, 1992); Andrew Dobson, *Green Political Thought*, 2nd edn. (London: Routledge, 1995); and Brian Baxter, *Ecologism: An Introduction* (Washington, DC: Georgetown University Press, 1999).

88. Rachel Carson, *Silent Spring* (Boston: Mariner/Houghton Mifflin, 2002 [1962]), p. 296.

89. See Hobsbawm, *The Age of Extremes*, p. 296.

90. Ibid. p. 325.

91. See Michael Kidron and Ronald Segal, *The State of the World Atlas* (London: Pluto Press, 1981), pp. 64–5.

92. Katsiaficas, *The Imagination of the New Left*, p. 4.

93. Edward Shils, "Dreams of Plenitude, Nightmare of Scarcity," in Seymour Martin Lipset and Philip G. Altbach, eds., *Students in Revolt* (Boston: Beacon Press, 1970), p. 5.

94. Frieden, *Global Capitalism*, p. 359.

95. Ibid. pp. 364–5.

96. Ibid. p. 367.

97. For a comprehensive treatment of neoliberalism as it relates to "Reaganism" and "Thatcherism," see, for example, Daniel Yergin and Joseph Stanislaw, *The Commanding Heights: The Battle for the World Economy* (New York: Touchstone, 1998); Stuart Hall and Martin Jacques, eds., *The Politics of Thatcherism* (London: Lawrence and Wisehart, 1983); Eric J. Evans, *Thatcher and Thatcherism*, 2nd edn. (London: Routledge, 1997); John Gray, *False Dawn: The Delusions of Global Capitalism* (New York: New Press, 1998); and David Harvey, *A Brief History of Neoliberalism* (Oxford: Oxford University Press, 2005).

98. F. A. Hayek, *The Road to Serfdom* (Chicago: University of Chicago Press, 1994 [1944]), pp. 225, 231, xxxviii.

99. Ibid. p. xxxiv.

100. Ibid. p. 41; and F. A. Hayek cited in Rachel S. Turner, "The 'Rebirth of Liberalism': The Origins of Neo-Liberal Ideology," *Journal of Political Ideologies* 12.1 (February 2007), p. 77.

101. F. A. Hayek, *The Constitution of Liberty* (Chicago: University of Chicago Press, 1960), p. 11.

102. Hayek, *The Road to Serfdom*, pp. 80–1.

103. Alex Ebenstein, *Friedrich Hayek: A Biography* (Chicago: University of Chicago Press, 2001), pp. 124–6; and *Hayek's Journey: The Mind of Friedrich Hayek* (New York: Palgrave-Macmillan, 2003), p. 119.

104. Freeden, *Ideologies and Political Theory*, p. 298.

105. Hayek, *The Constitution of Liberty*, p. 41. See also Freeden, *Ideologies and Political Theory*, p. 307.

106. Ibid. p. 311.

107. Ibid. p. 308.

108. See Turner, "The 'Rebirth of Liberalism,'" p. 75; and Jerry Z. Muller, *The Mind and the Market: Capitalism in Western Thought* (New York: Anchor Books, 2002), p. 378. For another argument in favor of an ideological affinity between Hayekism and socialism, see, for example, Simon Griffiths, " 'Comrade Hayek' or the Revival of Liberalism? Andrew Gamble's

Engagement with the Work of Friedrich Hayek," *Journal of Political Ideologies* 12.2 (2007), pp. 189–210.

109. F. A. Hayek, "The Intellectuals and Socialism," in *Studies in Philosophy, Politics and Economics* (London: Routledge, 1967), pp. 183, 194; and F. A. Hayek, "The Prospect of Freedom," cited in Turner, "The 'Rebirth of Liberalism,'" p. 75.

110. Hayek, *The Road to Serfdom*, p. 256.

111. "Mont Pelerin Society Statement of Aims," in Max Hartwell, *A History of the Mont Pelerin Society* (Indianapolis: Liberty Fund, 1995), pp. 7–11.

112. See Muller, *The Mind and the Market*, pp. 373–6.

113. Monica Prasad, *The Politics of Free Markets: The Rise of Neoliberal Economic Policies in Britain, France, Germany, & the United States* (Chicago: University of Chicago Press, 2006), p. 102. See also Graeme Lockwood, "Trade Union Governance: The Development of British Conservative Thought," *Journal of Political Ideologies* 10.3 (October 2005), pp. 355–71.

114. On the crucial role of neoliberal think tanks in the 1970s, see Richard Cockett, *Thinking the Unthinkable: Think-Tanks and the Economic Counter-Revolution, 1931–1983* (London: HarperCollins, 1995); Yergin and Stanislaw, *The Commanding Heights*, chapters 4 and 5; Mark Blyth, *Great Transformations* (Cambridge: Cambridge University Press, 2002); Sharon Beder, *Free Market Missionaries: The Corporate Manipulation of Community Values* (London: Earthscan, 2006), chapters 5–9; Prasad, *The Politics of Free Markets*, pp. 49–51; and Harvey, *A Brief History of Neoliberalism*, chapter 2. For a representative selection of "neoconservative" writings, see Mark Gierson, ed., *The Essential Neo-Conservative Reader* (Reading, MA: Addison-Wesley Publishing Company, 1996); and Irwin Stelzer, ed., *Neoconservatism* (London: Atlantic Books, 2004).

115. Irving Kristol, *Two Cheers for Capitalism* (New York: Basic Books, 1978). For a critical analysis of Kristol's ideological claims, see Ehrenberg, *Servants of Wealth*, pp. 11–15, 117–19, 156–7.

Chapter 5

1. Gregory C. Chow, *China's Economic Transformation* (Oxford: Blackwell, 2002), p. 93; and Harvey, *A Brief History of Neoliberalism*, pp. 122, 135.

2. See Lance Gore, *The Institutional Foundations of China's Post-Mao Hyper-Growth* (New York: Oxford University Press, 1998), pp. 65–71; Witold Rodzinski, *The People's Republic of China: A Concise Political History* (New York: Free Press, 1988), p. 227; and Yanlai Wang, *China's Economic Development and Democratization* (Aldershot, UK: Ashgate, 2003), pp. 103–6.

3. Cited in Rodzinski, *The People's Republic of China*, p. 211.

4. Ibid. p. 213.

5. See, for example, Ross Terrill, *The New Chinese Empire: And What It Means for the United States* (New York: Basic Books, 2003), p. 143.

6. Wang, *China's Economic Development and Democratization*, p. 101.

7. See Michael Webber, Mark Wang, and Zhu Ying, eds., *China's Transition to a Global Economy* (Houndmills, UK: Palgrave Macmillan, 2002), p. 241.

8. See Harvey, *A Brief History of Neoliberalism*, p. 120.

9. Mikhail Gorbachev, *Memoirs* (New York: Doubleday, 1996), p. 218.

10. Mikhail Gorbachev, *Perestroika: New Thinking for Our Country and the World* (New York: Harper & Row, 1987), pp. 35, 45–9.

11. Gorbachev, *Memoirs*, p. 165.

12. Gorbachev, *Perestroika*, p. 155. For a discussion of Gorbachev's reforms, see, for example, Stephen White, *After Gorbachev* (Cambridge: Cambridge University Press, 1993); Susan Sternthal, *Gorbachev's Reforms: De-Stalinization through Demilitarization* (Westport, CT: Praeger, 1997); and Anthony D'Agostino, *Gorbachev's Revolution* (New York: New York University Press, 1998).

13. Mikhail Gorbachev, "Statement by Mikhail Gorbachev, General Secretary of the CPSU Central Committee" (January 16, 1986), in *Selected Speeches and Articles*, 2nd edn. (Moscow: Progress Publishers, 1987), p. 318.

14. Gorbachev, *Perestroika*, pp. 136–55.

15. Gorbachev, *Memoirs*, p. 200.

16. Ibid. p. xxviii.

17. Ibid. p. 693.

18. Francis Fukuyama, "The End of History?" *National Interest* 16 (Summer 1989), pp. 3–4. See also Francis Fukuyama, *The End of History and the Last Man* (New York: Free Press, 1992).

19. Fukuyama, "The End of History?" p. 18.

20. Francis Fukuyama, "Economic Globalization and Culture: A Discussion with Dr. Francis Fukuyama," *Merrill Lynch Forum* <http://www.ml.com/woml/forum/global.htm> (2000); "Second Thoughts: The Last Man in a Bottle," *National Affairs* 56 (Summer 1999), pp. 16–44; and "Reflections on the *End of History*, Five Years Later," in Timothy Burns, ed., *After History? Francis Fukuyama and His Critics* (Lanham, MD: Rowman & Littlefield, 1994), p. 244.

21. Fukuyama, "The End of History?" p. 15.

22. Nayan Chanda, *Bound Together: How Traders, Preachers, Adventurers, and Warriors Shaped Globalization* (New Haven: Yale University Press, 2007), pp. x, 246.

23. One of the laudable exceptions to this trend is Roland Robertson's *Globalization*. The British sociologist's treatment of globalization as a "revolution in consciousness" affecting the entire world (as well as an objective dynamic) deeply influenced my own thinking on the subject.

24. Mikhail Gorbachev, "Underpinning a Secure World," in Ken Coates, ed., *Perestroika: Global Challenge* (Nottingham, UK: Spokesman, 1988), p. 27 (originally published in *Pravda*, September 17, 1987).

25. See Michael Mann, *Incoherent Empire* (London: Verso, 2003), pp. 22–3.

26. Theodore Levitt, "The Globalization of Markets," *Harvard Business Review* (May–June 1983), pp. 92–102.

27. Thomas L. Friedman, *The World Is Flat: A Brief History of the Twenty-First Century* (New York: Farrar, Straus and Giroux, 2005).

28. Levitt, "The Globalization of Markets," pp. 92–102. Both the phenomenal impact of Levitt's essay and the degree to which his ideological prescription took root in the global business community are reflected in a series of revealing interviews conducted by Jeffrey Garten with leading CEOs at the closing of the Roaring Nineties. See Jeffrey E. Garten, *The Mind of the CEO* (New York: Basic Books, 2001).

29. Chanda, *Bound Together*, p. 251.

30. See, for example, Kenichi Ohmae, *The Borderless World: Power and Strategy in the Interlinked World Economy* (New York: HarperBusiness, 1990); and *The End of the Nation-State: The Rise of Regional Economics* (New York: Free Press, 1995).

31. I have laid out this argument in much detail in my *Globalism: Market Ideology Meets Terrorism*, and *Globalization*.

32. For a brilliant treatment of this subject, see Nisha Shah, "Inventing the Internet: Metaphors of Globalization as Communications Technology," Paper presented at the 48th Annual International Studies Association Meeting, Chicago, IL, March 2007.

33. I am borrowing the catchphrase "Roaring Nineties" from Nobel-prize-winning economist Joseph Stiglitz whose characterization of the 1990s as a decade of exceptional economic growth draws heavily on the perspective of globalization as an economic process unfolding in a world "no longer divided on ideological grounds." See Joseph E. Stiglitz, *The Roaring Nineties: A New History of the World's Most Prosperous Decade* (New York: W. W. Norton, 2003), p. 3.

34. See Steger, *Globalism: The New Market Ideology*; Mark Rupert, *Ideologies of Globalization: Contending Visions of a New Order* (London: Routledge, 2000); and James H. Mittelman, *The Globalization Syndrome: Transformation and Resistance* (Princeton: Princeton University Press, 2000).

35. Steger, *Globalism*, 2nd edn., p. 51. I doubt whether these social elites actually constitute a coherent "transnational capitalist class," in a Marxist sense, as Leslie Sklair suggests. Mark Rupert's concept of a "transnational historic bloc of internationally-oriented capitalists, liberal statesmen, and their allies" comes closer to an accurate description of the loose, heterogeneous, and often disagreeing global alliance of power elites that I have in mind. See Leslie Sklair, *The Transnational Capitalist Class* (Oxford, UK: Blackwell, 2001); and Rupert, *Ideologies of Globalization*, pp. 16–17, 154.

36. James H. Mittelman, "Ideologies and the Globalization Agenda," in Manfred B. Steger, ed., *Rethinking Globalism* (Lanham, MD: Rowman & Littlefield, 2004), p. 18.

37. See Francis Fukuyama's cover endorsement of Thomas L. Friedman, *The Lexus and the Olive Tree: Understanding Globalization* (New York: Anchor Books, 2000).

See also William Bole, "Tales of Globalization," *America* 181.18 (December 4, 1999), pp. 14–16.

38. Friedman, *The Lexus and the Olive Tree*, pp. ix–xii, xxi.

39. Merrill Lynch advertisement cited in ibid. p. xvi.

40. Ibid. p. 9.

41. Ibid. p. 27.

42. Manuel Villar, Jr., "High-Level Dialogue on the Theme of the Social and Economic Impact of Globalization and Interdependence and Their Policy Implications," New York, September 17, 1998 <http://www.un.int/philippines/villar.html>.

43. For a critical assessment of Thatcher's policy from the perspective of the Roaring Nineties, see John Gray, *False Dawn: The Delusions of Global Capitalism* (New York: New Press, 1998), pp. 24–34.

44. Friedman, *The Lexus and the Olive Tree*, pp. 8–9.

45. Ibid. pp. 112–13.

46. Ibid. pp. 104–5.

47. Ibid. p. 113.

48. Ibid. pp. 109–10.

49. Garten, *The Mind of the CEO*, p. 248.

50. Friedman, *The Lexus and the Olive Tree*, p. 381.

51. Ibid. p. 464.

52. Ibid. pp. 45–6.

53. Ibid. pp. 171–87.

54. Ibid. p. 192.

55. "Economic Globalization and Culture: A Discussion with Dr. Francis Fukuyama" <http://www.ml.com/woml/forum/global2.html>.

56. See William I. Robinson, *Promoting Polyarchy: Globalization, U.S. Intervention, and Hegemony* (Cambridge: Cambridge University Press, 1996), pp. 56–62.

57. Benjamin R. Barber, "Globalizing Democracy," *The American Prospect Online* 11.20 (September 11, 2000) <http://www.prospect.org/archives/V11-20/barber-b.html>.

58. Taken in its broadest sense, "globalization" is a long-term historical process and consciousness that, over many centuries, has crossed distinct qualitative thresholds. For reasons I laid out in Chapter 4 of this book, the current, latest phase of globalization is unprecedented in its reach and intensity. See also Steger, *Globalization*, chapter 2.

59. Friedman, *The Lexus and the Olive Tree*, p. 204.

60. See, for example, George Ritzer, *The McDonaldization of Society: An Investigation into the Changing Character of Contemporary Social Life* (Thousand Oaks, CA: Pine Forge Press, 1993); Benjamin Barber, *Jihad Vs. McWorld* (New York: Ballantine Books, 1996); and Serge Latouche, *The Westernization of the World* (Cambridge: Polity Press, 1996). For more recent explorations of the relationship between globalization and American culture, see Ulrich Beck, Natan

Sznaider, and Rainer Winter, eds., *Global America? The Cultural Consequences of Globalization* (Liverpool: Liverpool University Press, 2003); William H. Marling, *How "American" Is Globalization?* (Baltimore: Johns Hopkins University Press, 2006); and Lane Crothers, *Globalization and American Popular Culture* (Lanham, MD: Rowman & Littlefield, 2006).

61. Friedman, *The Lexus and the Olive Tree*, pp. 9, 294–5. Evidently, Friedman borrowed the term "glocalization" from Roland Robertson who used it as a marker of the increasing interdependent and complex relationship between "the local" and "the global." See Robertson, *Globalization*, pp. 173–4.

62. Friedman, *The Lexus and the Olive Tree*, pp. 474–5.

63. Francis Fukuyama, "Economic Globalization and Culture: A Discussion with Dr. Francis Fukuyama," *Merrill Lynch Forum* <http://www.ml.com/woml/forum/global.htm> (2000).

64. Poll released by the Center on Policy Attitudes and the Center for International and Security Studies at the University of Maryland (June 4, 2004). <www.pipa.org/OnlineReports/Global_Issues/globescan_press-06_04.pdf>. For a summary of polls showing strong support for a market-globalist agenda, see Chanda, *Bound Together*, pp. 301–3. The receptivity of the global South to the market-globalist message is also emphasized in various articles collected in Manfred B. Steger, ed., *Rethinking Globalism* (Lanham: Rowman & Littlefield, 2004).

65. For the concept of a "strong discourse," see Zygmunt Bauman, *In Search of Politics* (Stanford, CA: Stanford University Press, 1999), pp. 28–9; and Pierre Bourdieu, *Acts of Resistance: Against the Tyranny of the Market* (New York: New Press, 1998), p. 95. For the idea of "performativity," see Judith Butler, "Gender as Performance," in Peter Osborne, ed., *A Critical Sense: Interviews with Intellectuals* (London: Routledge, 1996), p. 112.

66. Friedman, *The Lexus and the Olive Tree*, pp. 334–5.

67. See, for example, Anthony Giddens, *Beyond Left and Right: The Future of Radical Politics* (Stanford, CA: Stanford University Press, 1994), and *The Third Way: The Renewal of Social Democracy* (Cambridge: Polity, 1998); and Tony Blair and Gerhard Schröder, "The Third Way/*Die Neue Mitte*," *Dissent* (Spring 2000), pp. 51–65.

68. Norberto Bobbio, *Left & Right: The Significance of a Political Distinction* (Chicago: University of Chicago Press, 1996), pp. 60–71.

69. Martha C. Nussbaum, "Patriotism and Cosmopolitanism," in Joshua Cohen, ed., *For Love of Country* (Boston: Beacon Press, 1996), p. 4; and David Held, *Democracy and the Global Order: From the Modern State to Cosmopolitan Governance* (Cambridge: Polity Press, 1995).

70. See Hans Schattle, *Global Citizenship* (Lanham, MD: Rowman & Littlefield, 2007); and Sidney Tarrow, *The New Transnational Activism* (Cambridge: Cambridge University Press, 2005); pp. 68–9.

71. Ibid. pp. 40–60.

72. See Jackie Smith and Joe Bandy, "Introduction: Cooperation and Conflict in Transnational Protest," in Joe Bandy and Jackie Smith, eds., *Coalitions Across Borders: Transnational Protest and the Neoliberal Order* (Lanham, MD: Rowman & Littlefield, 2004), p. 14.

73. Subcomandante Marcos, "First Declaration of La Realidad," August 3, 1996 <http://www.apostate.com/politics/realidad2.html>.

74. See Christiane Grefe, Mathias Greffrath, and Harald Schumann, *ATTAC: Was wollen die Globalisierungskritiker?* (Berlin: Rowohlt, 2002).

75. Mary Kaldor, *Global Civil Society: An Answer to War* (Cambridge: Polity, 2003), p. 78. Other notable recent examples of this burgeoning literature on global civil society and transnational activism include, for example, Kevin McDonald, *Global Movements: Action and Culture* (Oxford: Blackwell, 2006); Donatella della Porta, Massimiliano Andretta, Lorenzo Mosca, and Herbert Reiter, *Globalization from Below: Transnational Activists and Protest Networks* (Minneapolis: University of Minnesota Press, 2006); Tarrow, *The New Transnational Activism*; Donatella della Porta and Sidney Tarrow, eds., *Transnational Protest and Global Activism* (Lanham, MD: Rowman & Littlefield, 2005); and Sanjeev Khagram, James V. Riker, and Kathryn Sikkink, eds., *Restructuring World Politics: Transnational Social Movements, Networks, and Norms* (Minneapolis: University of Minnesota Press, 2002).

76. George Soros, *The Crisis of Global Capitalism: Open Society Endangered* (New York: Public Affairs, 1998), pp. xv–xxix.

77. Perhaps the most prominent defector is the Nobel laureate Joseph Stiglitz, a former political appointee in the Clinton administration and chief economist of the World Bank, who let the decade of the Roaring Nineties pass before adding his voice to the growing chorus of market-globalist reformers. See Joseph E. Stiglitz, *Globalization and Its Discontents* (New York: Norton, 2002).

78. For a detailed account of the events in Seattle and the involvement of various global justice movements, see Jackie Smith, "Globalizing Resistance: The Battle of Seattle and the Future of Social Movements," in Jackie Smith and Hank Johnston, eds., *Globalization and Resistance: Transnational Dimensions of Social Movements* (Lanham, MD: Rowman & Littlefield, 2002), pp. 207–27; and Steger, *Globalism*, chapter 5.

79. See Jose Correa Leite, *The World Social Forum: Strategies of Resistance* (Chicago: Haymarket Books, 2005), p. 63.

80. Associated Press, "Police and Protesters Clash as Economic Summit Opens," *The New York Times* (July 20, 2001); and David E. Sanger and Alessandra Stanley, "Skirmishes Mark Big Protest March at Talks in Italy," *The New York Times* (July 22, 2001).

81. Grefe et al., *ATTAC*, p. 203.

82. Susan George, *Another World Is Possible If*...(London: Verso, 2004); and *The Lugano Report: On Preserving Capitalism in the Twenty-first Century* (London: Pluto Press, 1999).

83. George, *Another World Is Possible If*..., pp. xi–x.

84. "World Social Forum 2001 Charter of Principles" and "World Social Forum 2001 Call for Mobilization," in Leite, *The World Social Forum*, pp. 9–13, 181–6.

85. Della Porta, *Globalization from Below*, p. 68.

86. Michael Hardt and Antonio Negri, "Foreword," in William F. Fisher and Thomas Ponniah, eds., *Another World Is Possible: Popular Alternatives to Globalization at the World Social Forum* (London: Zed Books, 2003), p. xvii.

87. George, *Another World Is Possible If*..., p. 6.

88. Ibid. pp. 9, 20–1, 68.

89. For an overview of some of these reports, data, and statistics, see Chanda, *Bound Together*, p. 300–3. For market-globalist interpretations, see, for example, Martin Wolf, *Why Globalization Works* (New Haven: Yale University Press, 2005); and Jagdish Bhagwati, *In Defense of Globalization* (Oxford: Oxford University Press, 2005).

90. George, *Another World Is Possible If*..., pp. 100–7; and "World Social Forum 2001 Charter of Principles" and "World Social Forum 2001 Call for Mobilization," in Leite, *The World Social Forum*, pp. 9–13, 181–6.

91. George, *Another World Is Possible If*..., pp. 90–6.

92. Ibid., chapters 6–10. See also Fabian Globalization Group, *Just World: A Fabian Manifesto* (London: Zed Books, 2005); Naomi Klein, *Fences and Windows: Dispatches from the Front Lines of the Globalization Debate* (New York: Picador, 2002); and Fisher and Ponniah, *Another World Is Possible*.

93. George, *Another World Is Possible If*..., chapter 5.

94. Freeden, *Ideologies and Political Theory*, p. 485.

Chapter 6

1. See, for example, Patrick Buchanan cited in Martin Koppel, "Buchanan Courts Labor Officials with His 'America First' Politics," *The Militant* 63.42 (November 29, 1999).

2. "Neither Left Nor Right," *Southern Poverty Law Center Intelligence Report* (Winter 2000) <http://www.splcenter.org/intelligenceproject/ip-4m3.html>. I want to thank Mark Potok, the editor of the *Southern Poverty Law Center Intelligence Report* for his personal correspondence of January 25, 2001, clarifying my questions about the presence of the radical right in Seattle. See also Chip Berlet and Matthew N. Lyons, *Right-Wing Populism in America: Too Close for Comfort* (New York: Guilford Press, 2000), pp. 342–3.

3. See, for example, Hans-Georg Betz and Stefan Immerfall, eds., *New Politics of the Right: Neo-Populist Parties and Movements in Established Democracies* (New York:

St. Martin's Press, 1998); Pierre-Andre Taguieff, *L'illusion populiste* (Paris: Berg International, 2002); Jens Rydgren, ed., *Movements of Exclusion: Radical Right-Wing Populism in the Western World* (New York: Nove Science Publishers, 2005); and Daniele Albertazzi and Duncan McDonnell, *Twenty-First Century Populism: The Spectre of Western European Democracy* (Basingstoke, UK: Palgrave Macmillan, 2007).

4. See, for example, Ghita Ionescu and Ernest Gellner, eds., *Populism: Its Meaning and National Characteristics* (London: Weidenfeld and Nicolson, 1969); Margaret Canovan, *Populism* (New York: Harcourt Brace Jovanovich, 1981); John Lukacs, *Democracy and Populism: Fear and Hatred* (New Haven: Yale University Press, 2005); and Francisco Panizza, ed., *Populism and the Mirror of Democracy* (London: Verso, 2005).

5. Canovan, *Populism*, p. 299.

6. Ernesto Laclau, "Populism: What's in a Name?" in Panizza, ed., *Populism and the Mirror of Democracy*, p. 5. See also Ernesto Laclau, *On Populist Reason* (London: Verso, 2006); and Francisco Panizza, "The Ambiguities of Populism," *The Political Quarterly* 77.4 (2006), p. 512.

7. See, for example, Paul Taggart, "Populism and Representative Politics in Contemporary Europe," *Journal of Political Ideologies* 9.3 (October 2004), pp. 269–88.

8. See Margaret Canovan, "Trust the People! Populism and the Two Faces of Democracy," *Political Studies* 47.1 (1999), p. 6; and Yannis Stavrakakis, "Antinomies of Formalism: Laclau's Theory of Populism and the Lessons from Religious Populism in Greece," *Journal of Political Ideologies* 9.3 (October 2004), pp. 264–5.

9. Gianpietro Mazzoleni, "The Media and the Growth of Neo-Populism in Contemporary Democracies," in Gianpietro Mazzoleni, Julianne Stewart, and Bruce Horsfield, eds., *The Media and Neo-Populism: A Contemporary Comparative Analysis* (Westport, CT: Praeger, 2003), p. 4.

10. Taggart, "Populism and Representative Politics in Contemporary Europe," p. 275. See also Catherine Fieschi, "Introduction," *Journal of Political Ideologies* 9.3 (2004), p. 238.

11. Michael Kazin, *The Populist Persuasion: An American History*, rev. edn. (Ithaca, NY: Cornell University Press, 1998), p. 5. For a similar perspective on populism as "a particular style of communication," see Paul Taggart, *Populism* (Buckingham: Open University Press, 2000). Similarly, drawing on Michael Freeden's work, Koen Abts and Stefan Rummens refer to populism as "a thin-centered ideology concerning structures of power in society." See Koen Abts and Stefan Rummens, "Populism Versus Democracy," in *Political Studies* 55 (2007), p. 408.

12. Berlet and Lyons, *Right-Wing Populism in America*, p. 9.

13. Patrick Buchanan, press release July 2, 1999 <http://www.issues2000.org/Pat_Buchanan_Free_Trade_&_Immigration.html>; and Patrick J. Buchanan,

State of Emergency: The Third World Invasion and Conquest of America (New York: St. Martin's Press, 2007).

14. See Taggart, "Populism and Representative Politics in Contemporary Europe," pp. 278–80.

15. See Berlet and Lyons, *Right-Wing Populism in America*, pp. 11–13; and Peter Wiles, "A Syndrome, Not a Doctrine: Some Elementary Theses on Populism," in Ionescu and Gellner, eds., *Populism*, p. 170.

16. Taggart, "Populism and Representative Politics in Contemporary Europe," p. 282.

17. Kazin, *The Populist Persuasion*, pp. 28, 30.

18. Abts and Rummens, "Populism Versus Democracy," p. 409.

19. Lukacs, *Democracy and Populism*, pp. 65–6.

20. Chalmers Johnson, *Blowback: The Costs and Consequences of American Empire* (New York: Henry Holt, 2000). Since then, Johnson has expanded his argument. See *The Sorrows of Empire: Militarism, Secrecy, and the End of the Republic* (New York: Metropolitan Books, 2004); and *Nemesis: The Last Days of the American Republic* (New York: Metropolitan Books, 2006).

21. Jason Burke, *Al-Qaeda: The True Story of Radical Islam* (London: I. B. Tauris, 2004), pp. 4, 110.

22. Ibid. p. 3. As Burke notes, "al-Qaeda" also means "the rules" or "the basics."

23. See, for example, Mehdi Mozaffari, "What Is Islamism? History and Definition of a Concept," *Totalitarian Movements and Political Religions* 8.1 (March 2007), pp. 17–33; Greg Barton, *Jemaah Islamiyah: Radical Islamism in Indonesia* (Singapore: Ridge Books, 2005); Khaled Abou El Fadl, *The Great Theft: Wrestling Islam from the Extremists* (New York: HaperCollins, 2005); Olivier Roy, *Globalized Islam: The Search for a New Ummah* (New York: Columbia University Press, 2004); Azza Karam, ed., *Transnational Political Islam: Religion, Ideology and Power* (London: Pluto Press, 2004); Thomas W. Simons, *Islam in a Globalizing World* (Stanford, CA: Stanford University Press, 2003); Gilles Kepel, *The War for Muslim Minds* (Cambridge, MA: Belknap Press, 2004), and *Jihad: On the Trail of Political Islam* (London: I.B. Tauris, 2002); and Malise Ruthven, *A Fury for God: The Islamist Attack on America* (London: Granta Books, 2002).

24. Bruce Lawrence, "Introduction" in Osama Bin Laden, *Messages to the World: The Statements of Osama Bin Laden*, ed. Bruce Lawrence and trans. James Howarth (London: Verso, 2005), pp. xvii, xi. See also Bernard Lewis, "License to Kill," *Foreign Affairs* (November–December 1998).

25. Osama Bin Laden, "Under Mullah Omar" (April 9, 2001), in Bin Laden, *Messages to the World*, p. 96; and "The Winds of Faith" (October 7, 2001), pp. 104–5.

26. Ayman al-Zawahiri, "Loyalty and Enmity" (n.d.), in Raymond Ibrahim, ed. and trans., *The Al Qaeda Reader* (New York: Broadway Books, 2007), p. 102.

27. Osama Bin Laden, "From Somalia to Afghanistan" (March 1997), in ibid. pp. 50–1.

28. Osama Bin Laden, "The Saudi Regime" (November 1996), in ibid. p. 39.

29. Osama Bin Laden, "The Invasion of Arabia" (*c.*1995–6), in ibid. p. 15. See also Osama Bin Laden, "The Betrayal of Palestine" (December 29, 1994), in ibid. pp. 3–14.

30. See, for example, Bin Laden, "The Saudi Regime," pp. 32–3.

31. Mohammed Bamyeh, "Global Order and the Historical Structures of *dar al-Islam*," in Steger, *Rethinking Globalism*, p. 225.

32. Bin Laden, "The Betrayal of Palestine," p. 9.

33. Osama Bin Laden, "A Muslim Bomb" (December 1998), in Bin Laden, *Messages to the World*, p. 88.

34. Sayyid Qutb, "War, Peace, and Islamic Jihad," in Mansoor Moaddel and Kamran Talattof, eds., *Modernist and Fundamentalist Debates in Islam: A Reader* (New York: Palgrave Macmillan, 2002), p. 240.

35. Mary R. Habeck, *Knowing the Enemy: Jihadist Ideology and the War on Terror* (New Haven: Yale University Press, 2006), p. 62.

36. Osama Bin Laden, "Terror for Terror," (October 21, 2001), in Bin Laden, *Messages to the World*, p. 119.

37. Ayman al-Zawahiri, "I Am Among the Muslim Masses" (2006), in *The Al-Qaeda Reader*, pp. 227–8.

38. Roy, *Globalizing Islam*, p. 19.

39. For an insightful analysis of the tribal, national, and global dimensions in Bin Laden's discourse, see Denis McAuley, "The Ideology of Osama Bin Laden: Nation, Tribe and World Economy," *Journal of Political Ideologies* 10.3 (October 2005), pp. 269–87. For a brilliant discussion of globalizing dynamics involving tribal identities, see Paul James, *Globalism Nationalism Tribalism: Bringing the State Back In* (London: Sage, 2006).

40. For a more detailed exposition of the reasons behind al-Qaeda's shift from the near to the far enemy, see Gerges, *The Far Enemy*, and Kepel, *The War for Muslim Minds*.

41. Bin Laden, "A Muslim Bomb," p. 91.

42. Roy, *Globalized Islam*, chapter 7.

43. Osama Bin Laden, "Moderate Islam Is a Prostration to the West" (2003), in Ibrahim, ed., *The Al Qaeda Reader*, pp. 22–62. For a readable overview of the history and meanings of *jihad*, see David Cook, *Understanding Jihad* (Berkeley, CA: University of California Press, 2005).

44. Osama Bin Laden, "Among a Band of Knights" (February 14, 2003), in Bin Laden, *Messages to the World*, p. 202; "Resist the New Rome" (January 4, 2004), in ibid. p. 218; and "A Muslim Bomb," in ibid. p. 69.

45. Osama Bin Laden, "The World Islamic Front" (February 23, 1998), in ibid. p. 61; and "To the Americans" (October 6, 2002), p. 166.

46. See, for example, Bassam Tibi, "The Totalitarianism of Jihadist Islamism and Its Challenge to Europe and to Islam," *Totalitarian Movements and Political Religion* 8.1 (March 2007), pp. 35–54; and Hendrik Hansen and Peter Kainz, "Radical Islamism and Totalitarian Ideology: A Comparison of Sayyid Qutb's Islamism with Marxism and National Socialism," in ibid. pp. 55–76.

47. Osama Bin Laden, "Depose the Tyrants" (December 16, 2004), in ibid. pp. 245–75. Ayman al-Zawahiri, "*Jihad*, Martyrdom, and the Killing of Innocents" (n.d.), in *The Al Qaeda Reader*, pp. 141–71.

48. Bin Laden, "A Muslim Bomb," pp. 73, 87; and "The Winds of Faith," p. 105.

49. Bin Laden, "Moderate Islam Is a Prostration to the West," *The Al Qaeda Reader*, pp. 51–2, 30–1.

50. Osama Bin Laden, untitled transcript of the videotaped message (September 6, 2007) <http://www.msnbcmedia.msn.com/i/msnbc/sections/news/070907_bin_laden_transcript.pdf>.

51. Bin Laden, "To the Americans," pp. 167–8; and "Resist the New Rome," in *Messages to the World*, p. 214.

52. Osama Bin Laden, "Nineteen Students" (December 26, 2001), in ibid. p. 150; and untitled transcript of a videotaped message to the American people (September 6, 2007).

53. Bin Laden, "Terror for Terror," in *Messages to the World*, p. 112.

54. Osama Bin Laden, "The Towers of Lebanon" (October 29, 2004), in ibid. p. 242.

55. Faisal Devji, "Osama Bin Laden's Message to the World," *OpenDemocracy* (December 21, 2005), p. 2. See also Devji, *Landscapes of the Jihad*, p. 144.

56. Bin Laden, untitled transcript of a videotaped message to the American people (September 6, 2007).

57. See, for example, Stephen Roach, "Is It at Risk?—Globalization," *The Economist* (February 2, 2002), p. 65; John Ralston Saul, "The Collapse of Globalism and the Rebirth of Nationalism," *Harper's Magazine* (March 2005), pp. 33–43; Anatol Lieven, *America Right or Wrong: An Anatomy of American Nationalism* (New York, Oxford University Press, 2004); and Roger Scruton, *The West and the Rest: Globalization and the Terrorist Threat* (Wilmington: ISI Books, 2002).

58. Robert J. Samuelson, "Globalization Goes to War," *Newsweek* (February 24, 2003), p. 41.

59. See Gary Dorrien, *Imperial Designs: Neoconservatives and the New Pax Americana* (New York: Routledge, 2004), pp. 1–2.

60. Max Boot, "The Case for American Empire," *Weekly Standard* (October 29, 2001), pp. 27–30; and Niall Ferguson, *Colossus: The Rise and Fall of the American Empire* (New York: Penguin Books, 2004).

61. Martin Shaw, "The Political Structure of a Global World: The Role of the United States," in Bruce Mazlish, Nayan Chanda, and Kenneth Weisbrode, eds., *The Paradox of a Global USA* (Stanford: Stanford University Press, 2007), p. 28. See

also Neil Smith, *The Endgame of Globalization* (New York: Routledge, 2005); and Mann, *Incoherent Empire*.

62. Cited in Mann, *Incoherent Empire*, p. 2. For an excellent study of the evolution of neoconservative thought and American Empire, see Dorrien, *Imperial Designs*.

63. Francis Fukuyama, *America at the Crossroads: Democracy, Power, and the Neoconservative Legacy* (New Haven: Yale University Press, 2006), pp. 48–9.

64. *The National Security Strategy of the United States* (2002) <http://www. whitehouse.gov/nsc/nss.html>.

65. The terms "hard power" and "soft power" have been coined by Clinton's former Deputy Secretary of State, Joseph S. Nye. However, similar power dynamics have been described and analyzed in different terms by generations of political thinkers influenced by the writings of Antonio Gramsci. For the latest elaboration of Nye's perspective on power, see *Soft Power: The Means to Success in World Politics* (New York: PublicAffairs, 2004).

66. See Stiglitz, *The Roaring Nineties*, chapter 9, pp. 202–40.

67. Robert Jay Lifton, *Superpower Syndrome: America's Apocalyptic Confrontation with the World* (New York: Thunder's Mouth Press, 2003), pp. 187–8.

68. NSS (2002) <http://www.whitehouse.gov/nsc/nss.html>.

69. Ibid; and George W. Bush, "Securing Freedom's Triumph," *The New York Times* (September 11, 2002).

70. Bush cited in David Stout, "Bush Calls for World Bank to Increase Grants," *The New York Times* (July 17, 2001). Bush's "Three Pillar Speech" is taken from a transcript of his address in London on Iraq and the Mideast, *The New York Times* (November 19, 2003); and "Transcript of the George W. Bush's Inaugural Address," *The New York Times* (January 20, 2005).

71. Richard Falk, "Will the Empire Be Fascist?" *The Transnational Foundation for Peace and Future Research Forum* (March 24, 2003) <http://www.transnational. org/forum/meet/2003/Falk_FascistEmpire.html>. See also Richard Falk, *The Great Terror War* (New York: Olive Branch Press, 2003); and William H. Thornton, *New World Empire: Civil Islam, Terrorism, and the Making of Neoglobalism* (Lanham, MD: Rowman & Littlefield, 2005), p. 19.

72. Robert Mcfarlane and Michael Bleyzer, "Taking Iraq Private," *The Wall Street Journal* (March 27, 2003).

73. Robert D. Kaplan, "The Hard Edge of American Values," *The Atlantic Monthly Online* (June 18, 2003) <http://www.theatlantic.com/c...com/ unbound/interviews/int2003-06-18.htm>. See also Robert D. Kaplan, *Warrior Politics: Why Leadership Demands a Pagan Ethos* (New York: Vintage, 2003).

74. Norman Podhoretz, *World War IV: The Long Struggle Against Islamofascism* (New York: Doubleday, 2007).

75. Thomas P. M. Barnett, *The Pentagon's New Map: War and Peace in the Twenty-First Century* (New York: G. P. Putnam's Sons, 2004). The sequel to this book

is *Blueprint for Action: A Future Worth Creating* (New York: G. P. Putnam's Sons, 2005).

76. A milder version of this argument can be found in Walter Russell Mead's advocacy of an "American project—A grand strategic vision of what it is that the United States seeks to build in the World." See *Power, Terror, Peace, and War: America's Grand Strategy in a World of Risk* (New York: Knopf, 2004), p. 7.

77. Barnett, *The Pentagon's New Map*, pp. 31–2, 294–302.

78. Ibid., chapters 3 and 4.

79. Barnett, *Blueprint for Action*, p. xvii.

80. Barnett, *The Pentagon's New Map*, p. 245.

81. Manfred B. Steger, "American Globalism 'Madison Avenue-Style': A Critique of U.S. Public Diplomacy After 9-11," in Patrick Hayden and Chamsy el-Ojeili, eds., *Confronting Globalization: Humanity, Justice and the Renewal of Politics* (London: Palgrave Macmillan: 2005), pp. 227–41.

82. For a summary of these polls, see Andrew Kohut and Bruce Stokes, *America Against the World: How We Are Different And Why We Are Disliked* (New York: Times Books, 2006). See also Mark Hertsgaard, *The Eagle's Shadow: Why America Fascinates and Infuriates the World* (New York: Picador, 2003).

83. Barnett, *The Pentagon's New Map*, p. 50.

84. See Jan Nederveen Pieterse, *Globalization or Empire?* (New York: Routledge, 2004), p. v.

85. See Michael Ignatieff, *The Lesser Evil: Political Ethics in the Age of Terror* (Princeton: Princeton University Press, 2004); and Paul Berman, *Terror and Liberalism* (New York: W. W. Norton, 2003).

86. Thomas L. Friedman, *Longtitudes and Attitudes: The World in the Age of Terrorism* (New York: Anchor Books, 2003), p. 78.

87. George W. Bush, "Remarks at National Day of Prayer and Remembrance," National Cathedral, Washington, DC, September 14, 2001 <http://www.whitehouse.gov/news/releases/2001/09.html>.

88. NSS (2006); "President Bush Addresses American Legion National Convention" (August 31, 2006) <http://www.whitehouse.gov/news/releases/2006/08/ print/20060831-1.html>; "Transcript of President Bush's Address to Nation on U.S. Policy in Iraq," *The New York Times* (January 11, 2006); and "Transcript of President Bush's State of the Union Address," *The New York Times* (January 31, 2006).

89. Peter Singer, *The President of Good & Evil: Questioning the Ethics of George W. Bush* (New York: Plume Books, 2004), pp. 2, 207–12.

90. Dick Cheney cited in Cullen Murphy, *Are We Rome? The Fall of Empire and the Fate of America* (New York: Houghton Mifflin, 2007), p. 10.

91. Kevin Phillips, *American Theocracy: The Peril and Politics of Radical Religion, Oil, and Borrowed Money in the 21st Century* (New York: Viking, 2006), p. 236.

92. Chris Hedges, *American Fascists: The Christian Right and the War on America* (New York: Free Press, 2006), pp. 18–19, 205.

93. Mark Lilla, *The Stillborn God: Religion, Politics, and the Modern West* (New York: Knopf, 2007), p. 4.

94. Hans Maier, "Political Religion: A Concept and Its Limitations," *Totalitarian Movements and Political Religions* 8.1 (March 2007), p. 15.

95. Emilio Gentile, *Politics as Religion* (Princeton: Princeton University Press, 2006), p. xiv.

96. John Gray, *Black Mass: Apocalyptic Religion and the Death of Utopia* (London: Allen Lane, 2007), pp. 1–3.

97. See, for example, Stanley G. Payne, "On the Heuristic Value of the Concept of Political Religion and Its Application," *Totalitarian Movements and Political Religions* 6.2 (September 2005), pp. 163–74.

98. Nelson Goodman, *Ways of Worldmaking* (Indianapolis, IN: Hackett, 1978), p. 6.

99. The classic account of the "network society" remains Manuel Castells' seminal three-volume oeuvre *The Information Age: Economy, Society and Culture* (Oxford, UK: Blackwell, 1996–8). For a short introduction to the subject, see Darin Barney, *The Network Society* (Cambridge, UK: Polity, 2004).

100. See Beck, *What Is Globalization?* pp. 72–7.

101. For a discussion of such "fragmegration," see James N. Rosenau, *Distant Proximities: Dynamics Beyond Globalization* (Princeton, NJ: Princeton University Press, 2003).

Selected Bibliography

Ackerman, Peter and Jack Duvall, *A Force More Powerful: A Century of Nonviolent Conflict* (New York: Palgrave, 2000).

Adas, Michael, "Contested Hegemony: The Great War and the Afro-Asian Assault on the Civilizing Mission Ideology," in P. Duara (ed.), *Decolonization: Perspectives from Now and Then* (London: Routledge, 2004).

Adler, Max, *Marx und Engels als Denker* (Frankfurt: Makol Verlag, 1972 [1908; 1920]).

Albertazzi, Daniele and Duncan McDonnell, *Twenty-First Century Populism: The Spectre of Western European Democracy* (Basingstoke, UK: Palgrave Macmillan, 2007).

Albrow, Martin, *The Global Age: State and Society Beyond Modernity* (Stanford, CA: Stanford University Press, 1997).

Althusser, Louis, *For Marx* (London: Allen Lane, 1969).

Aly, Goetz, *Nazi Population Policy and the Murder of the European Jews* (New York: Oxford University Press, 1999).

Anderson, R. D., *France 1870–1914: Politics and Society* (London: Routledge and Kegan Paul, 1977).

Anderson, Benedict, *Imagined Communities: Reflections on the Origin and Spread of Nationalism*, rev. edn. (London: Verso, 1991).

Ansbro, John J., *Martin Luther King, Jr.: The Making of a Mind* (Maryknoll, NY: Orbis, 1984).

Appadurai, Arjun, *Fear of Small Numbers: An Essay on the Geography of Anger* (Durham & London: Duke University Press, 2006).

Archer, Robin, Diemut Bubeck, and Haujo Glock (eds.), *Out of Apathy: Voices of the New Left Thirty Years On* (London: Verso, 1989).

Aston, Nigel, *The French Revolution 1789–1804: Authority, Liberty and the Search for Stability* (Houndmills, UK: Palgrave Macmillan, 2004).

Atkin, Nicholas and Frank Tallett, *The Right in France: From Revolution to Le Pen*, 2nd edn. (London: I. B. Tauris, 2003).

Ball, Terence and Richard Bellamy (eds.), *The Cambridge History of Twentieth-Century Political Thought* (Cambridge: Cambridge University Press, 2003).

—— and Richard Dagger, *Political Ideologies and the Democratic Ideal* (New York: Pearson Longman, 2004).

Ball, Terence, James Farr, and Russell Hanson (eds.), "Ideology," in *Political Innovation and Conceptual Change* (Cambridge, UK: Cambridge University Press, 1989).

Barat, Leon P., *Political Ideologies: Their Origins and Impact*, 8th edn. (Upper Saddle River: Prentice-Hall, 2003).

Barber, Benjamin, *Jihad Vs. McWorld* (New York: Ballantine Books, 1996).

Barkawi, Tarak, *Globalization and War* (Lanham, MD: Rowman & Littlefield, 2006).

Barnett, Thomas P. M., *The Pentagon's New Map: War and Peace in the Twenty-First Century* (New York: G. P. Putnam's Sons, 2004).

——*Blueprint for Action: A Future Worth Creating* (New York: G. P. Putnam's Sons, 2005).

Barney, Darin, *The Network Society* (Cambridge, UK: Polity Press, 2004).

Barton, Greg, *Jemaah Islamiyah: Radical Islamism in Indonesia* (Singapore: Ridge Books, 2005).

Bauman, Zygmunt, *In Search of Politics* (Stanford, CA: Stanford University Press, 1999).

Baxter, Brian, *Ecologism: An Introduction* (Washington, DC: Georgetown University Press, 1999).

Bebel, August, *My Life* (Chicago, IL: University of Chicago Press, 1913).

Beck, Ulrich, *Risk Society: Toward a New Modernity* (London: Sage, 1992).

——*What Is Globalization?* (Cambridge: Polity Press, 2000).

——*Power in the Global Age: A New Global Political Economy* (Cambridge: Polity Press, 2005).

——Natan Sznaider, and Rainer Winter (eds.), *Global America? The Cultural Consequences of Globalization* (Liverpool, UK: Liverpool University Press, 2003).

Beder, Sharon, *Free Market Missionaries: The Corporate Manipulation of Community Values* (London: Earthscan, 2006).

Bell, Daniel, *The End of Ideology: On the Exhaustion of Political Ideas in the Fifties* (Glencoe, IL: Free Press, 1960).

Bellamy, Richard, "Introduction," in *Victorian Liberalism: Nineteenth-Century Political Thought and Practice* (London: Routledge, 1990).

——*Liberalism and Modern Society: A Historical Argument* (University Park: Penn State University Press, 1992).

Berkowitz, Peter, *Virtue and the Making of Modern Liberalism* (Princeton, NJ: Princeton University Press, 1999).

Berlet, Chip and Matthew N. Lyons, *Right-Wing Populism in America: Too Close for Comfort* (New York: Guilford Press, 2000).

Berman, Paul, *Terror and Liberalism* (New York: W. W. Norton, 2003).

Bernstein, Eduard, *Ferdinand Lassalle as a Social Reformer* (New York: Charles Scribner's Sons, 1893).

——*The Preconditions of Socialism* (Cambridge, UK: Cambridge University Press, 1993).

——*The Quest for Evolutionary Socialism: Eduard Bernstein and Social Democracy* (Cambridge: Cambridge University Press, 1997).

Betz, Hans-Georg and Stefan Immerfall (eds.), *New Politics of the Right: Neo-Populist Parties and Movements in Established Democracies* (New York: St. Martin's Press, 1998).

Bhagwati, Jagdish, *In Defense of Globalization* (Oxford: Oxford University Press, 2005).

Biddis, Michael D., *Father of Racist Ideology: The Social and Political Thought of Count Gobineau* (London: Weidenfeld & Nicolson, 1970).

—— "Introduction," in M. D. Biddiss (ed.), *Arthur de Gobineau, Selected Political Writings* (London: Jonathan Cape, 1970).

Billig, Michael, *Banal Nationalism* (London: Sage, 1995).

Bin Laden, Osama, *Messages to the World: The Statements of Osama Bin Laden*, ed., Bruce Lawrence and trans., James Howarth (London: Verso, 2005).

Blyth, Mark, *Great Transformations* (Cambridge: Cambridge University Press, 2002).

Bobbio, Norberto, *Left & Right: The Significance of a Political Distinction* (Chicago, IL: University of Chicago Press, 1996).

Bosworth, R. J. B., *Mussolini* (London: Arnold, 2002).

Bourdieu, Pierre, *Acts of Resistance: Against the Tyranny of the Market* (New York: New Press, 1998).

—— *The Logic of Practice* (Stanford, CA: Stanford University Press, 1990).

Bracher, Karl Dietrich, *The German Dictatorship* (Harmondsworth, UK: Penguin, 1971).

Brandenberger, David, *National Bolshevism: Stalinist Mass Culture and the Formation of Modern Russian National Identity, 1931–1956* (Cambridge, MA: Harvard University Press, 2002).

Breitman, George (ed.), *Malcolm X Speaks* (New York: Pathfinder, 1965).

Bronner, Stephen Eric, *Moments of Decision: Political History and the Crisis of Radicalism* (New York: Routledge, 1992).

—— *A Rumor About the Jews: Reflections on Antisemitism and the Protocols of the Learned Elders of Zion* (New York: St. Martin's Press, 2000).

Brozat, Martin, *Hitler and the Collapse of Weimar Germany* (Leamington Spa: Berg, 1987).

Buchanan, Patrick J., *State of Emergency: The Third World Invasion and Conquest of America* (New York: St. Martin's Press, 2007).

Buchheim, Hans, *Totalitarian Rule: Its Nature and Characteristics* (Middletown, CT: Wesleyan University Press, 1967).

Burke, Jason, *Al-Qaeda: The True Story of Radical Islam* (London: I.B. Tauris, 2004).

Burleigh, Michael, *The Third Reich: A New History* (New York: Hill and Wang, 2001).

Burns, Timothy (ed.), *After History? Francis Fukuyama and His Critics* (Lanham, MD: Rowman & Littlefield, 1994).

Bush, Barbara, *Imperialism and Postcolonialism* (Harlow, UK: Pearson, 2006).

Bushnell, David and Neill Macaulay, *The Emergence of Latin America in the Nineteenth Century* (New York: Oxford University Press, 1994).

Butler, Judith, "Gender as Performance," in P. Osborne (ed.), *A Critical Sense: Interviews with Intellectuals* (London: Routledge, 1996).

Calhoun, Craig, *Nationalism* (Minneapolis: University of Minnesota Press, 1997).

Canovan, Margaret, *Populism* (New York: Harcourt Brace Jovanovich, 1981).

—— *Nationhood and Political Theory* (Cheltenham, UK: Edward Elgar, 1996).

Cappon, Lester J. (ed.), *The Adams-Jefferson Letters: The Complete Correspondence Between Thomas Jefferson and Abigail and John Adams* (Chapel Hill: University of North Carolina Press, 1959).

Carr, E. H., *Socialism in One Country: 1924–1926*, 2 vols. (London: Macmillan, 1958–9).

Carson, Rachel, *Silent Spring* (Boston, MA: Mariner/Houghton Mifflin, 2002 [1962]).

Carsten, F. L., *The Rise of Fascism* (Berkeley: University of California Press, 1967).

Carver, Terrell, *Marx & Engels: The Intellectual Relationship* (Bloomington: Indiana University Press, 1983).

Castells, Manuel, *The Information Age: Economy, Society and Culture* (Oxford, UK: Blackwell, 1996–8).

Castoriadis, Cornelius, *The Imaginary Institution of Society* (Cambridge: Polity Press, 1987).

Ch'en, Jerome (ed.), *Mao Papers. Anthology and Bibliography* (Oxford: Oxford University Press, 1970).

Chanda, Nayan, *Bound Together: How Traders, Preachers, Adventurers, and Warriors Shaped Globalization* (New Haven, CT: Yale University Press, 2007).

Chatterjee, Partha, *Nationalist Thought and the Colonial World: A Derivative Discourse?* (Minneapolis: University of Minnesota Press, 1993).

Chow, Gregory C., *China's Economic Transformation* (Oxford, UK: Blackwell, 2002).

Clarke, Peter, *Liberals and Social Democrats* (Cambridge: Cambridge University Press, 1978).

Cockett, Richard, *Thinking the Unthinkable: Think-Tanks and the Economic Counter-Revolution, 1931–1983* (London: HarperCollins, 1995).

Cohen, Daniel, *Globalization and Its Enemies* (Cambridge, MA: MIT Press, 2006).

Cohen, Joshua (ed.), *For Love of Country* (Boston, MA: Beacon Press, 1996).

Cohen, Stephen F., *Bukharin and the Bolshevik Revolution* (New York: Oxford University Press, 1980).

Colaiaco, James A., *Martin Luther King Jr.: Apostle of Militant Nonviolence* (New York: St. Martin's Press, 1993).

Collins, Irene, *Liberalism in Nineteenth-Century Europe* (London: The Historical Association, 1957).

Connolly, William E., *Political Theory and Modernity* (Cambridge: Basil Blackwell, 1988).

Cook, David, *Understanding Jihad* (Berkeley: University of California Press, 2005).

Courtois, Stéphane, Nicolas Werth, Jean-Louis Panné, Andrzej Paczkowski, Karel Bartosek, and Jean-Louis Margolin, *The Black Book of Communism: Crimes, Terror, Repression* (Cambridge, MA: Harvard University Press, 1999).

Craiutu, Aurelian, *Liberalism Under Siege: The Political Thought of the French Doctrinaires* (Lanham, MD: Lexington Books, 2003).

Crothers, Lane, *Globalization and American Popular Culture* (Lanham, MD: Rowman & Littlefield, 2006).

Cummins, Ian, *Marx, Engels, and National Movements* (New York: St. Martin's Press, 1980).

D'Agostino, Anthony, *Gorbachev's Revolution* (New York: New York University Press, 1998).

Dalton, Dennis, *Mahatma Gandhi: Nonviolent Power in Action* (New York: Columbia University Press, 1993).

Dann, Otto and John Dinwiddy (eds.), *Nationalism in the Age of the French Revolution* (London: Hambledon Press, 1988).

Davidowicz, Lucy, *The War Against the Jews, 1933–1945* (New York: Bantam, 1975).

Davies, Peter, *The Extreme Right in France, 1789 to the Present* (London: Routledge, 2002).

De Maistre, Joseph, *Considerations on France*, trans. Richard A. Lebrun (Montreal, Canada: McGill-Queen's University Press, 1974).

Della Porta, Donatella, Massimiliano Andretta, Lorenzo Mosca, and Herbert Reiter, *Globalization from Below: Transnational Activists and Protest Networks* (Minneapolis: University of Minnesota Press, 2006).

Denning, Michael, *Culture in the Age of Three Worlds* (London: Verso, 2004).

Dobson, Andrew, *Green Political Thought*, 2nd edn. (London: Routledge, 1995).

Dorrien, Gary, *Imperial Designs: Neoconservatives and the New Pax Americana* (New York: Routledge, 2004).

Downs, Anthony, *An Economic Theory of Democracy* (New York: Harper & Row, 1957).

Doyle, William, *The Ancien Regime*, 2nd edn. (Houndmills, UK: Palgrave Macmillan, 2001).

——*The French Revolution: A Very Short Introduction* (Oxford, UK: Oxford University Press, 2001).

Dreyfus, Hubert, *Being in the World* (Cambridge, MA: MIT Press, 1991).

Dubcek, Alexander, *Hope Dies Last: The Autobiography of Alexander Dubcek* (New York: Kodansha International, 1993).

Dumont, Louis, *German Ideology: From France to Germany and Back* (Chicago, IL: University of Chicago Press, 1994).

Dunlop, John B., *The Faces of Contemporary Russian Nationalism* (Princeton, NJ: Princeton University Press, 1983).

Dwork, Deborah and Robert Jan Van Pelt, *Holocaust: A History* (New York: W. W. Norton, 2003).

Eatwell, Roger, *Fascism: A History* (London: Pimlico, 2003).

Ebenstein, Alex, *Friedrich Hayek: A Biography* (Chicago, IL: University of Chicago Press, 2001).

——*Hayek's Journey: The Mind of Friedrich Hayek* (New York: Palgrave Macmillan, 2003).

Eckersley, Robin, *Environmentalism and Political Theory: Toward an Ecocentric Approach* (London: UCL Press, 1992).

Edwards, J. W., and Louis de Rose, *United We Stand: A Message for All Americans* (Ann Arbor, MI: Mundus, 2001).

Ehrenberg, John, *Servants of Wealth: The Right's Assault on Economic Justice* (Lanham, MD: Rowman & Littlefield, 2006).

El Fadl, Khaled Abou, *The Great Theft: Wrestling Islam from the Extremists* (New York: HarperCollins, 2005).

Elliott, Anthony and Charles Lemert, *The New Individualism: The Emotionalism Costs of Globalization* (London: Routledge, 2006).

Ellis, Richard J., *The Dark Side of the Left: Illiberal Egalitarianism in America* (Lawrence: University Press of Kansas, 1998).

Ernesto, Laclau, *On Populist Reason* (London: Verso, 2006).

Evans, Eric J., *Political Parties in Britain 1783–1867* (London: Methuen, 1985).

——*Thatcher and Thatcherism*, 2nd edn. (London: Routledge, 1997).

Evans, Richard J., *The Coming of the Third Reich* (London: Penguin Books, 2003).

Fabian Globalization Group, *Just World: A Fabian Manifesto* (London: Zed Books, 2005).

Falk, Richard, *The Great Terror War* (New York: Olive Branch Press, 2003).

Fanon, Frantz, *The Wretched of the Earth* (New York: Grove Press, 1963).

——*A Dying Colonialism* (New York: Grove Press, 1965).

——*Black Skin, White Masks* (New York: Grove Press, 1967).

Ferguson, Niall, *Colossus: The Rise and Fall of the American Empire* (New York: Penguin Books, 2004).

——*The War of the World: Twentieth-Century Conflict and the Descent of the West* (New York: Penguin Press, 2006).

Festenstein, Matthew and Michael Kenny (eds.), *Political Ideologies: A Reader and Guide* (Oxford: Oxford University Press, 2005).

Feuchtwanger, Edgar, *Imperial Germany 1850–1918* (London: Routledge, 2001).

Fisher, William F. and Thomas Ponniah (eds.), *Another World Is Possible: Popular Alternatives to Globalization at the World Social Forum* (London: Zed Books, 2003).

Fitzpatrick, Sheila, *Everyday Stalinism: Ordinary Life in Extraordinary Times: Soviet Russia in the 1930s* (New York: Oxford University Press, 1999).

Footman, David, *Ferdinand Lassalle: Romantic Revolutionary* (New Haven, CT: Yale University Press, 1947).

Forman, Michael, *Nationalism and the International Labor Movement: The Idea of the Nation in Socialist and Anarchist Theory* (University Park: Pennsylvania State University Press, 1998).

Fredrickson, George M., *Racism: A Short History* (Carleton: Scribe Publications, 2002).

Freeden, Michael, *Liberalism Divided: A Study in British Political Thought 1914–1939* (Oxford: Clarendon Press, 1986).

——"The Family of Liberalisms: A Morphological Analysis," in J. Meadowcroft (ed.), *The Liberal Tradition: Contemporary Reappraisals* (Cheltenham, UK: Edward Elgar, 1996).

——*Ideologies and Political Theory* (Oxford: Oxford University Press, 1996).

——(ed.), *Reassessing Political Ideologies: The Durability of Dissent* (London: Routledge, 2001).

——*Ideology: A Very Short Introduction* (Oxford: Oxford University Press, 2003).

Friedan, Betty, *The Feminist Mystique* (New York: W. W. Norton, 1963).

Frieden, Jeffrey A., *Global Capitalism: Its Fall and Rise in the Twentieth Century* (New York: W. W. Norton, 2006).

Friedlaender, Saul, *Nazi Germany and the Jews, Vol. 1: The Years of Persecution* (London: Weidenfeld and Nicolson, 1997).

Friedman, Thomas L., *The Lexus and the Olive Tree: Understanding Globalization* (New York: Anchor Books, 2000).

——*The World Is Flat: A Brief History of the Twenty-First Century* (New York: Farrar, Straus, and Giroux, 2005).

Friedrich, Carl J. (ed.), *Totalitarianism* (Cambridge, MA: Harvard University Press, 1954).

——Michael Curtis, and Benjamin R. Barber, *Totalitarianism in Perspective: Three Views* (New York: Praeger 1969).

Fueredi, Frank, *Colonial Wars and the Politics of Third World Nationalism* (London: I. B. Tauris, 1994).

Fukuyama, Francis, *The End of History and the Last Man* (New York: Free Press, 1992).

——*America at the Crossroads: Democracy, Power, and the Neoconservative Legacy* (New Haven, CT: Yale University Press, 2006).

Furet, Francois, *The Passing of an Illusion: The Idea of Communism in the Twentieth Century* (Chicago, IL: University of Chicago Press, 2000).

Gandhi, Mahatma, *The Collected Works of Mahatma Gandhi* (*CWMG*) 100 vols. (New Delhi: Publications Division, Ministry of Information and Broadcasting, Government of India, 1958–94).

Garrow, David, *Bearing the Cross: Martin Luther King, Jr., and the Southern Christian Leadership Conference* (New York: Vintage, 1986).

Garten, Jeffrey E., *The Mind of the CEO* (New York: Basic Books, 2001).

Geddis, John Lewis., *The Cold War: A New History* (New York: Penguin Press, 2005).

Geertz, Clifford, *The Interpretation of Cultures* (New York: Basic Books, 1973).

Gentile, Emilio, *The Origins of Fascist Ideology: 1918–1925* (New York: Enigma Books, 2005).

——*Politics as Religion* (Princeton, NJ: Princeton University Press, 2006).

George, Susan, *The Lugano Report: On Preserving Capitalism in the Twenty-first Century* (London: Pluto Press, 1999).

——*Another World Is Possible If . . .* (London: Verso, 2004).

Giddens, Anthony, *Beyond Left and Right: The Future of Radical Politics* (Stanford, CA: Stanford University Press, 1994).

——*The Third Way: The Renewal of Social Democracy* (Cambridge: Polity Press, 1998).

Gierson, Mark (ed.), *The Essential Neo-Conservative Reader* (Reading, MA: Addison-Wesley, 1996).

Gilbert, Martin, *A History of the Twentieth Century Vol 1: 1900–1933* (London: HarperCollins, 1997).

——*A History of the Twentieth Century: The Concise Edition of the Acclaimed World History* (New York: HarperCollins, 2002).

Gilpin, Robert, *The Challenge of Global Capitalism: The World Economy in the 21st Century* (Princeton, NJ: Princeton University Press, 2000).

Gladstone, David, *The Twentieth-Century Welfare State* (New York: St. Martin's Press, 1999).

Glendon, Mary Ann, *Rights Talk: The Impoverishment of Political Discourse* (New York: Free Press, 1990).

Goldhagen, Daniel Jonah, *Hitler's Willing Executioners: Ordinary Germans and the Holocaust* (New York: Vintage Books, 1996).

Goodman, Nelson, *Ways of Worldmaking* (Indianapolis: Hackett, 1978).

Gorbachev, Mikhail, *Perestroika: New Thinking for Our Country and the World* (New York: Harper and Row, 1987).

——*Selected Speeches and Articles*, 2nd edn. (Moscow: Progress Publishers, 1987).

——*Memoirs* (New York: Doubleday, 1996).

Gordon, Lewis R., T. Denean Sharpley-Whiting, and Reneé T. White (eds.), *Fanon: A Critical Reader* (Oxford: Blackwell, 1996).

Gore, Lance, *The Institutional Foundations of China's Post-Mao Hyper-Growth* (New York: Oxford University Press, 1998).

Gould, Andrew C., *Origins of Liberal Dominance: State, Church, and Party in Nineteenth-Century Europe* (Ann Arbor: University of Michigan Press, 1999).

Gray, John, *Liberalism*, 2nd edn. (Minneapolis: University of Minnesota Press, 1995).

——*False Dawn: The Delusions of Global Capitalism* (New York: New Press, 1998).

——*Black Mass: Apocalyptic Religion and the Death of Utopia* (London: Allen Lane, 2007).

Green, T. H., "On the Different Senses of 'Freedom' as Applied to Will and the Moral Progress of Man," in P. Harris and J. Morrow (eds.), *Lectures on the Principles of Political Obligation and Other Writings* (Cambridge: Cambridge University Press, 1986).

Greenfeld, Liah, *Nationalisms: Five Roads to Modernity* (Cambridge, MA: Harvard University Press, 1992).

—— *The Spirit of Capitalism: Nationalism and Economic Growth* (Cambridge, MA: Harvard University Press, 2001).

—— "Is Modernity Possible Without Nationalism?," in S. Michel (ed.), *The Fate of the Nation-State* (Montreal: McGill-Queen's University Press, 2004).

Grefe, Christiane, Mathias Greffrath, and Harald Schumann, *ATTAC: Was wollen die Globalisierungskritiker?* (Berlin: Rowohlt, 2002).

Griffin, Roger (ed.), *Fascism* (Oxford: Oxford University Press, 1995).

Griffiths, Richard, *Fascism* (London: Continuum, 2005).

Guehenno, Jean-Marie, *The End of the Nation-State* (Minneapolis: University of Minnesota Press, 1995).

Guevara, Ernesto Che, *Guerilla Warfare* (Lincoln: University of Nebraska Press, 1998).

Habeck, Mary R., *Knowing the Enemy: Jihadist Ideology and the War on Terror* (New Haven, CT: Yale University Press, 2006).

Habermas, Jürgen, *The Philosophical Discourse of Modernity* (Cambridge, MA: MIT Press, 1987).

Hall, Stuart and Martin Jacques (eds.), *The Politics of Thatcherism* (London: Lawrence and Wisehart, 1983).

Hanhimaki, Jussi and Odd Arne Westad (eds.), *The Cold War: A History in Documents and Eyewitness Accounts* (Oxford: Oxford University Press, 2003).

Hannaford, Ivan, *Race: The History of an Idea in the West* (Baltimore, MD: Johns Hopkins University Press, 1996).

Hannerz, Ulf, *The Transnational Connection* (London: Routledge, 1996).

Hardiman, David, *Gandhi in his Time and Ours: The Global Legacy of his Ideas* (New York: Columbia University Press, 2003).

Hartz, Louis, *The Liberal Tradition in America: An Interpretation of American Political Thought Since the Revolution* (New York: Harcourt Brace & Company, 1991).

Harvey, David, *A Brief History of Neoliberalism* (Oxford: Oxford University Press, 2005).

Hayden, Patrick and Chamsy el-Ojeili (eds.), *Confronting Globalization: Humanity, Justice and the Renewal of Politics* (London: Palgrave Macmillan, 2005).

Hayek, F. A., *The Constitution of Liberty* (Chicago, IL: University of Chicago Press, 1960).

—— "The Intellectuals and Socialism," in *Studies in Philosophy, Politics and Economics* (London: Routledge, 1967).

—— *The Road to Serfdom* (Chicago, IL: University of Chicago Press, 1994 [1944]).

Hazareesingh, Sudhir, *Political Traditions in Modern France* (New York: Oxford University Press, 1994).

Head, Brian W., *Ideology and Social Science: Destutt de Tracy and French Liberalism* (Dordrecht, Holland: Martinus Nijhoff, 1985).

Hedetoft, Ulf and Mette Hjort (eds.), *The Postnational Self: Belonging and Identity* (Minneapolis: University of Minnesota Press, 2002).

Hedges, Chris, *American Fascists: The Christian Right and the War on America* (New York: Free Press, 2006).

Held, David, *Democracy and the Global Order: From the Modern State to Cosmopolitan Governance* (Cambridge: Polity Press, 1995).

Hertsgaard, Mark, *The Eagle's Shadow: Why America Fascinates and Infuriates the World* (New York: Picador, 2003).

Heywood, Andrew, *Political Ideologies: An Introductions*, 3rd edn. (Houndmills, UK: Palgrave Macmillan, 2003).

Himmelfarb, Gertrude (ed.), *Essays in Politics and Culture* (New York: Anchor Books, 1963).

Hirschman, Albert O., *The Rhetoric of Reaction: Perversity Futility Jeopardy* (Cambridge, MA: Harvard University Press, 1991).

Hitler, Adolf, *Mein Kampf*, trans. Ralph Manheim (Boston, MA: Houghton Mifflin, 1971).

Hobhouse, L. T., In J. Meadowcroft (ed.), *Liberalism and Other Writings* (Cambridge: Cambridge University Press, 1994).

Hobsbawm, Eric, *The Age of Empire: 1875–1914* (New York: Pantheon Books, 1987).

——*Nations and Nationalism Since 1780* (Cambridge: Cambridge University Press, 1992).

——*The Age of Extremes: A History of the World* (New York: Vintage, 1996).

——and Antonio Polito, *On the Edge of the New Century* (New York: New Press, 2000).

Ibrahim, Raymond ed., and trans., *The Al Qaeda Reader* (New York: Broadway Books, 2007).

Ignatieff, Michael, *The Lesser Evil: Political Ethics in the Age of Terror* (Princeton, NJ: Princeton University Press, 2004).

Ilic, Melanie (ed.), *Stalin's Terror Revisited* (Houndmills, UK: Palgrave Macmillan, 2006).

Ionescu, Ghita and Ernest Gellner (eds.), *Populism: Its Meaning and National Characteristics* (London: Weidenfeld and Nicolson, 1969).

Iyer, Raghavan (ed.), *The Moral and Political Writings of Mahatma Gandhi*, 3 vols. (Oxford: Clarendon Press, 1986–7 [1916]).

Jacoby, Russell, *The End of Utopia: Politics and Culture in an Age of Apathy* (New York: Basic Books, 1999).

James, Paul, *Globalism Nationalism Tribalism: Bringing Theory Back in* (London: Sage, 2006).

Johnson, Chalmers, *Blowback: The Costs and Consequences of American Empire* (New York: Henry Holt, 2000).

——*The Sorrows of Empire: Militarism, Secrecy, and the End of the Republic* (New York: Metropolitan Books, 2004).

——*Nemesis: The Last Days of the American Republic* (New York: Metropolitan Books, 2006).

Judt, Tony, *Postwar: A History of Europe Since 1945* (London: Penguin, 2005).

Kahan, Alan S., *Liberalism in Nineteenth-Century Europe: The Political Culture of Limited Suffrage* (New York: Palgrave Macmillan, 2003).

Kaldor, Mary, *Global Civil Society: An Answer to War* (Cambridge: Polity Press, 2003).

Kaplan, Robert D., *Warrior Politcs: Why Leadership Demands a Pagan Ethos* (New York: Vintage, 2003).

Karam, Azza (ed.), *Transnational Political Islam: Religion, Ideology and Power* (London: Pluto Press, 2004).

Katsiaficas, George, *The Imagination of the New Left: A Global Analysis of 1968* (Boston, MA: South End Press, 1987).

Kautsky, Karl, *Das Erfurter Program: In seinem grundsaetzlichen Teil erlaeutert* (Berlin: Verlag J. H. W. Dietz Nachfolger, 1974) [1922]).

Kazin, Michael, *The Populist Persuasion: An American History*, rev. edn. (Ithaca, NY: Cornell University Press, 1998).

Kelly, Christine A., *Tangled Up in Red, White, and Blue: New Social Movements in America* (Lanham, MD: Rowman & Littlefield, 2001).

Kenez, Peter, *A History of the Soviet Union from the Beginning to the End*, 2nd edn. (New York: Cambridge University Press, 2006).

Kennedy, Emmet, *A Philosophe in the Age of Revolution: Destutt de Tracy and the Origins of "Ideology"* (Philadelphia, PA: The American Philosophical Society, 1978).

Kepel, Gilles, *Jihad: On the Trail of Political Islam* (London: I.B. Tauris, 2002).

—— *The War for Muslim Minds* (Cambridge: Belknap Press, 2004).

Kershaw, Ian, *Hitler1889–1945 Vol. 1: Hubris* (London: Penguin, 2001).

Keynes, John M., *The General Theory of Employment, Interest, and Money* (New York: Harcourt, Brace, 1936).

Khagram, Sanjeev, James V. Riker, and Kathryn Sikkink (eds.), *Restructuring World Politics: Transnational Social Movements, Networks, and Norms* (Minneapolis: University of Minnesota Press, 2002).

Kidron, Michael and Ronald Segal, *The State of the World Atlas* (London: Pluto Press, 1981).

King, Martin L., Jr., *Where Do We Go from Here: Chaos or Community?* (New York: Harper and Row, 1967).

—— *A Testament of Hope: The Essential Writings and Speeches of Martin Luther King, Jr.*, ed. (New York: James M. Washington, HarperCollins, 1991).

Kinloch, Graham C. and Raj P. Mohan (eds.), *Ideology and the Social Sciences* (Westport, CT: Greenwood Press, 2000).

Kirkpatrick, Jeane J. and Odd Arne Westad, *The Global Cold War: Third World Interventions and the Making of Our Times* (Cambridge: Cambridge University Press, 2005).

Klein, Naomi, *Fences and Windows: Dispatches from the Front Lines of the Globalization Debate* (New York: Picador, 2002).

Kohut, Andrew and Bruce Stokes, *America Against the World: How We Are Different and Why We Are Disliked* (New York: Times Books, 2006).

Kolakowski, Leszek, *Main Currents of Marxism, Vol. 1: The Founders* (Oxford, UK: Oxford University Press, 1978).

—— *Main Currents of Marxism, Vol. 2: Its Origins, Growth and Dissolution, The Golden Age* (Oxford: Oxford University Press, 1978).

—— *Main Currents of Marxism, Vol. 3: The Breakdown* (Oxford: Oxford University Press, 1978).

Kristeva, Julia, *Nations Without Nationalism* (New York: Columbia University Press, 1993).

Kristol, Irving, *Two Cheers for Capitalism* (New York: Basic Books, 1978).

Laqueur, Walter, *Black Hundred: The Rise of the Extreme Right in Russia* (New York: HarperCollins, 1994).

—— *Fascism: Past, Present, Future* (Oxford: Oxford University Press, 1996).

Lasswell, Harold D., *Politics: Who Gets What, When and How* (New York: Meridian Books, 1958).

Latouche, Serge, *The Westernization of the World* (Cambridge: Polity Press, 1996).

Le Bon, Gustave, *Psychologie des foules* (Paris: Alcan, 1895).

Leite, Jose C., *The World Social Forum: Strategies of Resistance* (Chicago, IL: Haymarket Books, 2005).

Lenin, V. I., *Collected Works* (Moscow: Progress Publishers, 1972).

Lieberman, Benjamin, *Terrible Fate: Ethnic Cleansing in the Making of Modern Europe* (Chicago, IL: Ivan R. Dee, 2006).

Lieven, Anato, *America Right or Wrong: An Anatomy of American Nationalism* (New York: Oxford University Press, 2004).

Lifton, Robert J., *Superpower Syndrome: America's Apocalyptic Confrontation with the World* (New York: Thunder's Mouth Press, 2003).

Lilla, Mark, *The Stillborn God: Religion, Politics, and the Modern West* (New York: Knopf, 2007).

Lipset, Seymour M., *Political Man: The Social Bases of Politics* (Garden City, NY: Anchor, 1963).

—— and Philip G. Altbach (eds.), *Students in Revolt* (Boston, MA: Beacon Press, 1970).

Longerith, Peter, *Politik der Vernichtung: Eine Gesamtdarstellung der nationalsozialistischen Judenverfolgung* (Munich: Beck, 1998).

Lukacs, John, *Democracy and Populism: Fear and Hatred* (New Haven, CT: Yale University Press, 2005).

Luttwak, Edward, *Turbo-Capitalism: Winners and Losers in the Global Economy* (New York: HarperCollins, 2000).

Lyons, Martyn, *Napoleon Bonaparte and the Legacy of the French Revolution* (London: Macmillan, 1994).

Mandelbaum, Michael, *The Ideas That Conquered the World: Peace, Democracy and Free Markets in the Twenty-First Century* (Washington, DC: Public Affairs, 2002).

Manent, Pierre, *An Intellectual History of Liberalism* (Princeton, NJ: Princeton University Press, 1995).

Mann, Michael, *Incoherent Empire* (London: Verso, 2003).

——*Fascists* (Cambridge: Cambridge University Press, 2004).

Marling, William H., *How "American" Is Globalization?* (Baltimore, MD: Johns Hopkins University Press, 2006).

Marshall, T. H., *Class, Citizenship, and Social Development* (Garden City, NY: Doubleday, 1965).

Marx, Karl and Friedrich Engels, *Werke*, 39 vols. (Berlin: Dietz Verlag, 1956–78).

Mazlish, Bruce, Nayan Chanda, and Kenneth Weisbrode (eds.), *The Paradox of a Global USA* (Stanford, CA: Stanford University Press, 2007).

Mazzoleni, Gianpietro, Julianne Stewart, and Bruce Horsfield (eds.), *The Media and Neo-Populism: A Contemporary Comparative Analysis* (Westport, CT: Praeger, 2003).

McCelland, J. S. (ed.), *The French Right from de Maistre to Maurras* (London: Jonathan Cape, 1970).

McDonald, Kevin, *Global Movements: Action and Culture* (Oxford: Blackwell, 2006).

McLellan, David, *Ideology*, 2nd edn. (Minneapolis: University of Minnesota Press, 1995).

McMahon, Robert J., *The Cold War: A Very Short Introduction* (Oxford: Oxford University Press, 2003).

Mead, Walter R., *Power, Terror, Peace, and War: America's Grand Strategy in a World of Risk* (New York: Knopf, 2004).

Merquior, J. G., *Liberalism Old and New* (Boston, MA: Twayne, 1991).

Mill, John S., "Coleridge," in H. Gertrude (ed.), *Essays on Politics and Culture* (New York: Anchor Books, 1963).

——"Representative Government," in *Utilitarianism, Liberty, Representative Government* (London: Dent, 1910).

——*On Liberty* (New York: Macmillan, 1987).

Miller, Susanne and Heinrich Potthoff, *A History of German Social Democracy: From 1848 to the Present*, trans. J. A. Underwood (Lexington Spa: Berg, 1986).

Mittelman, James H., *The Globalization Syndrome: Transformation and Resistance* (Princeton, NJ: Princeton University Press, 2000).

——*Whither Globalization: The Vortex of Knowledge and Ideology* (London and New York: Routledge, 2004).

Moaddel, Mansoor and Kamran Talattof (eds.), *Modernist and Fundamentalist Debates in Islam: A Reader* (New York: Palgrave Macmillan, 2002).

Moravchik, Joshua, *Heaven on Earth: The Rise and Fall of Socialism* (San Francisco, CA: Encounter Books, 2002).

Moses, Greg, *Revolution of Conscience: Martin Luther King, Jr., and the Philosophy of Nonviolence* (New York: Guilford Press, 1997).

Mosse, George L., *The Nationalization of the Masses: Political Symbolism and Mass Movements in Germany from the Napoleonic Wars Through the Third Reich* (New York: Howard Fertig, 1975).

Mosse, George L., *The Crisis of German Ideology: Intellectual Origins of the Third Reich* (New York: Schocken Books, 1981).

Muller, Jerry Z., *The Mind and the Market: Capitalism in Western Thought* (New York: Anchor Books, 2002).

Murphy, Cullen, *Are We Rome? The Fall of an Empire and the Fate of America* (New York: Houghton Mifflin, 2007).

Neocleous, Mark, *Fascism* (Minneapolis: University of Minnesota Press, 1997).

Nimni, Ephraim, *Marxism and Nationalism: Theoretical Origins of a Political Crisis* (London: Pluto, 1991).

Nisbet, Robert, *Conservatism* (Milton Keynes: Open University Press, 1986).

Nkrumah, Kwame, *The Autobiography of Kwame Nkrumah* (Edinburgh: T. Nelson, 1957).

Nolte, Ernst, *Three Faces of Fascism: Action Française, Italian Fascism, National Socialism* (New York: Mentor Books, 1969).

Nye, Joseph S., *Soft Power: The Means to Success in World Politics* (New York: Public-Affairs, 2004).

Oates, Stephen B., *Let the Trumpet Sound: The Life of Martin Luther King, Jr.* (New York: New American Library, 1982).

Ohmae, Kenichi, *The Borderless World: Power and Strategy in the Interlinked World Economy* (New York: HarperBusiness, 1990).

——*The End of the Nation-State: The Rise of Regional Economies* (New York: Free Press, 1995).

Oncken, Hermann, *Lassalle: Zwischen Marx und Bismarck* (Stuttgart, Germany: W. Kohlhammer, 1966 [1904]).

Panizza, Francisco (ed.), *Populism and the Mirror of Democracy* (London: Verso, 2006).

Parel, Anthony J. (ed.), *Hind Swaraj and Other Writings* (Cambridge, UK: Cambridge University Press, 1997).

Parry, D. L. L. and Pierre Girard (eds.), *France Since 1800: Squaring the Hexagon* (Oxford: Oxford University Press, 2002).

Paterson, Thomas G., *On Every Front: The Making and Unmaking of the Cold War*, 2nd rev. edn. (New York: R. S. Means, 1992).

Patomaki, Heikki and Teivo Teivainen, *A Possible World Democratic Transformation of Global Institutions* (London: Zed Books, 2004).

Paxton, Robert O., *The Anatomy of Fascism* (New York: Vintage, 2004).

Payne, Stanley G., *A History of Fascism: 1914–1945* (Madison, MD: University of Wisconsin Press, 1995).

Peukert, Detlev, *Inside Nazi Germany: Conformity, Opposition, and Racism in Everyday Life* (London: Penguin, 1989).

Phillips, Kevin, *American Theocracy: The Peril and Politics of Radical Religion, Oil, and Borrowed Money in the 21st Century* (New York: Viking, 2006).

Pieterse, Jan N., *Globalization or Empire?* (New York: Routledge, 2004).

Pipes, Richard, *The Formation of the Soviet Union: Communism and Nationalism 1917–1923* (Cambridge, MA: Harvard University Press, 1964).

——*A Concise History of the Russian Revolution* (New York: Vintage, 1995).

Podhoretz, Norman, *World War IV: The Long Struggle Against Islamofascism* (New York: Doubleday, 2007).

Powell, David, *British Politics, 1910–35: The Crisis of the Party System* (London: Routledge, 2004).

Prasad, Monica, *The Politics of Free Markets: The Rise of Neoliberal Economic Policies in Britain, France, Germany, and the United States* (Chicago, IL: University of Chicago Press, 2006).

Pulzer, Peter, *Germany, 1870–1945: Politics, State Formation, and War* (Oxford, UK: Oxford University Press, 1997).

Puri, Rashmi-Sudha, *Gandhi on War and Peace* (New York: Praeger, 1987).

Rémond, René, *La Droite en France* (Paris: Aubier, 1963).

Renan, Ernest, "What Is a Nation," in D. Omar and M. Ishay (eds.), *The Nationalism Reader* (Atlantic Highlands, NJ: Humanities Press, 1995).

Ricoeur, Paul, *Lectures on Ideology and Utopia* (New York: Columbia University Press, 1986).

Riddell, John (ed.), *The Communist International in Lenin's Time. Workers of the World and Oppressed People, Unite! Proceedings and Documents of the Second Congress, 1920*, 2 vols. (New York: Pathfinder, 1991).

Ritzer, George, *The McDonaldization of Society: An Investigation into the Changing Character of Contemporary Social Life* (Thousand Oaks, CA: Pine Forge Press, 1993).

Robertson, Roland, *Globalization: Social Theory and Global Culture* (Thousand Oaks, CA: Sage, 1992).

Robinson, William I., *Promoting Polyarchy: Globalization, U.S. Intervention, and Hegemony* (Cambridge: Cambridge University Press, 1996).

Robson, John, "Civilization and Culture as Moral Concepts," in J. Skorupski (ed.), *The Cambridge Companion to Mill* (Cambridge: Cambridge University Press, 1998).

Rodzinski, Witold, *The People's Republic of China: A Concise Political History* (New York: Free Press, 1988).

Rosenau, James N., *Distant Proximities: Dynamics Beyond Globalization* (Princeton, NJ: Princeton University Press, 2003).

Roy, Olivier, *Globalized Islam: The Search for a New Ummah* (New York: Columbia University Press, 2004).

Roy, Ravi K., Arthur T. Denzau, and Thomas D. Willett, *Neoliberalism: National and Regional Experiments with Global Ideas* (New York: Routledge, 2007).

Rupert, Mark, *Ideologies of Globalization: Contending Visions of a New Order* (London: Routledge, 2000).

Ruthven, Malise, *A Fury for God: The Islamist Attack on America* (London: Granta Books, 2002).

Rydgren, Jens (ed.), *Movements of Exclusion: Radical Right-Wing Populism in the Western World* (New York: Nove Science, 2005).

Sargent, Lyman T., *Contemporary Political Ideologies: A Comparative Analysis*, 12th edn. (Belmont, CA: Wadsworth, 2003).

Sassen, Saskia, *Territory, Authority, Rights: From Medieval to Global Assemblages* (Princeton, NJ: Princeton University Press, 2006).

—— *A Sociology of Globalization* (New York: W. W. Norton, 2007).

Schattle, Hans, *Global Citizenship* (Lanham, MD: Rowman & Littlefield, 2007).

Schram, Stuart R. (ed.), *Quotations from Chairman Mao Tse-Tung* (New York: Praeger, 1968).

—— *The Political Thought of Mao Tse-Tung* (New York: Praeger, 1969).

Schwarzmantel, John, *Socialism and the Idea of the Nation* (London: Harvester Wheatsheaf, 1991).

—— *The Age of Ideology: Political Ideologies from the American Revolution to Postmodern Times* (London: Macmillan Press, 1998).

Scruton, Roger, *The Meaning of Conservatism*, 3rd rev. edn. (Houndmills, UK: Palgrave Macmillan, 2001).

—— *The West and the Rest: Globalization and the Terrorist Threat* (Wilmington: ISI Books, 2002).

Searle, John, *The Construction of Social Reality* (New York: Free Press, 1995).

Simons, Thomas W., *Islam in a Globalizing World* (Stanford, CA: Stanford University Press, 2003).

Singer, Peter, *The President of Good & Evil: Questioning the Ethics of George W. Bush* (New York: Plume Books, 2004).

Siracusa, Joseph, *Nuclear Weapons: A Very Short Introduction* (Oxford: Oxford University Press, 2008).

Skilling, H. G., *Czechoslovakia's Interrupted Revolution* (Princeton, NJ: Princeton University Press, 1976).

Sklair, Leslie, *The Transnational Capitalist Class* (Oxford, UK: Blackwell, 2001).

Slaughter, Anne-Marie, *A New World Order* (Princeton, NJ: Princeton University Press, 2004).

Smiles, Samuel, *Self-Help, with Illustrations of Conduct and Perseverance* (London: Cosimo, 1925).

Smith, Anthony, *Nationalism and Modernism: A Critical Survey of Recent Theories of Nations and Nationalism* (London & New York: Routledge, 1998).

Smith, Neil, *The Endgame of Globalization* (New York: Routledge, 2005).

Smith, Jackie and Hank Johnston (eds.), *Globalization and Resistance: Transnational Dimensions of Social Movements* (Lanham, MD: Rowman & Littlefield, 2002).

—— and Joe Bandy (eds.), *Coalitions Across Borders: Transnational Protest and the Neoliberal Order* (Lanham, MD: Rowman & Littlefield, 2004).

Soros, George, *The Crisis of Global Capitalism: Open Society Endangered* (New York: Public Affairs, 1998).

Stalin, J. V., *On the Great Patriotic War of the Soviet Union* (Moscow: Foreign Languages Publishing House, 1944).

—— *Works*, 13 vols. (London: Lawrence & Wishart, 1952–5).

Staum, Martin S., *Minerva's Message: Stabilizing the French Revolution* (Montreal: McGill-Queen's University Press, 1996).

Steenson, Gary P., *"Not One Man! Not One Penny!" German Social Democracy, 1863–1914* (Pittsburgh, PA: University of Pittsburgh Press, 1981).

Steger, Manfred B., *The Quest for Evolutionary Socialism: Eduard Bernstein and Social Democracy* (Cambridge: Cambridge University Press, 1997).

—— *Gandhi's Dilemma: Nonviolent Principles and Nationalist Power* (New York: St. Martin's Press, 2000).

—— *Judging Nonviolence: The Dispute Between Realists & Idealists* (New York: Routledge, 2003).

—— (ed.), *Rethinking Globalism* (Lanham, MD: Rowman & Littlefield, 2004).

—— *Globalism: Market Ideology Meets Terrorism*, 2nd edn. (Lanham, MD: Rowman & Littlefield, 2005).

Stelzer, Irwin (ed.), *Neoconservatism* (London: Atlantic Books, 2004).

Sternhell, Zeev, *Neither Left Nor Right: Fascist Ideology in France* (Berkeley: University of California Press, 1986).

—— *The Birth of Fascist Ideology* (Princeton, NJ: Princeton University Press, 1994).

Sternthal, Susan, *Gorbachev's Reforms: De-Stalinization Through Demilitarization* (Westport, CT: Praeger, 1997).

Stiglitz, Joseph E., *Globalization and Its Discontents* (New York: W. W. Norton, 2002).

—— *The Roaring Nineties: A New History of the World's Most Prosperous Decade* (New York: W. W. Norton, 2003).

Stuermer, Michael, *The German Empire, 1870–1918* (New York: The Modern Library, 2000).

Taggart, Paul, *Populism* (Buckingham: Open University Press, 2000).

Taguieff, Pierre-Andre, *L'illusion populiste* (Paris: Berg International, 2002).

Talmon, J. L., *The Myth of the Nation and the Vision of Revolution: The Origins of Ideological Polarisation in the Twentieth Century* (Berkeley: University of California Press, 1981).

Tarrow, Sidney, *Power in Movement*, 2nd edn. (Cambridge: Cambridge University Press, 1998).

—— *The New Transnational Activism* (Cambridge: Cambridge University Press, 2005).

—— and Donatella della Porta (eds.), *The New Transnational Activism; Transnational Protest and Global Activism* (Lanham, MD: Rowman & Littlefield, 2005).

Taylor, Charles, *Modern Social Imaginaries* (Durham, UK & London: Duke University Press, 2004).

—— *A Secular Age* (Cambridge, MA: Belknap Press of Harvard University Press, 2007).

Terrill, Ross, *The New Chinese Empire: And What It Means for the United States* (New York: Basic Books, 2003).

Thompson, John B., *Studies in the Theory of Ideology* (Berkeley: University of California Press, 1984).

——*Ideology and Modern Culture: Critical Social Theory and the Era of Mass Communication* (Stanford, CA: Stanford University Press, 1990).

Thornton, William H., *New World Empire: Civil Islam, Terrorism, and the Making of Neoglobalism* (Lanham, MD: Rowman & Littlefield, 2005).

Tian, Chenshan, *Chinese Dialectics: From Yijing to Marxism* (Lanham, MD: Lexington Books, 2005).

Tilly, Charles, *Social Movements, 1768–2004* (Boulder, CO: Paradigm, 2004).

Toulmin, Stephen, *Cosmopolis: The Hidden Agenda of Modernity* (Chicago, IL: University of Chicago Press, 1990).

Tracy, Destutt de, *A Treatise on Political Economy: To Which is Prefixed a Supplement to a Preceding Work on the Understanding or, Elements of Ideology* (New York: Augustus Kelley, 1970 [1817]).

Traugott, Mark (ed.), *Repertoires and Cycles of Collective Action* (Durham, UK: Duke University Press, 1995).

Trotsky, Leon, *The Defence of Terrorism: A Reply to Kautsky* (London: G. Allen & Unwin, 1921).

Tse-Tung, Mao, *Selected Works of Mao Tse-Tung*, 1 vol. (Peking: Foreign Languages Press, 1965).

Tucker, Robert C. (ed.), *What Is to Be Done?*, in *The Lenin Anthology* (New York: W. W. Norton, 1975).

Tudor, Henry (ed.), *The Preconditions of Socialism* (Cambridge, UK: Cambridge University Press, 1993).

Urry, John, *Global Complexity* (Cambridge: Polity Press, 2003).

Vincent, Andrew, *Nationalism & Particularity* (Cambridge, UK: Cambridge University Press, 1992).

Waldron, Peter, *The End of Imperial Russia, 1855–1917* (New York: St. Martin's Press, 1997).

Walicki, Andrzej, *A History of Russian Thought: From the Enlightenment to Marxism* (Stanford, CA: Stanford University Press, 1979).

Wang, Yanlai, *China's Economic Development and Democratization* (Aldershot, UK: Ashgate, 2003).

Waters, Malcolm, *Globalization* (London: Routledge, 1995).

Waxman, Chaim I. (ed.), *The End of Ideology Debate* (New York: Funk & Wagnalls, 1968).

Webber, Michael, Mark Wang, and Zhu Ying (eds.), *China's Transition to a Global Economy* (Houndmills, UK: Palgrave Macmillan, 2002).

Weiss, John, *Conservatism in Europe* (New York: Harcourt Brace Jovanovich, 1977).

Welch, Cheryl B., *Liberty and Utility: The French Idéologues and the Transformation of Liberalism* (New York: Columbia University Press, 1984).

Westad, Odd A., *The Global Cold War: Third World Interventions and the Making of Our Times* (Cambridge: Cambridge University Press, 2005).

White, Stephen, *After Gorbachev* (Cambridge: Cambridge University Press, 1993).

Wolf, Martin, *Why Globalization Works* (New Haven, CT: Yale University Press, 2005).

Wolff, Robert P., *The Poverty of Liberalism* (Boston, MA: Beacon Press, 1968).

Wolin, Sheldon S., *Politics and Vision* (exp. edn.) (Princeton, NJ: Princeton University Press, 2004).

Yergin, Daniel and Joseph Stanislaw, *The Commanding Heights: The Battle for the World Economy* (New York: Touchstone, 1998).

Young, Robert C., *Postcolonialism: An Historical Introduction* (Malden, MA: Blackwell, 2001).

Zizek, Slavoj, *Iraq: The Borrowed Kettle* (London: Verso, 2004).

——*Mapping Ideology* (London: Verso, 1994).

Zunes, Stephen, Lester R. Kurtz, and Sarah Beth Asher, *Nonviolent Social Movements: A Geographical Perspective* (Malden, MA: Blackwell, 1999).

Index

306

CPSIA information can be obtained at www.ICGtesting.com
Printed in the USA
BVOW011638130613

323221BV00002B/7/P